Bobbin Lace

Bobbin Lace

Form by the Twisting of Cords

Kaethe and Jules Kliot

A NEW LOOK AT A TRADITIONAL TEXTILE ART

472 PHOTOGRAPHS · 20 COLOR PLATES

Crown Publishers, Inc. New York

Inquiries should be addressed to Crown Publishers, Inc.
419 Park Avenue South, New York, N.Y. 10016

Library of Congress Catalog Card Number: 73–82937
Printed in the United States of America
Printed simultaneously in Canada by
General Publishing Company Limited

Design by Nedda Balter

Acknowledgments

Thanks to a small group of dedicated enthusiasts who have organized and called themselves "The International Old Lacers," bobbin lace has been kept alive in its traditional forms together with its tools and materials. It is to this group that we are indebted and in particular to a wonderful and patient teacher, Mrs. Gertrude Biederman, for the sharing of her years of knowledge and resources with us through her teachings of both the simplicities and the many intricacies of this lace form.

Much of contemporary bobbin lace expression appears within this book, and we are thankful to the creators of these pieces who have shared their work and experience with us.

As first-time authors writing a book on contemporary bobbin lace, we have relied solely on the excitement that this textile technique has offered us to carry us through our many anxieties.

Special thanks must be given to Grace Davis who gave us so much of her time and editorial expertise in the editing and proofreading of the manuscript.

Note: all photographs by authors unless otherwise credited.

Contents

Preface

Bobbin lace, for all its complex appearances, is simply a technique for fabricating an open-type designed fabric by the twisting, or plaiting, of threads. The simplicity of the basic technique, together with one of the richest heritages of fabric art, makes bobbin lace one of the most rewarding expressions in contemporary textile crafts.

Without the limits of loom or frame, of fixed threads or rigid perimeters, virtually complete freedom of form, color, and design is possible, using only the two basic motions of this lace form.

One can work with four cords and form a simple braid or with many hundreds of cords to form the most intricate of traceries. Though traditional lace was generally worked with white bleached threads finer than a human hair, together with intricate patterns passed down from generation to generation, our contemporary forms explode with all the colors and materials available today and with designs and forms of totally new dimensions.

The term "lace" no longer need imply doilies, frilly collars, or dresser scarves worked from traditional patterns on stuffed pillows. It can, instead, imply a complete freedom of expression with designs either preplanned or momentarily inspired. The stuffed pillow can give way to the board and the board can give way to free suspension, however each individual feels most comfortable in the execution of any particular piece. The basic tool, the bobbin, can be a finely carved piece of bone or hardwood, a simple nail, or a clean-picked chicken bone.

Patterns can imitate those of weaving or can enrich weaving forms by being integral with them or as finishing terminations. For these reasons bobbin lace should have strong appeal to weavers as well as other textile workers.

Like macramé, which was also a lace technique when executed with fine threads at the turn of the century, bobbin lace should have the same wide appeal as a rebirth of an unfairly neglected fine craft.

Rather than a skill emphasizing superb craftsmanship in the duplication of traditional patterns, contemporary bobbin lace is worked without patterns and is keyed to personal expression in terms of both design and technique.

As contemporary expressions using bobbin lace techniques have barely scratched the surface in areas of creative textile crafts, this book is geared to the textile enthusiast who would like to learn the basic techniques, develop his own language in the use of them, and finally explore the potential of this art form.

The step-by-step instructions, photographically illustrated, are aimed at making the techniques simple enough to become second nature as you proceed to explore their many variations.

The chapters that follow offer simple and useful projects to aid you in your explorations, as well as more advanced techniques based on our own "affair" with bobbin lace.

Introduction

Chapter I

A TEXTILE TECHNIQUE

The term "lace," as applied to contemporary textile techniques, refers to an openwork fabric where the combination of open spaces and dense textures forms the design. Although traditional lace implied fine openwork, contemporary lace is not restricted by dimension. Bobbin lace applies to only one method of making such an openwork pattern, a method with perhaps the greatest potential in terms of textile exploration, a method that gives the worker the freedom of pure design.

In relating bobbin lace to other textile techniques, it is useful to think of all techniques as falling into one of two categories: *single thread textiles* and *multiple thread textiles*.

As the name implies, single thread textiles are formed by a single continuous thread by making one stitch at a time in sequence along the entire length of this thread. Techniques such as knitting, netting, knotless netting, tatting, crochet, and needle lace fall into this category. A needle, hook, or shuttle are some of the simple tools used for these techniques, although many times the hand alone is sufficient.

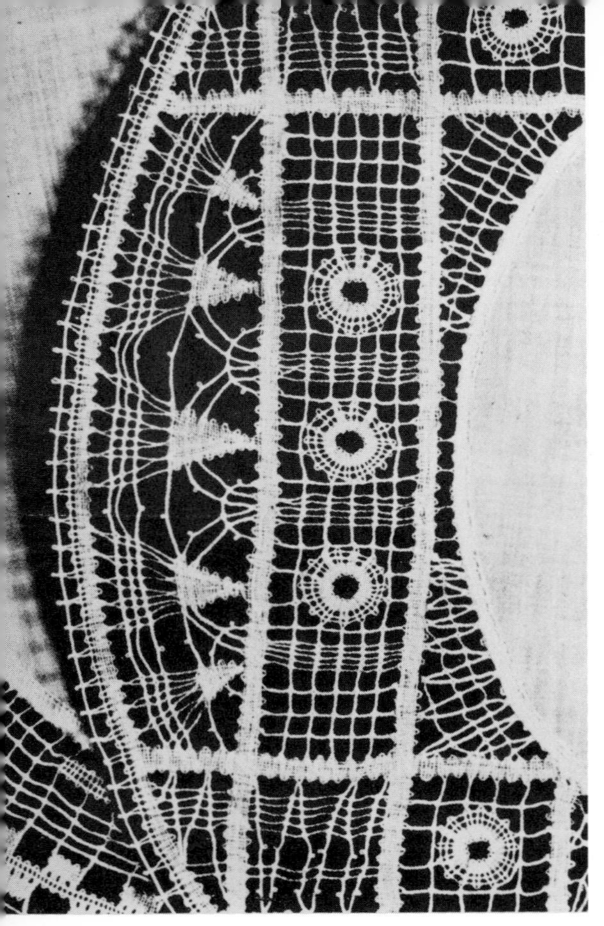

An early example of contemporary bobbin lace. Student lace design from the government-sponsored Schneeberg Lace School (Germany). From Stickereien und Spitzen (Embroidery and Lace), *October 1931.*

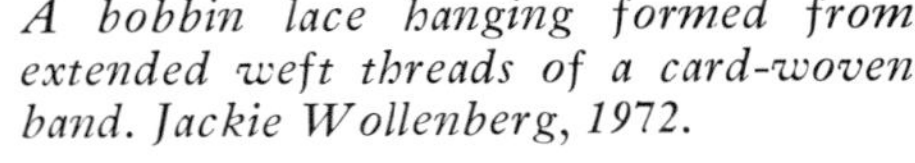

A bobbin lace hanging formed from extended weft threads of a card-woven band. Jackie Wollenberg, 1972.

Multiple thread textiles are formed by the manipulation of many identical threads, with stitches being made with at least two of these threads. Weaving, in all its many forms, is certainly the most common technique in this category. Bobbin lace, sprang, and macramé are other multiple thread textile forms.

In weaving there is always a warp that is made up of any number of threads in fixed relation to each other. This entire warp is supported at each end to hold it in tension. When a single weft thread is passed through selected warp threads, the threads become interlaced forming the fabric. Among the multiple thread textiles, weaving has the distinction of being the only one that permits the making of many stitches with a single pass of a (weft) thread.

Sprang, like weaving, has a warp of any number of threads supported at each end and in fixed relation to each other. A fabric is produced, however, without a weft thread. The stitches are formed by twisting and intertwining the warp threads. A single stick woven through these threads at their center keeps all the stitches in place.

Macramé is a suspended warp technique involving any number of independent threads that can have their relationship to each other changed. Threads are only supported at one end with tension required only for specific holding threads. Stitches are formed by knotting the threads together and/or around each other.

Bobbin lace combines many of the favorable characteristics of the other multiple thread techniques. The fabric is formed from strands suspended at only one end as in macramé, but which are individually weighted for tension on the free end with handles, or bobbins. These threads are given complete freedom to move about in relation to each other. A fabric is made by the twisting, or plaiting, of these threads to form a series of stitches. A single pair

A contemporary expression in bobbin lace by Joannes Chaleye, 1910, Vogtland.

A sixteen-year-old student working with 1,000 bobbins on a single piece at the Abbe Berraly School (Belgium). From Bobbins of Belgium *by Charlotte Kellogg, 1920.*

of these suspended threads forms a working unit, and any of these units can be added or deleted at will. Not limited by any fixed number of threads or regular perimeters, bobbin lace is free to move in any direction. As in weaving, where warp and weft cross to form a stitch, in bobbin lace the crossing of threads by means of a TWIST or CROSS forms a stitch.

Unlike weaving, bobbin lace threads are interchangeable in terms of becoming either a warp or weft thread, depending on the design of a particular stitch. While weaving, with its sequential repetition of identical stitches, emphasizes pattern and texture, bobbin lace, with its freedom of stitch and direction, emphasizes design. It is this unique combination of assets that makes bobbin lace the most versatile of textile techniques.

As it evolved, bobbin lace was traditionally worked with uncut, unbroken threads. Each piece was worked on a stationary cushion with ground and design being worked together simultaneously. Each thread was worked through the entire piece until finally terminated at an edge. As designs became finer and more complex, it was not uncommon for a single piece to require over a thousand bobbins.

By the end of the seventeenth century an alternate method was developed whereby a lace piece was worked detail by detail. These separate parts were then joined and the spaces filled in by a ground to complete the piece. Generally worked on a round cushion, the number of bobbins could be reduced to about two dozen. It is this latter method, permitting maximum flexibility, that contemporary bobbin lace follows.

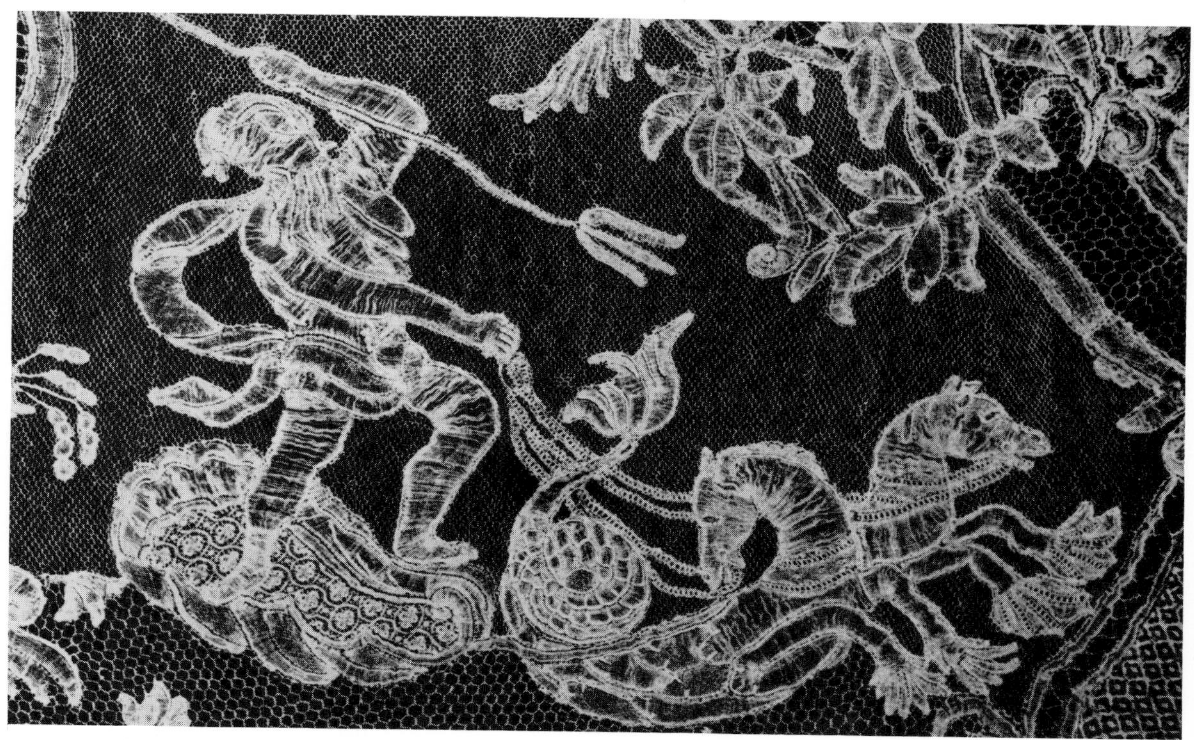

A traditional lace design from the Regency period (France about 1720). From the Alfred Lescure Collection, after Overloop.

HISTORICAL ORIGINS

The origin as well as the history of bobbin lace is rich with theory, intrigue, myths, and legends. Whether born from the web of a spider or evolving as an extension of the simple braiding of hanging threads, evidence of fabrics formed by twisted threads can be found dating back over six thousand years in Egypt, northern Europe, and China.

In ancient Egypt, slaves executed what is now called Mummy lace by a technique now known as sprang. Threads supported at both top and bottom were twisted together, forming a twined mesh symmetrical about the center. Without a rigid frame, short lengths of thread supported only at one end, such as the hanging warp threads of a woven fabric, could be similarly manipulated to form braids. Handles, which acted as weights, supported by the free ends of these threads, simplified the plaiting process. The freedom to manipulate these threads by these handles, or bobbins, was eventually to be explored and refined into what is now called bobbin lace. Although evidence of bone bobbins has been found in ancient Rome, this textile form lay dormant for thousands of years, not to surface again until the fifteenth century.

It is primarily through the scanning of old paintings that have survived that the history of lace has been compiled. The reproduction of lace patterns was a challenge to the skills of artists who painted lace adornments of the clothing of men and women.

It was during the middle of the fifteenth century when the traditions of

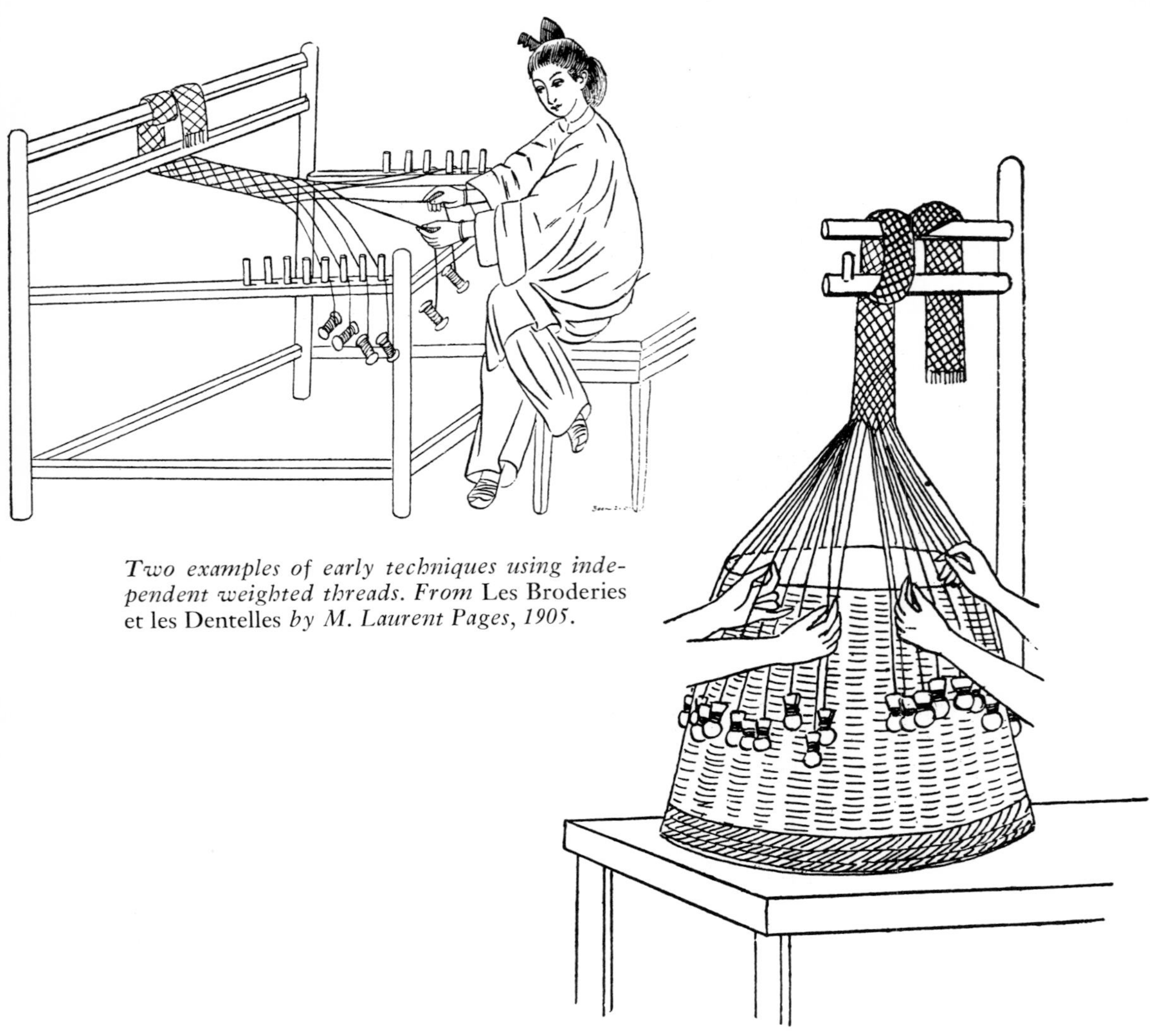

Two examples of early techniques using independent weighted threads. From Les Broderies et les Dentelles *by M. Laurent Pages, 1905.*

bobbin lace began. Its growth and development, intertwined with the religious, political, and social structures of Europe, is fascinating with a great deal of source material available. With its first modern home in Italy, this lace form was soon to spread with the momentum of the Renaissance. By the end of the fifteenth century it had spread to Antwerp and Flanders where some of the finest lace was to be made. These areas, traditionally of weavers, readily accepted lace as a new fabric technique. The valley of the Lys around Flanders was the finest flax region of the world. The linen made from this flax was to be the most desired and revered lacemaking material.

The development of this lace form was phenomenal during the sixteenth and seventeenth centuries with insatiable demands by 1700 by the Roman Catholic Church, as well as the aristocracy of Europe.

From early geometric designs, complex patterns and traceries evolved, each being indigenous to the particular regions where the lace was executed. Most designs of this early period had religious themes and motifs, with most work being commissioned by the Roman Catholic Church.

Although all bobbin lace is formed from the same basic stitches, the combinations of these stitches were to take on the names of the cities of

The height of lace style. Mary Sidney, Countess of Pembroke. From Chats on Old Lace and Needlework *by Lowes, 1908.*

A doily worked with traditionally fine threads. About 1800. Author's collection.

A bobbin lace bed jacket worked about 1920 with silk thread. Author's collection.

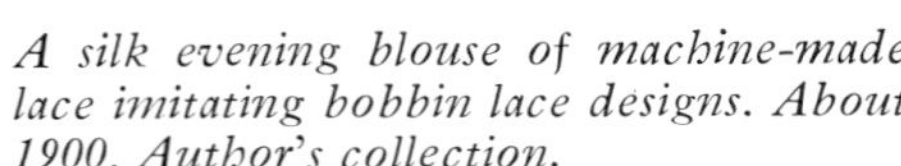

A silk evening blouse of machine-made lace imitating bobbin lace designs. About 1900. Author's collection.

their origin. Bruges, Brussels, Chantilly, Mechlin, and Valenciennes are only a few of the respected lace styles. With the political and social upheavals came the migration of the lace workers and the influx of patterns and styles into new areas. The competition of the courts of Europe, to secure the finest laces and to keep the tremendous amounts of monies spent on lace at home, led to the buying and even the abduction of lacemakers. The patterns and specific techniques went with them, and the eventual result was the merging of many of the techniques and the production of new and more complex designs. It was this migration that was to result in over fifty categorized variations of bobbin lace. While the designs became more complex, the lace itself became more filmy and exquisite, as it was made from finer and finer threads. It was not unusual for a worker to spend a whole year or more on a single yard of lace.

At the beginning of the eighteenth century, lace reached its peak under the reign of Louis XIV. The state subsidized lace schools, laceworkers were encouraged to immigrate, and new designs and techniques were rewarded. Most lace was now destined for the courts and the new designs were the products of well-known painters. To protect the national lace and encourage its growth, the death penalty was imposed on those who might attempt to carry lace secrets beyond the borders. Importation of foreign laces was prohibited with both England and France issuing edicts to this effect with the threat of severe penalties. Such edicts, of course, led to a lace underground whereby Brussels lace, which was the finest and most treasured, was smuggled back and forth across the Channel. Many stories have been recounted of the dressing of corpses in yards and yards of fine lace and then transporting the whole sealed coffin across the Channel.

The production of many of the laces required very specific working environments. A fine lace known as "Blonde" could only be worked by

A post-World War I lace school in Belgium, the Abbe Berraly School at Turnhout. Nine-year-old children making lace. From Bobbins of Belgium *by Charlotte Kellogg, 1920.*

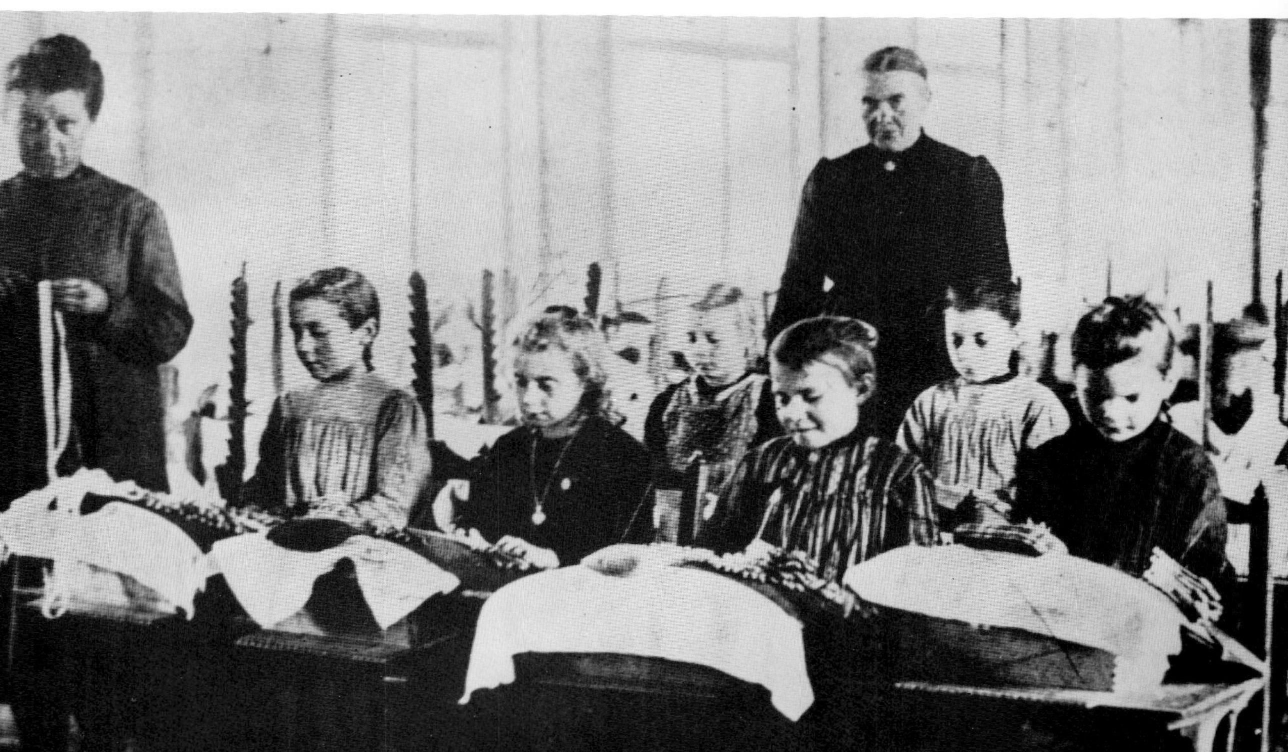

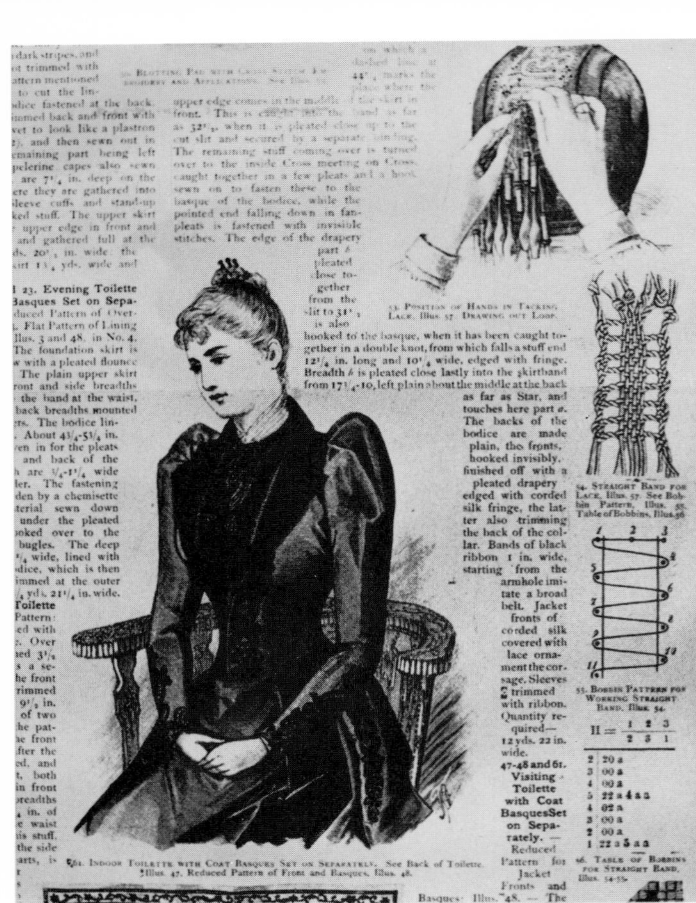

upper edge comes in the middle of the skirt in front. This is caught into the band as far as 32½, when it is pleated close up to the cut slit and secured by a separate binding. The remaining stuff coming over is turned over to the inside Cross meeting on Cross, caught together in a few pleats and a hook sewn on to fasten these to the basque of the bodice, while the pointed end falling down in fan-pleats is fastened with invisible stitches. The edge of the drapery part *b* pleated close together from the slit to 31½ is also hooked to the basque, when it has been caught together in a double knot, from which falls a stuff end 12½ in. long and 10¼ wide, edged with fringe. Breadth *b* is pleated close lastly into the skirtband from 17¼-10, left plain about the middle at the back as far as Star, and touches here part *a*. The backs of the bodice are made plain, the fronts, hooked invisibly, finished off with a pleated drapery edged with corded silk fringe, the latter also trimming the back of the collar. Bands of black ribbon 1 in. wide, starting from the armhole imitate a broad belt. Jacket fronts of corded silk covered with lace ornament the corsage. Sleeves trimmed with ribbon. Quantity required—12 yds. 22 in. wide.

47-48 and 61. Visiting Toilette with Coat Basques Set on Separately. — Reduced Pattern for Jacket Fronts and Basques: Illus. 48. — The

23. Evening Toilette Basques Set on Sepa-

53. Position of Hands in Tacking Lace. Illus. 57. Drawing out Loop.

54. Straight Band for Lace. Illus. 57. See Bobbin Pattern, Illus. 55. Table of Bobbins, Illus. 56

55. Bobbin Pattern for Working Straight Band. Illus. 54.

56. Table of Bobbins for Straight Band. Illus. 54-55.

61. Indoor Toilette with Coat Basques Set on Separately. See Back of Toilette, Illus. 47. Reduced Pattern of Front and Basques, Illus. 48.

Lace designs as presented through periodicals of the late nineteenth century. Author's collection.

94 MARCH, 1891. THE SEAS

wide, sloped off at the joining seam. Double strings draw the stuff in at the waist, stripes of stuff being set under after the fine line on Illus. 68. A bias band 1½ in. wide piped above with white finishes off the lower edge of the apron, which is buttoned at the back. A pretty and suitable bobbined edging will be found at Illus. 57, in No. 11, Vol. VII. Quantity required —31½ in. 31½ in. wide.

42 and 8. Dress with Pelerine Trimming for Little Girls. — Flat Pattern: Illus. 6 and 68, in No. 9, Vol. VII. — Our illustrations show a dress made of different stuffs, and trimmings; that is to say, of pale blue, fancy cloth bordered with dark stripes, and of fine cheviot trimmed with velvet. The pattern mentioned may be used to cut the lining of the bodice fastened at the back, this being trimmed back and front with stripes of velvet to look like a plastron (see Illus. 42), and then sewn out in tucks, the remaining part being left plain. The pelerine capes also sewn out in tucks, are 7¼ in. deep on the shoulders where they are gathered into the seam. Sleeve cuffs and stand-up collar of tucked stuff. The upper skirt tucked at the upper edge in front and at the sides and gathered full at the back, is 2 yds. 20½ in. wide; the foundation skirt 13¼ yds. wide and 16¼ long.

43-44 and 23. Evening Toilette with Long Basques Set on Sepa-

49. Cloth for Voider: Colour

50. Blotting Pa... broidery and ...

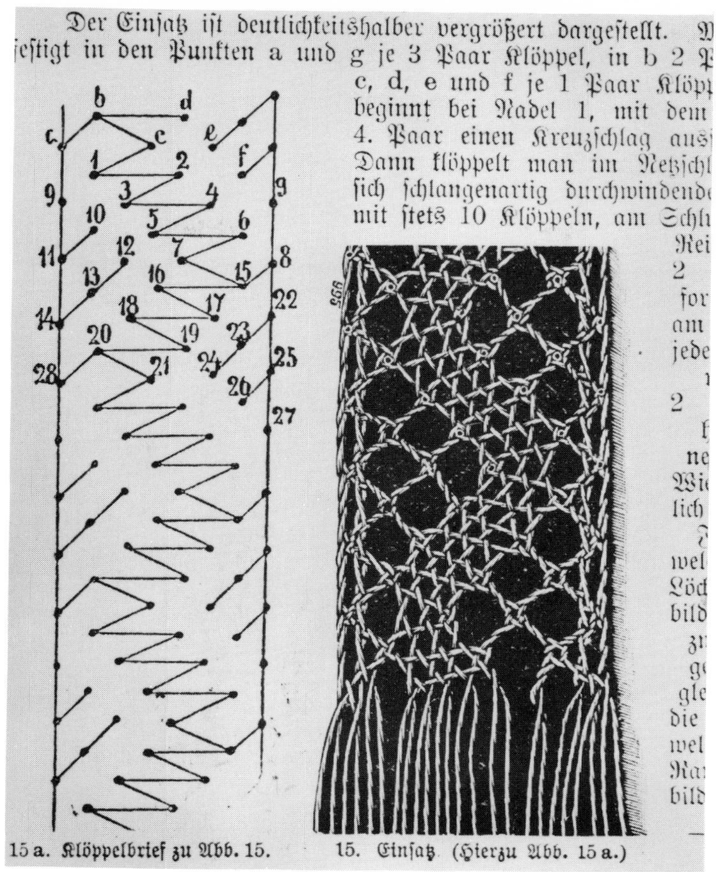

Der Einsatz ist deutlichkeitshalber vergrößert dargestellt. M
festigt in den Punkten a und g je 3 Paar Klöppel, in b 2 P
c, d, e und f je 1 Paar Klöpp
beginnt bei Nadel 1, mit dem
4. Paar einen Kreuzschlag aus
Dann klöppelt man im Netzschl
sich schlangenartig durchwindende
mit stets 10 Klöppeln, am Schl
Rei
2
for
am
jede
2
ne
Wi
lich
wel
Löd
bild
gle
die
wel
Ra
bild

15 a. Klöppelbrief zu Abb. 15.   15. Einsatz. (Hierzu Abb. 15 a.)

women having especially dry hands. In summer it was worked in the open air, while in winter it was worked in special rooms built over cow houses where the animals' breath warmed the air. Any form of flame heat would cause soot damage to the fine threads. Valenciennes lace was worked only in dark damp cellars, the moist atmosphere being necessary to prevent the fine threads from breaking. It was under such conditions that the useful life of the laceworker terminated before the age of thirty. Poor eyesight and pulmonary diseases were common among these workers.

It was the flax of Flanders from the valley of the Lys that could be spun into these superfine threads. The flax was spun in dark damp rooms where only a single ray of light was allowed to enter. This thread was said to be so fine that it could not be seen and had to be manipulated by touch only. Handspun, a pound of this material was valued at over a thousand dollars.

As each lacemaking nation tried to protect its own interests, heavy duties and excess taxes were levied. It was this overprotection that was to lead to the decline of lace forms. To check overextravagance, sumptuary edicts were issued that limited and, in some cases, prohibited the wearing of it. This led to simpler dress forms and a decline in the demand for lace. The end of the eighteenth century marked the end of the great lace era. Lace designs became coarser with more primitive patterns. The development of sheer cloths and industrialized processes further lessened the demands for lace. The final death blow to the industry came with the French Revolution. Lace, which was associated with the aristocracy, was now banned, the wearing of it a crime.

Although lace centers survived in other areas, primarily Belgium, bobbin lace was never to gain its previous support.

At the beginning of the nineteenth century, with the use of coarser threads and heavy designs, there was little in common with the traditional lace motifs. At this time machine-made tulle, or netting, came into wide use with the development by John Heathcoat of the bobbin net machine. This netting was used as a background and simply ornamented with applications of details done with either needle or bobbins. Cotton was soon to replace the finer and stronger linens. Industrial and commercial development led to machine-made laces, and by 1870 handmade lace virtually vanished except for a few strongholds of the tradition in France and Belgium. Even these areas were destined for extermination as entire lace regions were physically devastated during World War I.

After the war, concerned groups and government agencies made noble efforts to restart the industry. Grants were given for the redevelopment of schools, attempts were made at organizing the workers, and by 1920 lace was having what was to be a short-lived revival. Two hundred schools were soon operating in Belgium alone. The effort was, however, futile. With the depression and finally World War II, the lace industry was to be buried for good. Today, in Bruges, which was the last stronghold of bobbin lace, there is virtually no trace of this noble tradition.

SOCIAL TRADITIONS

Lace, both bobbin and needle types, had a parallel development. While bobbin lace probably evolved from the finishing off of extended warp threads on a woven fabric, needle lace evolved from the sewn finishing of a cut fabric. Both techniques were eventually to free themselves of the woven fabric and become textile forms in their own right. Bobbin lace, integral with the woven fabric, and originally executed by slaves, remained among the lower ranks of social systems. As a supplementary source for income, it

A street scene in Bruges (Belgium), about 1900. From Bobbins of Belgium *by Charlotte Kellogg, 1920.*

Working a lace edging on a vertical pillow in the Spanish tradition with several hundred bobbins. From Hispanic Lace and Lace Making, *May 1939.*

was worked by the common people over most of the agricultural areas of Europe and soon became part of the traditions of the people of these areas. As demand for lace increased, a highly structured trade system evolved.

In a lacemaking village every house would have at least one pillow on which lace was worked in spare moments from the work of the fields and home. Villagers would often gather in the streets to work on their pillows while carrying on their other social activities. During harvest periods, this industry would virtually come to a standstill. Worked in this fashion, lacemaking was a true "home industry" spread wide over the countryside. Periodically, a first buyer would come through the villages and collect the finished pieces, leaving in return an equivalent amount of lace thread. This buyer would resell these pieces to a dealer, who in turn would sell them to a larger dealer. Such a system permitted many intermediaries, thinning profit margins, and keeping basic wages to the lacemaker at a minimum. The equivalent of five cents was not an uncommon daily wage. Thus, from the beginning, the lacemaker was predestined to be the victim of a social and economic slavery. Due to the scattered nature of these villages, the women were never able to protect themselves through syndicates, or guilds. The attempts at revival and reform after World War I accomplished little.

As part of the social tradition, the techniques as well as the parchment patterns were passed down from mother to daughter, generation to generation. It was not until the latter part of the nineteenth century that lace

Pages from a student's notebook showing patterns and finished samplers. Late nineteenth century. Author's collection.

schools became a significant factor in the teaching of lace. With the demand for lace diminishing, many government-supported schools and programs were begun as a means of preserving this noble industry. Although preschool training was often given at home to children of four years old, formal school training began with children at age five. Working with few bobbins at first, an advanced student at the age of sixteen was capable of working with a thousand or more bobbins, spending an entire year on a single piece. A typical school day began at 8:00 in the morning and did not terminate until 6:30 that evening.

Needle lace, as an extended sewing technique, was made with a single needle by the looping, twisting, weaving, and knotting of a single thread. These techniques developed in the courts as a craft of the noblewoman. Its traditions were aristocratic and, thus, never had the wide appeal of bobbin lace.

Adrienne Webb, still working lace in the traditional manner using contemporary bobbins.

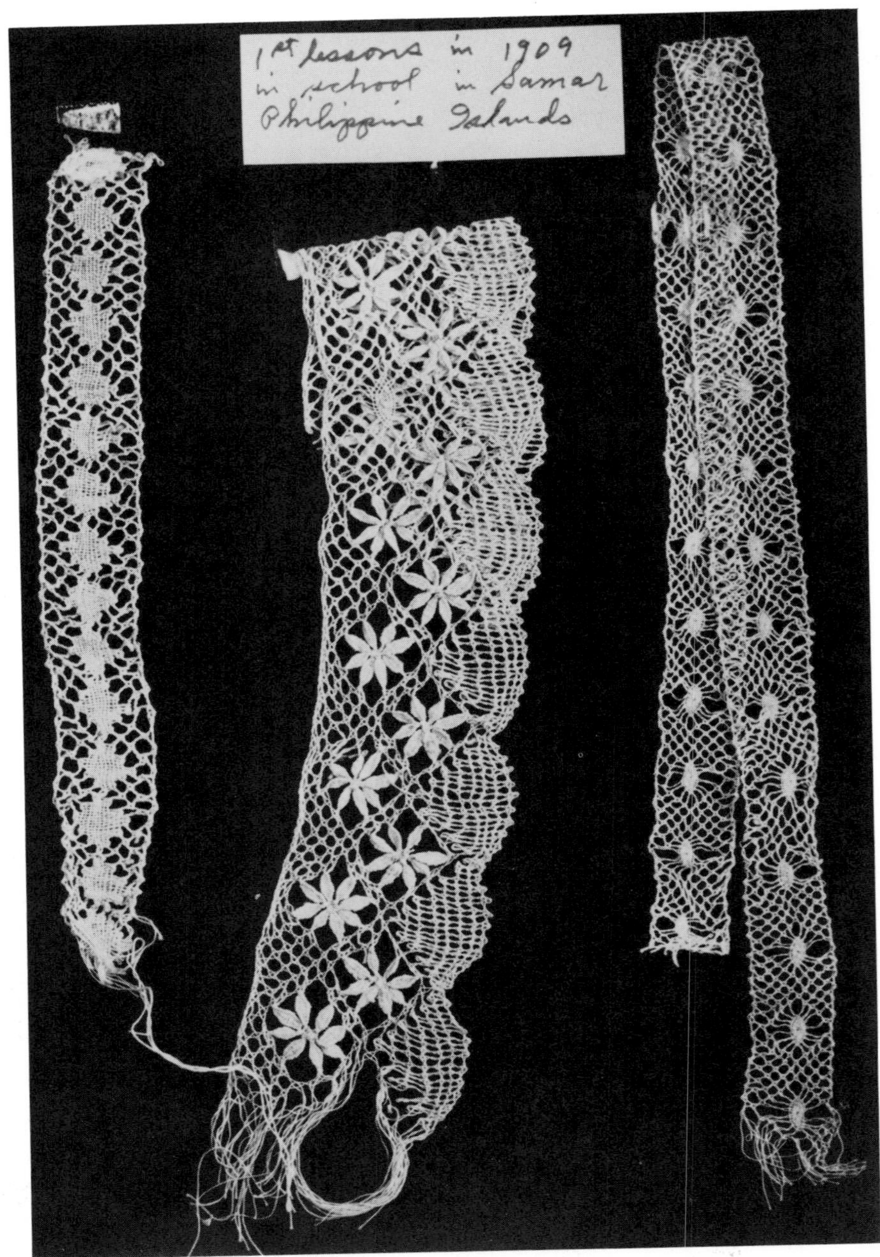

First worked pieces of lace by Adrienne Webb, 1909.

The weakest area of bobbin lace traditions, in terms of twentieth-century appeal, was the sharply divided processes between idea and execution. It was rare for any individual to execute a piece of lace from concept to finished piece. When lace designs reached their height of complexity, it became customary for a lacemaker to make only one kind of lace, to work only one design, year after year. Although this constant repetition developed skill, it precluded any sense of joy. The concept of exploring new ways to use the lacemaker's skills was unheard of. The joy of creation was not the joy of the lacemaker.

An original lace design always began with the lace designer, who was perhaps the most highly regarded within the lace industry. Thomas Wright in his fascinating historical treatise, *The Romance of the Lace Pillow,* wrote in 1919 of the lace designer:

> Much of the work of these designers is beyond criticism, and our indebtedness to their originality, fecundity, and versatility has never been sufficiently acknowledged. The patterns elaborated by them are their most jeweled thoughts stereotyped in parchment, just as the work of an inspired author is the expression of his inmost soul imparted, as Blake would put it, "fearfully and tremblingly" to the printed page. They did great things, for their thoughts were hitched to the stars. In moments of ecstasy, say the old philosophers, the soul divests itself of the body. In the finest of lace, as in a precious book, we seem to come into contact with the detached soul of a great personality.

How well thoughts such as this might express our contemporary approach to the arts in view of the psychological inroads so boldly explored in the rich and often psychedelic designs emanating as part of our now expressions. The revival of bobbin lace seems to have been waiting for this moment in time.

Lace designers and prickers working out lace patterns. From Hispanic Lace and Lace Making, *May 1939.*

When a design was carefully laid out, it was turned over to the "pricker" who would translate this design into a pattern of pinpoints, each pin indicating the location of a single stitch. This was a very complicated process as every bobbin would have to be accounted for as its thread traversed the pattern. With each point noted and the stitch pattern designated, the entire layout would be translated onto a stiff piece of parchment. This was the pattern form on which the lacemaker directly worked. These patterns were very precious and carefully guarded by each family and lace district. These patterns left no room for improvisation. Each worked piece would be identical to every other worked piece made from the same pattern.

The clear division of these tasks permitted a much higher degree of complexity in lace designs but at the same time severely hindered the development of bobbin lace as a creative skill. The few lacemakers of today are still dependent on the pattern. These can still be found and are still being made, reproduced, and traded among lacemakers.

With these traditions so ingrained in bobbin lace, it is easy to understand why it has for so long avoided any role in contemporary textiles.

A lace edging being worked over a parchment pattern. Bobbins are of bamboo. Adrienne Webb.

Equipment And Materials

Chapter 2

As with other textile techniques, equipment can be as simple or elaborate as one wishes. Along with the rich heritage of bobbin lace have come collectors of bobbin lace equipment. Most of these traditional tools are quite expensive and are most often simply collected rather than used.

The actual working of bobbin lace requires a minimum of equipment. The tools that are required are simple enough so that they can be made or improvised from common elements.

In working contemporary lace, equipment will also be dependent on the size of the project as well as the materials used.

THE BOBBIN

No matter what the form or technique used in working bobbin lace, the bobbin is the one tool that is difficult to dispense with. The prime function of the bobbin is to act as a weight for the suspended thread. As such, the earliest bobbins were simply a stone or piece of wood that could be attached to the end of the hanging thread to keep it in tension. With the refinement

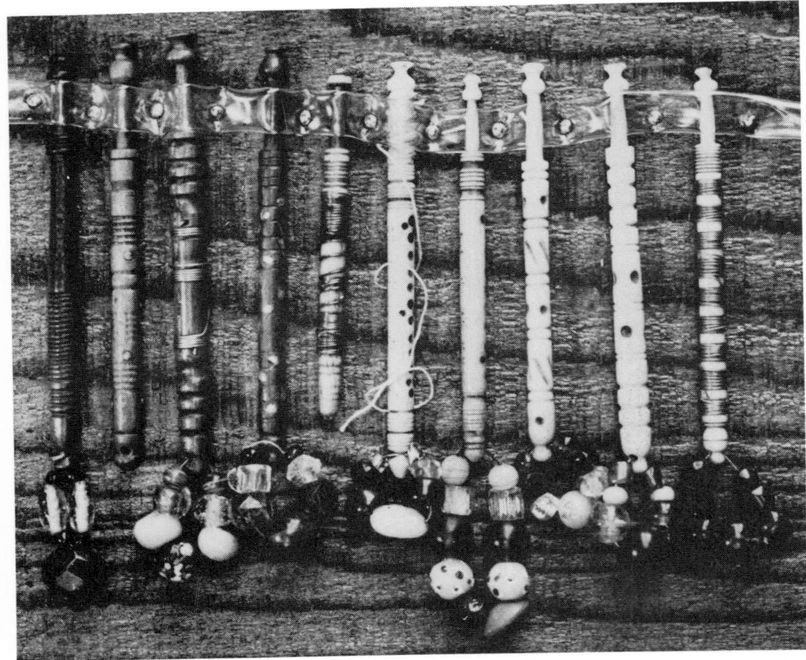

A collection of traditional lace bobbins. The beaded bobbins with the fine necks (above) are English with the beads added for weight control. The decorative wood ones (below) are Danish and have the traditional ball end. The turned bobbins (right) are made from exotic hardwoods primarily for collectors.

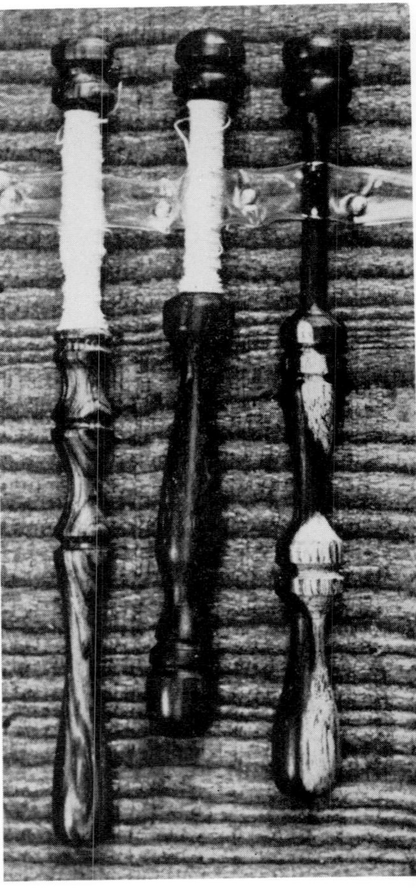

of lace techniques, the bobbin took on the additional functions of storing the unused thread (as the warp beam does on a loom), keeping the fine threads protected from dirt, and acting as a useful handle to allow easy manipulation of the attached threads.

As the lace regions developed their characteristic lace styles, so did they develop their characteristic lace bobbins. Some had straight shafts, others distinct sculptural forms. In Saxony a hooded bobbin was developed with a wooden hood to cover the unused thread. Weights were often added to the bobbin shaft to increase the tension in the thread. Characteristic beads and those from unusual origins were typically used for this purpose. Most bobbins had a narrow neck at the top portion on which the threads were wound. An additional small neck or notch was often provided to secure the supporting knot of the attached thread.

Materials were typically bone or found hardwood, although bobbins were formed of almost any material. Ivory, silver, and brass were used to decorate bobbins as well as basic bobbin materials. Bobbins were molded, blown from glass, turned on lathes, or simply carved. Many were inlaid with silver and brass or just wound with lengths of these materials. As mementos, gifts, and keepsakes, many of the old bobbins are decorated with inscriptions relating to almost anything.

As the weaver will treasure a smooth fine shuttle, so the lacemaker treasures the fine bobbin. Use and age only enhance these as they obtain their smooth polished finish.

The size and weight of the bobbin will depend on the material being used. For fine threads, a light 4-inch bobbin is quite satisfactory. For heavy threads and cords, bobbins can get up to 9 inches long before they become too awkward to handle. The cord or thread is wound on the upper third of the bobbin, allowing the lower two-thirds to serve as the handle. When fine white threads are used, a recess to receive the wound thread will tend to keep it clean. The portion below this recess should be shaped for holding in the hand. For cords and heavier materials, a simple straight shaft can be used with a single notch to receive the supporting knot. Where thread length is limited, such as the hanging warp threads of a woven piece, a narrow notch

A selection of available bobbins suitable for contemporary bobbin lace. From the left: large winders useful for heavy ropes; a standard 6-inch contemporary bobbin with a small neck on one end used to secure the cord; with a small notch on the opposite end, this same bobbin can be used to secure the ends of hanging cords; large and medium contemporary bobbins; large and medium tapestry bobbins. For traditional as well as contemporary work: small Danish bobbins; large and small hooded bobbins; turned and polished decorative Bobbins. At the lower right is a simple table-mounted bobbin winder suitable for any of the smaller bobbins.

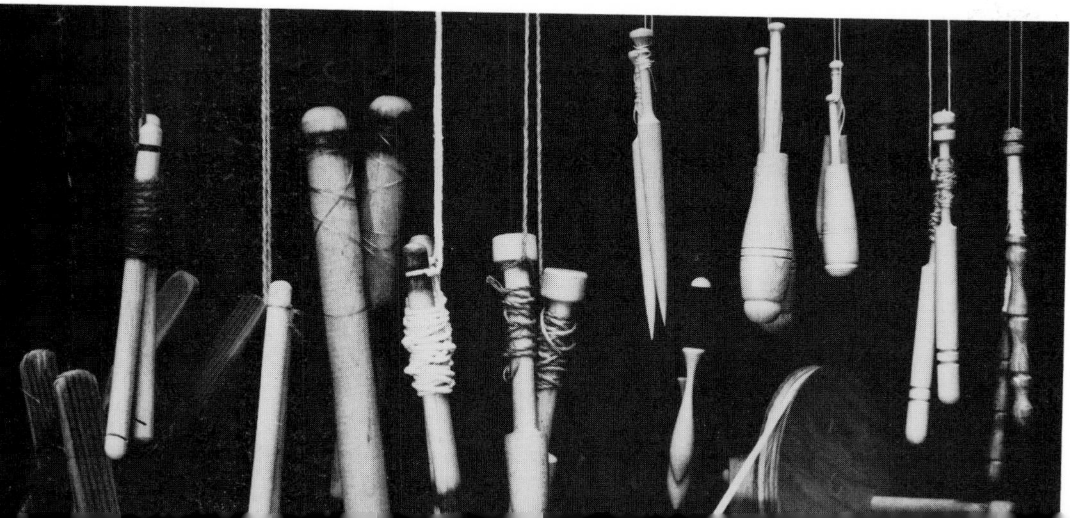

A piece of traditional lace being worked with turned shaft bobbins by Adrienne Webb.

or saw cut in one end of the bobbin will secure the thread at its end without requiring knotting. If this notch is put on the lower, or handle, end, it will not interfere with normal thread attachment.

Bobbins can easily be made from straight dowel stock of various sizes or improvised using chicken leg bones that have been cleaned and bleached, ordinary sticks or straight twigs, pencils, clothespins, and so on. Common construction nails, which come in many sizes and weights, can be used, although the double-headed "duplex" or form nails work better. Tubular porcelain electrical insulators work well and have a lovely sound. Weavers can use their fly shuttle bobbins or tapestry bobbins as working bobbins.

If the weight of your bobbin is not sufficient, additional weight can be hung from the bobbin by a wire.

A selection of improvised bobbins. From the left: two pairs of cleaned chicken bones; weavers' fly shuttles; double-headed "duplex" nails; railroad ties; porcelain electrical insulators; pencils with a small notch cut in one end.

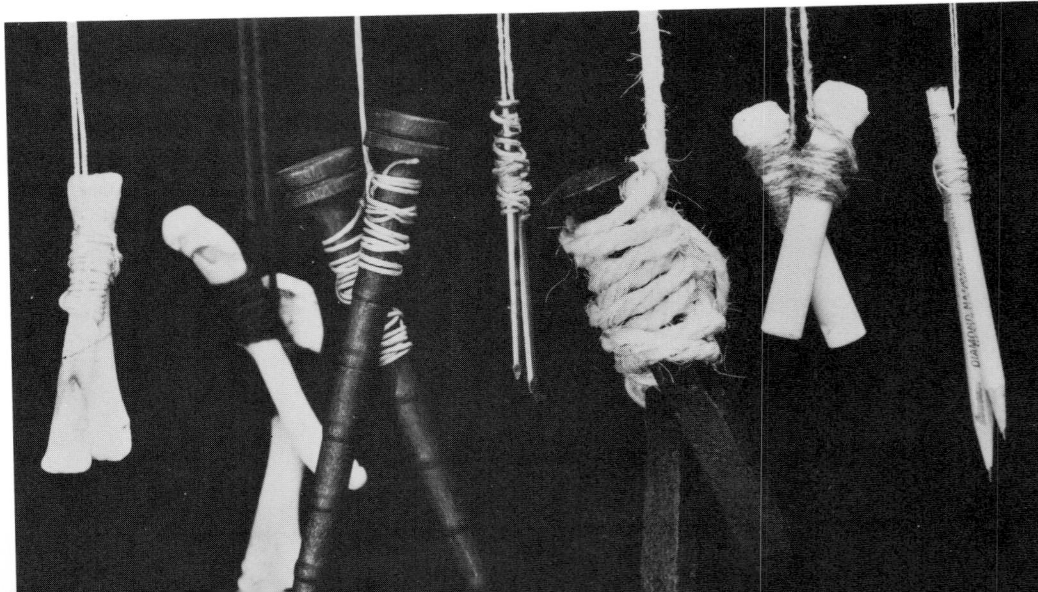

THE PILLOW

Most lace requires a firm "pinable" surface on which to work. The pillow, which can be in virtually any shape, dimension, or form, serves as this surface. A pin inserted into the pillow must be able to remain in position when the weight of several bobbins is supported by it.

Traditional lace was always worked on very hard stuffed pillows. These were made of canvas and stuffed tightly with straw, which was hammered hard with a mallet. Pins were inserted with difficulty into these pillows, many getting bent or broken in the process. The stuffed pillow was generally covered with a removable slipcover of a more decorative fabric. A pattern, usually of parchment, was pinned to the pillow and the lace worked over the pattern. Characteristic pillows developed in specific lace areas depending on the type of lace made and the techniques used in working it. In general, three basic types of pillows developed: the "tubular" type, a cylindrical form that could be rotated; the "cookie" type, which was a flat cushion generally round; and the "French" type, a revolving cylinder set in a well in a sloping padded flat pillow. The "cookie" and "tubular" types are useful for many forms of contemporary lace and can be made without too much difficulty.

TUBULAR PILLOW: The tubular pillow is used for making continuous tapes and yardage. A shawl, for example, is ideally worked on this type pillow. When working over a pattern, the pattern is pinned to the pillow in a continuous loop. As the work progresses, the pillow is rotated exposing a new work area. A good size to work on is 8 inches diameter by 16 inches long.

To make a pillow of this size, you will need a piece of feather ticking or 8-ounce canvas for the liner, 18 by 24 inches. A piece of material of the same size of smooth cloth will be needed for the cover. This material can be the same as the liner or it can be some other smooth material such as felt, velvet, or cotton. A washable material is preferred as it will need to be periodically removed and cleaned. A plain color should be selected as you will be working, many times, directly on this surface. For the pillow ends you will need two pairs of 3-inch-diameter circles, one pair for the liner and one pair for the cover.

Sew each of the rectangular pieces of material into a tube using a ¼-inch seam allowance. Form the tube by sewing the two 18-inch sides together. Leave both ends open. Take a strong cord and sew a gathering string along each open end using a ¼-inch margin. Pull one end together tightly and sew in place so end will not open. Turn right side out and fill liner with sawdust. You will need six to eight pounds depending on material. This can generally be obtained as a waste material from your local lumberyard. It should be clean and without chips. Fill the liner in 2-inch layers, beating down after each layer with your fist or a mallet. When full, pull in this end with the gathering string, leaving a small hole. Test the pillow for firmness. With the pillow lying down, you should not be able to make an impression in it if you push hard with your thumb. If it is not firm enough, add more sawdust using a kitchen funnel through the small end opening. Tamp pillow on its closed end to further compact the filling as well as flatten the end. When the pillow is full, pull the gathering cord tight and sew the opening together. Take the cut fabric circle and sew into place over each end. Now pull the slipcover over the liner and draw each end together. Sew up and cover ends with circles sewn into place. The cover should fit snugly without sliding over the liner.

Making a tubular pillow: Closing one end of the liner prior to filling.

Compressing sawdust in layers.

Closing up the liner.

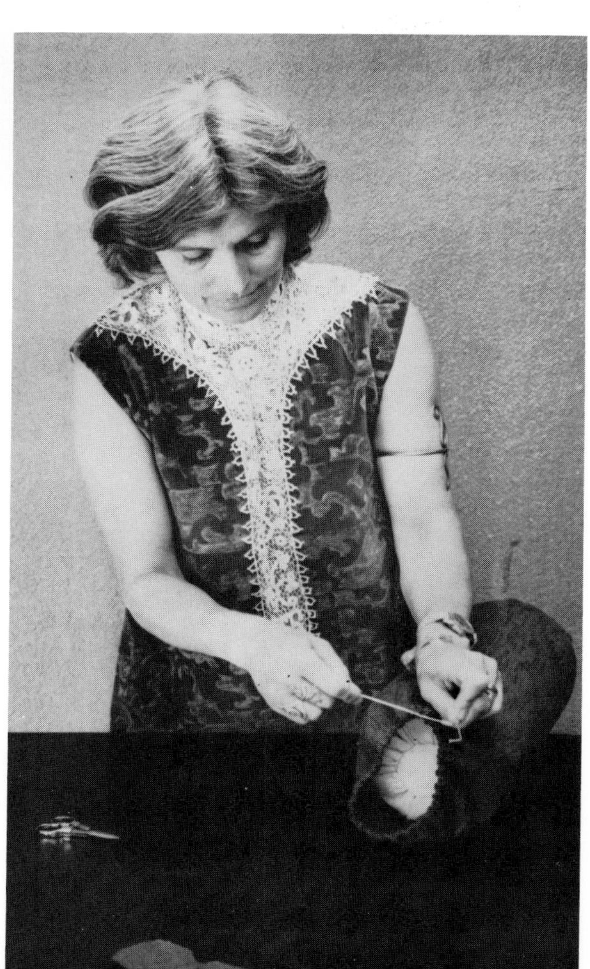

Closing slipcover with drawstring.

Sewing on end piece completing the pillow.

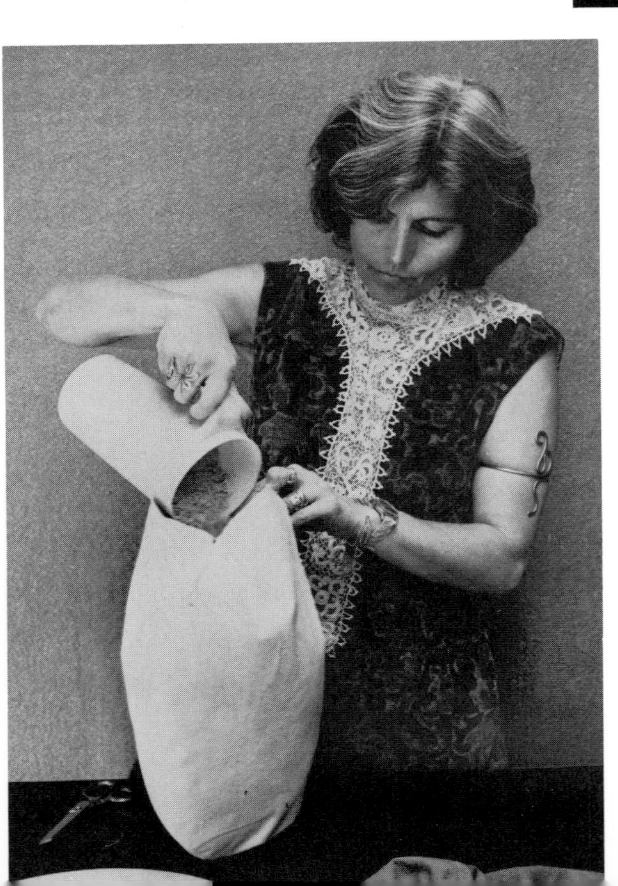

Making a cookie pillow: Filling the liner with loose sawdust.

COOKIE PILLOW: The cookie pillow is the type commonly used for making flat, nonlinear pieces such as collars, inserts, doilies, and so on. A 15-inch-diameter pillow is a good working size. You will need a firm base, which can be cut out of ¼-inch plywood or hardboard. It should be approximately 10 inches in diameter. For the liner you will need two pieces of material 16 inches in diameter. For the cover you will need one piece of material 22 inches in diameter.

Make the liner by sewing the two circular pieces together around their edges leaving a 3-inch opening. Seam allowance should be ¼ inch. Fill the liner full with sawdust without packing and sew up opening. Prepare the cover by sewing a ¼-inch hem around the material edge and pulling a drawstring through. Take the filled liner and slam it firmly on the table with the flat side down. Beat down and shape so one face is flat and the other domes up. Beat firmly compacting the sawdust. Place the cover material upside down on a table and lay the filled liner on top also upside down (flat side up). On top of this lay your base. Now pull the cover up over the base, pull the drawstring tightly, and tie the ends together. Turn the pillow right side up and beat around the edges to get a nice shape.

FLAT BOARD PILLOW: The flat board is most suited for contemporary lace forms. It is not only economical but can be had in almost any size or shape. An excellent material is fiber ceiling board used for acoustical ceilings. It is available in ½ inch thicknesses and in sizes up to 4 by 8 feet. Good working sizes are 12 by 16 inches and 16 by 24 inches. A circular piece cut into a 16-inch-diameter disk is ideal for working round or symmetrical shapes. With a nail through its center to another board, rotation is possible, permitting the piece to be worked from any direction. As bobbin lace requires much pinning, it is recommended that a cover be made for the board to keep the surface from becoming too shabby. A slipcover can be made, sized for a loose fit over the board. The cover can then be made tight by pulling and pinning at intervals of 1 inch all along the edge. This technique permits use of both sides of the board. Another technique is to simply glue your cover material to the board surface. An excellent adhesive that is easy to use is spray mounting adhesive. The disadvantage with glueing is that the cover cannot be removed for cleaning.

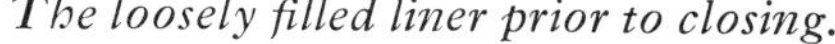

The loosely filled liner prior to closing.

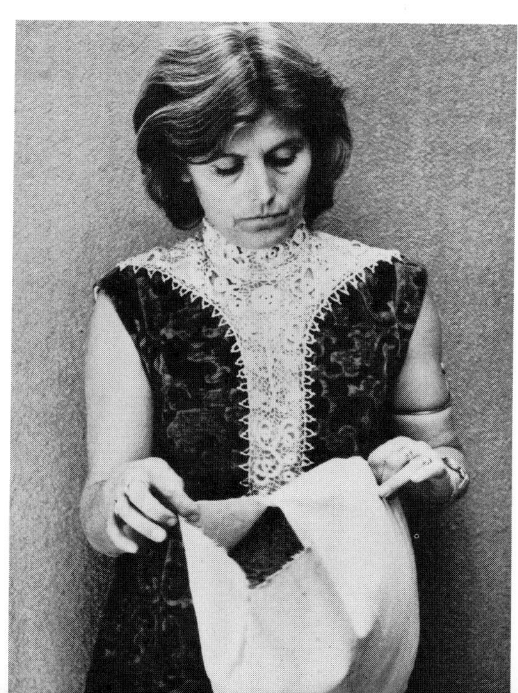

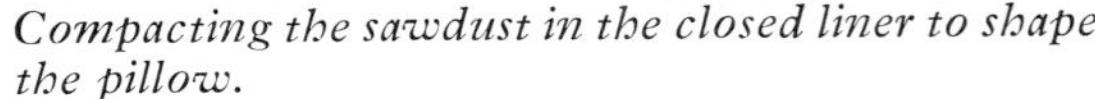

Compacting the sawdust in the closed liner to shape the pillow.

Securing the slipcover with drawstring.

PINS

Pins are used to work the pattern as well as to keep the bobbins in order. In working traditional lace over a fine pattern, the pins need to have very small heads and fine shafts as space is at a premium. Where fine threads are worked, brass or stainless steel pins should be used so as not to stain the threads. Considering these requirements, the stronger the pin the better. The length of the pin is somewhat dependent on the type of pillow used as well as the cord. A stuffed pillow will require a longer pin than the flat board. The inserted pin should be strong enough to support the weight of several bobbins.

Most work will require at least two different pin sizes: a small size for working the design and a large size for organizing and holding groups of bobbins out of the way. As pins tend to get bent and lost, it is good to start with about a gross of the small pins and about a dozen of the large ones.

For fine work, fine-head insect pins are excellent. They do not rust and come in a variety of sizes. Sizes 4, 6, and 7 are suitable for the finest of threads available today For heavier threads and cords, glass-headed florist pins work well. They have good sharp points and are easy to push into the pillow. If longer pins are required, hatpins can be used.

When working on a flat board, heavy "bank" pins, which are about 1½ inches long, seem to work the best. The head is small and they are very strong.

Except for large-scale work, "T"- and "O"-headed pins should be avoided; the heads will constantly be in the way of the work.

A selection of pins suitable for bobbin lace work. The large center pins are hatpins. These are used with stuffed pillows to keep groups of bobbins organized. The upper pins are glass-headed florist pins. The longer ones are for working designs on stuffed pillows, the smaller ones for working on a flat board. The lower right pins are fine-headed insect pins for working fine pieces. At the lower left are large heavy steel bank pins, the best for working on a flat board.

PILLOW STANDS

As the working of bobbin lace requires tension in the working threads, the pillow or board needs to be held in a position that will allow the bobbins to hang and thus weight the threads or cords. Although it is possible to work horizontally by letting the bobbins hang off the edge of the table, this is awkward and the least desirable method.

The tubular pillow is best supported by a simple cradle stand. This will support the pillow and keep it from rolling, while at the same time permitting manual rotation as the work progresses. Such a stand can be made from two pieces of wood with a circular cutout to match the curve of the pillow or it can be made by straps or slings supported from uprights. If using pieces of wood, the two pieces can be spaced and held in place with two dowels. In making such a stand, space the two end pieces or slings approximately two-thirds the pillow length. A floor stand for a tubular pillow can be made simply from a bar stool from which the seat has been removed. Two slings can be supported by the top ends of the legs. Strips of leather or canvas binding can be used for the slings.

Selection of lace stands and pillows. From the left: bar stool with a leather cradle for a tubular pillow; a round lace board on an adjustable table stand (secured at the center it is free to rotate); lace stand without board; adjustable table stand for supporting either a board or cookie type pillow; a decorative table stand for a tubular pillow; an adjustable floor stand for any board, cookie, or tubular pillow. The top is positively secured at any angle and is adjustable to any working height. The cantilever design permits sitting close to the work. See Chapter 3 for a simple easel-type table stand.

The flat board or flat pillow is best supported by an adjustable easel-type stand. The pillow should be supported at an angle of at least 45°. Many designs require working from different directions, as when working out from the center of a circular piece. For this reason it is desirable that the stand permit rotation of the board or pillow. If using a circular board, a nail driven through the center to the stand permits easy rotation. A clip is then required to hold the board in its selected position.

While a table stand is light and portable, a sturdy adjustable floor stand has the advantages of permitting the working at any height, angle, and with any type pillow.

PATTERN STOCK

Although not a necessary part of contemporary lace techniques, the pattern was of prime importance in working the traditional designs. The pattern indicated the full size and design of the finished lace with various graphic symbols used to note the various stitches and stylized designs. Every stitch was marked by a dot indicating a specific pin location. Ink markings further indicated the direction that the pattern was to be worked, the location of the gimp, and so on. The lace was worked directly on the pattern, which was pinned to the pillow, so it was subjected to heavy use. Heavy durable stock was required, which could be cleaned easily. Parchment was the most ideal material as it was transparent enough to allow tracing from a working layout and it was durable enough to serve many generations.

A selection of hand-drawn lace patterns on parchment, stiff paper, and card stock.

In contemporary lace, the pattern can take the place of a cartoon as used in tapestry. Every stitch need not be indicated but only outlines of worked areas, notations of stitch type, and maybe even texture sketches. This can be as simple or as detailed as one wishes. For one-time use, a heavy paper can be used, although a medium heavy board such as ordinary card stock will hold up much better. This is available in many colors and can be found in ordinary stationery stores or can be obtained from a local print shop. For ease in working, select a color contrasting to that of your thread. For heavier use, lightweight poster board is a good material.

If you have a paper pattern, it is a simple matter to transfer it to a piece of card stock. Lay the paper over the stock and with a needle or pricker, transfer the critical points. Another method is to glue the paper pattern, or a photo or electrostatic duplicate of it, to a card. Mounting adhesives, which are available in easy-to-use spray cans, make this a simple process.

USEFUL AIDS

As with most craft techniques, tools and aids seem to accumulate. Many find a use for only one project, while others become an essential part of your working equipment. The following list is in no way meant to be complete. It should, however, start you thinking of ways to make the working of any particular project simpler. Many of these items relate to other textile techniques as well. Some are just ordinary household items while others are just an improvised tool meant for something quite different.

BOBBIN WINDER: When many bobbins and fine threads are used the savings in time by the use of a bobbin winder can be considerable. In addition to speed, the bobbin winder places the thread on the bobbin without changing the natural thread twist. Both electric and manual winders are available with prices ranging from $9.50 to $30. Before purchasing a winder make sure it will handle the type of bobbin that you are planning to use.

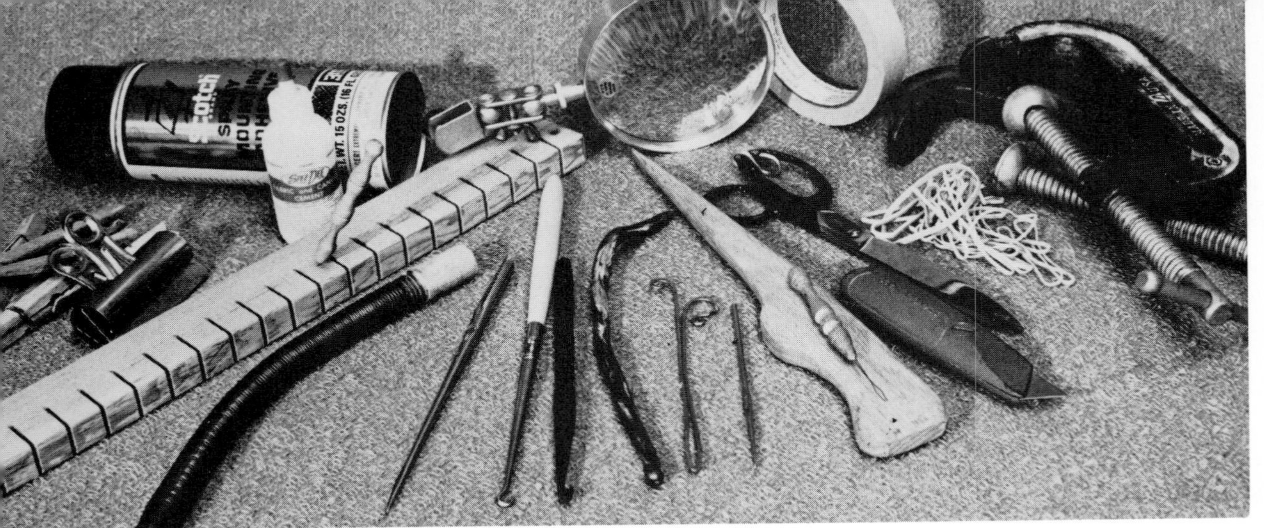

Useful aids. From the left counterclockwise: spray mounting adhesive; squeeze bottle of fabric cement; clothespins and paper clip; suspended-warp spacer beam; pricker (stuck in spacer beam); soft flexible spring; larding needle; selection of hooks for drawing threads and cords through small openings; wedge; mat knife; scissors; rubberbands; "C" clamps; masking tape; magnifying glass.

Most winders are not universal, although adapters are often available to extend their use.

WARPING BOARD: As with other multiple thread techniques, the measuring of the individual cords can become an unmanageable burden. A warping board, or set of warping pins, as used by the weaver is an ideal method of measuring your cords. When not available, a system can be improvised using two nails or simply the backs of two chairs.

CROCHET HOOK: An indispensable tool for handling cords and threads. The crochet hook is useful for splicing, sewings, adding threads, and so on. It is good to have several sizes available for the handling of a variety of materials. A shoe buttonhook is excellent for the larger cords.

SOFT SPRING: Stretched out and tied or nailed to your pillow, a spring will help keep your threads in place. A roller shade spring is excellent for this purpose.

SPACER BEAM: Another tool borrowed from the weaver, this is excellent when working large pieces where a board is not practical and suspension techniques are employed. The beam is simply a length of wood approximately 1 by 2 inches and about 12 inches long. Saw cuts are made along the length of the board approximately halfway through the board and about ½ inch apart. Clamped to a sturdy support, this beam will keep your cords in order.

FABRIC CEMENT: A good quick-drying fabric cement that stays resilient is indispensable for making splices, finishing and securing ends, and pointing your cord when threading beads.

MASKING TAPE: Ordinary masking tape can be used for grid lines on your board. It can be as temporary or as permanent as you wish, and will not damage most fabric cover materials. Used in this way it can outline your work, defining its perimeters as well as acting as a guide when working angular lines. When working with stiff materials, masking tape can be used to hold the cord on your bobbins.

YARN END WEAVER: A good tool for terminating threads at the end of a piece as well as for splicing in new cords.

WEDGE: Easily made from a tapered piece of wood, this tool is useful for adjusting openings and making sewings when working with heavy materials.

CLOTHESPINS, PAPER HOLDER: Useful, inexpensive tools for attaching additional weights onto a cord, for keeping cords in place, and as emergency bobbins. The old type one-piece clothespins, if you can find them, make excellent bobbins when working with medium weight cords.

LAYOUT PAPER: Any grid paper makes laying out of a pattern a simpler task. A 10- or 8-per-inch ruling is a good working scale.

PRICKER: A needle or pin mounted on the end of a handle is the traditional tool for making and transferring patterns and designs.

CLAMPS: Two "C" clamps can prove very useful. They can be used for measuring your cord, supporting your work when working in suspension, clamping a spacer beam to a support, and so on.

MAGNIFYING GLASS: When working with fine threads or when examining any fine piece, it can prevent much eyestrain.

LARDING NEEDLE: Clamped to the end of your cord, this tool will simplify many sewing operations.

SCISSORS, KNIFE: For cutting your materials.

PENCIL, PAPER: For making sketches and keeping notes of your work.

Cord measuring devices: warping board; nails in a piece of wood; two "C" clamps; warping posts.

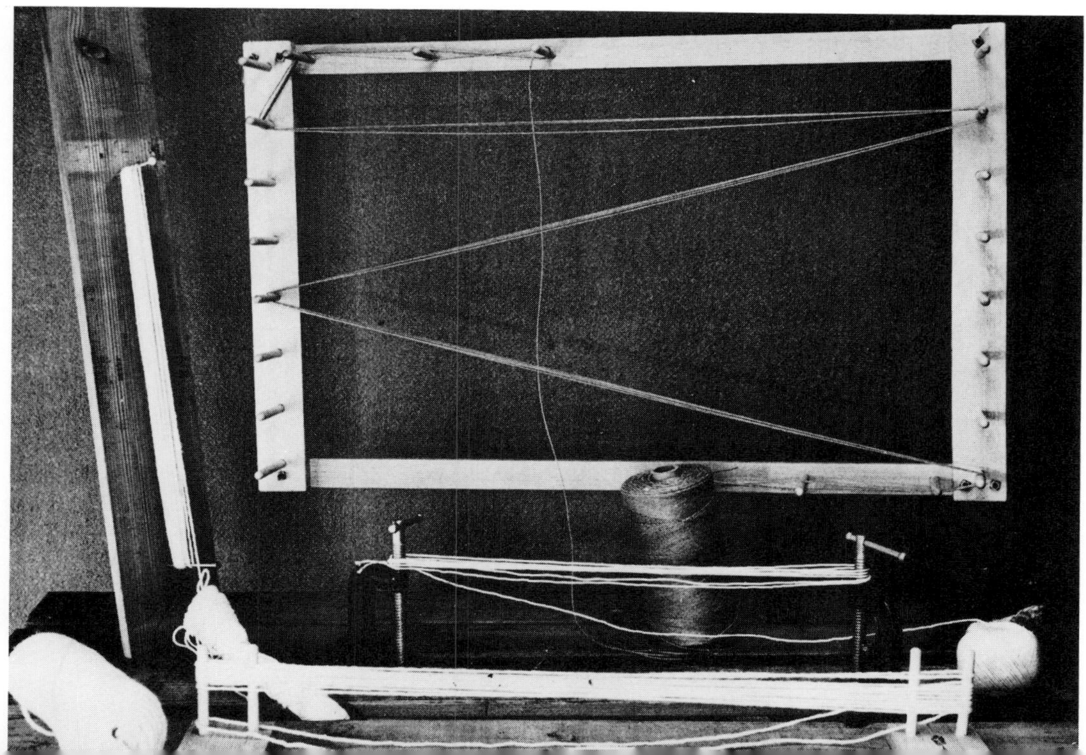

MATERIALS

There are virtually no limitations in terms of the materials that might be suitable for bobbin lace. In its traditional forms, only fine linen and silk threads were used, selected for their extreme fineness and durability. As a contemporary textile art, without scale limitations, any cord can be successfully used. With the popularity of textile crafts, macramé in particular, cords and twines of all types and colors are easily found.

In addition to the general cords and twines, other materials can be successfully used. As knots are not part of the fabric, materials that would ordinarily kink can be worked. Thus, wire, monofilament nylon, reeds, grasses, and so on can be useful and important materials.

Besides regular craft suppliers, your search for materials can extend to hardware stores, sporting goods stores, cane workers, cordage companies, and fabric centers. Natural environments are excellent sources for soft branches, grasses, vines, seaweed, and so on.

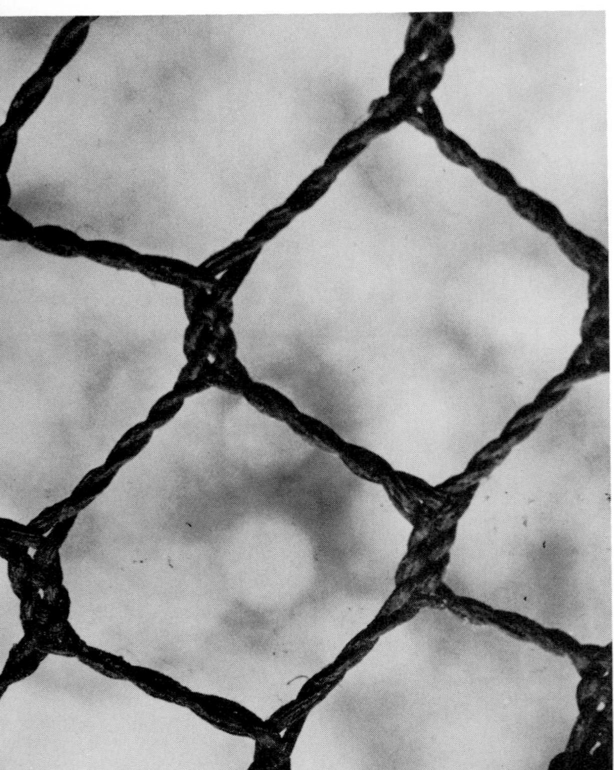

Waxed linen.

Tightly twisted marlin (treated jute).

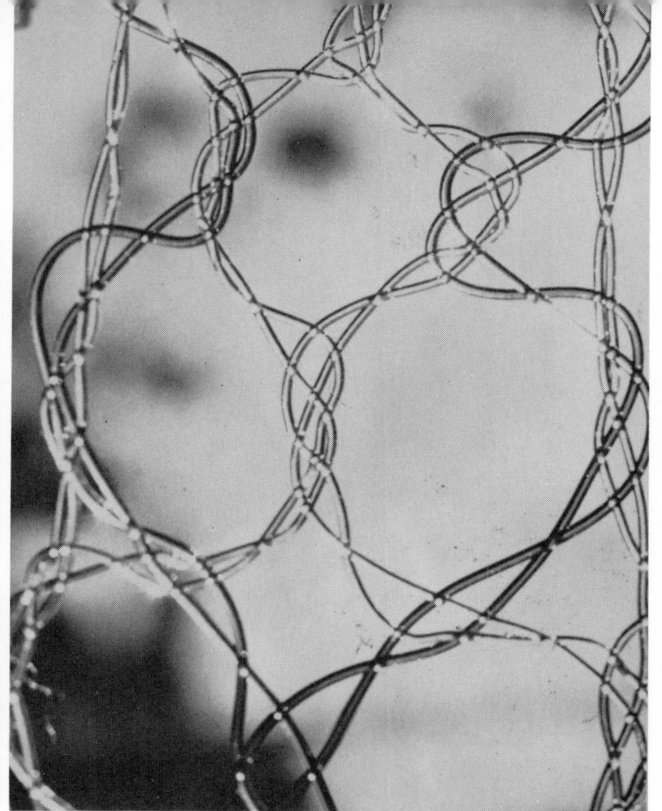

Nylon monofilament.

Plastic coated cord.

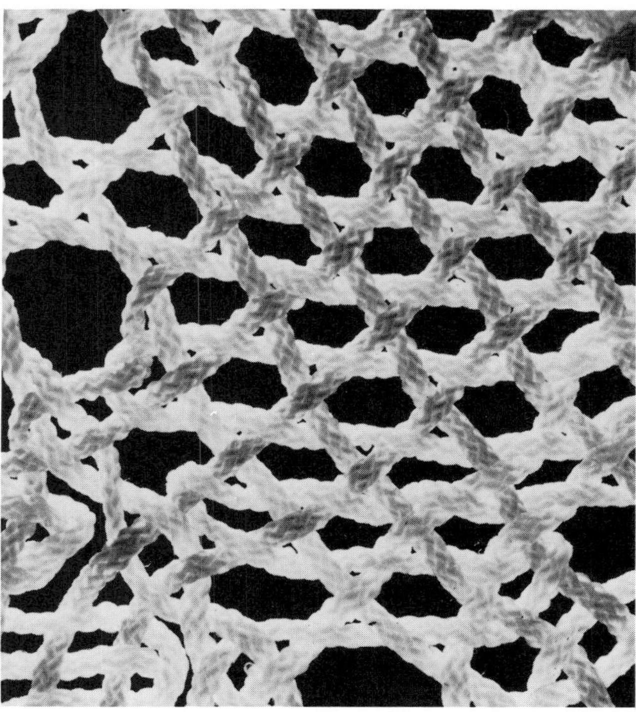

Braided nylon.

Standard marlin.

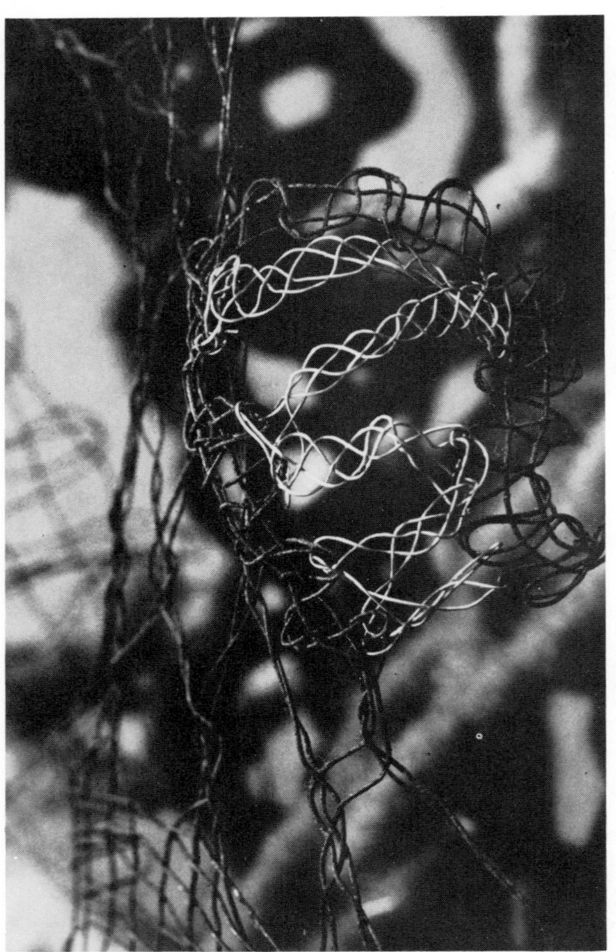

Wire, from a piece by Sharon Bazis.

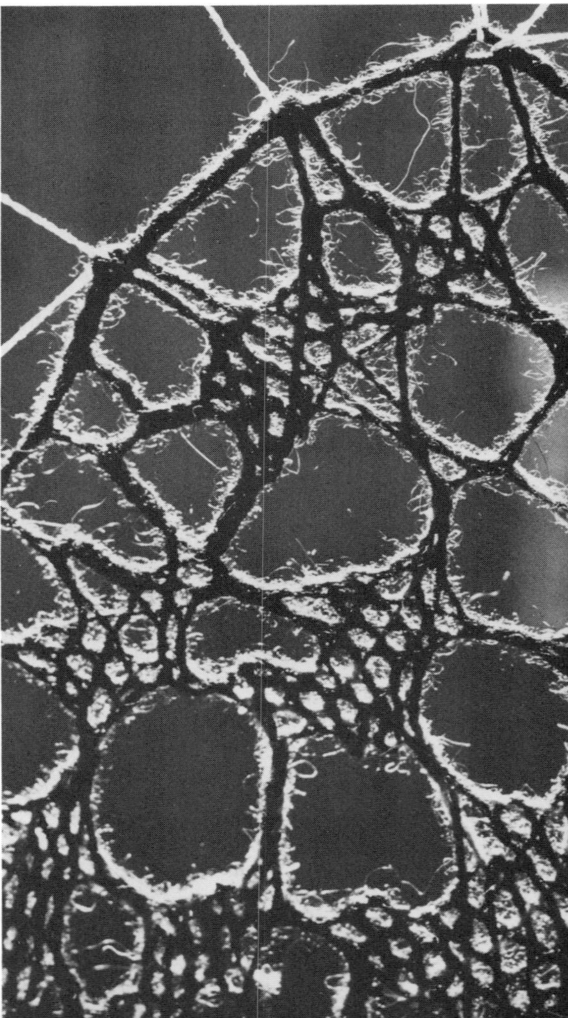

Rug wool, from a piece by the author.

Rattan, from a piece by Christina Santner.

TWIST: Before discussing the various cords, it is important to note that all cords, threads, and ropes have a twist. The twist will either be a right-hand or left-hand twist and is commonly referred to as an "S" or "Z" twist. When winding the cord around the end of a bobbin, you will tend to increase or decrease the twist. Winding an "S" twist cord counterclockwise will tighten the twist, and winding it clockwise will loosen the twist. It is a good practice in winding to maintain the natural twist by rolling the thread on, or to wind the thread around the bobbin in such a manner as to increase the twist.

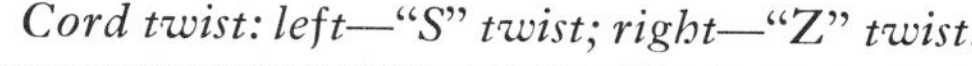

Cord twist: left—"S" twist; right—"Z" twist.

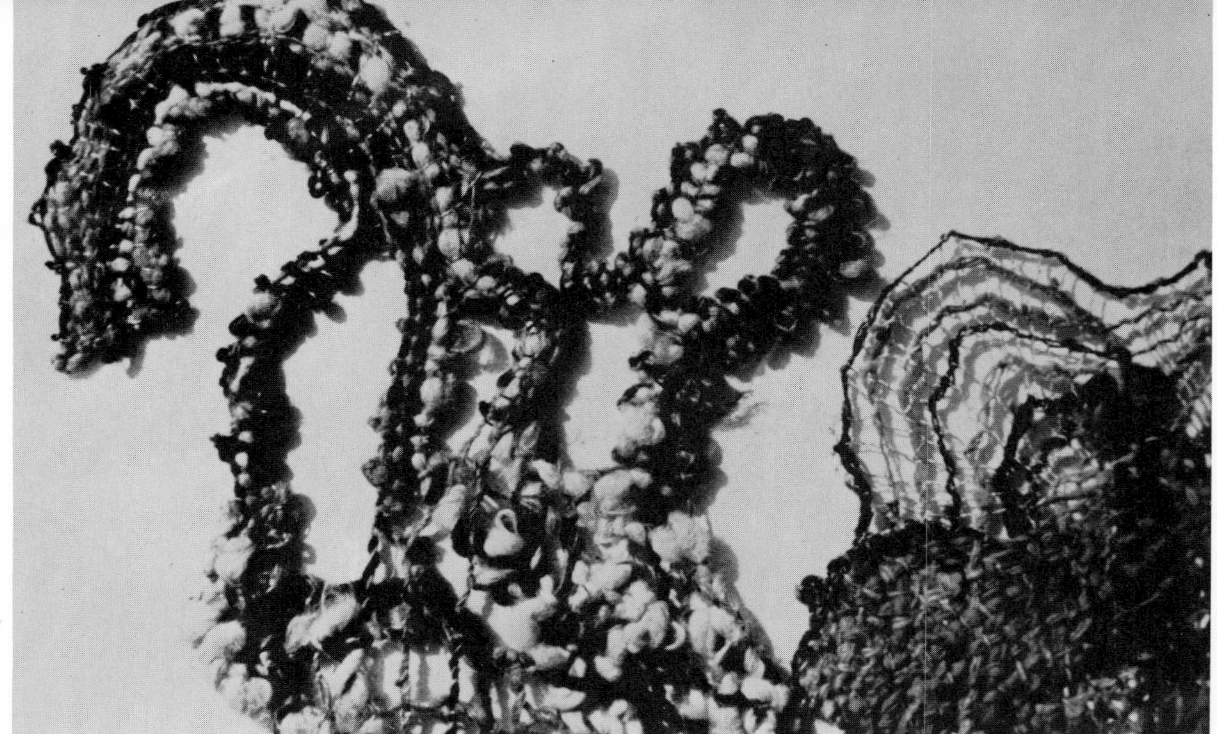

Handspun and novelty yarns used as a means to a rich textural surface. Detail of "Typography." Mary Ellen Cranston-Bennett. Photo: artist.

CORD DESIGNATIONS: Most cords can be defined in terms of material, ply, and size of ply. The number of single individual strands twisted together to form a cord is referred to as the ply. A 2-ply cord will be made up of two individual strands, a 3-ply cord will likewise be made up of three strands. The size of each individual ply is designated by a number that generally refers to a relation of spun length to fixed weight of material. Thus, the higher the number, the finer the ply. A 3-ply yarn designated as 3/22 will be heavier then another 3-ply designated as 3/62.

Threads

Threads are the traditional lace material. The finest of the linen threads are no longer available, although some fine materials can still be found. Threads are generally graded in numbers, the higher the number, the finer the threads. Lace threads were generally bleached, of 2-ply construction, and with a smooth finish. Of the linen lace threads, 120/2 is about the finest that is still available. Although this would be considered coarse in the working of many an old pattern, one pound of this material contains over 54,000 feet or almost ten miles of material. Linen is still the strongest and longest lasting of available threads. Cotton can be used for thread if properly conditioned. A "gassed" cotton thread indicates a thread from which the fine fuzz has been burned off. Silk and metallic threads are also available for lacemaking.

Cords

As a working material, cords can be divided into two general categories: soft materials and hard materials. Each has distinct characteristics in terms of design. Soft materials tend to emphasize pattern and color with the stitches being of less importance.

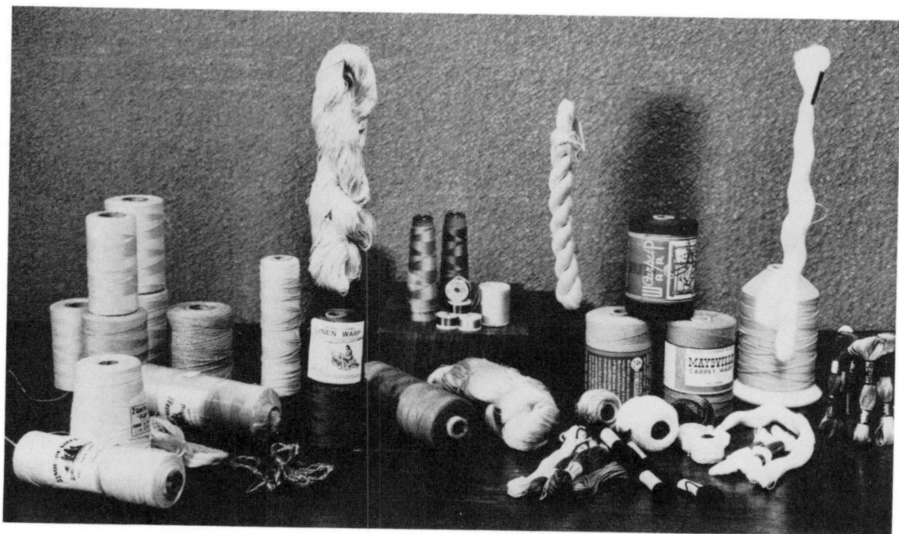

Lace threads. From the left: spools and hanks of linen threads and warps; silk threads; cotton threads and warps; cotton embroidery threads.

SOFT MATERIALS: Some of the more common soft materials are:

Rug yarns: Wool has coarse resilient fibers and is beautiful to work with. It holds stitches well and is available in many colors and weights. Cotton is a softer material and thus has less body. It works best for solid areas with minimal openings. Nylon has resiliency like wool, but has much more elasticity. Appearancewise, this material has a sheen that should be considered when making this selection.

Jute: Jute is a stiffer and coarser material than wool and is available in a variety of sizes and colors. It is inexpensive and can be obtained in much larger sizes than standard rug yarns. The main disadvantage of jute is that it wears poorly and rots easily. Marlin, a treated jute, overcomes these disadvantages but is tacky and has a distinct preservative odor. If you can put up with these disadvantages, you will find marlin a beautiful material to work with and excellent for outdoor pieces.

Flax: Flax or linen can be obtained in various weights and firmness. It has a much softer texture than jute and is probably the finest material to work with. It has great strength and durability and can be obtained in forms ranging from fine threads to heavy ropes. In heavier weights it is sold ordinarily as a "sack" twine in ½-pound-skein form. Common plys are 3, 5, 7, and 10. In lighter weights it can be found as a gilling twine or weaving yarn. A popular weaving size is 14/2, which is excellent for lace and comes in a wide variety of colors.

Sisal: Sisal is a coarse fiber and can be found in various qualities, the better grades being smoother and finer. It is the least expensive of the fibers and comes untreated, natural, and in colors, and in a treated form with either oil (baler twine) or creosote (tree rope) preservative. Although stiffer than the other fibers, it lends itself well to large-scale, open lacy textures.

Soft lace cords. From the left: linen; jute; sisal; wool, nylon and cotton rug yarns.

HARD MATERIALS: Hard materials tend to emphasize stitch and technique. They permit very crisp patterns and, therefore, are ideal when learning the basic techniques. Many of these materials are tightly twisted or cabled. When such cords are cut they tend to untwist. To prevent this, knot the cut ends or seal with a drop of fabric adhesive. Some of the more common materials are:

Cotton: Seine twine is a tightly twisted cord and is available in a medium or hard lay. It comes in many well-graded sizes from a #6, which is very fine, and up to a #72, which is a good ⅛-inch diameter. Larger sizes are also manufactured but are not as easy to locate. For large sizes, cotton rope can be used. These are specified by diameter in inch fractions such as ¼ inch, ⅜ inch and so on.

Linen: Cabled linen, which is also referred to as "cuttyhunk," is a beautiful material to work with. It is smooth, long wearing, and can be washed repeatedly. Sizes are limited however, with the maximum size being equivalent to a #18 cotton seine twine. Linen can also be found in braided form. Its main advantage aside from a texture difference is that there is no tendency for it to untwist.

Nylon: Nylon cords and ropes are available as cabled seine twines and as braided cords and ropes. Nylon comes in many sizes and its characteristic smooth shiny surface gives a piece a clean crisp quality. Some of the finer braided materials are available as fishing lines, the heavier ones as parachute cords.

Hard lace cords. From the left: polypropylene; cotton seine; linen cuttyhunk (cabled); braided nylon parachute cords; plastic-coated nylon.

Miscellaneous Materials

This category includes materials that are not ordinarily thought of as textile materials but which do lend themselves to the plaiting techniques of bobbin lace. Different weighting techniques are generally required as winding on bobbins is often impractical. Included in this category are:

Monofilament nylon: The beauty of this material lies in its translucent quality, which controls and bends light in magical ways. Although ordinarily found as a fishing line in fine sizes, it is also available in heavy sizes up to 1/8 inch.

Wire: Copper, zinc, nickel, aluminum, and silver wires can be used beautifully for bobbin lace. In finer sizes wire can be worked into jewelry, while in heavier sizes wire worked into a piece can give it structure and form. Most wire is available as a single strand in many sizes. Copper wire is available in both multistrand and single strand forms. The multistrand type can be untwisted and worked out from the main bundle.

Plastic tubing: This is another material where the translucent quality becomes a tool to work with.

Reeds: Reeds, including all types of grasses and raffias, are available in a wide variety of textures and sizes. The grasses can generally be worked dry, while most of the reeds should be worked wet. Shaped reeds can be used as structural supporting members as well as part of the decorative fabric. Although many of these materials can be purchased, some are native to almost every area and can be found. Seaweed and water grasses are suitable as are tall field grasses.

Miscellaneous materials: reeds, raffia, plastic tubing, nylon monofilament, gold braid, wire, sea grass.

Decorative Elements

Decorative elements can be described as objects that become part of the finished piece but not part of the textile fabric. Much of bobbin lace works best if kept taut in a frame or over a solid surface. Old picture frames can often be found or wood and wire can be used to advantage to make your own frame. Standard size wire rings are available or can be fabricated. Reeds can be shaped to almost any form with the ends overlapped and tied. Larger size reeds should be soaked first and then tied.

For a solid surface on which to mount a piece, a painted board or fabric-coated board is a relatively simple task. A piece of driftwood, bark, or even stone can be far more interesting and even establish the concept for a piece. Where a frame is not used, some hanging support of rigid material can be your structural element. A dowel or broomstick is a simple device. Again, a natural branch, a piece of driftwood, a rusty piece of iron, a nail, or almost any old finding can complement a piece. A hand-forged piece of brass or cast piece of metal can be specifically designed for your work.

Other items you will be looking for are buckles, purse handles, neck rings, jewelry findings, and so on. Some of these can inspire a project while others will be a necessary and functional part of them.

Beads can also form part of your fabric. A single bead might form the focus of your project or many inexpensive beads can just add to the pattern. Manufactured beads are numerous in many materials and colors. Beads can also be made out of wood, seed pods, slices of horn, papier-mâché, clay, and leather. The most elaborate tool needed to fabricate your own beads is a hand drill.

COLOR AND DYEING TECHNIQUES

Color can be an important design tool in working contemporary lace. Traditional lace was always worked with fine bleached white threads with total emphasis on texture and design as expressed by open and closed areas. With the independent control of cords that is inherent in bobbin lace, individual colored cords can be used to create designs where color and value are the prime elements.

Although many of the cords are available in a variety of colors, far greater rewards are to be had by dyeing natural cords to your own specifications. Aside from the cost savings, dyeing allows you to obtain many shades of one color and to achieve special effects such as variations of color throughout a piece of cord as well as multicolored cords. Techniques of tie-dyeing lend themselves well to skeins or hanks of cord.

With primary emphasis on simplicity and ease of dyeing, discussion here is related to the use of packaged household dyes. Some packaged dyes work primarily as tints while others, such as Putnam dyes, permit deep rich colors. All natural materials including cotton, rayon, wool, linen, silk, and even wood can be permanently dyed. Among the synthetics, nylon is the only material that dyes well. Polyesters such as Dacron, acetates, polypropylene, and glass fibers will not take packaged dye. This characteristic can be used to advantage in planning a piece with color. If a finished lace piece is dyed that incorporates some nondyeable materials, the finished dyed piece will retain strong contrasts of the different materials in terms of color. It should be noted that all dyeable materials do take dye differently, the texture, material, and predyed color all having some effect. If you plan to dye any piece after completion, it is a good practice to test the various yarns for dyeing prior to dyeing the finished piece.

If you are in doubt as to a particular material, a simple burn test can be made. Any of the natural fibers will burn leaving an ash. Cotton, linen, and rayon smell of burning paper, while wool, silk, and animal fibers will have the odor of burning hair or feathers. Nylon will melt and bead up as will most synthetics.

PREPARATION OF MATERIAL FOR DYEING: There are many ways of preparing yarns for dyeing, depending on the result and type of control you desire. For perfectly uniform color the yarns must be wound into skeins and tied loosely. This is best accomplished with a skein winder or a hand-held niddy noddy, which is inexpensive and easy to store. The beginning and end of the skein should be twisted together and tied around the skein, forming a figure eight as it goes around and between the strands. Two or three similar ties should likewise be made equidistant around the skein. These ties should all be loose so as not to cause streaks. If controlled streaking is desired, the skein can be tied tightly at various places. These areas will not dye and will remain in the original yarn color. Retying and dyeing in a different color dyebath will produce other color combinations. For variegated yarn having different colors, the skein should be suspended above the dyebath with only a portion of it submerged in the bath. When the first dyeing is complete, the skein is rotated and another section of the skein is placed in another dyebath. Four or five colors can be achieved this way, depending, of course, on the size of your skein. Each color will repeat at regular intervals. Irregular variegated effects can be obtained by dyeing yarn that is wound in a relatively loose ball or pull skein. Dyed in this form, the outer layers will dye darker than the inner layers. Tightly wound balls of cord can similarly be dyed. Strong contrasts of dark, light, and no color will result with the inner cord receiving no dye at all.

In addition to predyeing your cords, the finished article can also be dyed. This has the obvious advantage of not having to worry about running short or having to dye an excess of material. Where twists in your stitches are tight, there is likely to be some difference in shading of the dyed color. Remember that different materials will take color differently as will most wood beads.

Preparing yarn for dyeing: winding into skeins with a niddy noddy, or skein winder; pull-skeins tied for spotted effects. Note the pulling of a pull-skein apart for a more uniform dye.

Tying a skein in a loose figure eight prior to dyeing.

PREPARATION OF DYEBATH: In preparing a dyebath, it is good practice to first dissolve each package of dye, which comes in a dissolvable packet, in a quart jar of boiling water. Do not open these packages as the dye powder is very fine and can be quite messy. A total quart of the mixed dye added to a water bath will dye approximately one pound of cord or yarn the color as shown on the dye package. This should be used as the basis for designing your dyebath. For less than a pound of material a proportionately less amount of dye solution should be used. For deeper or lighter shades, increase or decrease the amount of dye solution relative to the weight of material. Dyes prepared in this fashion permit a simple method for mixing colors. Proportionate amounts of mixed dye solution from your quart jars can be mixed in another jar, the total mixed dye then being your working solution. Thus, a quart of this new color will dye one pound of material. It is a good practice to keep a record of these mixes in case duplication should be necessary. Any unused dye will keep indefinitely in its jar for future use.

If bright colors are desired on some of the darker of the natural fibers such as linen and jute, a stripping agent such as Putnam's No-Kolor should be used prior to dyeing. Similarly, if you are dyeing yarn that has previously been dyed, and bright colors are desired, it is best to first strip out the original color.

Preparation of dyes: dye packages are dissolved in quart jars to make a concentrated working solution (note the dissolvable package on the right). Amounts from these jars are then added to your dye pot for desired color and then water added to completely cover your material.

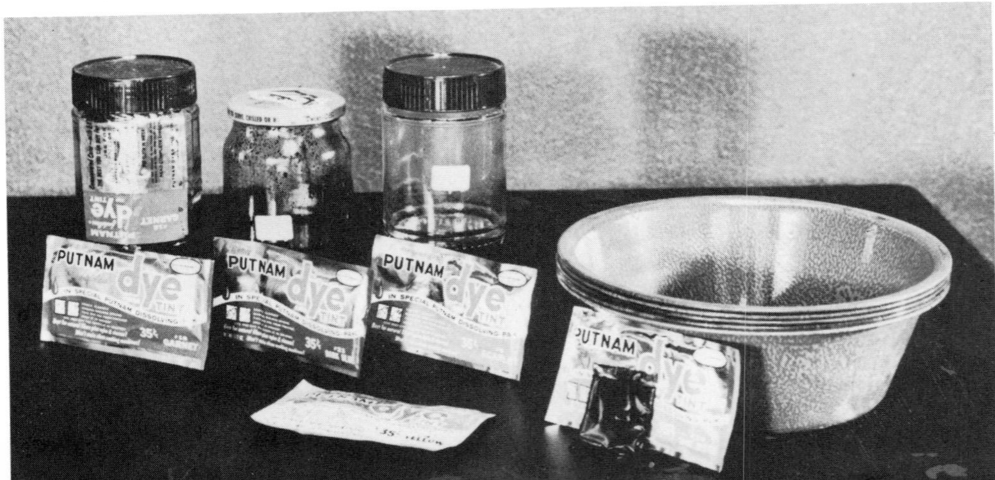

DYEING: Although washing machine methods can be used in dyeing, the most successful results and the most colorfast colors will be obtained by using a simmering method. This is done on the stove using any ordinary cooking pot. For the clearest colors use only stainless steel or enameled pots. An iron or aluminum pot will have an effect on the color that might or might not be desirable. To make the dyebath, simply fill the pot with cool water so that it will just cover your material. Add to this the determined amount of dissolved dye from your quart jar.

Before placing your prepared material into this bath, wash it in a warm detergent solution and then rinse thoroughly in clear warm water making certain that all the detergent is rinsed out. This wet material is then placed in the dye pot and the solution slowly brought to a simmer or slow boil. Periodically gently lift the material to stir the solution. Continue simmering until the dye solution becomes clear, indicating that all the dye has combined with the material. Some colors will take only 20 minutes, while many of the deeper colors will take over an hour. After 20 minutes or so, salt can be added in the ratio of 3 to 4 ounces per pound of material to shorten the dye process. When the dyebath has cleared, the material can be removed and rinsed in water of the same temperature as the dyebath. Time permitting, it is a better practice to let the material cool in the dyebath until it reaches room temperature. Then rinse off in cool water. Always avoid temperature extremes in handling yarns. Many fibers, wool in particular, will mat and become harsh if subjected to rapid temperature changes. Do not remove your material from the dyebath before it has been exhausted. If in doubt as to how dark a color is desired, always dye to a lighter shade. You can always repeat the process to get it darker.

When dyeing is complete and yarns have been rinsed, gently squeeze to remove excess water and hang on a clothesline out of direct sunlight to drip dry. If balls of cord have been dyed, wind them into skeins to speed drying. If pull skeins have been dyed, pull out the center third of the skein before hanging to dry.

If the above methods are followed, which are really quite simple, you wil find dyeing an absolutely painless process. There should be no mess from powders, no staining, and no residues. There are no chemicals to mix, and there should be no fear of toxicity from the dyed material. The rewards are many with unlimited potential in designing with color.

A variety of dyed yarns showing various tying effects and the results of dyeing cord wound in a ball.

The Basic Techniques

Chapter 3

One of the most delightful surprises of bobbin lace is the simple technique from which all bobbin lace patterns are made. The TWIST and CROSS actions are all that need be mastered to accomplish unlimited and rich patterns.

Countless patterns can be found from which traditional lace has been formed. The real rewards, however, come from combining the TWISTS and CROSSES in unique and original ways.

The handling of your threads by way of their bobbins should be one of ease and should be done in a relaxed manner with a natural rhythm as you make the TWISTS and CROSSES. As there are no knots, there is no tugging or pulling other than the normal pull of the bobbins and the occasional tug to align your work. Practice the motions, stitches, and grounds of this chapter until they are mastered with all motions becoming automatic. With this accomplished, emphasis can be placed on innovation and exploration, the real joys of bobbin lace.

Thread was the traditional bobbin lace material and this term will sometimes be referred to in describing the material secured to the bobbin, although a cord, rope, or even a wire might be used as the working material.

The materials and tools required for the learning of the basic techniques include: a "pinnable" board; a stand to hold it in an inclined position; eight pairs of bobbins; heavy pins; a scissors; two colors of a medium weight cord.

PREPARATION

To learn and work the basic motions, stitches, and grounds you will need eight bobbin pairs or a total of sixteen bobbins. A simple shaft bobbin made from a 3/8-inch round dowel is quite suitable. These should be cut between 6 and 7 inches long, and the ends rounded. Cut a groove completely around each bobbin approximately 1/2 inch from one end. For your starting cord use cotton seine twine or an equivalent in a size between numbers 24 and 36. You will need two colors of this cord; one can be natural and the other a darker color. If a color cannot be found, dye about 25 yards of the natural cord. For a pillow, a flat board type is recommended approximately 12 by 16 inches. Prepare this board as described in Chapter 2. Bobbin lace is most easily worked with your board in a generally vertical position. Use a stand or some other prop to keep your board at a good working angle. If the board is too close to horizontal, the weight of the bobbins will be unable to maintain tension in the cords. A couple of dozen heavy straight pins about 1 1/2 inches long should be sufficient for these exercises.

WINDING THE BOBBINS

With few exceptions, all bobbin lace is worked with bobbins in pairs. These pairs are prepared prior to starting the work.

To prepare a single bobbin pair, cut a length of cord twice as long as that required for one bobbin. When many threads or cords are required, a warping frame or board is an extremely useful tool for measuring your cords. If this is not available, wrap your cord around two nails, the back of two chairs, or some other pair of supports.

Holding a bobbin in one hand, the object is to wind approximately one-half of your cord onto the upper portion of the bobbin, keeping it below the groove. Prior to winding, the center of your cord can be noted with a kink or slipknot. Ideally the thread or cord should be wound on the bobbin without changing its twist. This is particularly critical with the firmer cords. Winding the cord around the bobbin will either increase or decrease the twist, depending on the direction that it is wound. If the bobbin is rolled in your hand, the cord will wind on without changing its twist. In this method, direction is not important so long as all bobbins are wound in the same direction. A bobbin winder permits rapid winding in this manner. The softer cords can be wound around the bobbin without serious consequences. If hand winding, this is generally a faster method. If your cord has a "Z" twist, wind in a clockwise direction. If it has an "S" twist, wind counter-clockwise. Winding in this way will increase the natural twist of the cord. If the cord becomes overtwisted and starts to kink, simply let it untwist. Pull firmly while winding, distributing the cord uniformly. Avoid pileups on the shaft, which will cause loose loops and cause your bobbin to unwind.

You are now ready to secure the cord at the notch at the top of the bobbin. This is done with a half hitch and can easily be learned by following the illustrations. Form a loop with the index finger of your right hand. Twist this loop once or twice, whichever works better with the cord you are using, and then flip the resulting loop over onto the bobbin head. Pull the free end of your cord taut to secure this knot in the groove. This knot not only secures the cord to the bobbin, but allows controlled release of the cord. A simple twist of the bobbin in a direction opposite to that wound will unwind the cord from the bobbin while still maintaining the knot. To shorten your cord, slip a finger under the cord just below the knot and then wind the bobbin in the direction to that wound.

In the same manner, using another bobbin, wind the other half of your cord starting from the free end. This completes the preparation of one bobbin pair.

If contrasting colors are desired in a bobbin pair, simply knot the two cords together between the two bobbins. If possible, try to avoid these and any other knots. By rearranging bobbins of bobbin pairs, contrasting cords can often be introduced without knots. Techniques for accomplishing this are explained in later chapters.

For ease in manipulating the bobbins, always keep your suspended bobbins at the same level. Wind or unwind the cord from the bobbins as required.

PINNING

The pin has many functions in bobbin lace. It is used to hold your piece to the pillow, to hold your pattern to the pillow, to keep your bobbins in place, to hold the cords when they change direction, and to locate the center

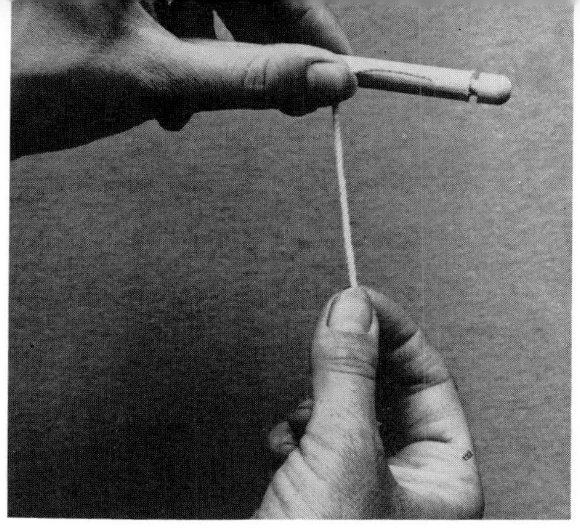

Hold the bobbin and the end of your cord in one hand with approximately one inch of the cord extending beyond your finger.

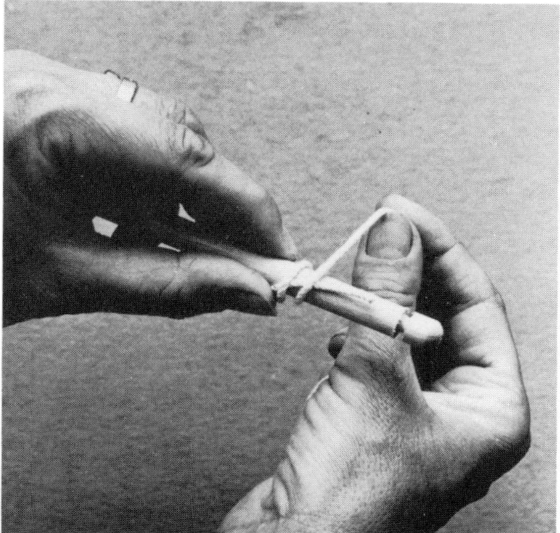

With your other hand, wind the cord around the bobbin and the extended cord end.

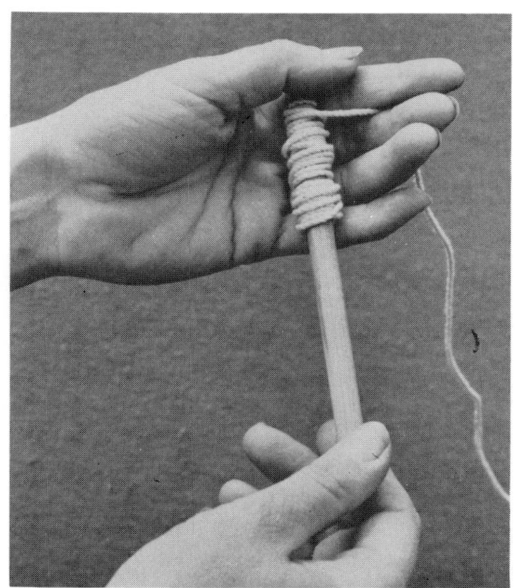

Rotating the bobbin with one hand, guide the cord on with the other. Keep the cord on the upper portion of your bobbin.

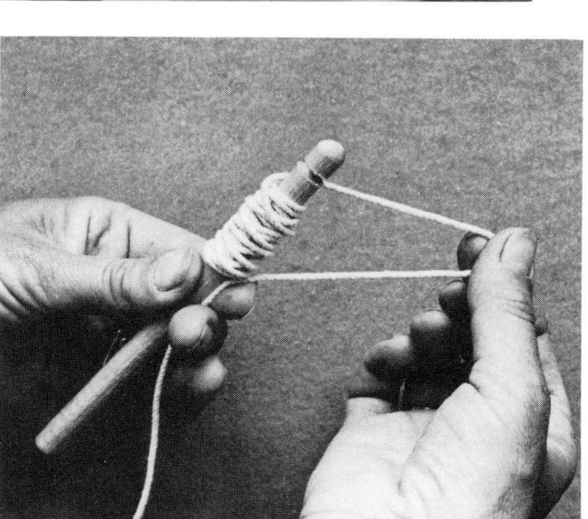

At completion of winding form a loop with the free cord.

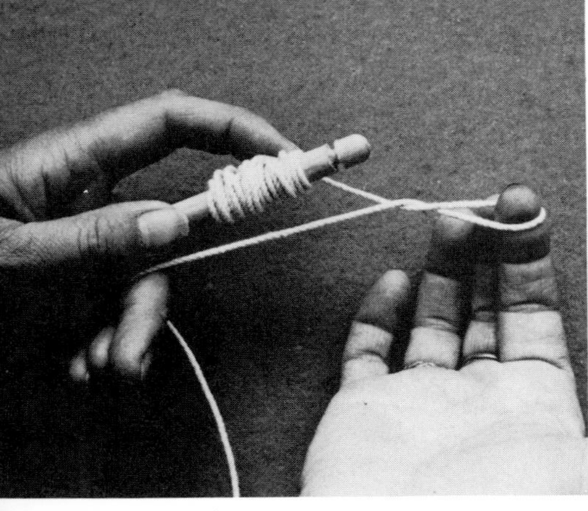

With your index finger twist the loop.

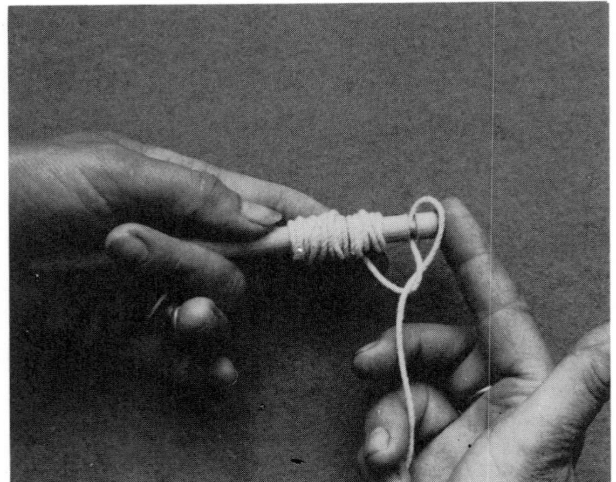

Flip the formed loop over and onto the bobbin head.

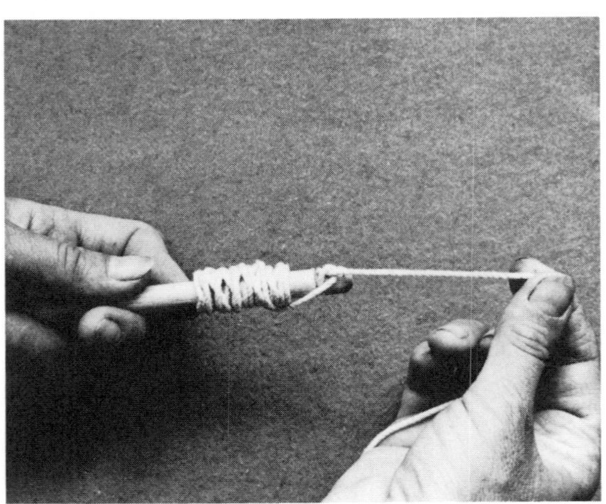

Pull the free end of your cord, securing the knot into the bobbin neck.

of a stitch. When used to control the working threads, the operation of inserting the pin into your board is referred to as PIN. When used to hold a stitch in place, it generally comes after a CROSS—TWIST motion and is placed under the cross. When a pattern is used, this point would be noted as a pinpoint or pricking point.

As the inserted pin often takes the weight of the bobbin and its cord as well as an occasional tug, it should be placed into the pillow or board at an angle away from the work. This not only gives it strength but keeps it out of the way.

THE BASIC MOTIONS

With few exceptions, it can be said that in bobbin lace ALL MOTIONS ARE MADE SIMULTANEOUSLY WITH TWO BOBBIN PAIRS. To learn the basic motions you will need two bobbin pairs. Wind each bobbin of each pair with approximately one yard of cord. Wind one of the bobbin pairs with a cord of a contrasting color. PIN two pins near the top of your board approximately 1 inch apart. Hang one of your bobbin pairs on each pin.

The basic and only motions of bobbin lace are the TWIST and the CROSS. Combined in various ways, these form stitches that in turn are combined to form the many patterns and grounds that form all bobbin lace designs.

With palms up, hold one bobbin pair in each hand. Now make a TWIST:

> A TWIST is the crossing of the two cords of one bobbin pair RIGHT OVER LEFT, or counterclockwise. Unless specifically noted as being worked with only one pair, the TWIST is always worked with two pairs simultaneously.
>
> TWIST both hands counterclockwise holding onto the bobbins. This will place the right bobbin cord over the left bobbin cord of each pair. Return your hands to their normal palm-up position, leaving the bobbins in their new position.

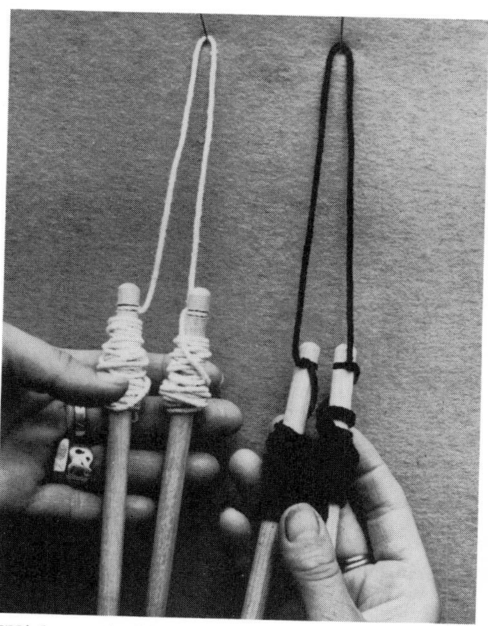

With two bobbin pairs pinned to your board, hold one pair in the palm of each hand.

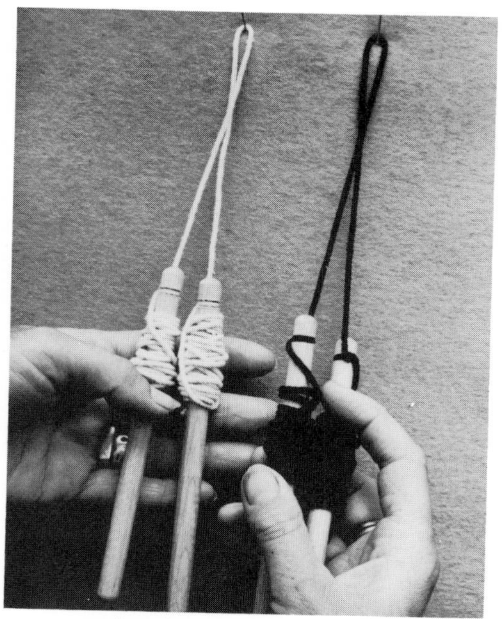

TWIST *each pair simultaneously placing the* RIGHT CORD OVER THE LEFT CORD.

You can now follow the TWIST motion with a CROSS:

> A CROSS is the crossing of the two inner cords of two bobbin pairs LEFT OVER RIGHT, or clockwise.
>
> Drop the right bobbin from the pair in your left hand over the left bobbin in your right hand and into your right hand. Transfer the left bobbin from your right hand into your left hand. These motions are done simultaneously and become quite automatic with practice.

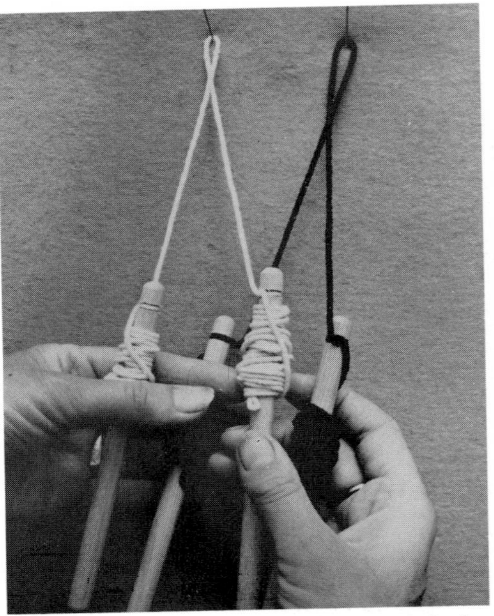

Form a CROSS *with the inner two cords by placing the* LEFT CORD OVER THE RIGHT CORD. *The inner bobbins will exchange hands.*

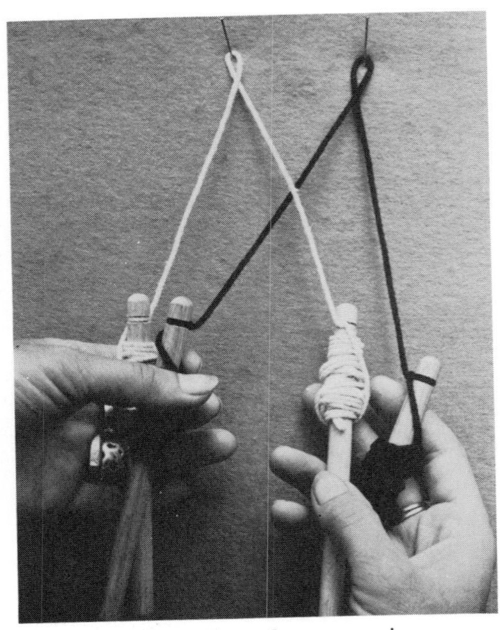

The complicated CROSS *motion.*

THE BASIC STITCHES

The combination of the basic motions in a particular sequence while working with only two bobbin pairs defines a stitch. Using the same two bobbin pairs as used for the basic motions, pinning each to your board approximately 1 inch apart, work the following stitches.

Half Stitch

The *half stitch* always begins with both pairs in the TWIST position. The combination of the motions

CROSS—TWIST

forms the *half stitch*. If you work with additional pairs and use one pair from your initial stitch and an adjacent bobbin pair, the *half stitch* can be repeated to form a weave.

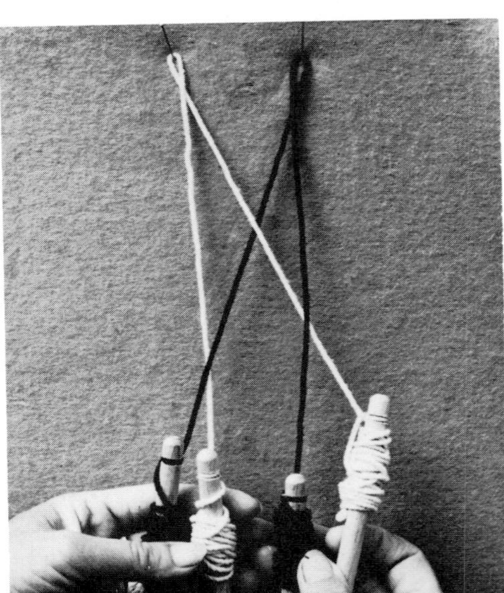

Continuing from your CROSS *motion make another* TWIST *motion with the new bobbin pairs.*

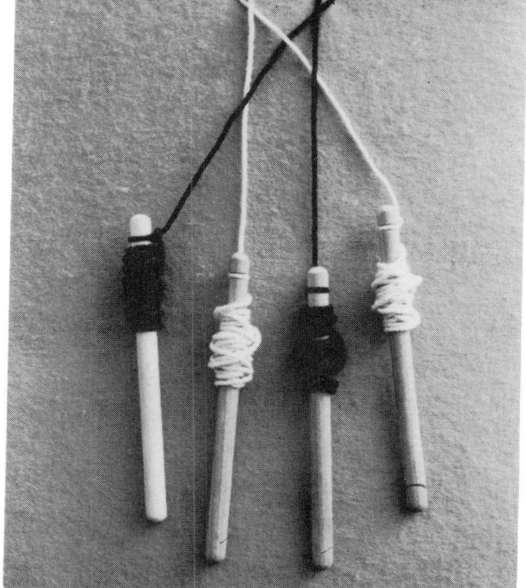

A CROSS *followed by a* TWIST *forms the half stitch.*

Whole Stitch

If the *half stitch* is continued once again with the same bobbin pairs, the result is the *whole stitch.* A pin is generally inserted after the first TWIST to locate the center of the stitch as well as to keep the stitch in place. Thus, the combination of

CROSS—TWIST—PIN—CROSS—TWIST

forms the *whole stitch.* If you work with additional pairs, another *whole stitch* can be made using two adjacent bobbin pairs.

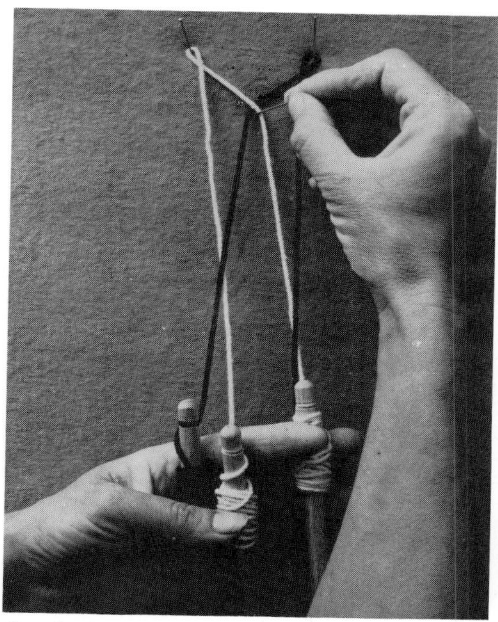

Continuing from your half stitch, hold all bobbins in one hand and PIN *under the cross formed with the other hand.*

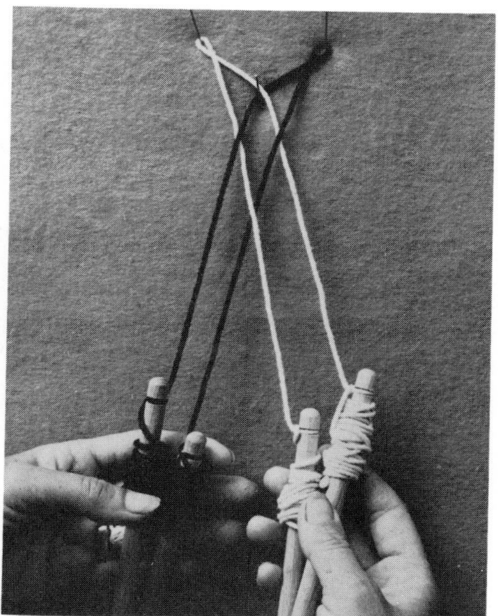

Make another CROSS *with the inner bobbins, again exchanging hands.*

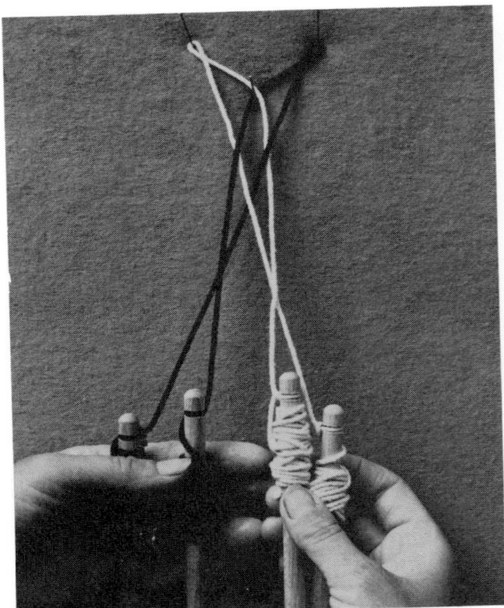

Follow with a TWIST *completing a whole stitch.*

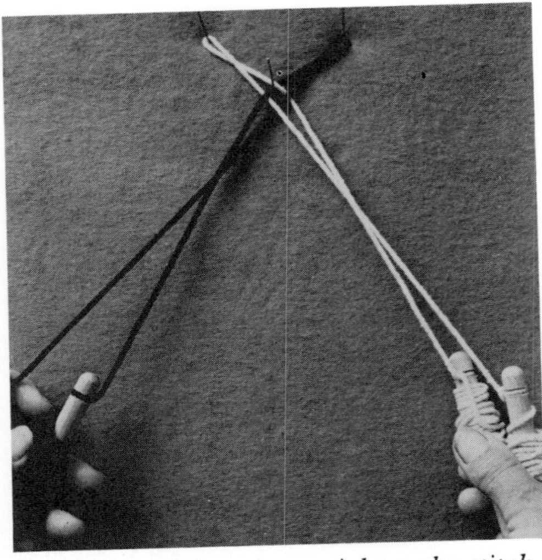

Pull both bobbin pairs to tighten the stitch, drawing it up to the pin. The sequence of CROSS—TWIST—PIN—CROSS—TWIST *forms the whole stitch. Note that the completed stitch leaves both bobbin pairs in the* TWIST *position.*

Braid

If the *whole stitch* is repeated two or more times using the same bobbin pairs, a *braid* is formed. Pins are generally not used in a *braid* except under the first and last CROSS for support.

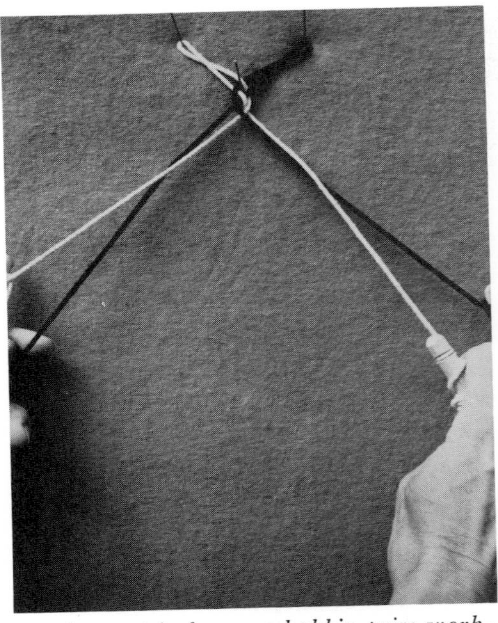

Continue with the same bobbin pairs working CROSS—TWIST *motions to form a braid.*

A completed length of braid.

Linen Stitch

The *linen stitch* is formed without any initial twist in the bobbin pairs. The combination of

CROSS—TWIST—CROSS

with two bobbin pairs forms the *linen stitch.* This stitch closely resembles a simple tabby weave. If you work with additional pairs and use one pair from your initial stitch and an adjacent bobbin pair, this stitch can be repeated to form a tabbylike weave. This repetitive sequence is referred to as a *weaving ground.*

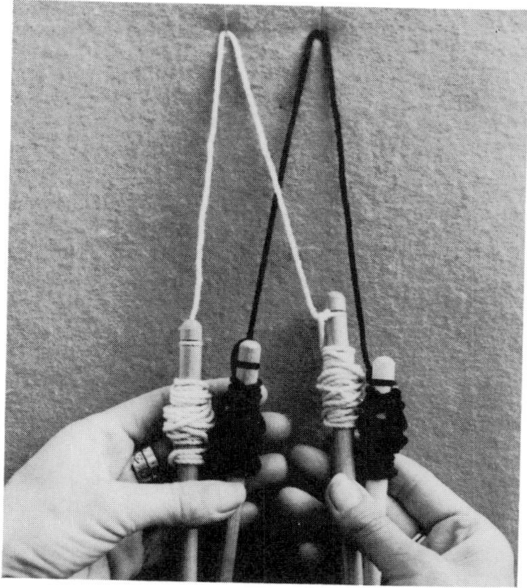

Starting with two hanging pairs make a CROSS. . .

Another CROSS.

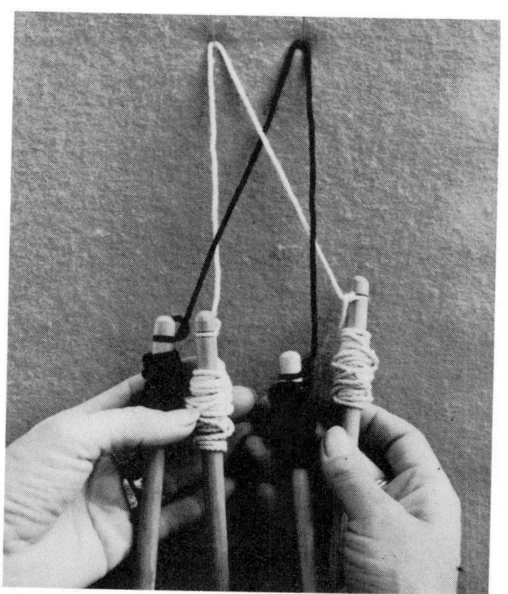

. . .*follow with a* TWIST.

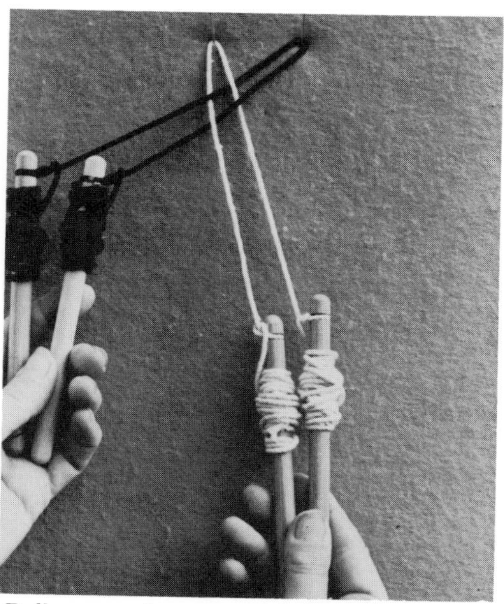

Pull your pairs up completing a linen stitch (CROSS—TWIST—CROSS).

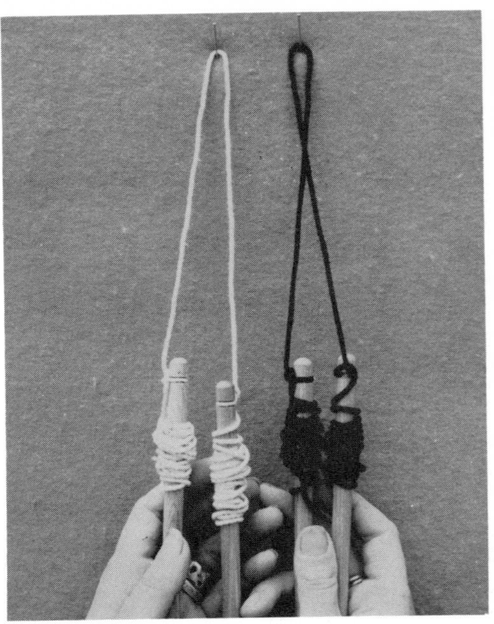

TWIST *the right pair only.*

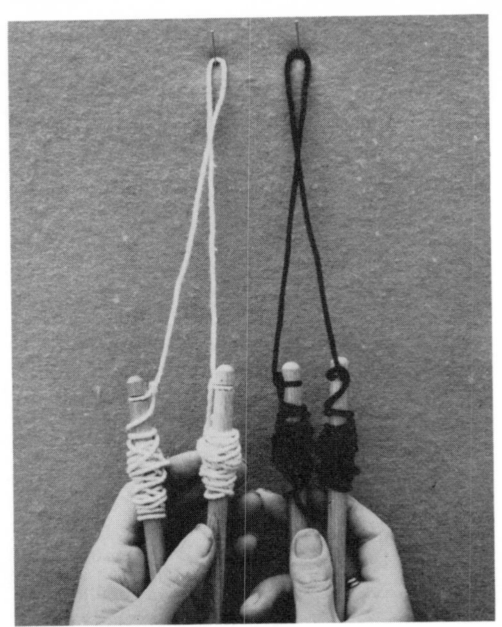

Begin the stitch sequence with a TWIST *in the left or starting pair.*

Leaf Stitch

The *leaf stitch* is identical to a tabby weave with only one thread weaving back and forth across the others. The TWIST motions of this stitch are made with only one bobbin pair. The outside bobbin of one pair is the "weaver" as it weaves across the other three hanging threads, which are kept vertical. The pair with the weaver is the starting pair. The *leaf stitch* is formed with an initial TWIST in the nonstarting bobbin pair. The sequence of the motions

TWIST—CROSS—TWIST

with two bobbin pairs forms the *leaf stitch.* The first TWIST is made with one pair and the second TWIST with the other. A continuation of these motions with the same bobbin pairs, where the last TWIST and the first TWIST are made with the same pair, forms a *filling.*

Follow with a CROSS,

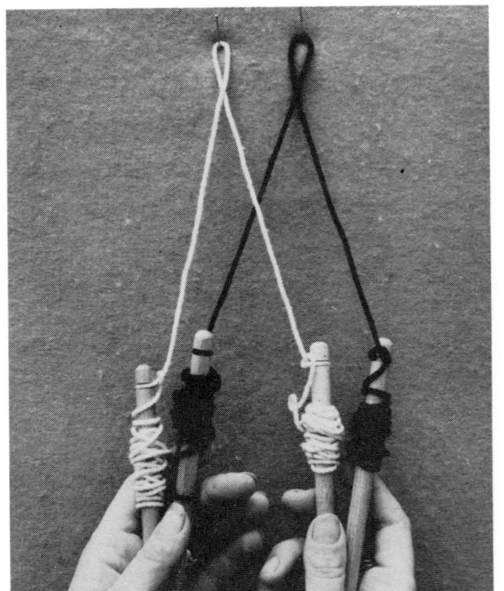

then a TWIST *with the right pair. This completes one leaf stitch.*

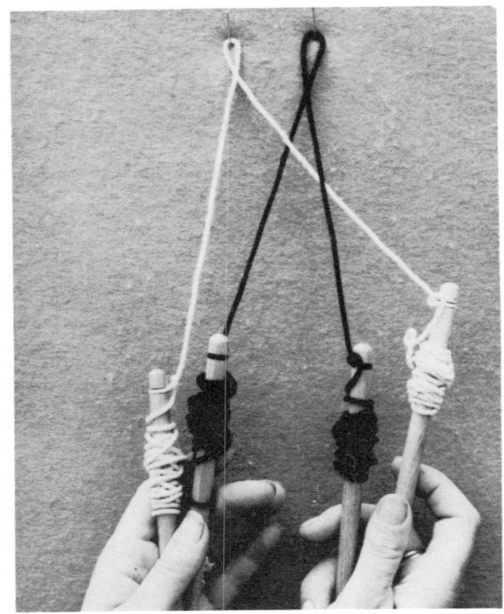

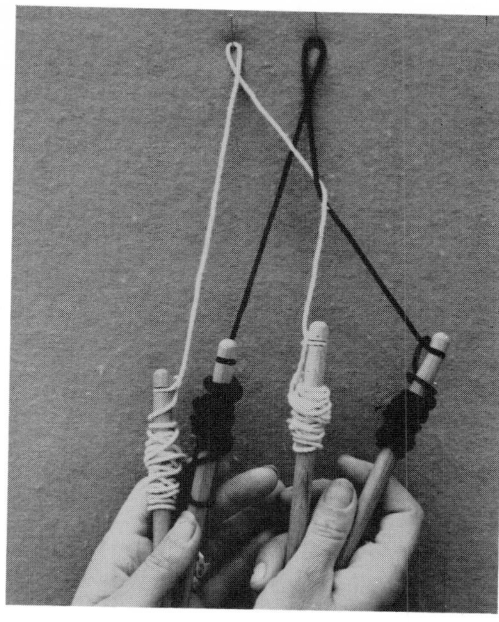

The following stitch begins with the last pair of the previous stitch. Give the right pair a TWIST.

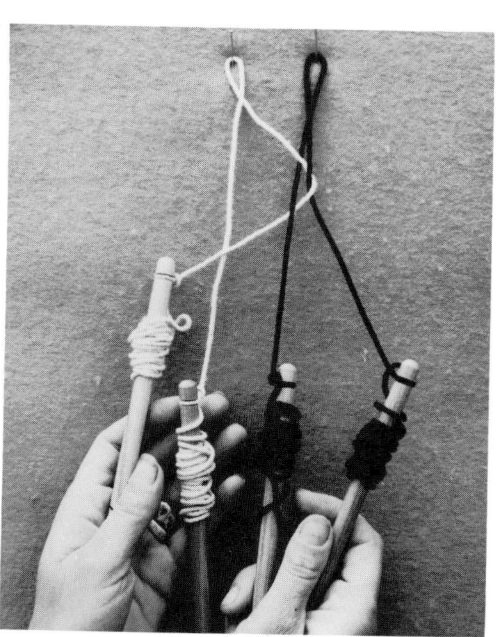

Follow with a CROSS *and then a* TWIST *with the left pair.*

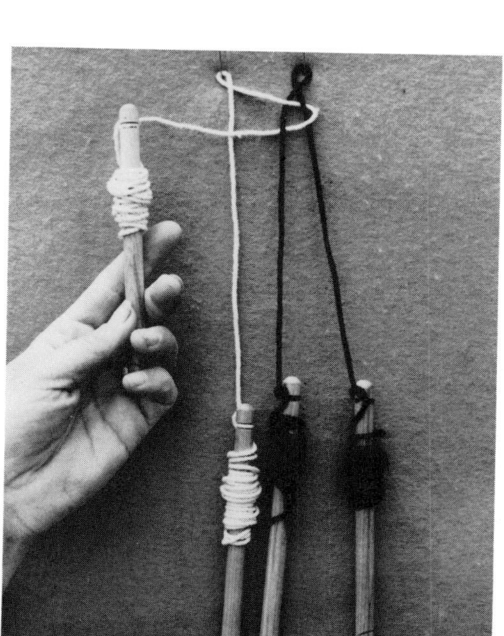

Pull your weaver horizontal completing the second stitch.

GROUNDS

With the basic motions and stitches defined, you are now ready to work the basic grounds. A ground is simply a repetitive pattern of a stitch or stitches using multiple bobbin pairs. Most grounds can be used as a netting to hold designed elements together as well as the structure of the designed element.

Grounds are traditionally uniform, although in contemporary lace forms distortions can be incorporated as a distinct design technique.

There are dozens of standard grounds and many modifications of these that have developed over the many years of traditional lace working. You can be as innovative in creating grounds as you can in creating patterns in any of the other textile techniques.

In working these grounds, you are encouraged to work directly on your board. If you have difficulty in judging your stitch spacing, you can pin a piece of graph paper to your board and work directly over it.

For consistency, bobbins will always be counted in pairs beginning at the left and counting to the right. The borders of your ground will define its outline.

If the first stitch of a ground ends in a TWIST, all starting bobbin pairs should be given an initial TWIST. If a stitch ends in a CROSS, an initial TWIST is not required.

Weaving Ground

This is probably the most useful and flexible of the grounds. While most grounds can be used as a netting to hold design elements together or as part of the designed element, the *weaving ground* is only used to form the designed element. This ground closely resembles a woven tabby weave but differs in that two weaver threads weave back and forth across the other threads instead of one. It is primarily used to make narrow braids, which in turn are used to form strong lines in a design. It is easily shaped to any configuration, however, and can be used to form dense areas of any configuration.

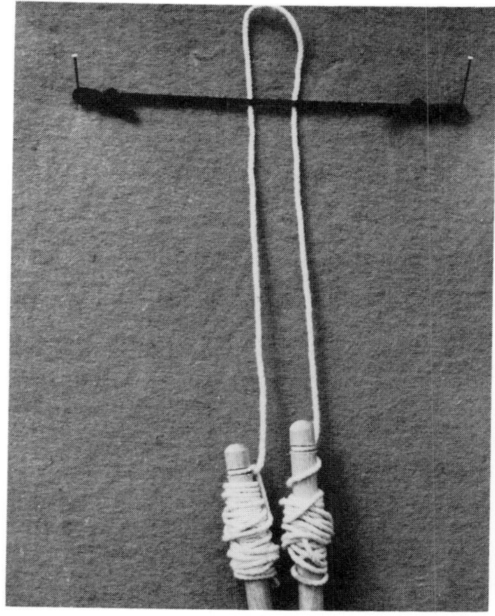

The half hitch is a simple way to secure a pair of bobbins to a starting cord or other support when beginning the work. Place your bobbin pair under your starting cord.

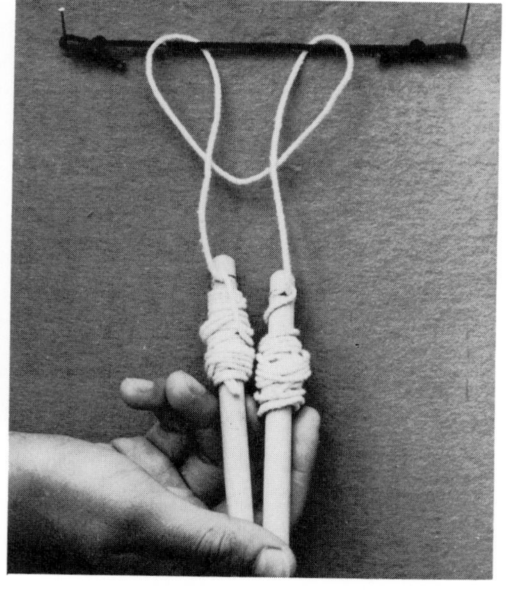

Pass the two bobbins through the loop formed, drawing the loop back over the starting cord.

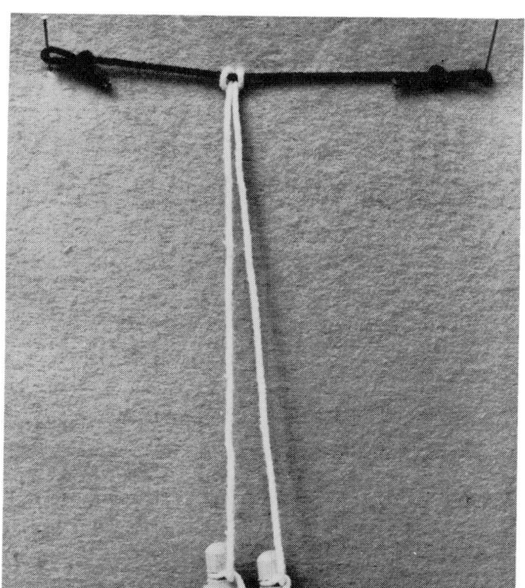

Pull both bobbins downward completing the mounting.

The ground is formed by the continuous working of *linen stitches*, each stitch being formed from one pair from the previous stitch and a new adjacent pair. It can be defined as a

CROSS—TWIST—CROSS continuous operation with one constant pair and each adjacent pair in sequence.

To work a sampler, prepare six bobbin pairs. Wind each of five of these pairs with approximately one yard of cord. Wind each bobbin of the remaining pair with three yards of cord, winding one bobbin of this pair with a contrasting color cord. Pin a starting cord approximately 8 inches long near the top of your board. Half hitch the pair with the contrasting color cord to the left. Half hitch the other five pairs to the right of this pair, spacing them about ½ inch apart.

In the *weaving ground* one hanging pair will weave back and forth across the others. This constant pair is referred to as the "weaver" pair and, accordingly, requires a longer cord than the other pairs. For this sampler the first pair on the left will be the weaver pair.

Proceed to work your sampler:

1. Take the weaver pair in your left hand and give it a TWIST. PIN to the right of this pair just under its support.
2. Pick up the second bobbin pair with your right hand and make a *linen stitch* (CROSS—TWIST—CROSS) with these pairs. The weaver pair will now be in your right hand.
3. Set the pair in your left hand down and transfer the weaver pair back to your left hand. Pick up the next adjacent pair (third pair) with your right hand. With these two pairs make a *linen stitch*.
4. Complete the first row making *linen stitches* with the weaver pair and each hanging pair in sequence.
5. At the end of the row PIN under the weaver pair, establishing the right extremity of your ground.
6. Give the weaver pair a TWIST and return it to the left edge, working *linen stitches* with all hanging pairs. At the edge, again PIN under the weaver pair.

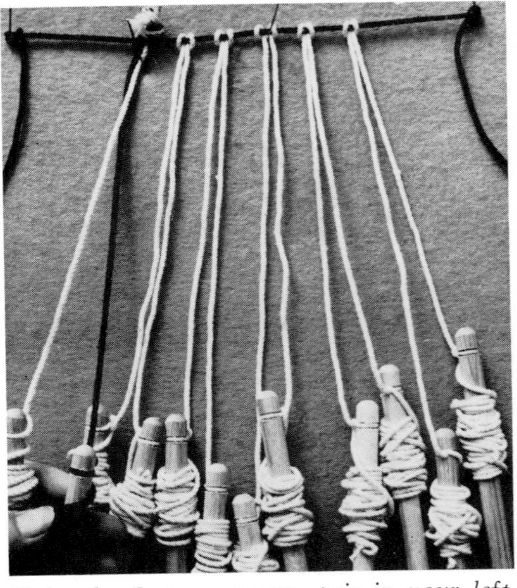

Take the first or weaver pair in your left hand and TWIST. PIN *to the right of this pair.*

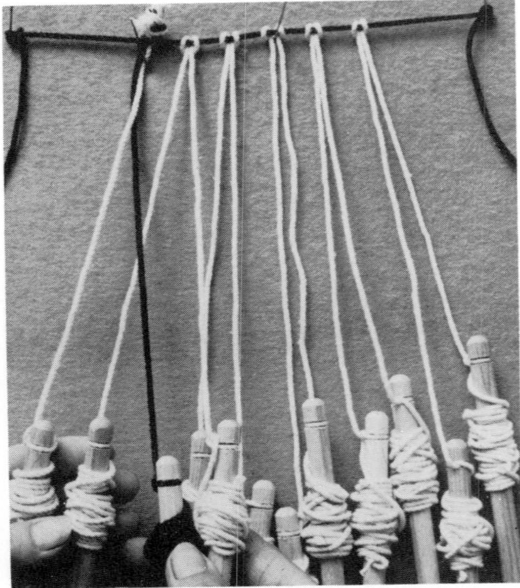

With the first and second pairs make a CROSS,

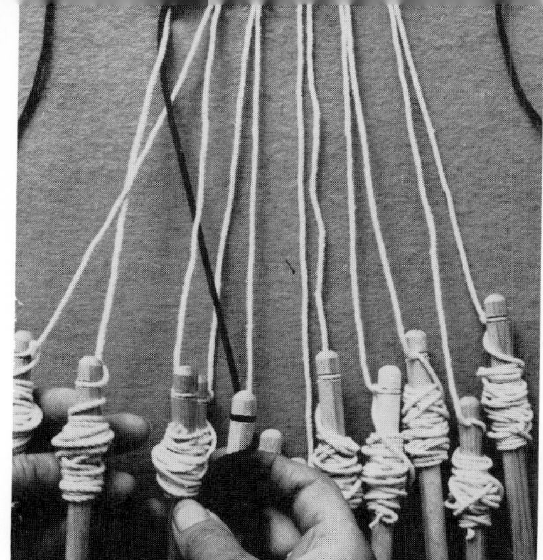

followed by a TWIST,

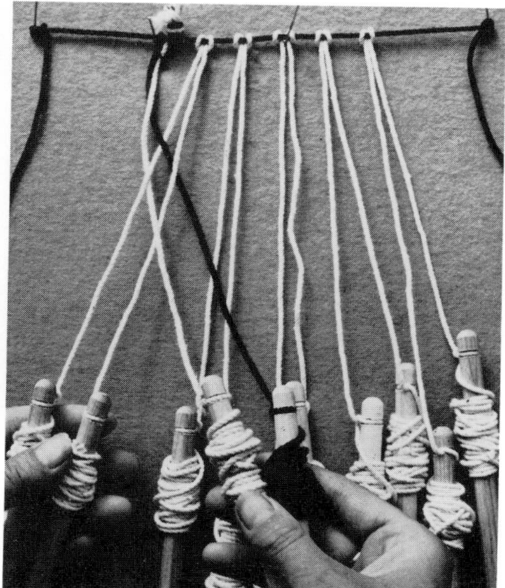

then another CROSS, *completing the first stitch.*

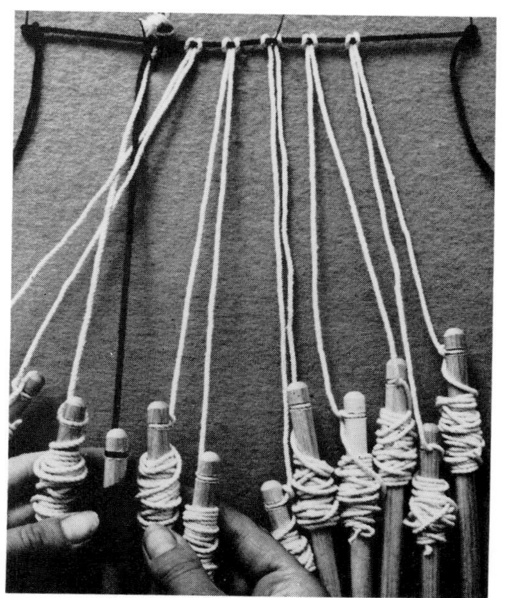

Set down the pair from your left hand and transfer the weaver pair from your right hand to your left hand. Pick up the third pair with your right hand. With these two pairs make another

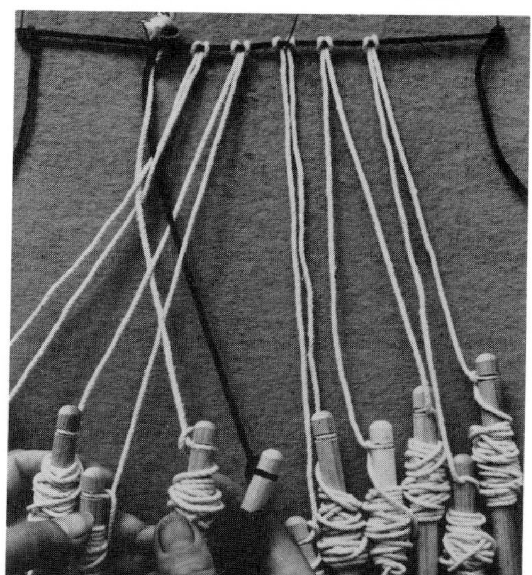

linen stitch (CROSS—TWIST—CROSS). *This completes the second stitch. Note that both pairs have changed hands.*

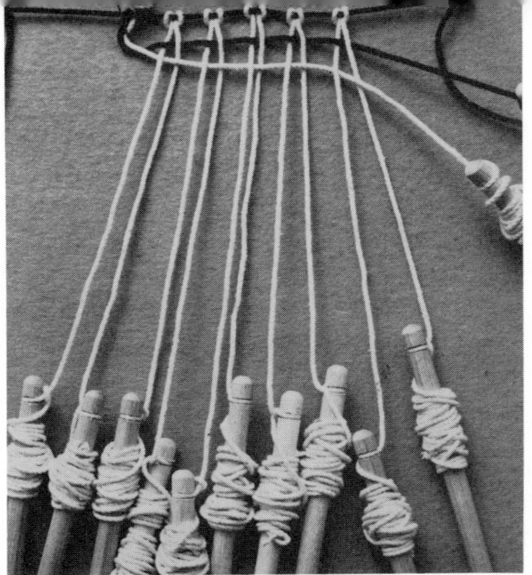

Work across row in this manner with the weaver pair working to the right.

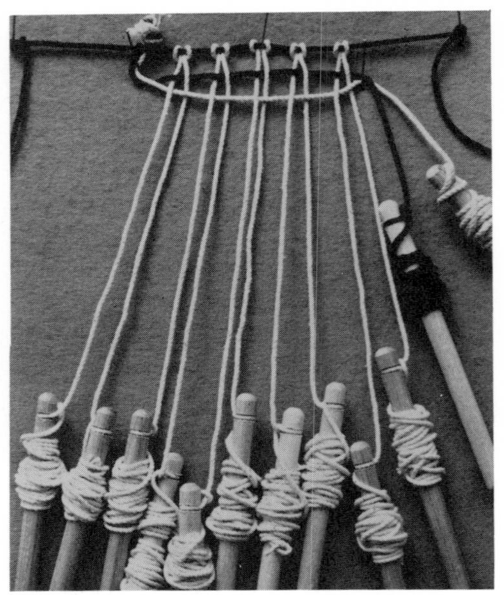

PIN *under the weaver pair and give this pair a* TWIST.

With the weaver pair and the adjacent end pair make another linen stitch.

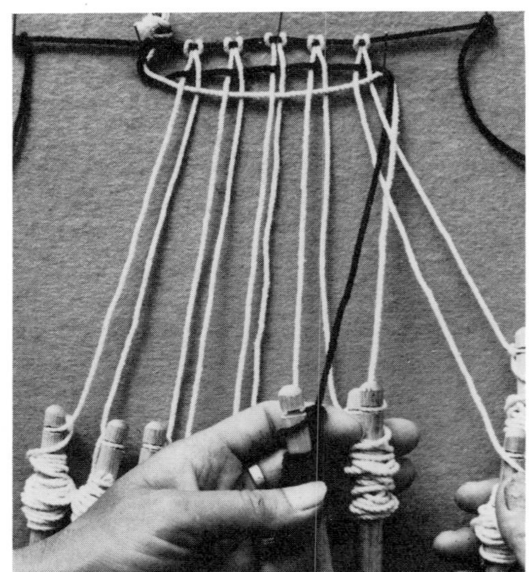

Continue with linen stitches to the left completing the second row. PIN *at end of row under the weaver pair.*

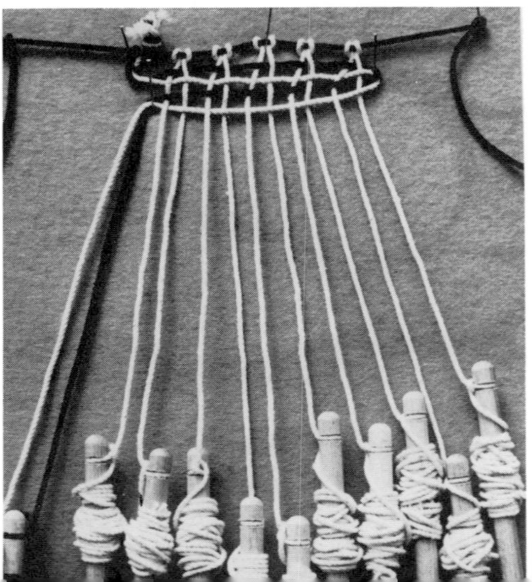

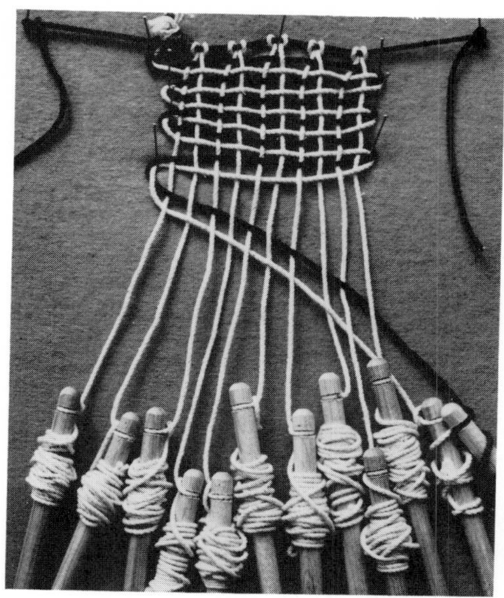

Working linen stitches back and forth in this manner forms the weaving ground. With a single TWIST *in the weaver pair at the end of each row, each of the cords of the weaver pair will alternate.*

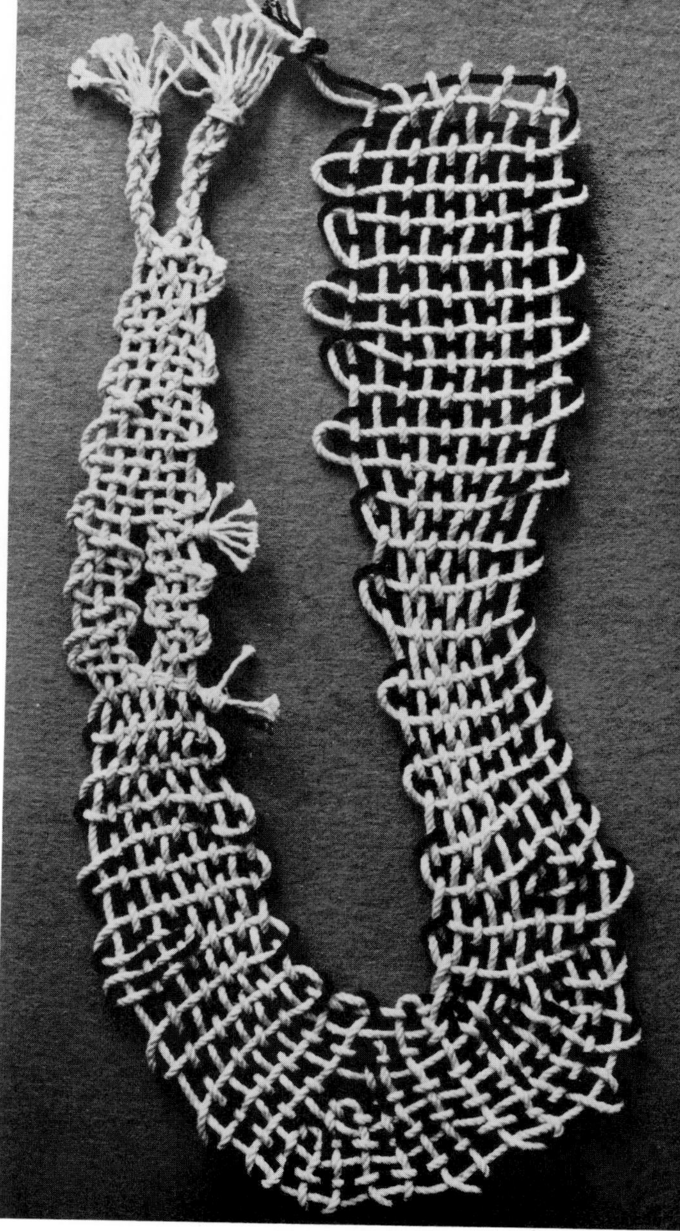

A completed weaving ground sampler. Note how curves or contours are formed by not returning the weaver pair completely across the row. When the weaver pair cords have run out, another pair is used as the weaver pair.

Continue back and forth in this manner creating your fabric. Work for uniformity and the making of all operations smooth and continuous.

If done correctly, the contrasting color of your weaver pair will alternate with the main color of this pair. If it does not, a TWIST at the edge pin is missing or your right-over-left motion is backward. After each row, adjust your cords by pulling down on the hanging bobbins while holding the weaver pair horizontal. The weaver pair should weave horizontally without sagging. If you cannot maintain it horizontal, your spacing is probably too tight. Try changing the mounting distance between your pairs to widen your ground or use a thinner cord.

When you can accomplish uniformity in your ground, change the shape of your piece by varying your pin spacings. Try forming curves or contours by manipulating your weaver pair. For sharp curves, return the weaver pair before it reaches the inside edge of your curve. Demonstrate the interchangeability of warp and weft by changing your weaver pair.

Half-Stitch Ground

This ground is worked in the same manner as the *weaving ground.* As implied by its name, it is formed by the repetition of *half stitches.* Although it is worked like the *weaving ground*, it is more open and is used as a netting as well as the basis for a designed element.

The *half-stitch ground* can be defined as a CROSS—TWIST continuous operation with one new pair and the adjacent pair from the previous stitch.

Again you will need six bobbin pairs. Wind each bobbin of each of five pairs with one yard of cord. Wind one bobbin of the remaining pair with three yards of a contrasting color cord, the other bobbin with one yard of the main color cord. Tie these two cords together between the two bobbins. Begin with a starter cord as you did in the *weaving ground* sampler. Half hitch the contrasting color pair at the left with the contrasting color to the left. Hang the other five bobbin pairs to the right of this pair using a half hitch and spacing them approximately ½ inch apart.

In the *half-stitch ground*, only the first bobbin of the starting bobbin pair is the "weaver." This cord will weave back and forth horizontally, while all other cords will weave on a diagonal. The cord on this first bobbin should, accordingly, be proportionately longer than the other cords. For the sampler the first pair will be the starting pair.

Proceed to work your sampler:

1. Take the first two bobbin pairs and give them an initial TWIST. PIN to the right of the first pair just under its support. With these two pairs make a *half stitch* (CROSS—TWIST).
2. Put the bobbin pair in your left hand down and transfer the right pair to your left hand. With your right hand, pick up the next bobbin pair (third pair) and give this pair an initial TWIST. Your left pair is already in the twist position. With these two pairs make a *half stitch.*
3. Repeat this sequence across the row. At the end of the row PIN under the last pair, establishing the right edge.
4. Give this edge pair one additional TWIST and follow with a *half stitch* with the adjacent pair to the left.
5. Work *half stitches* to the left, joining one new pair with each stitch. PIN at the edge under the last pair.

Continue back and forth in this manner working for uniformity. Except for the first row, where all hanging pairs are given an initial TWIST, all hanging pairs will be in the TWIST position from the previous stitch, and ready for the *half stitch* of the new row. At the end of each row, the edge pair is given an additional TWIST before working back.

If worked correctly, the contrasting color cord on your first bobbin will weave back and forth while the remaining cords will weave diagonally. As you work, pull bobbins downward while holding the weaver cord horizontal. This will keep your lines straight and the ground uniform.

When you have completed several rows, try altering the ground by changing the edge pin spacing. Try changing the openness of your ground in this manner.

If you delete the TWIST on your end pair or give it an additional TWIST, you can change the cord that is used as the weaver. In this manner you can change the direction of the contrasting color cord from horizontal to diagonal. By systematically changing the weaver you can work with all cords of the same length. Interesting effects can also be achieved by working this ground using three or more different colors of cords as well as materials of different weights and textures.

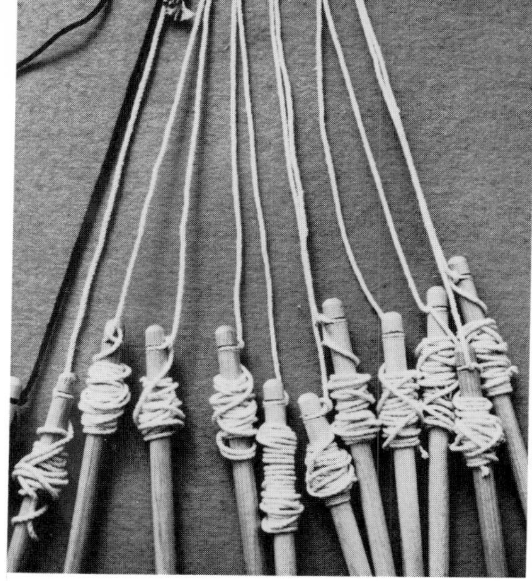

Mount six bobbin pairs on a starting cord. The first cord of the first pair is of a contrasting color.

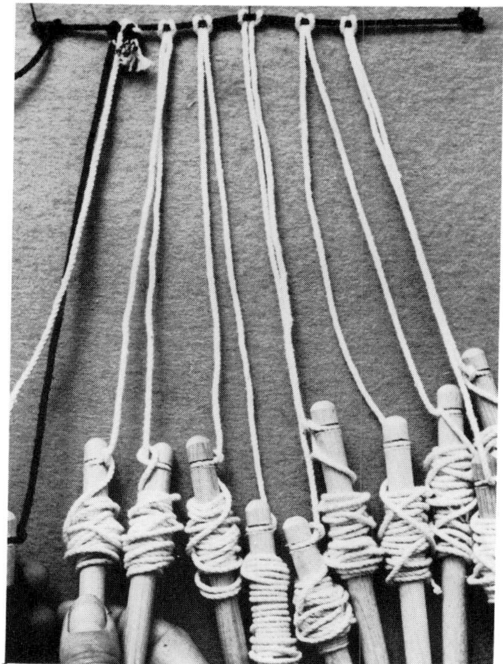

Take the first two bobbin pairs and give them an initial TWIST.

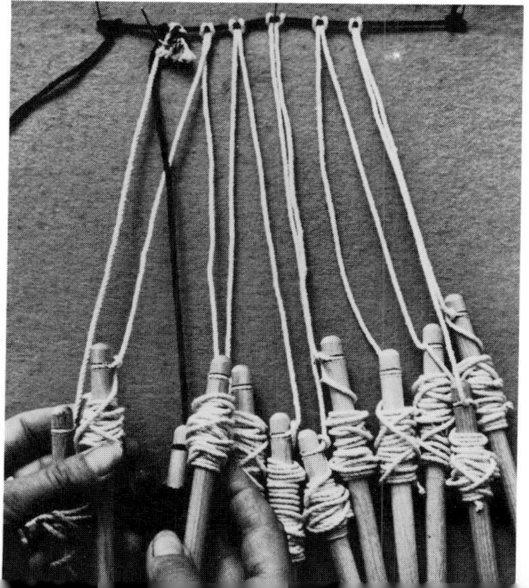

PIN *to the right of the first pair; then with the first and second pairs make a* CROSS *followed by a . . .*

. . . TWIST. *This completes the first stitch.*

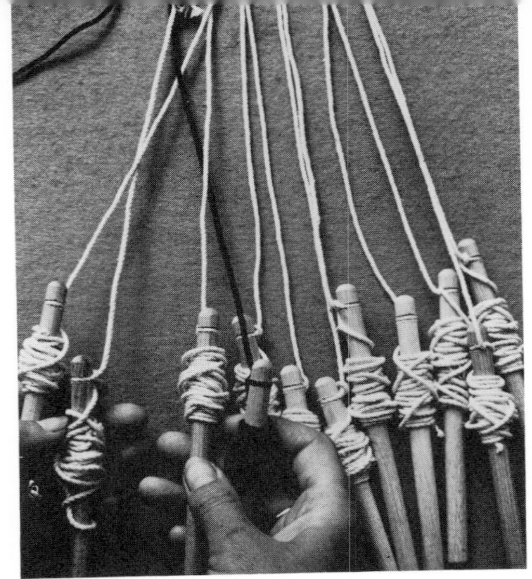

Put the bobbin pair that was in your left hand down and transfer the right pair to your left hand. With your right hand pick up the next (third) bobbin pair and give this pair an initial TWIST. *Note that the left pair is already in the twist position: With these two pairs . . .*

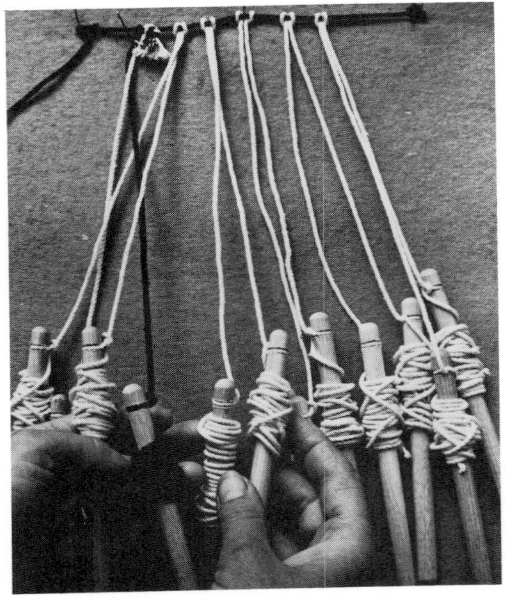

. . . *make another half stitch* (CROSS—TWIST).

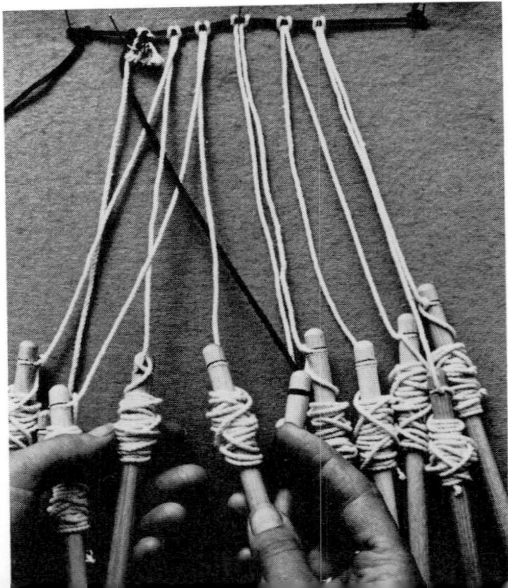

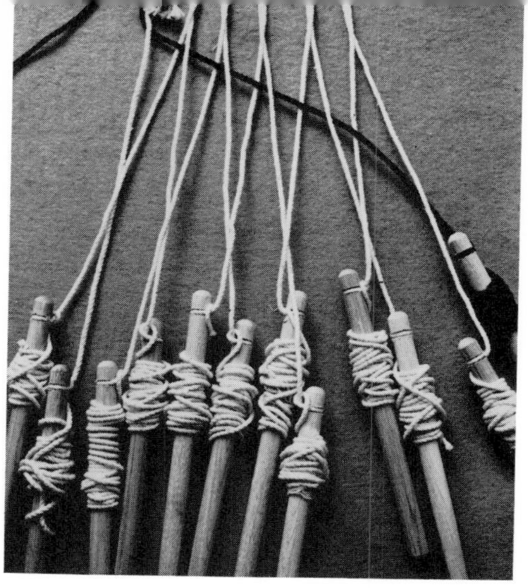

After giving each new starting pair an initial TWIST, *work across row with half stitches.*

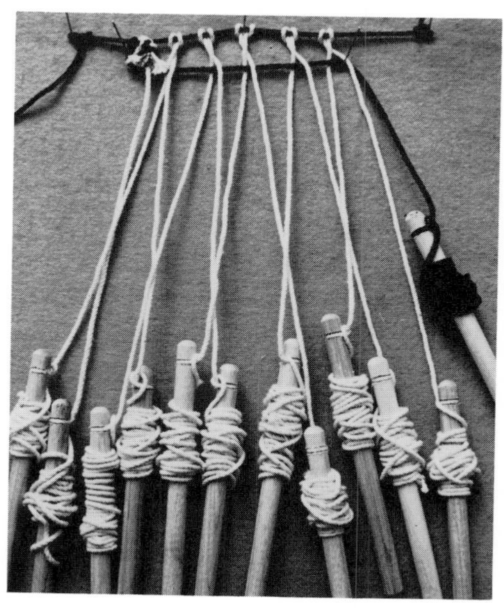

PIN *at end of row under the last twisted pair. This pair includes one bobbin from the first hung pair (the weaver) and one bobbin from the last hung pair.*

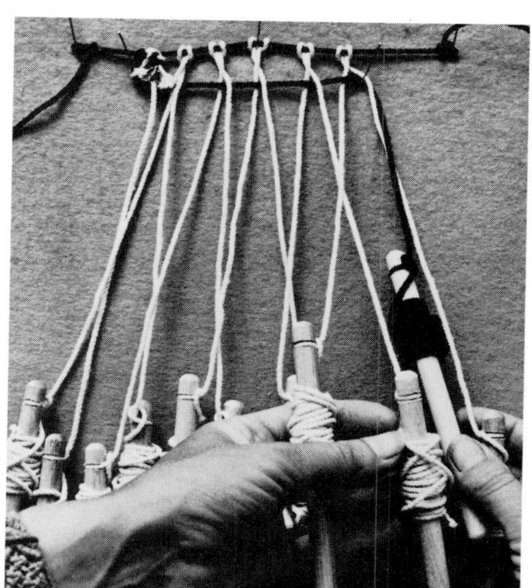

Give the end pair an additional TWIST.

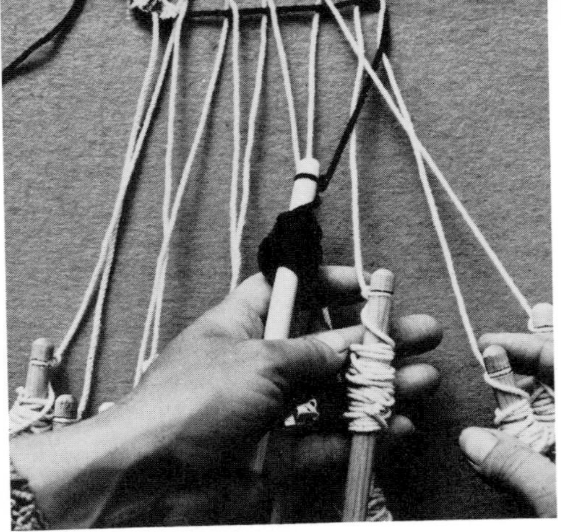

With the last pair and the adjacent pair to the left make another half stitch, the first stitch of the second row.

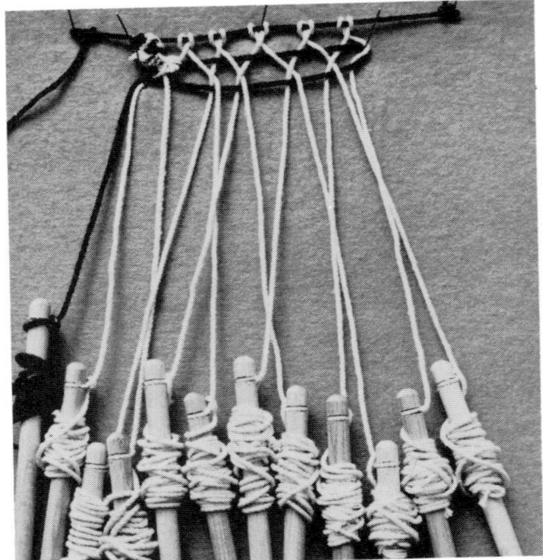

Continue working to the left with half stitches, completing the second row. PIN *under the last pair. Note that all hanging pairs are in the* TWIST *position.*

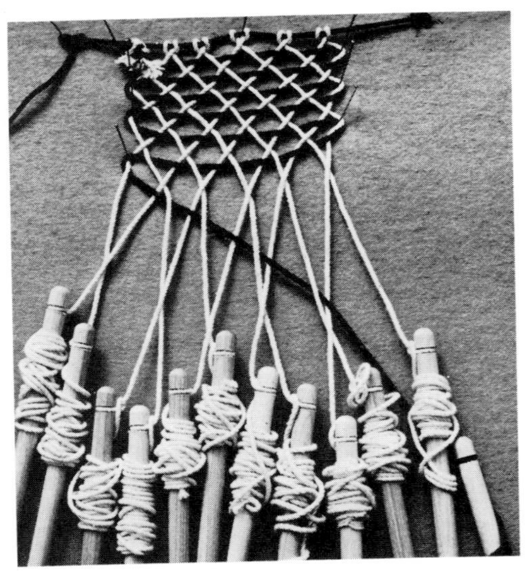

A completed half-stitch ground sampler. Note how the initial weaver cord (the dark cord) interchanges with one of the diagonal cords. This is simply done by eliminating one of the twists at the end of a row.

Working back and forth in this manner forms the half-stitch ground. The first contrasting color cord should weave back and forth horizontally while all other cords weave diagonally.

Whole-Stitch Ground

This ground, often called the *Torchon ground,* is formed by the repetition of *whole stitches* using two new adjacent bobbin pairs for each new stitch.

For each alternate row the stitches are staggered with each stitch being formed with the adjacent bobbin pairs from the two stitches directly above. This principle of splitting the groups of one row for use in the succeeding row is the typical method for working most of the grounds of bobbin lace.

The *whole-stitch ground* can be described as the sequence of CROSS—TWIST—PIN—CROSS—TWIST repeated with two adjacent bobbin pairs.

Prepare eight bobbin pairs for this pattern. Wind two of the pairs with a contrasting color cord. With the contrasting color pairs in the center, half hitch each bobbin pair to a starter cord spacing them approximately ¾ inch apart.

Proceed to work your sampler:

1. Take the second and third bobbin pairs, holding one in each hand, and give them an initial TWIST. With these same pairs now form a *whole stitch* (CROSS—TWIST—PIN under the cross formed—CROSS—TWIST). Put both pairs down.
2. Take the fourth and fifth bobbin pairs and repeat step 1.
3. Take the sixth and seventh bobbin pairs and again repeat step 1. This completes the stitches of the first row.
4. Now take the first pair and give it three or four TWISTS. With this pair and the left pair from your first stitch above, form another *whole stitch.* This is the first stitch of your second row.
5. The next stitch is formed from the right pair of the first stitch of the first row and the left pair of the second stitch of the first row. With these pairs make a *whole stitch.*

Continue in this manner completing four or five rows. Maintain a uniform spacing, keeping your rows and columns straight and the diagonal line of stitches at a 45° angle. Except for the first row, where all hanging pairs are given an initial TWIST, all hanging pairs will be in the TWIST position from the previous stitch and ready to form the new *whole stitch.* It should be noted that the first and last pairs are only used in alternate rows to form a stitch. Put enough TWISTS in these pairs to cross the rows where not used.

With a little practice, this ground can be worked without the intermediate stitch pins. The outside pins should still be used where the cords change direction. Try working the ground in this manner, adjusting the spacing of your stitches until the stitch itself determines the spacing. The size as well as the stiffness of your cord will determine a natural spacing. Working in this manner, try changing your spacing by adding TWISTS after each *whole stitch.* Keep tension uniform as you work and all bobbins hanging at a uniform level.

Using the contrasting color pairs suggested, large diamond forms will be formed within the ground. If your other pairs have different textures or colors, complex patterns will result with strong diagonal lines.

In its traditional fine scale, this ground was generally worked diagonally. After completing the first stitch of the first row in this sampler, you would work the first stitch of the second row. You would again return to the first row where you would work the second stitch, followed by the second stitch of the second row and the first stitch of the third row. The ground can generally be worked quicker in this sequence as one bobbin pair of each stitch is used in the making of the following stitch. While this is practical when working on small or narrow pieces, when working large pieces this method becomes awkward as the diagonal line quickly runs off your board.

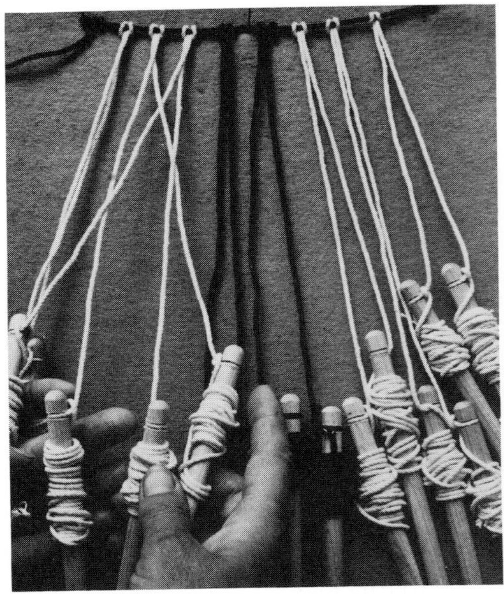

With the second and third pairs make an initial TWIST. *Follow with a* CROSS—TWIST, *then*

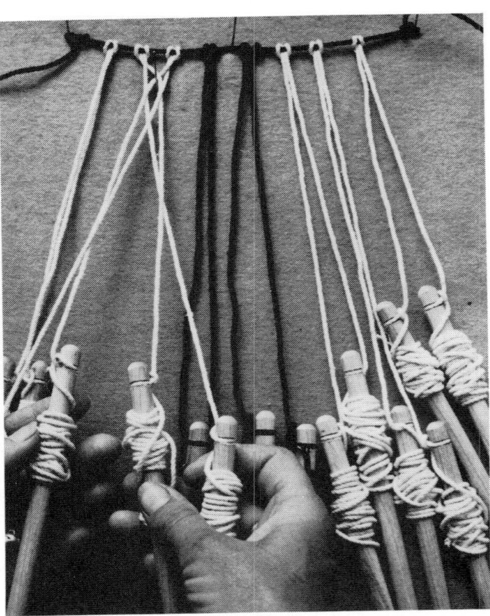

PIN *under the cross formed and follow with another* CROSS—TWIST, *completing the first whole stitch.*

With the fourth and fifth pairs make another whole stitch (CROSS—TWIST—PIN—CROSS—TWIST) *after an initial* TWIST.

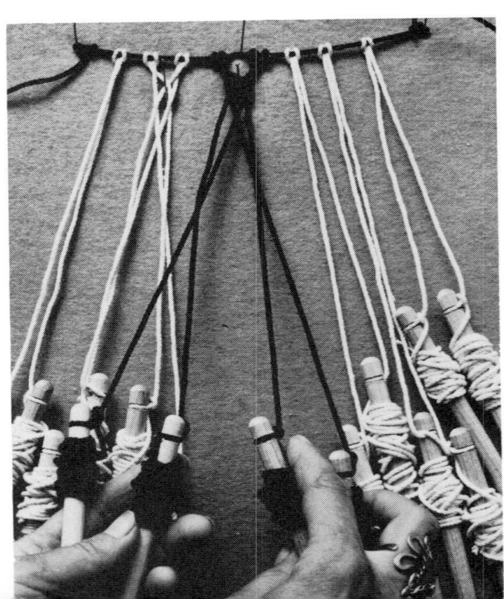

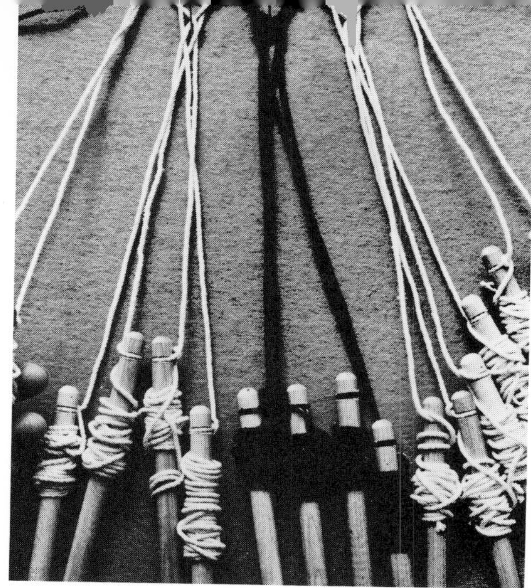

Complete this row by making a whole stitch with the sixth and seventh pairs. The first and last pairs are not used to form stitches in this row. Before beginning the next or alternate row give the first pair three or four TWISTS.

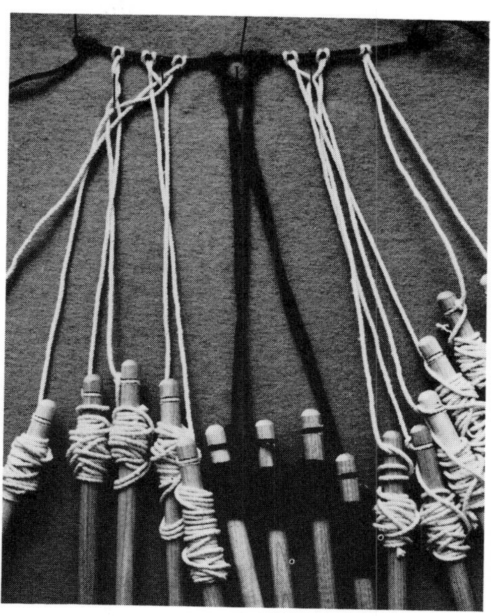

With the hanging pair and the left pair from the first stitch above make a new whole stitch.

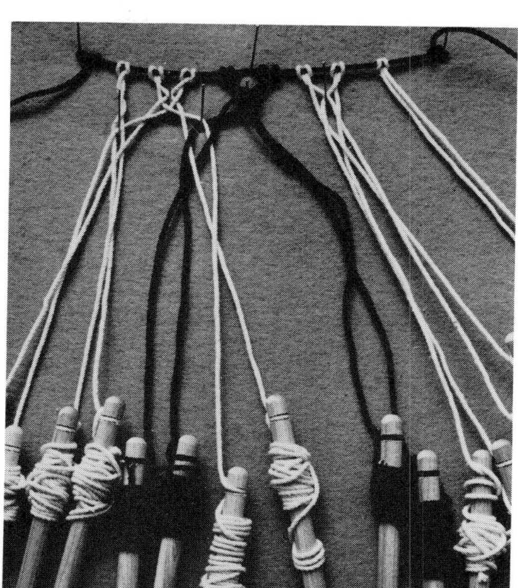

The next stitch is typically made with the left pair from the right stitch above and the right pair from the left stitch above.

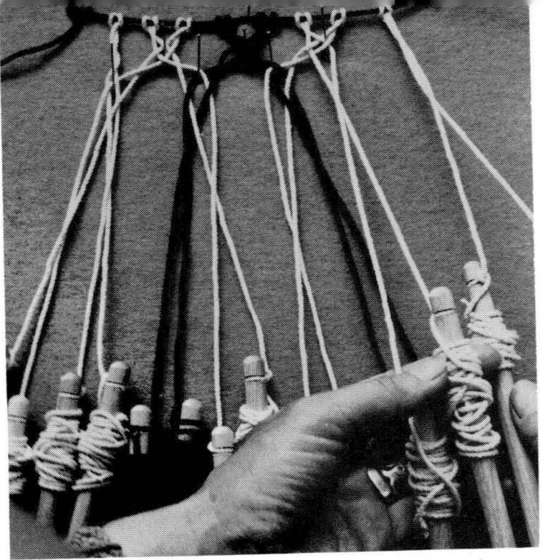

Complete the second row. The last pair, as the first pair, is given extra TWISTS *to cross the first row. Note that all suspended pairs are in the* TWIST *position.*

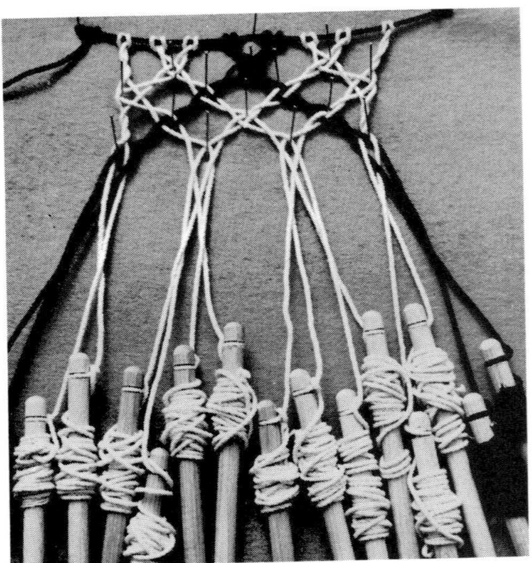

Repetition of whole stitches with adjacent bobbin pairs forms the whole-stitch ground. The first and last pairs, which are only used in alternate rows, are twisted to cross the rows where not used.

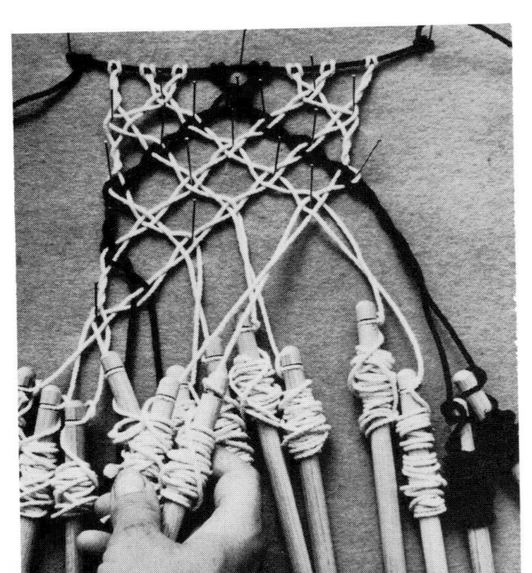

A finished whole-stitch ground sampler. Note how all lines run diagonally. Symmetrical pairs of contrasting color cords will form large intersecting diamonds within the ground.

This ground can also be worked on a diagonal working from right to left.

Brussels Ground

This ground, which is worked on the same principle as the *whole stitch ground*, is formed by the repetition of short *braids* using two new adjacent bobbin pairs for each new stitch. The design formed is a series of interlocking hexagons with each *braid* separated by a TWIST.

Each *braid* of this ground is formed by the working of two *whole stitches*. A PIN is used to locate the center of these *braids*. The sequence of motions can be described as

CROSS—TWIST—CROSS—TWIST—PIN—CROSS—TWIST—CROSS—TWIST repeated with two adjacent bobbin pairs.

Prepare your bobbins in the same manner as for the *whole-stitch ground*.

Proceed to work your sampler:

1. Take the second and third bobbin pairs and give them an initial TWIST. With these same pairs make a *whole stitch*—PIN under the last cross formed—and make another *whole stitch*. Put down both pairs.
2. Take the fourth and fifth pairs and repeat step 1.
3. Take the sixth and seventh pairs and again repeat step 1, completing the stitches of the first row.
4. Now take the first pair and give it three or four TWISTS. With this pair and the left pair of your first stitch form a new stitch. This is the first stitch of the second row.

Continue across row in this manner, making your *braids* with the right pair from the left *braid* above and the left pair from the right *braid* above. Complete four or five rows working for straight rows and columns. Except for the first row, all hanging pairs will be in the TWIST position from the previous stitch formed. Only in the first row does each hanging pair receive an initial TWIST prior to the first *whole stitch*. As in the *weaving ground* the first and last pairs are used only in alternate rows to form a stitch. Put enough TWISTS in these pairs to cross the rows where not used.

The color pairs of this ground do not change columns and, thus, run essentially vertically, forming hexagonal shapes between the short *braids*.

Try working this ground without the intermediate stitch pins. Adjust your stitch spacing, letting the formed stitch, pulled with uniform tension, determine a natural spacing. Try varying your ground by making additional TWISTS after each *braid* and by varying the length of the individual *braids*.

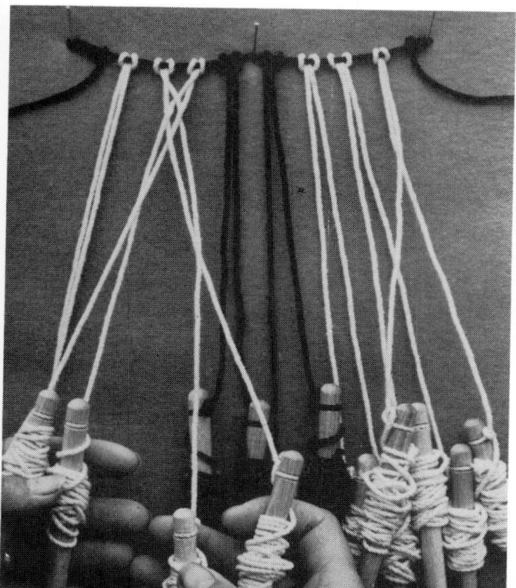

With the second and third pairs make an initial TWIST. *Follow with a whole stitch* (CROSS—TWIST—CROSS—TWIST), *then,*

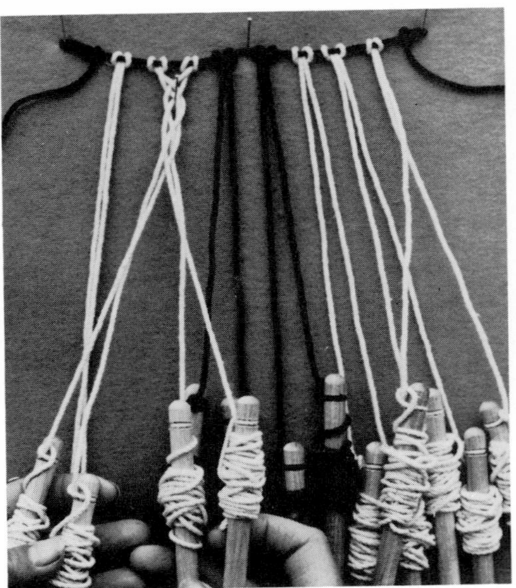

PIN *under the last cross formed. Follow with another whole stitch completing the first braid.*

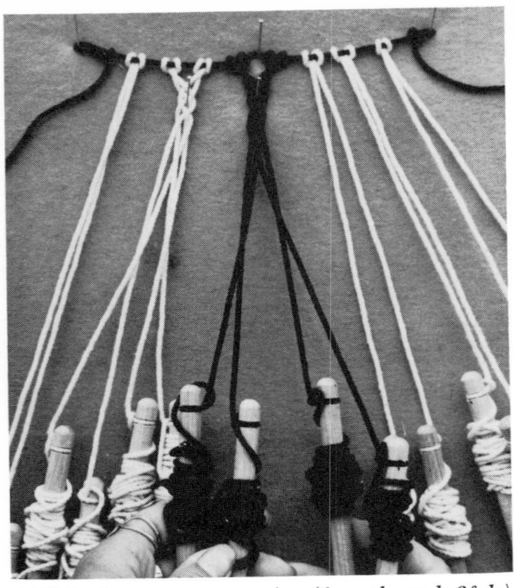

With the next two pairs (fourth and fifth) make a second braid by making an initial TWIST *followed by two whole stitches, with a* PIN *between them* (CROSS—TWIST—CROSS—TWIST—PIN—CROSS—TWIST—CROSS—TWIST).

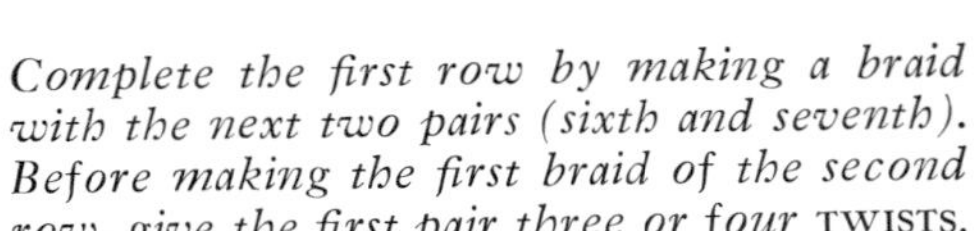

Complete the first row by making a braid with the next two pairs (sixth and seventh). Before making the first braid of the second row, give the first pair three or four TWISTS.

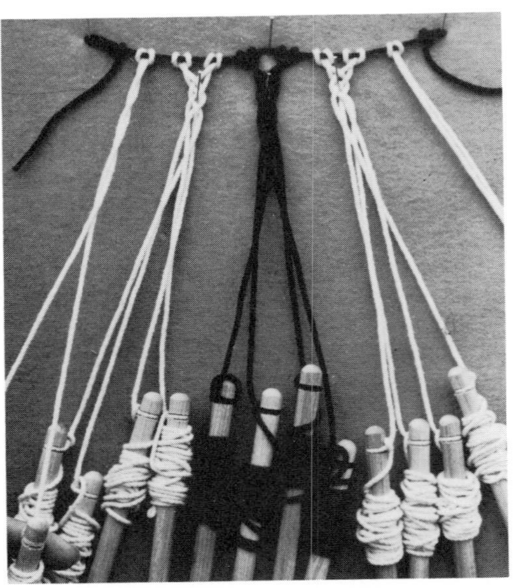

With the first pair and the left pair of your first stitch above make the first braid of the second row.

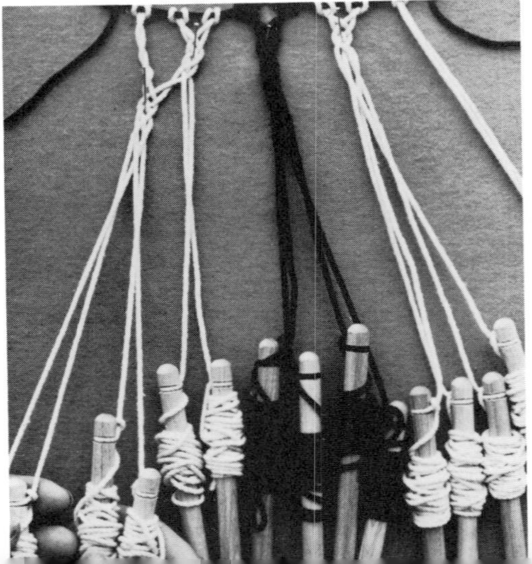

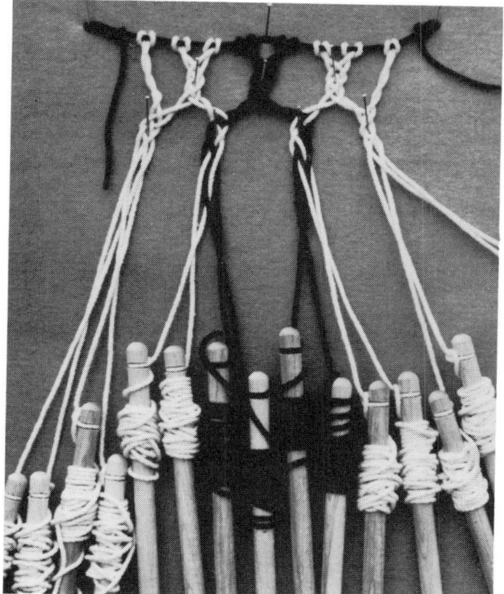

Complete the second row using all bobbin pairs to form the stitches. Each stitch is typically made from the right pair of the left braid above and the left pair of the right braid above.

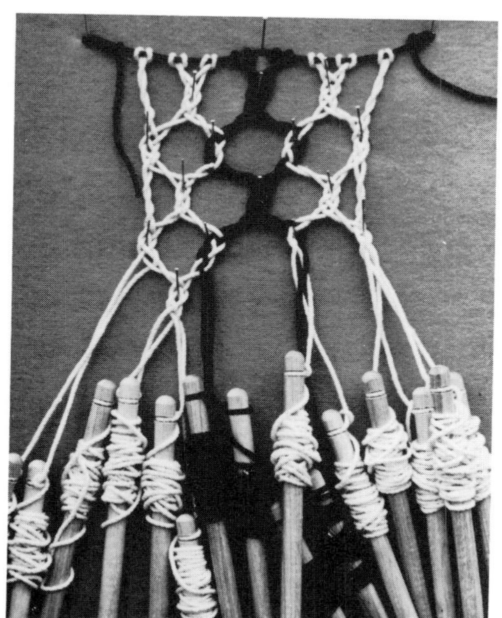

Repetition of braids with adjacent bobbin pairs forms the Brussels ground. Note that all suspended pairs are in a TWIST.

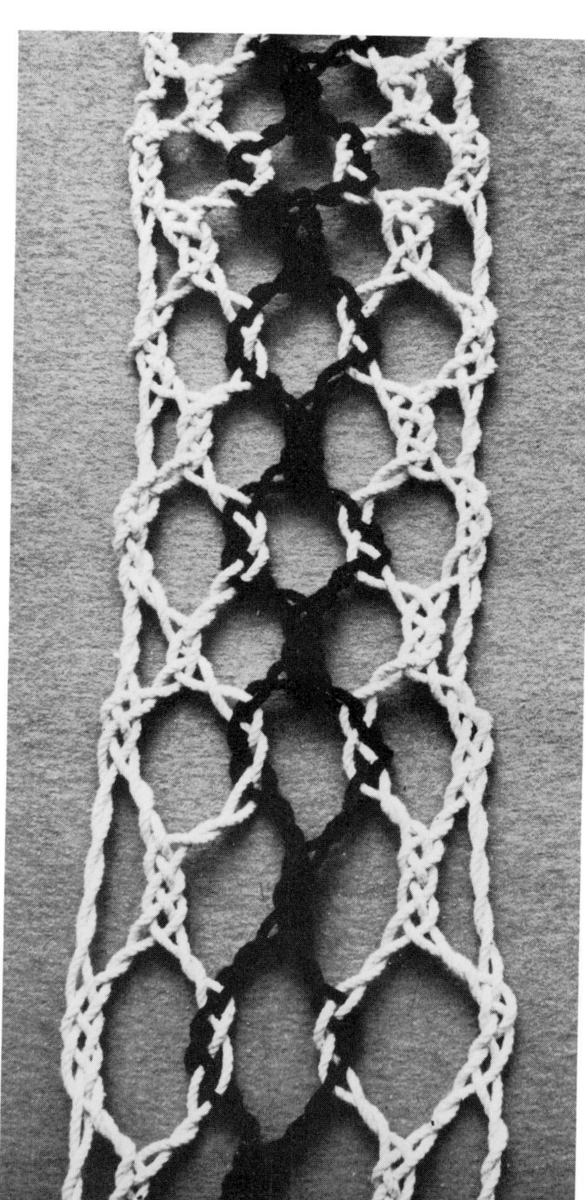

A finished Brussels ground sampler. Note how the contrasting color pair runs vertically forming hexagonal shapes. At the lower portion, an extra TWIST *has been introduced between the braids to widen the ground.*

Sampler

Chapter 4

This sampler is designed to help you understand and become familiar with the working of the basic stitches and grounds as they are combined to produce distinct designs.

The sampler illustrated is made from braided nylon, in a size equivalent to a #15 seine twine. Two colors are used, white and yellow, to illustrate how color can be a planned and integral part of a design.

You will need ten bobbin pairs to work this sampler. Material can be almost anything, although one of the firmer materials is recommended for clarity of stitches. The directions are based on the use of nylon in the weight noted or a #15 cotton seine twine. Make any necessary allowances for heavier or lighter materials.

Cut six strands of white and four strands of yellow or other contrasting color cord, each approximately 2½ yards long. Wind each strand onto a pair of bobbins.

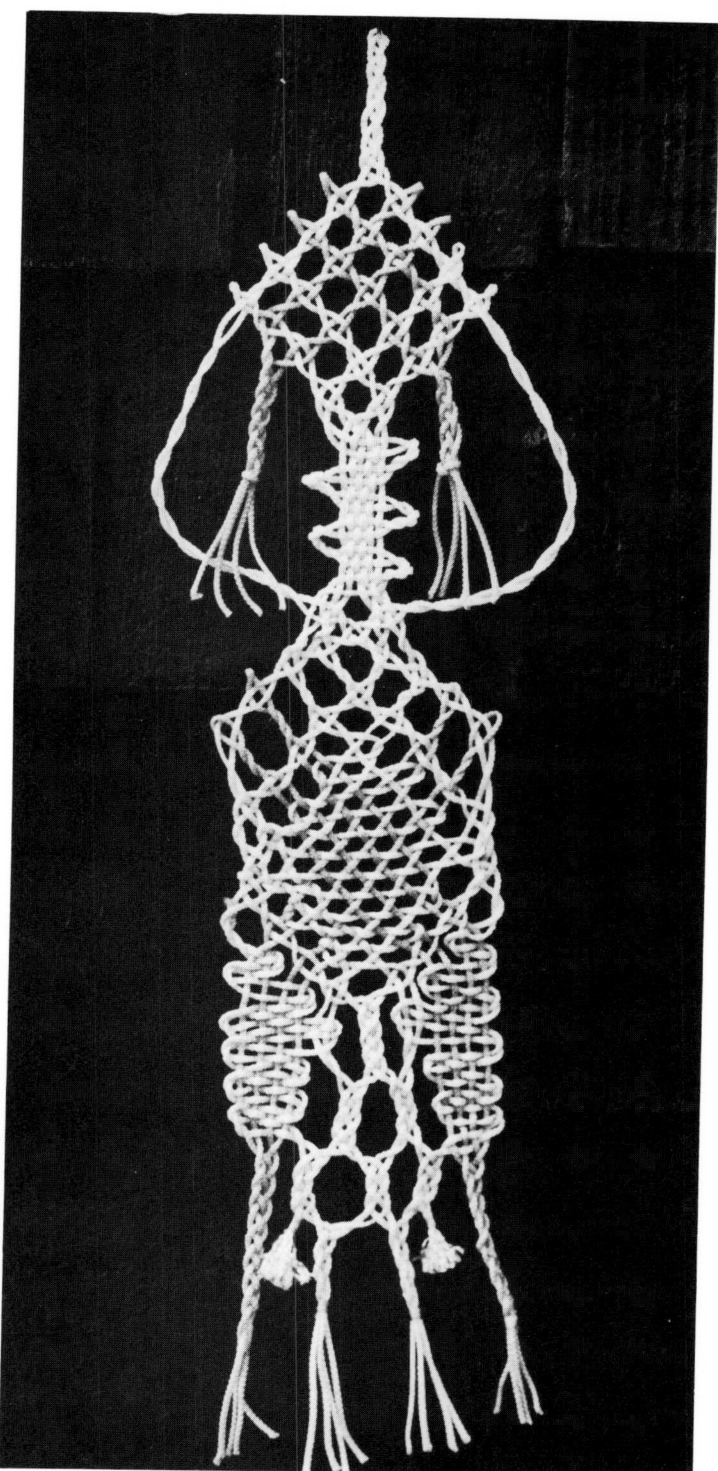

Bobbin lace sampler made from two shades of braided nylon cord.

PIN *two white bobbin pairs to the center of your board and make a braid 1½ inches long.* PIN *under last stitch for support.*

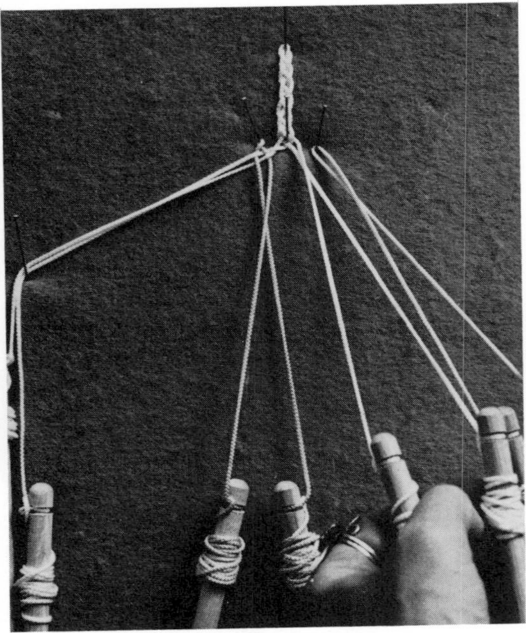

PIN *one yellow bobbin pair on each side of the braid approximately ½ inch from and 45° down from the braid pin. Give these pairs an initial* TWIST *and then form a whole stitch* (CROSS—TWIST—PIN—CROSS—TWIST) *with the left pair and the left pair from the braid. Do the same with the right pair and the right pair from the braid.*

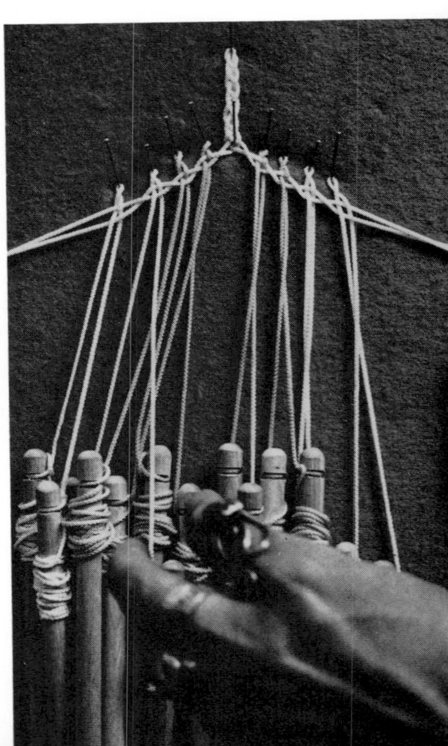

PIN *another yellow bobbin pair followed by two white bobbin pairs on each side and in line with the first yellow bobbin pair. Continue working whole stitches with each of these pairs in sequence with the white pair from the braid.*

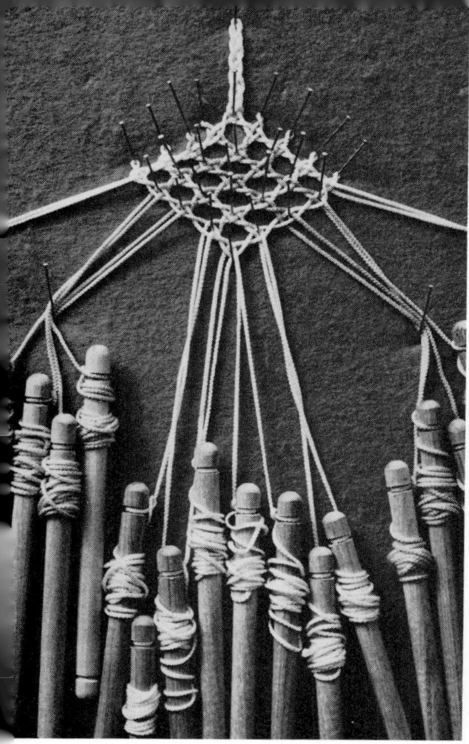

Starting in the center and working left to right diagonally, work the whole stitch with all pairs. Repeat for the next three rows creating a diamond shape.

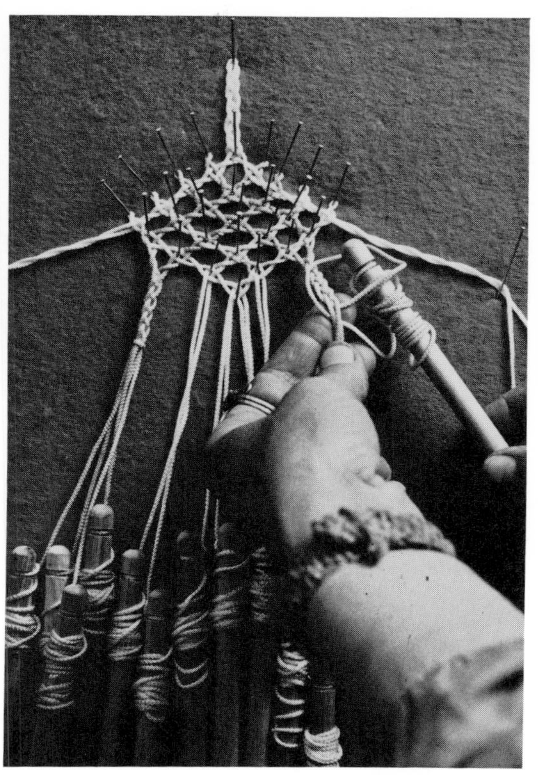

Leave the outside white bobbin pairs on each side unused. Braid the yellow cords in pairs forming two 1½-inch braids. Tie off with an overhand knot.

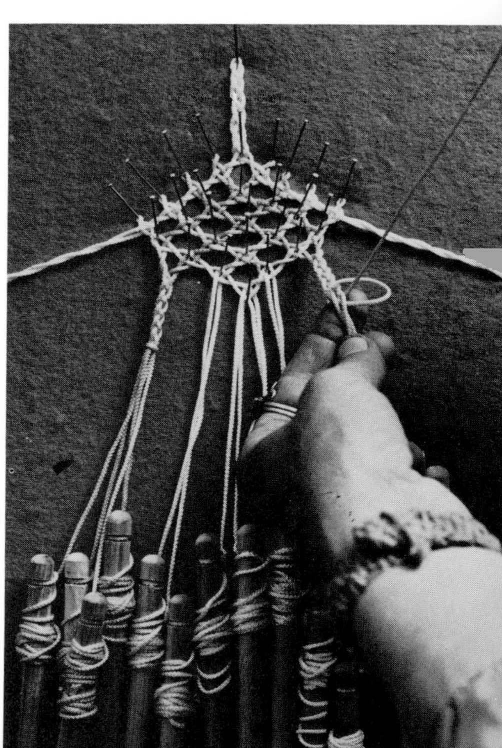

Using the four center pairs work the weaving ground (linen stitches) using the left bobbin pair and the weaver. At each edge give the weavers three or four TWISTS. PIN *and return. This will give an extra loop on the edges. Repeat for six rows.*

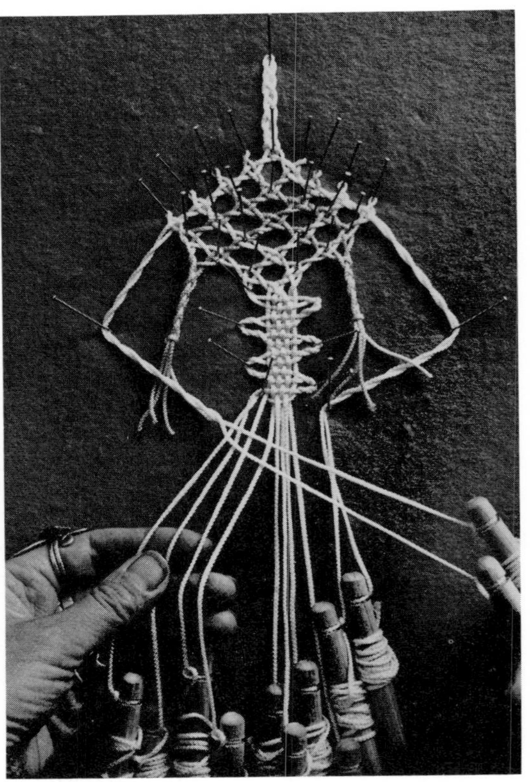

Cut the cords from the two braids leaving a ¾-inch fringe. Take the outside white pairs and give them fourteen to sixteen TWISTS *each.* PIN *out into a loop surrounding the yellow braid.*

Bring each of these twisted pairs down to the bottom of the completed weaving ground. Make a linen stitch with each of these pairs in turn with the two outer pairs from the ground. Make a whole stitch at the center with the two twisted pairs.

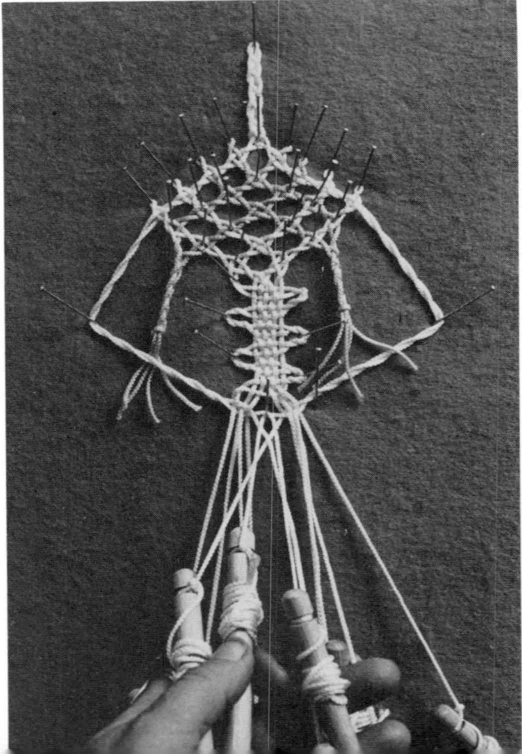

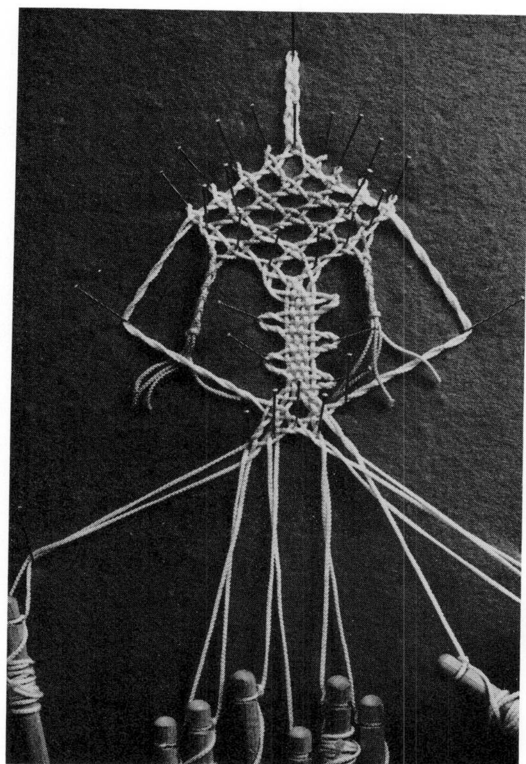

Working out from the center and to the left, take the first bobbin pair from the weaving ground and give it one TWIST. *Now make a whole stitch with this pair and the left pair from the center whole stitch. Now take the second or left outside pair from the weaving ground and give it two* TWISTS. *Follow with a whole stitch combining this pair with the left pair from the previous whole stitch. Do the same with the right pair from the center whole stitch working to the right.*

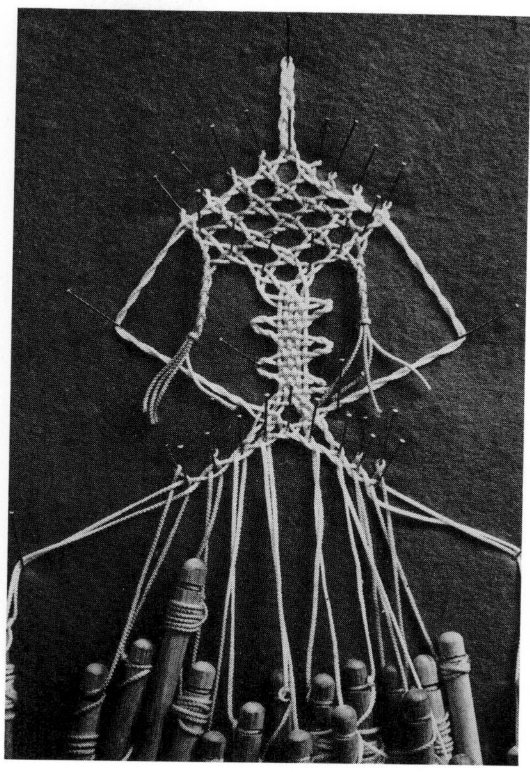

Take two of the cut-off yellow bobbin pairs and rewind them with a bobbin on each end forming four yellow bobbin pairs. PIN *two pairs on each side of the last whole stitch about ½-inch apart and down at about a 45° angle. This will add four new pairs of cord to your work. Make whole stitches combining these with the outer pairs from the previous step.*

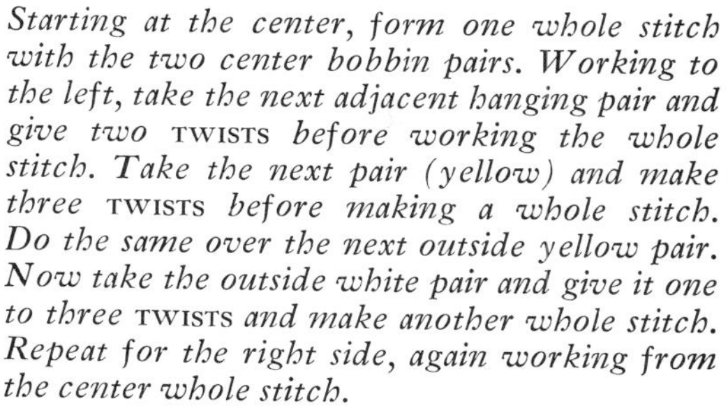

Starting at the center, form one whole stitch with the two center bobbin pairs. Working to the left, take the next adjacent hanging pair and give two TWISTS *before working the whole stitch. Take the next pair (yellow) and make three* TWISTS *before making a whole stitch. Do the same over the next outside yellow pair. Now take the outside white pair and give it one to three* TWISTS *and make another whole stitch. Repeat for the right side, again working from the center whole stitch.*

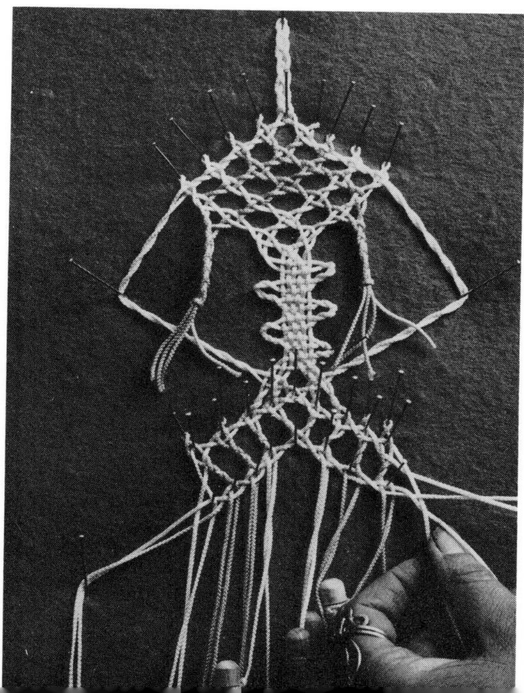

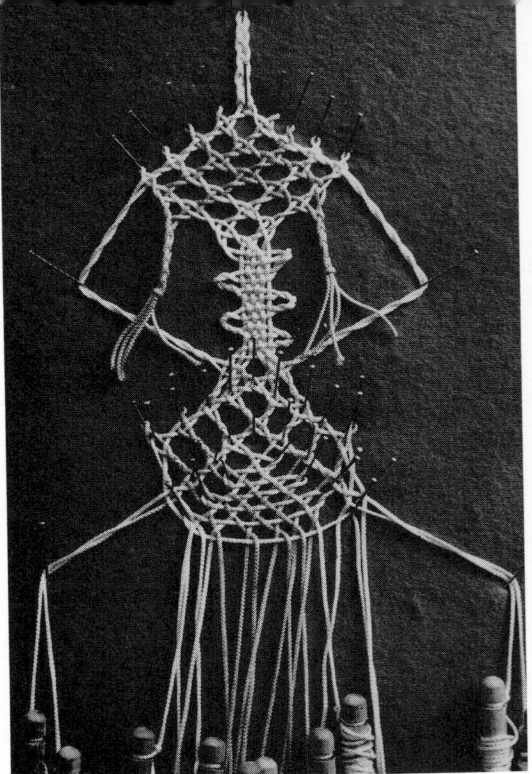

Starting at the center, work a half-diamond shape with half stitches (CROSS—TWIST). Take the two center pairs and without an initial twist make two half stitches and PIN. Return to the left making half stitches. At the left side pick up the first yellow pair and without an initial twist, incorporate it into the half-stitch ground. Be sure to give one extra TWIST before each return so the white cord remains the weaver, weaving back and forth horizontally. Continue working back and forth with half stitches, adding a new pair at each edge until all pairs except the outside pairs have been incorporated into the ground.

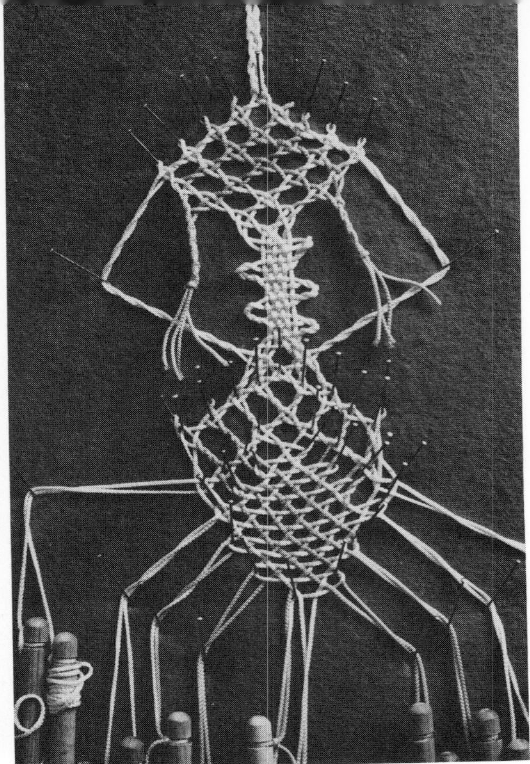

Now decrease forming the lower half of the diamond form. Drop a bobbin pair each time you come to an edge as you continue the half-stitch ground. PIN the dropped pairs out of the way.

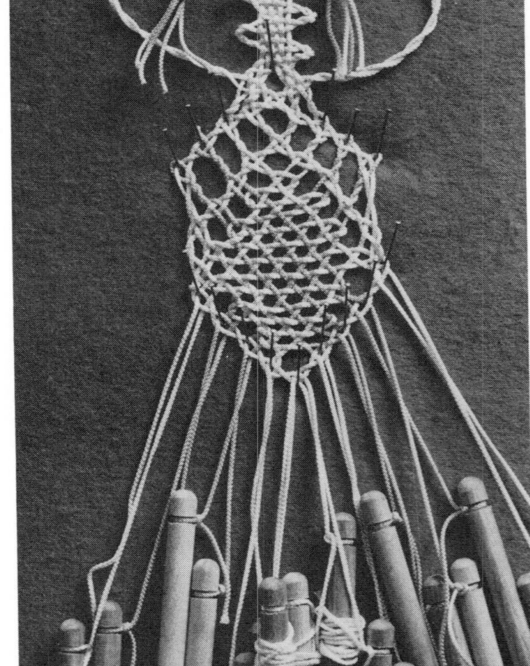

Take the left edge pair, give it two TWISTS, and follow with a whole stitch with the adjacent pair. Continue whole stitches with all pairs working to the center. Repeat for the right side.

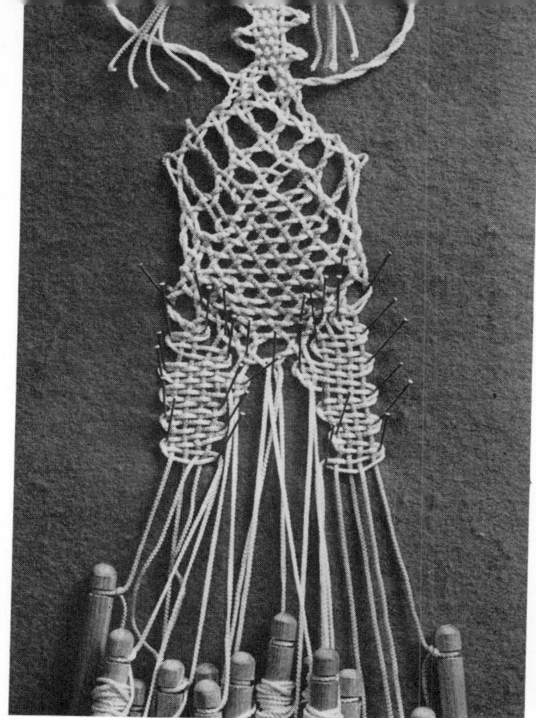

Starting at the left outside edge, take the outside pair of bobbins, give them two TWISTS *and make a linen stitch over adjacent pair.* PIN *and return to outside edge. Repeat, working back and forth adding next two pairs on next two successive rows. On the next row drop the last added pair and repeat working five more rows over the yellow pairs. The weaver pair should end up on the inner edge. Repeat on the right side.*

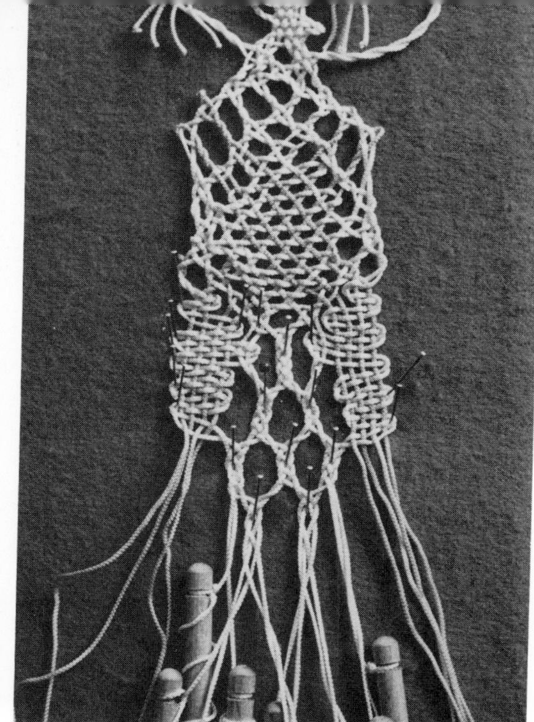

With the center two pairs, work a 1-inch braid, PINNING *through the center of the braid. With the hanging pairs from this braid and the two adjacent hanging pairs, work two Brussels stitches (each Brussels stitch is two whole stitches). Work the next row making three Brussels stitches incorporating the next adjacent weaver pairs. Complete the Brussels ground by making two Brussels stitches in the fourth row.*

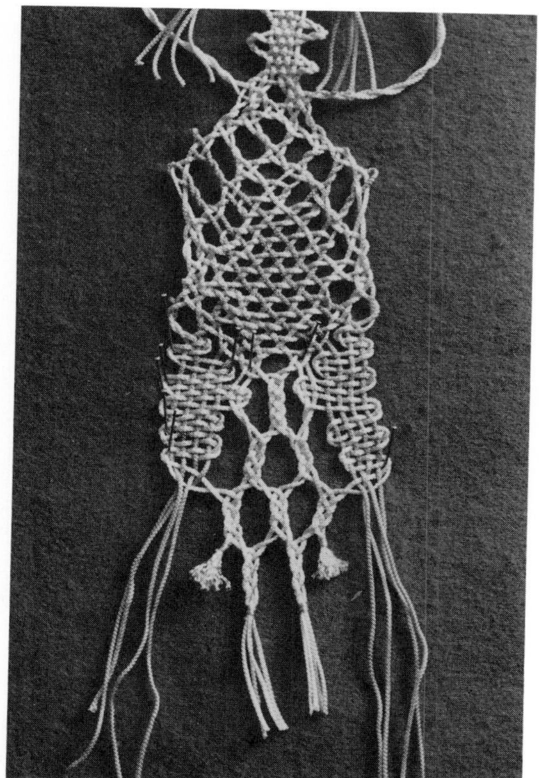

Tie off the two Brussels stitches by wrapping with a fine thread. Cut off bobbins leaving a 1- to 2-inch fringe. Tie off the adjacent hanging pairs from the Brussels stitch in a similar manner.

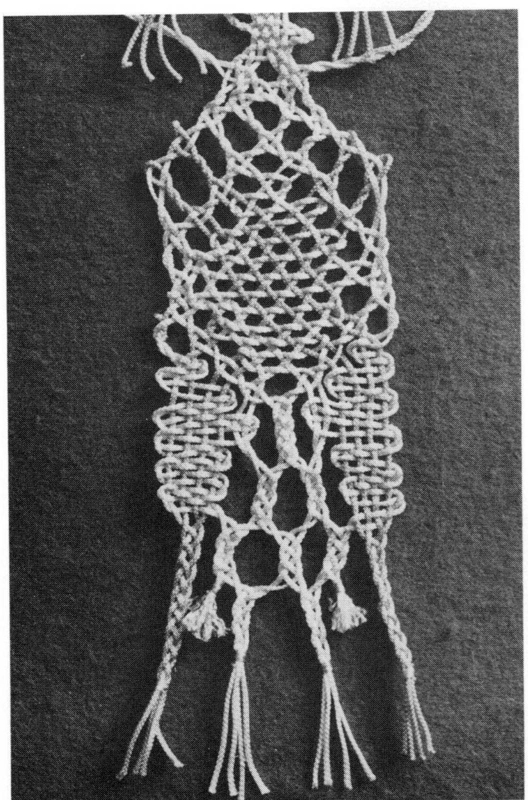

Braid the hanging yellow pairs from the outer weaving grounds forming a 1½-inch braid. Tie off by wrapping, then cut cords leaving a short fringe.

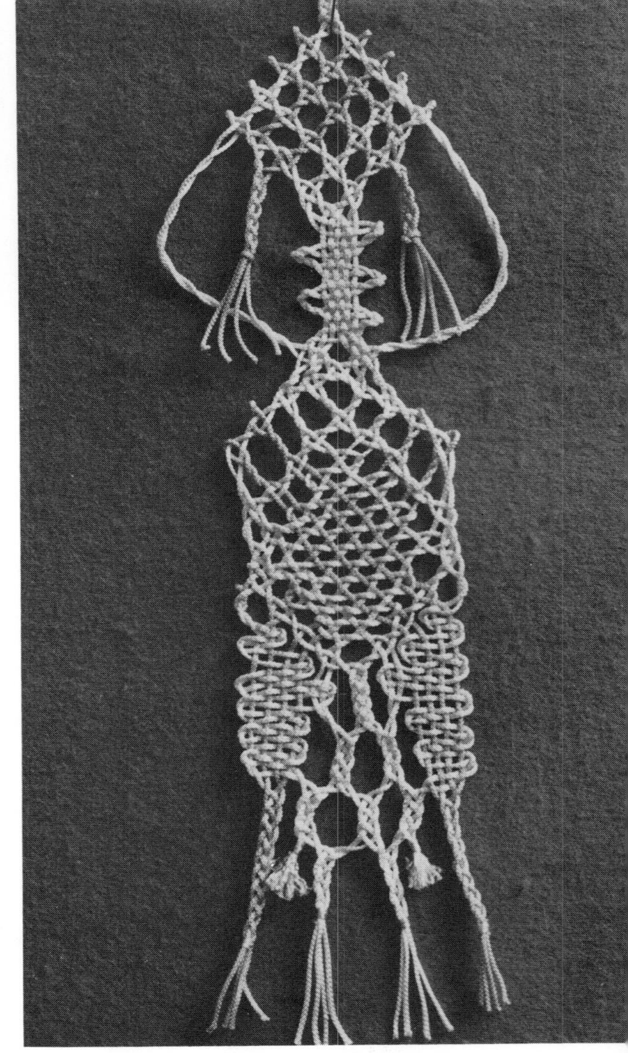

The finished sampler.

When you have completed this sampler, try working another sampler using the basic grounds and stitches. Use materials of different textures and try other stitch combinations. Before working your sampler, make a rough sketch or cartoon and see if you can follow it.

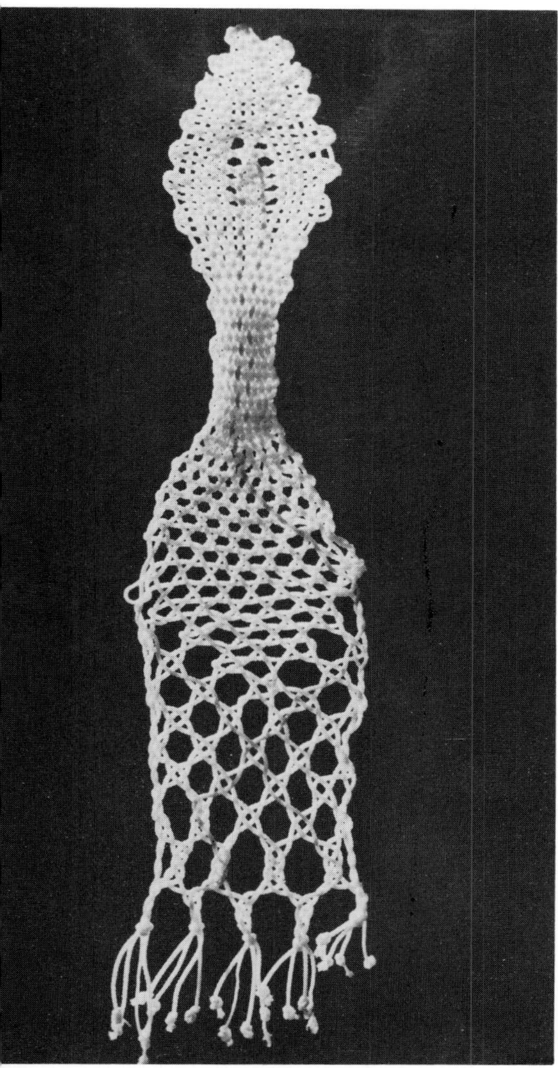

Another sampler worked with braided nylon.

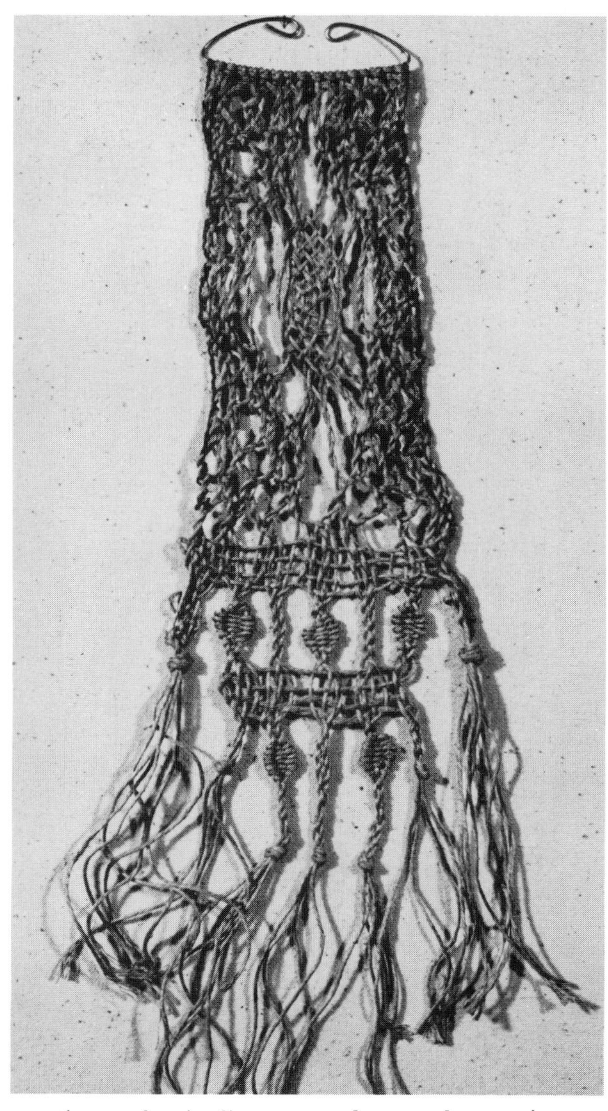

A sampler in linen started on a brass wire. Clarise Bois.

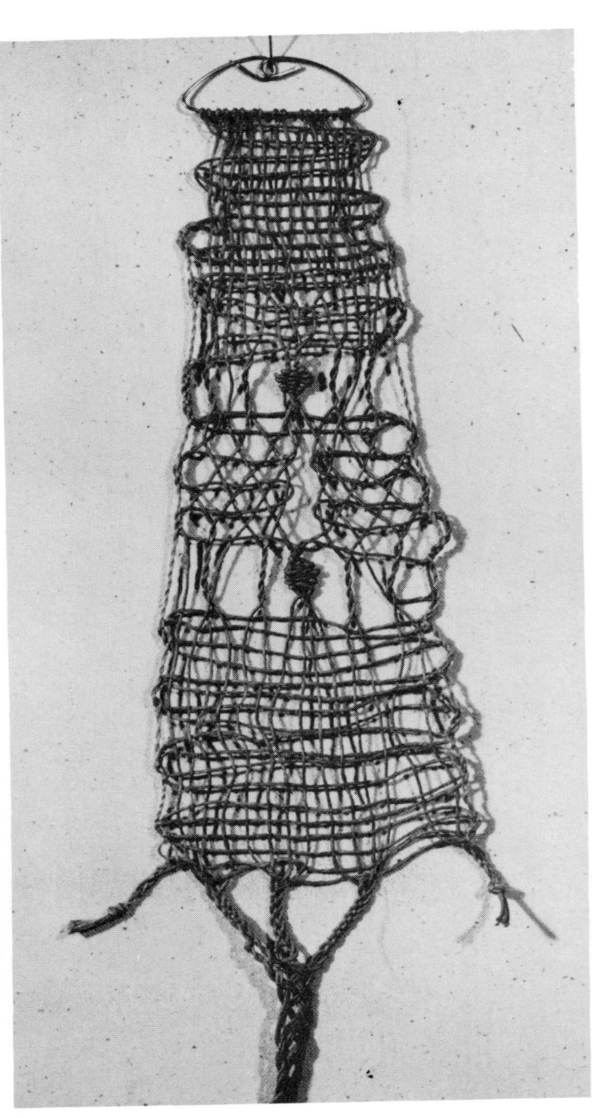

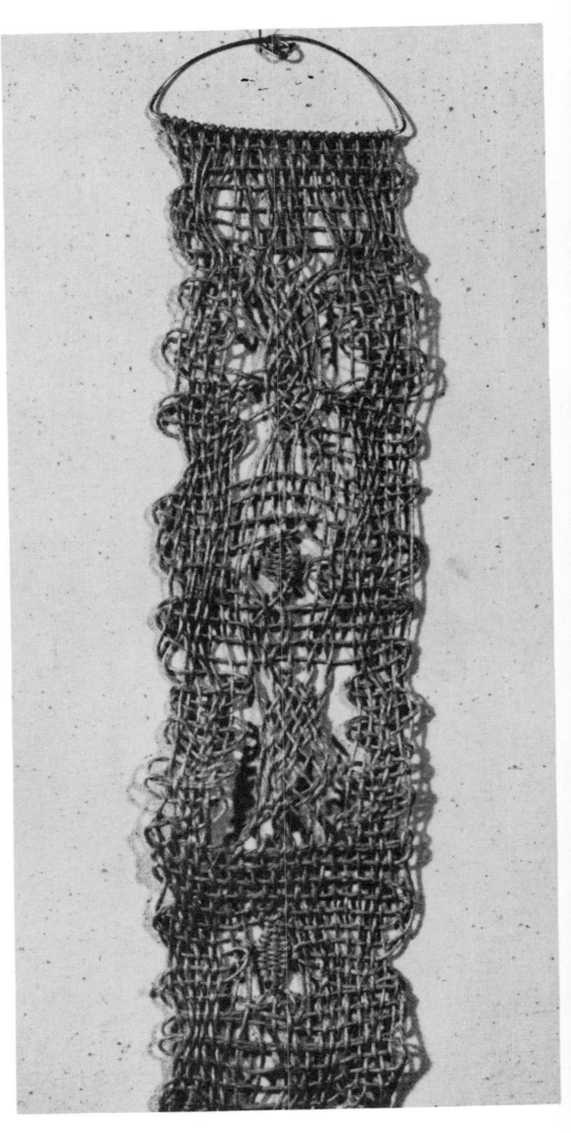

Two more samplers in linen by Clarise Bois.

LIFE CYCLE. Kaethe Kliot. Fabricating large screen working bobbin lace in suspension.

EMBRYO. Kaethe Kliot. Rug wool and linen.

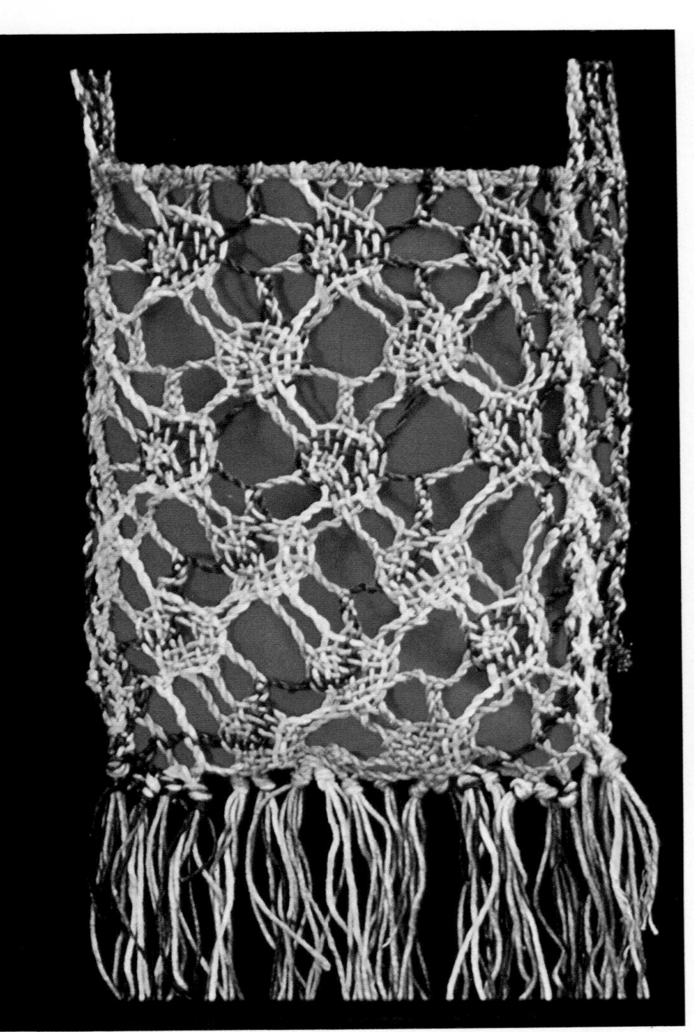

SHOULDER BAG. Kaethe Kliot. Patterns through control of stitch and thread. Dyed linen.

NECKPIECE. Kaethe Kliot. Linen.

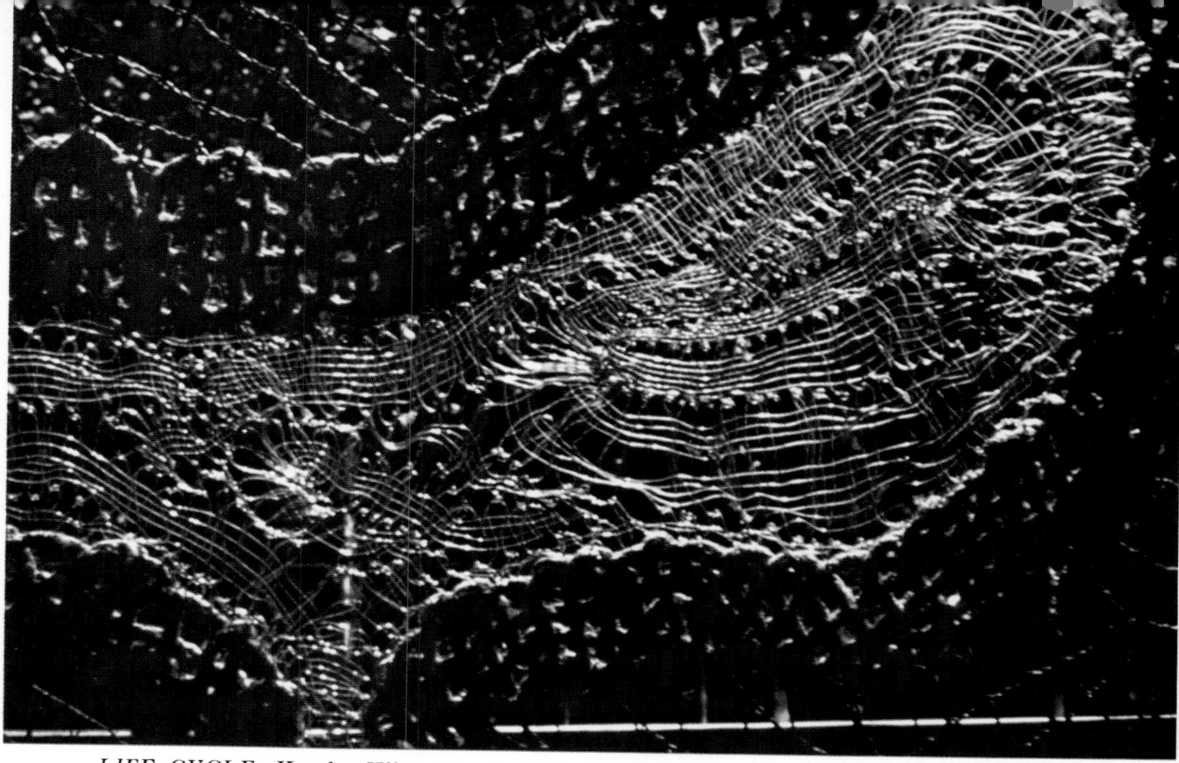

LIFE CYCLE. Kaethe Kliot. Detail of completed screen showing luminescent quality of the monofilament nylon.

SHOULDER BAG. Kaethe Kliot. Detail of reverse side.

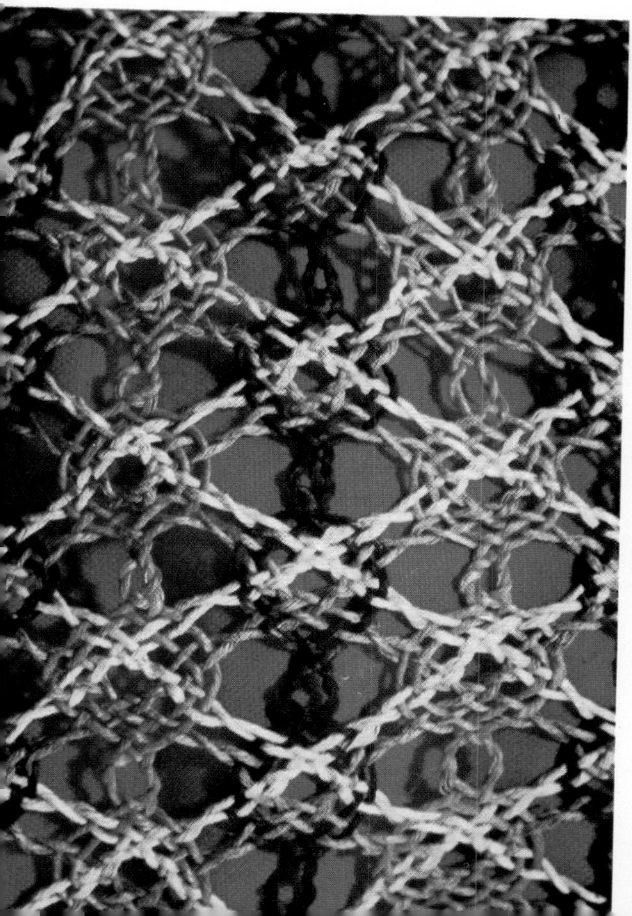

LIFE CYCLE. Kaethe Kliot. Detail of completed screen made with marlin, waxed linen, and monofilament nylon.

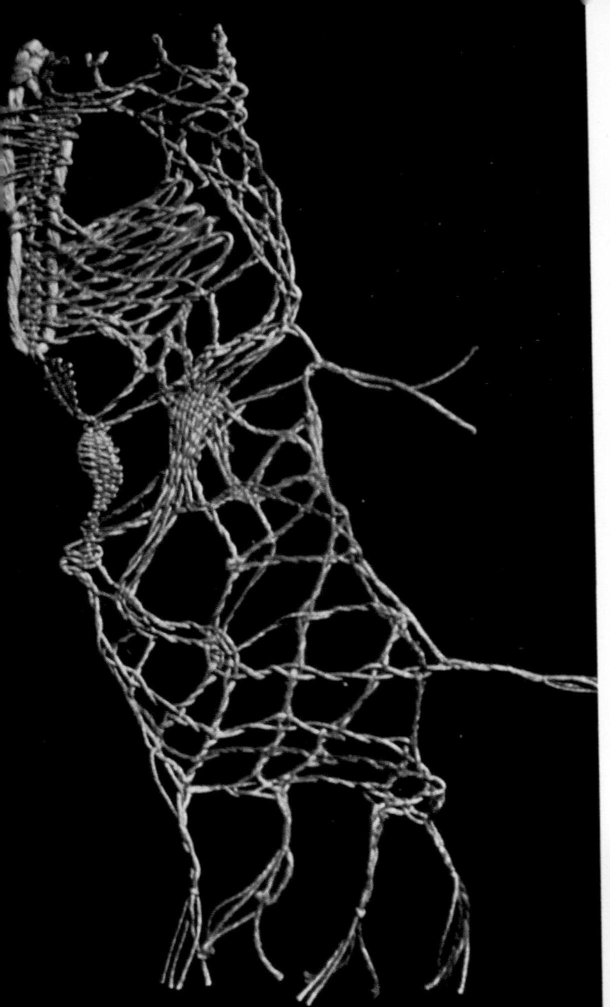

BEAST. Linda Harrell. Exploration of form and material in a lace sampler. Linen.

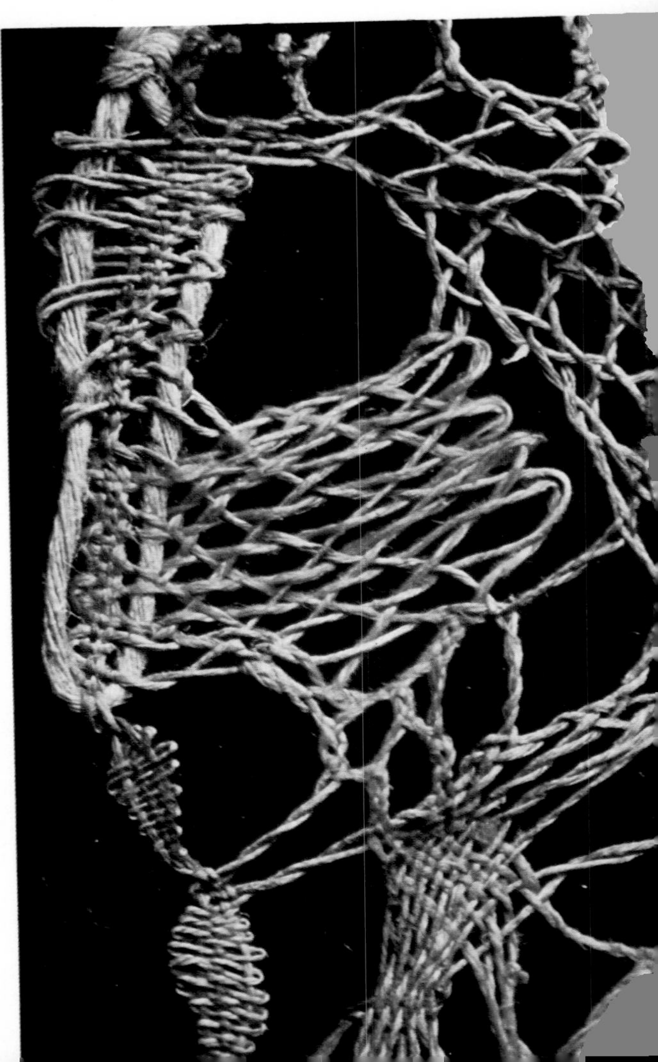

BEAST. Linda Harrell. Detail.

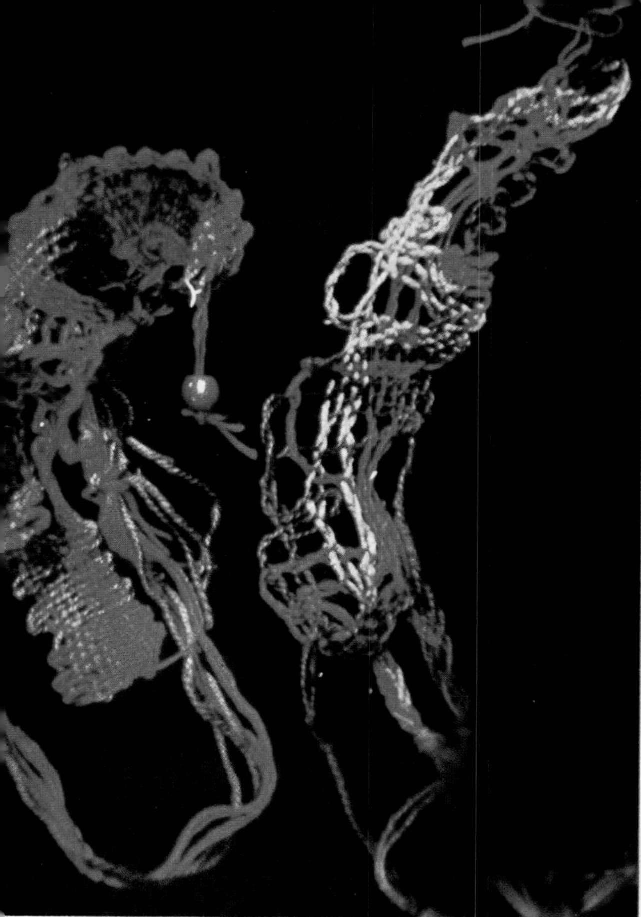

SAMPLERS. Helen Dietge. Rug wool and novelty yarns.

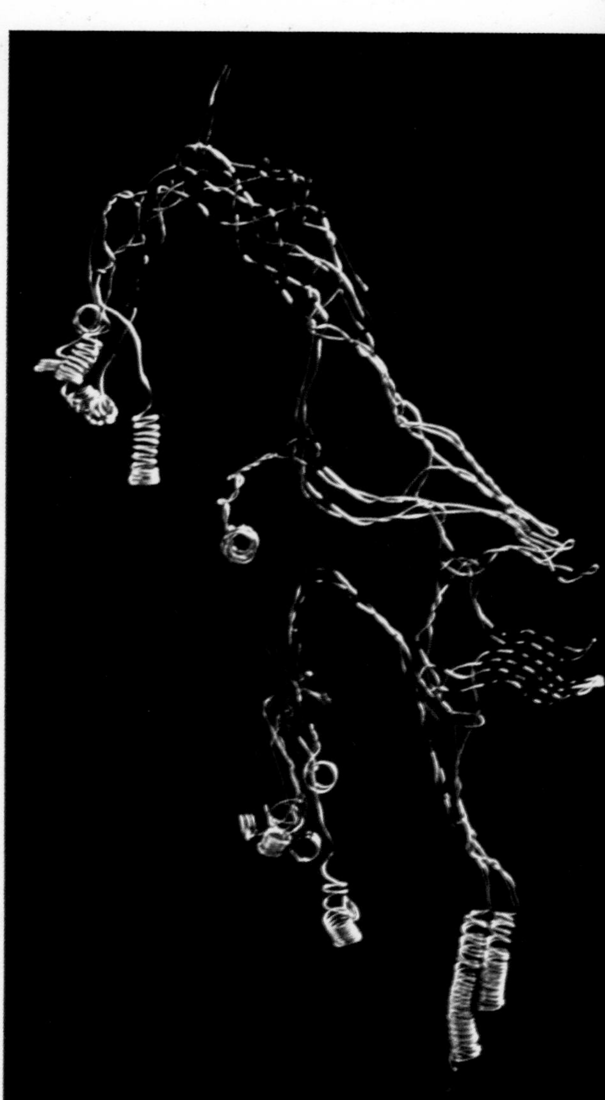

HORSE. Natalie Batchie. Wire.

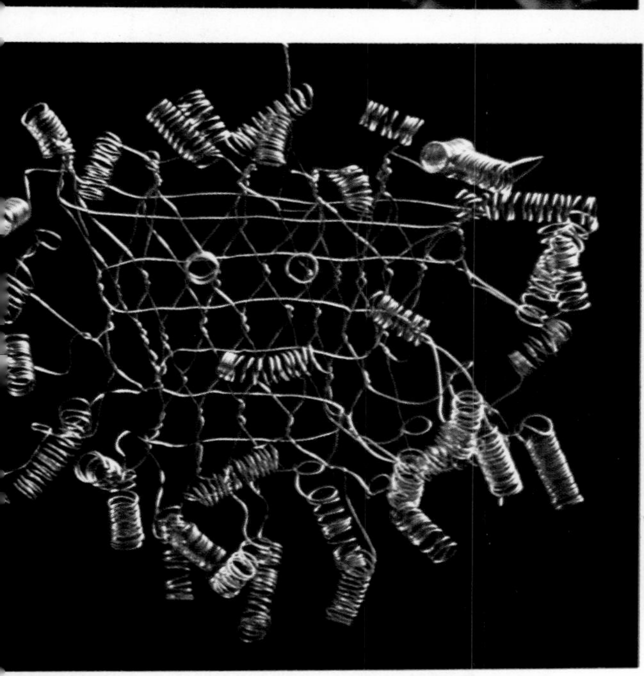

MASK. Florence McLelland. Wire.

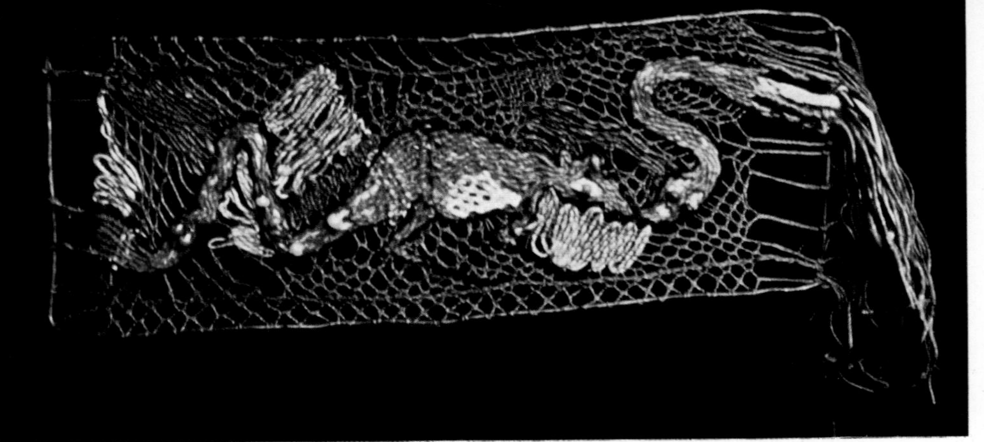

WALL HANGING. Lydia Van Gelder. Animal forms in linen.

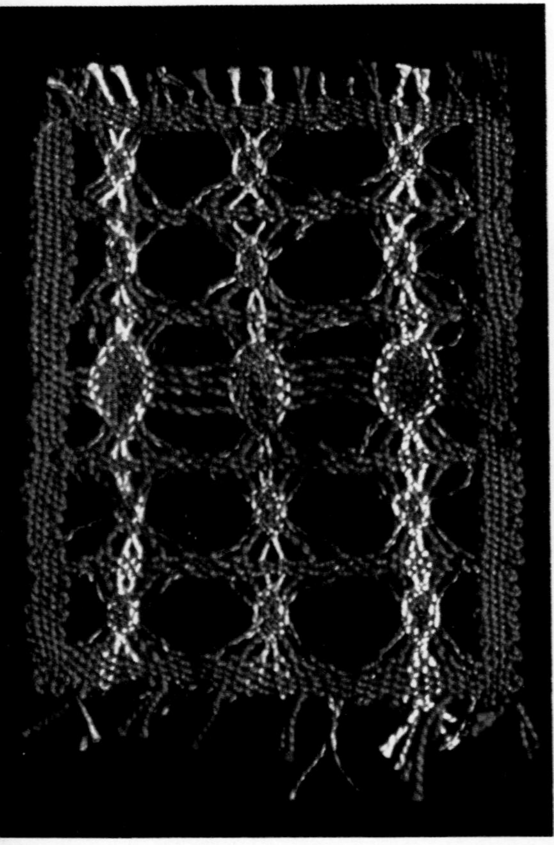

SAMPLER. Kaethe Kliot. Dyed linen.

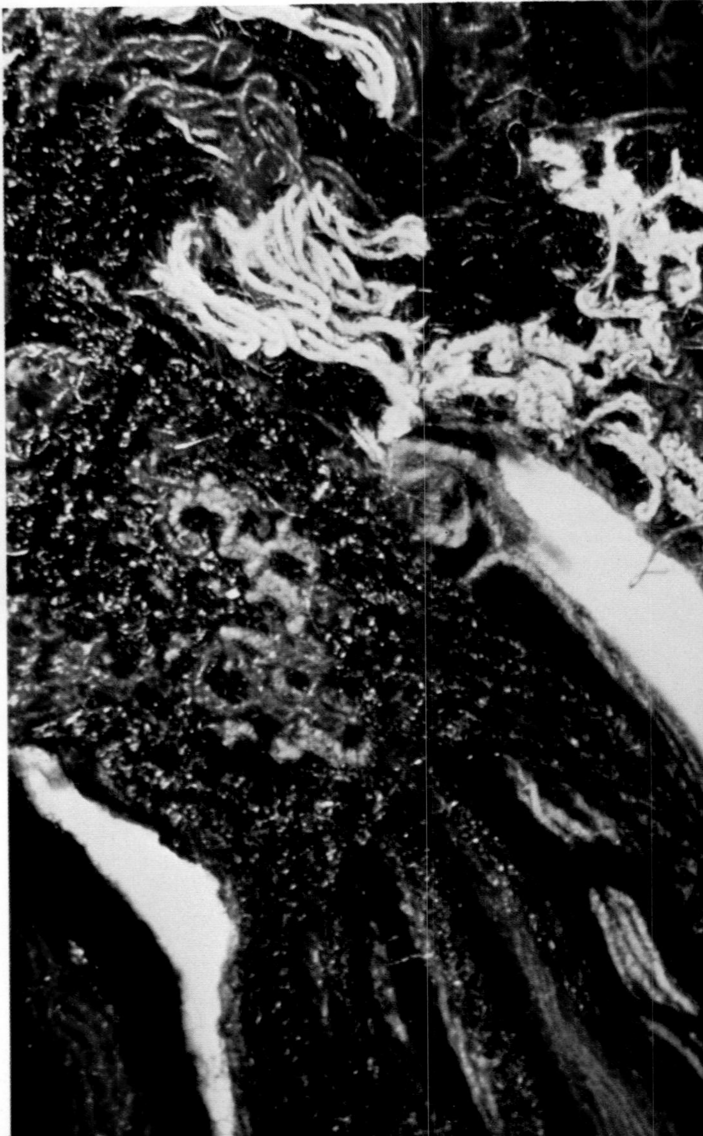

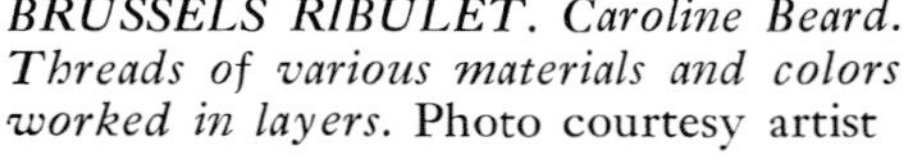

BRUSSELS RIBULET. Caroline Beard. Threads of various materials and colors worked in layers. Photo courtesy artist

SAMPLER. Kaethe Kliot. Bouclé and gold thread worked in layers.

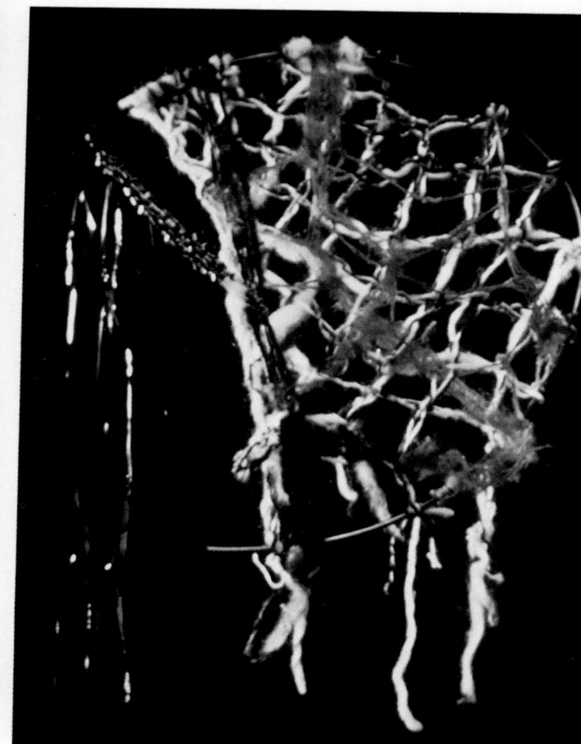

FREE HANGING. Kaethe Kliot. Silk, hand spun, magnetic tape, and wool.

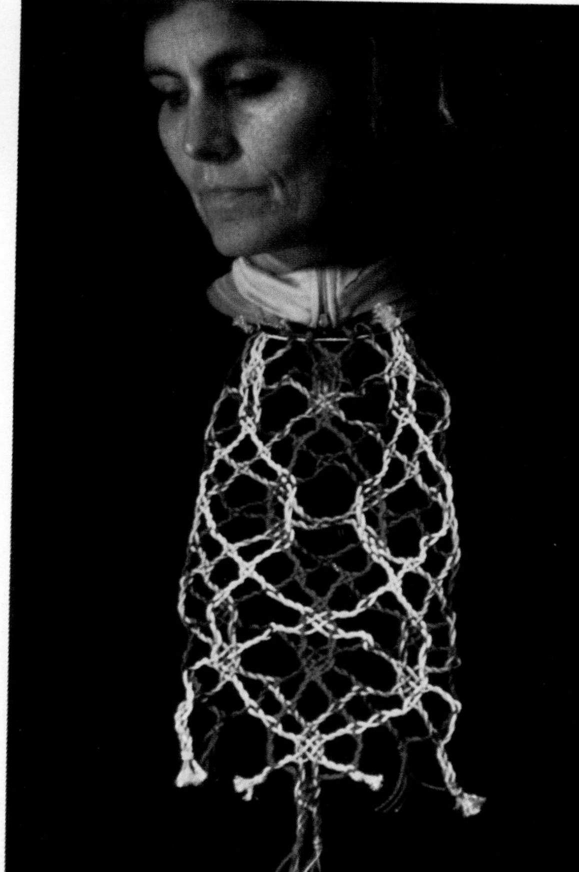

NECKPIECE. Kaethe Kliot. Pattern in color through the control of threads. Braided nylon.

FIGURE. Luba Krejci. Traveling exhibit, 1965.

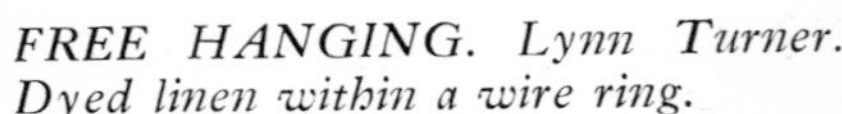

FREE HANGING. Lynn Turner. Dyed linen within a wire ring.

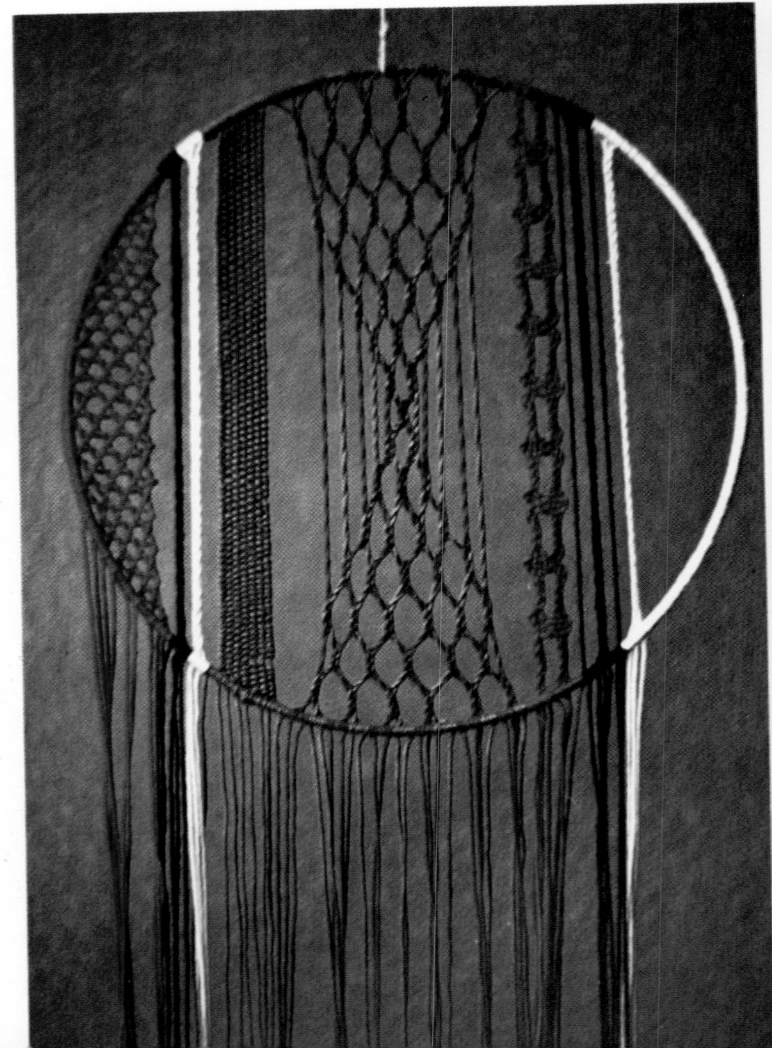

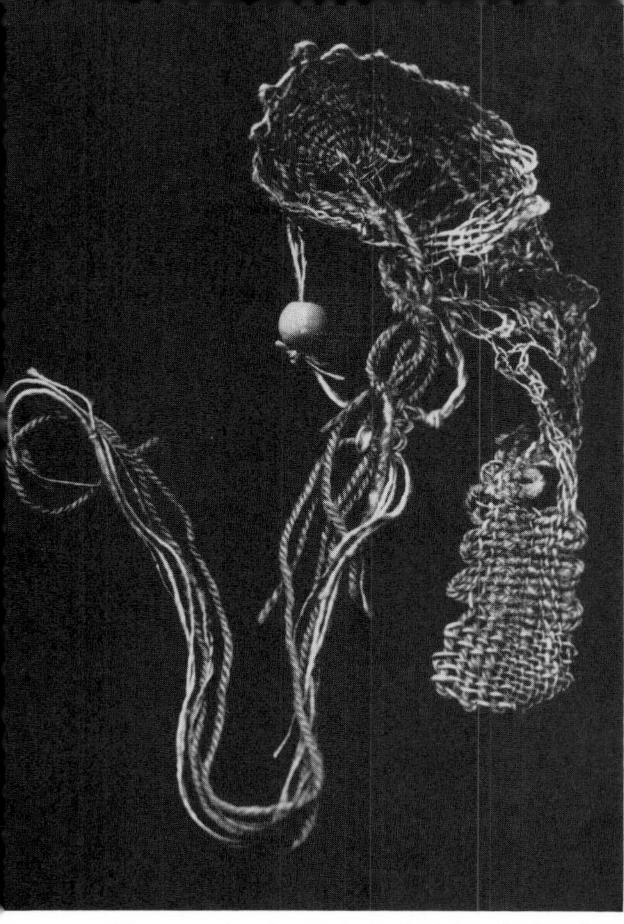

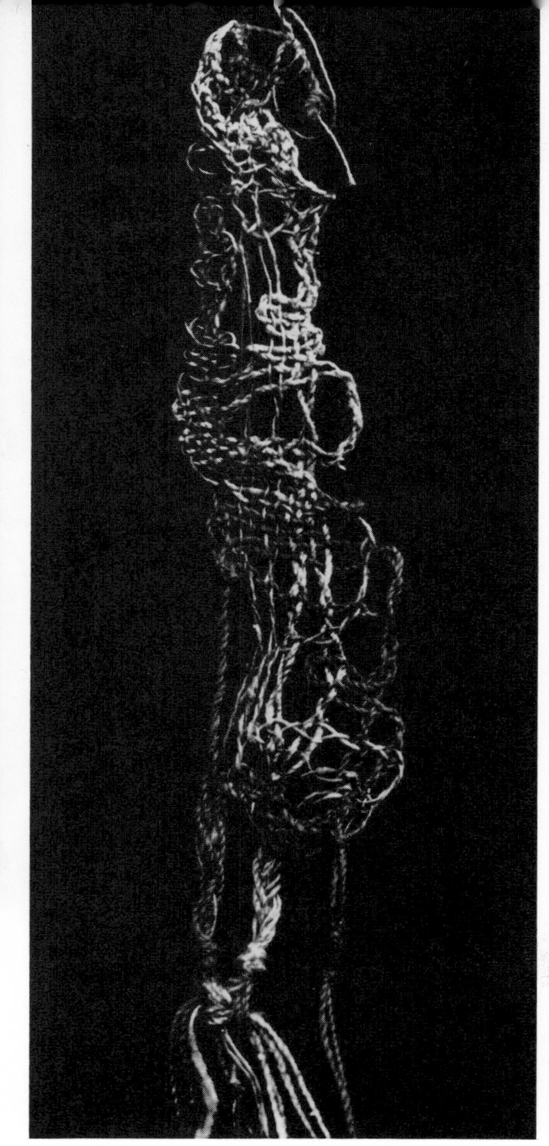

Two samplers in wool emphasizing the freedom of movement of bobbin lace threads. Helen Dietge.

A sampler in wool using two colors. Eleanor Grivin.

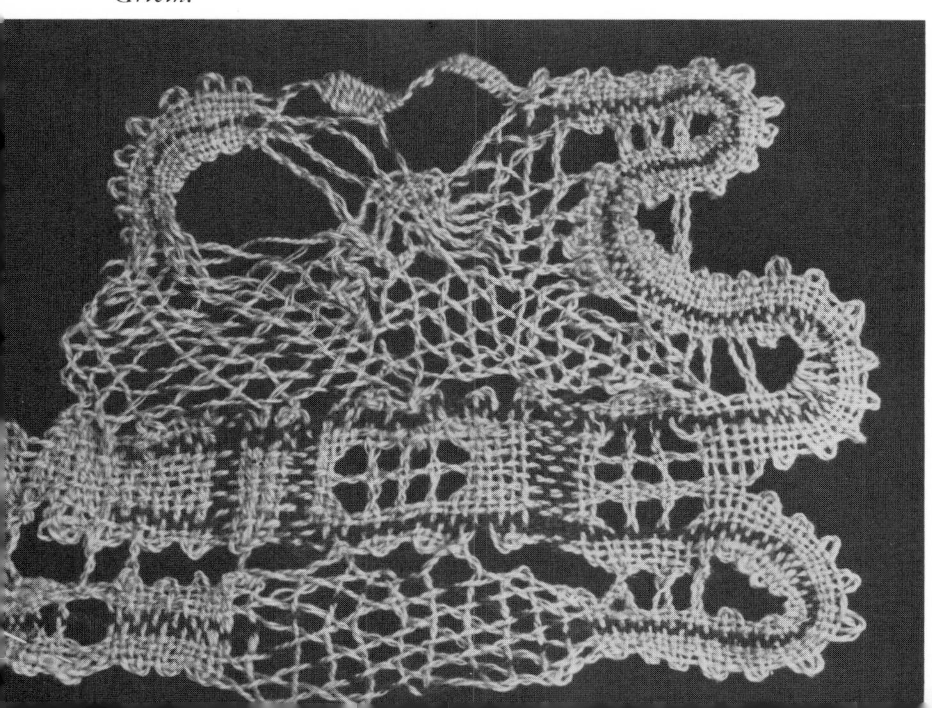

Special Techniques And Stitches

Chapter 5

Over the many years of the development of bobbin lace, countless techniques were developed to simplify the working of the complex designs as well as to provide standard methods for handling the many threads.

The basic stitches as previously described define the simple crossing of threads or bobbin pairs. The crossing of threads has always been an event, and exploration of these crossings has led to more elaborate combinations of the basic stitches.

Some of the more common techniques and stitches are presented in this chapter as additional tools to work with.

HEADINGS

The simplest method of starting a piece of bobbin lace is to hang your bobbin pairs on pins. This results in a finished edge integral with the piece. This was the only method used in working traditional lace.

For hangings or when lace is to be integral with a flexible or rigid frame, various methods of mounting can be considered. A few methods are demonstrated here to open up some of the possibilities for exploring the design potential of this edge.

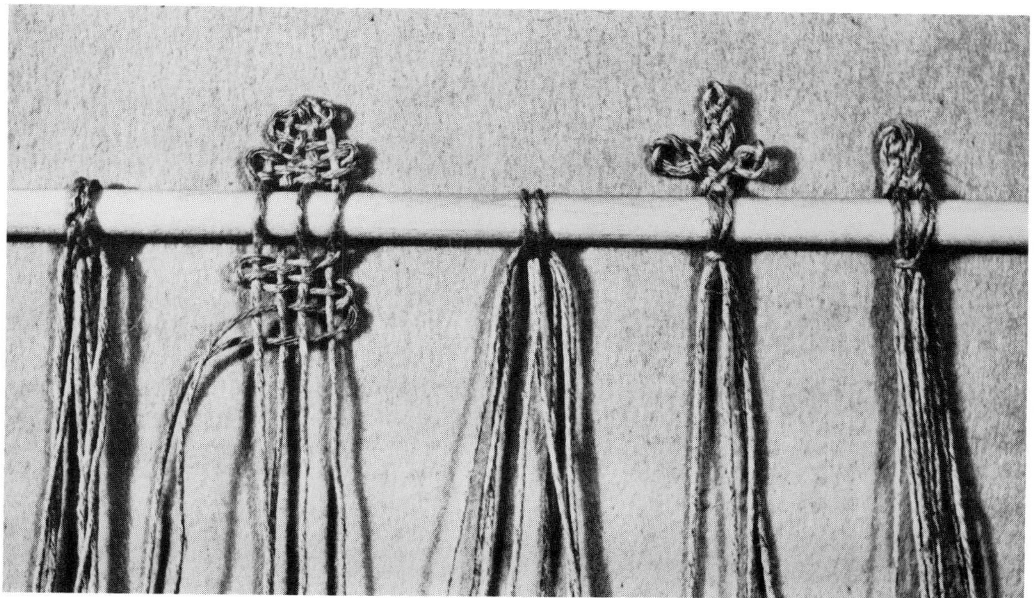

A variety of headings. From left to right: braided half hitch; linen stitch; single half hitch; double picot; hanger.

BRAIDED HALF HITCH: This mounting must be formed prior to winding your bobbins. With two pairs of threads form a *braid* long enough to go around your mounting. When starting, allow a small loop above the start of the *braid*. When the *braid* is finished the free ends are passed through this loop, forming a half hitch around your support. Additional pairs can be combined with this heading by simply laying them through the hitch.

Braided half hitch; formed with two pairs, it is mounted with two additional pairs.

LINEN STITCH HANGING: This mounting can be done with three or more pairs. Hang all pairs except the weaver pair on one pin. Hang the weaver pair on an adjacent pin. Work a *weaving ground* of a desired length and then hang over mounting bar with half the threads going on each side. Work at least two rows of *linen stitches* below the mounting bar before working your piece.

Linen stitch heading worked with three pairs. Note how threads are divided as they go over mounting bar.

SINGLE HALF HITCH: Half hitch one or two bobbin pairs to your mounting. Add as many additional pairs to this mounting as required by laying them through the hitch. Note that each thread laid through the hitch will result in one bobbin pair.

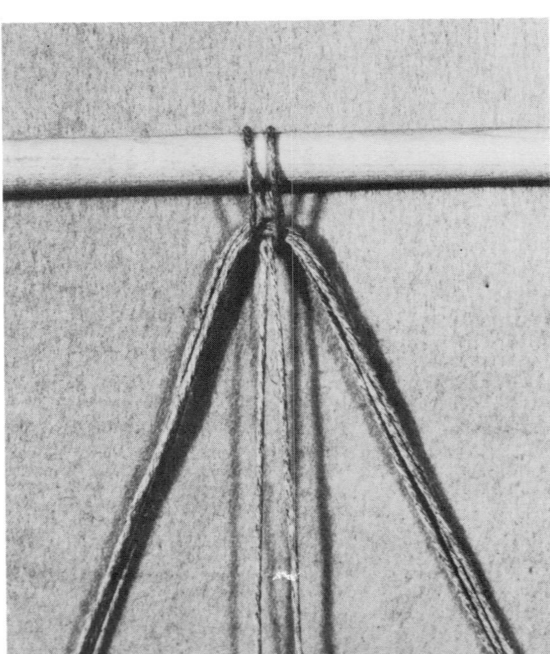

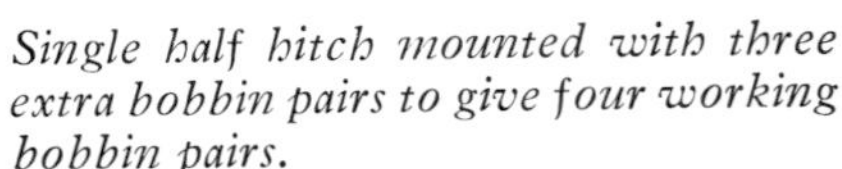

Single half hitch mounted with three extra bobbin pairs to give four working bobbin pairs.

DOUBLE PICOT: Form a short *braid* and then work a *picot* on each side. Work a *linen stitch* with both pairs. Split pairs as shown and hang heading over your mounting bar. Secure heading by making an overhand knot below the mounting bar.

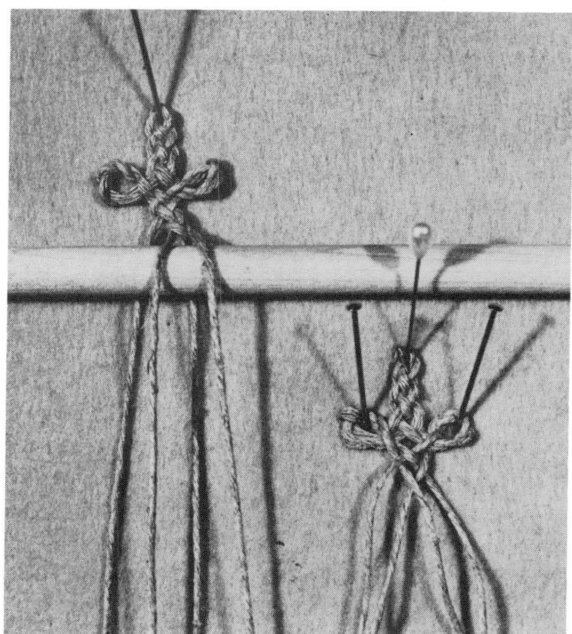

Double picot heading.

HANGER: A hanger can be used as an edge detail or as a functional device by which your piece can be supported. Using two pairs or four pairs (worked as two), form a *braid* of any length. Split pairs, hanging the heading over the mounting bar. Secure with an overhand knot.

Try other stitch combinations for mountings. "Picots," "spiders," and "fillings" can all be worked into decorative headings.

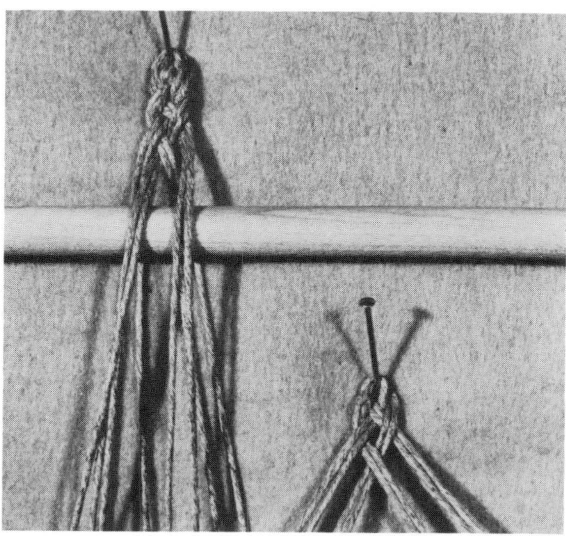

Hanger formed with double threads resulting in four starting pairs.

CROSSING OF PAIRS

The crossing of bobbin pairs in varying numbers can be used as the basis of many weblike forms. Many grounds and delicate traceries can be formed based on these crossings.

The crossing of two pairs is simply done with a *linen stitch*. As additional pairs join the crossing, more elaborate designs are possible.

Before starting your crossing, TWIST all pairs so the twists reach the point of the intended intersection.

CROSSING OF THREE PAIRS—METHOD 1: This method forms a crossing with a tight center.

1. With the two left pairs make a *half stitch* (CROSS—TWIST). Do the same with the two right pairs, then again with the two left pairs.
2. PIN at the center with three bobbin pairs falling on either side.
3. With the two right pairs make a *half stitch*. Do the same with the two left pairs, then again with the two right pairs.
4. Continue working your pairs with TWISTS.

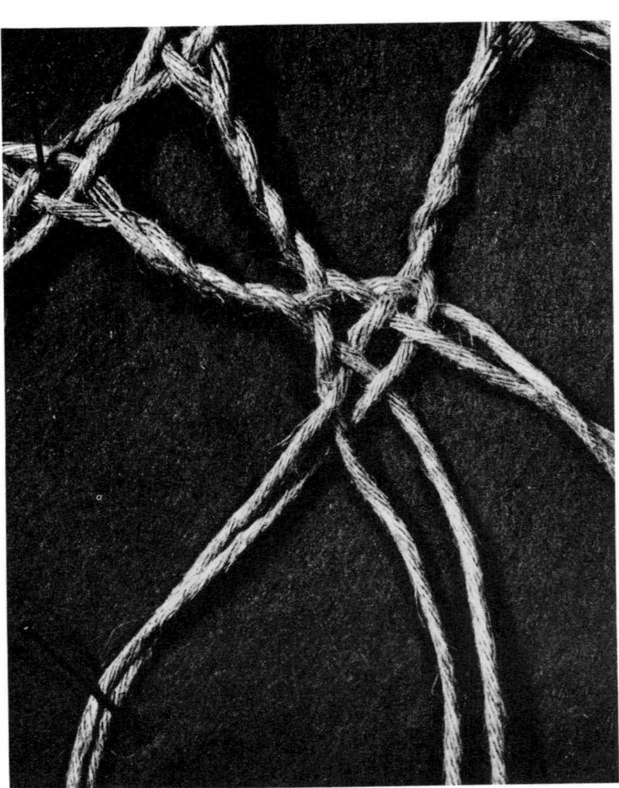

The crossing of three pairs with half stitches forming a tight center crossing.

CROSSING OF THREE PAIRS—METHOD 2: This method forms a crossing with a hole in the center.

1. With the two left pairs make a *whole stitch* and PIN.
2. With the two right pairs make a *whole stitch*.
3. With the two left pairs make a *whole stitch*.
4. Continue working your pairs with TWISTS.

The crossing of three pairs with whole stitches forming an open center crossing.

CROSSING OF FOUR PAIRS: As you work this crossing, PIN as required to keep pairs in place.

1. With the center pairs make a *linen stitch.*
2. With the two left pairs make a *linen stitch.* Do the same with the two right pairs.
3. With the two center pairs make another *linen stitch* and PIN. This is the center of the crossing.
4. Repeat steps 2 and 3.
5. Continue working your pairs with TWISTS.

The crossing of four pairs with linen stitches. The crossing can be left in this form or worked again after the pinning.

The completed crossing. Note how the outer pairs continue in the same direction while the inner pairs reverse their direction.

CROSSING OF SIX OR MORE PAIRS: This crossing is made by a repetition of *half stitches*.

1. With the center pairs make a *half stitch*.
2. Working to the left, take the left center pair and adjacent pair and make a *half stitch*. With the left pair from this stitch and the adjacent pair make another *half stitch*. Repeat until the outer pair has been worked. Do the same with the right center pair working to the right.
3. Repeat steps 1 and 2.
4. Repeat step 3 until all pairs have crossed.

The interchange of threads in this crossing can be used to advantage when working with threads of contrasting colors.

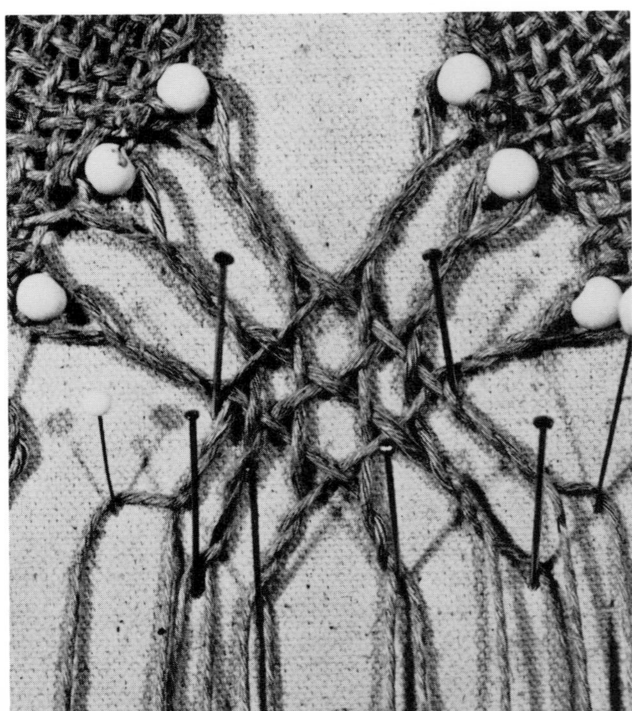

The crossing of six pairs with half stitches. Note the complex interchanging of individual threads as they leave the crossing in new pair formations.

The complete six pair crossing used as a central design motif.

CROSSING OF BRAIDS

When *braids* intersect or cross, the primary object is to make the intersection secure while at the same time keeping the work flat. Intersections can become major design motifs or they can be relatively inconspicuous. While two *braids* form the most common intersection, three and four *braid* intersections can be planned as powerful focuses of a piece.

CROSSING OF TWO BRAIDS—METHOD 1: Each pair of each *braid* is treated as a single thread.

1. Make a *whole stitch* (CROSS—TWIST—PIN—CROSS—TWIST) with all four pairs.
2. Pull into place and continue forming your *braids*.

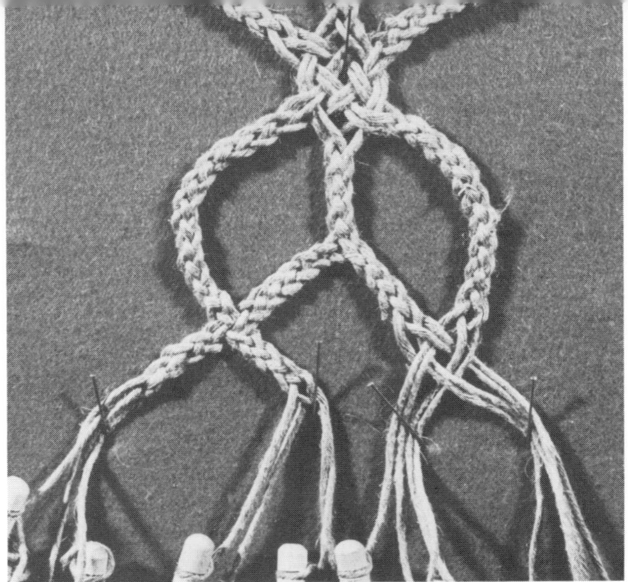

The crossing of two braids with each pair of each braid treated as a single thread.

CROSSING OF TWO BRAIDS—METHOD 2: Each thread is treated independently.

1. With the center two pairs make a *linen stitch* (CROSS—TWIST—CROSS).
2. Take the left pair and the adjacent outside pair and make another *linen stitch*. Do the same with the two right pairs.
3. With the center two pairs make another *linen stitch*.
4. Pull into place and continue forming your two *braids*.

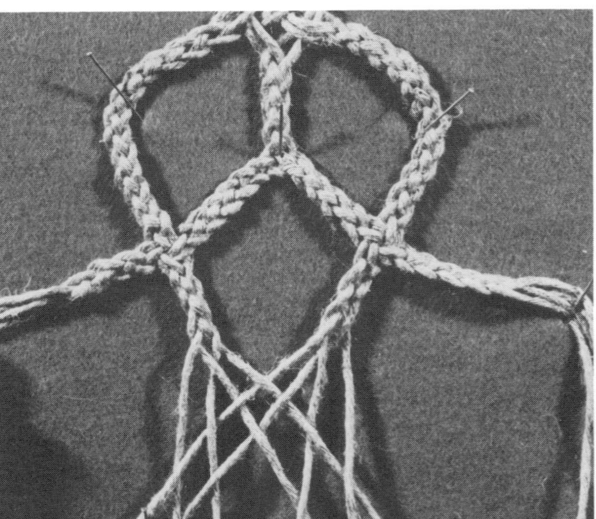

The crossing of two braids with each thread treated independently. All pairs are worked with linen stitches.

The completed crossing of two braids.

CROSSING OF THREE BRAIDS: Each pair of each *braid* is treated as a single thread. Make sure that these pairs do not twist as you work them. PIN between the three *braid* pairs to keep them in place.

1. Take the left pair from the center *braid* and CROSS it with the adjacent left pair, then TWIST it with the outside left pair. Do the same with the right pair from the center *braid* working to the right.
2. TWIST the center two pairs. With the left pair CROSS with the adjacent left pair, then TWIST with the outer left pair. Do the same with the right center pair working to the right.
3. Repeat step 2.
4. Pull into place and continue forming your three *braids*.

This crossing will have an opening in the center. This opening can be made large or small, depending on how you pull your threads.

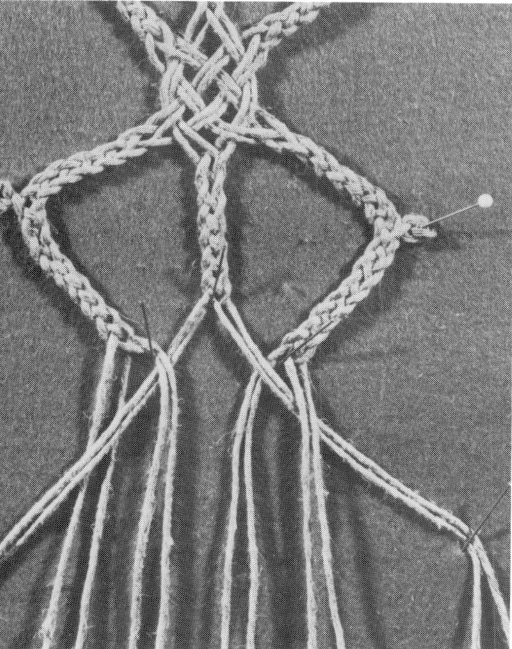

The crossing of three braids. Each pair of each braid is treated as a single thread. The first crossing (step 1).

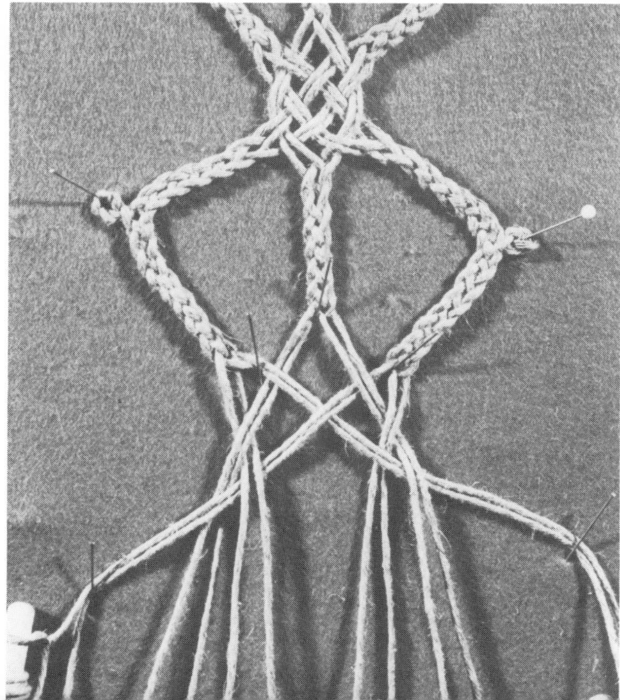

The second crossing (step 2).

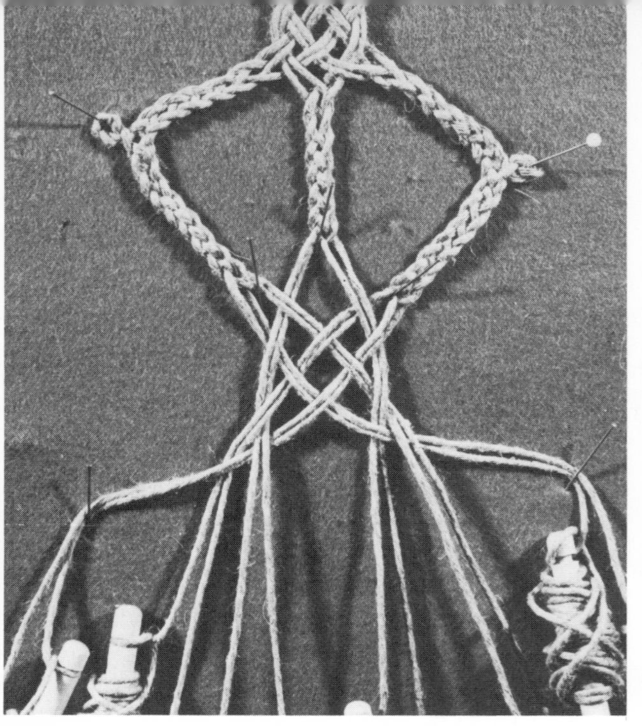

The final crossing (step 3).

All pairs are pulled tight and formed again into braids.

CROSSING OF FOUR BRAIDS: Treat each pair of each *braid* as a single thread, making sure that they do not twist. PIN between the four *braid* pairs to keep them in place.

1. With the center four pairs make a *half stitch* (CROSS—TWIST).
2. With the left four pairs make another *half stitch*. Do the same with the right four pairs.
3. Repeat steps 1 and 2 and then PIN. This is the middle of the crossing.
4. Repeat steps 1 and 2 two more times completing the crossing.
5. Pull into place and continue forming your four *braids*. As with the three-braid crossing, there will be an opening in the center. The size of this opening is determined by the pulling of your threads.

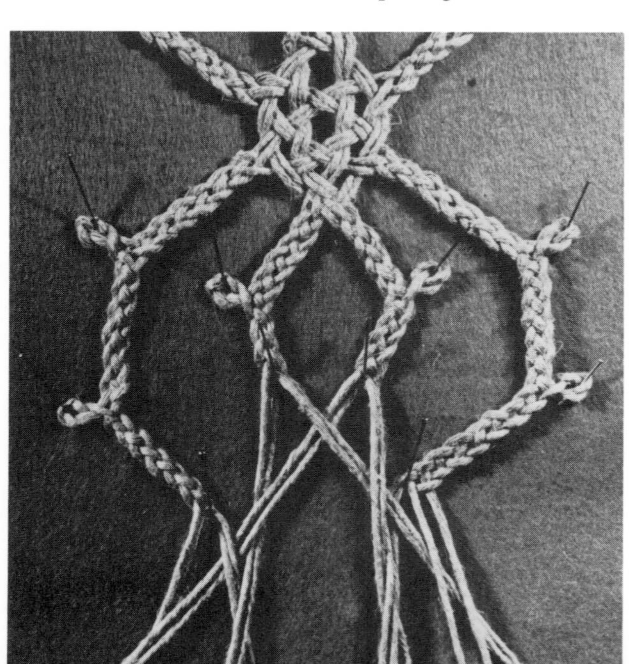

The crossing of four braids. Each pair of each braid is treated as a single thread. The first crossing (steps 1 and 2).

The second crossing that completes half the complete stitch (step 3).

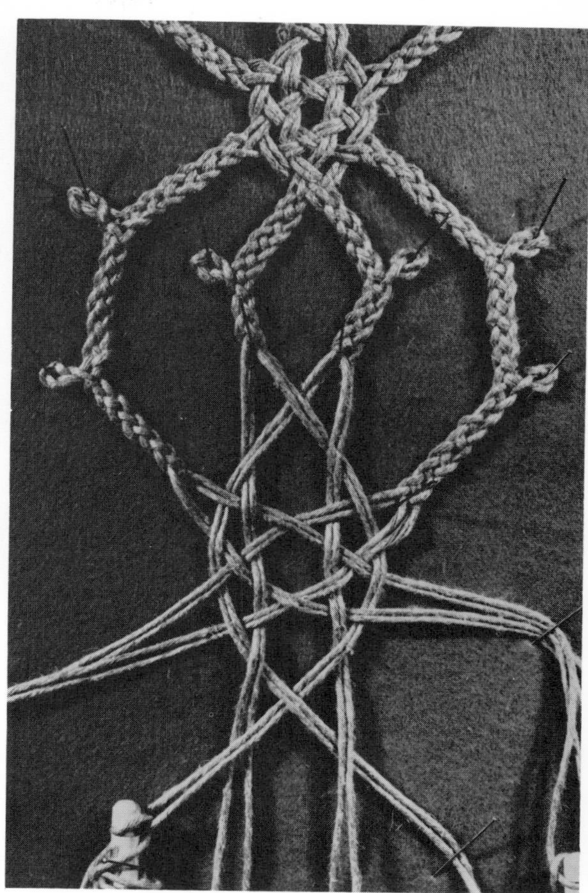

All pairs have crossed (step 4).

All pairs are pulled tight and formed again into braids.

SPIDERS

A "spider" is the name given to a particular crossing that forms a dense circular area in a design that has a spiderlike appearance. It is always formed with an even number of bobbin pairs. Eight-legged spiders and twelve-legged spiders are formed by the crossing of four and six pairs respectively and are the most common, although far more complex crossings are possible. Spiders are an integral design element in many traditional lace patterns and grounds.

In working the spider, control of tension is important. The body can be made to lay flat or arch up, forming a cuplike form.

Begin by twisting each leg or bobbin pair until the twist reaches the area of the body. Pairs will enter the upper half of the body symmetrically about its vertical axis.

1. With the two center pairs make a *linen stitch.*
2. With the right center pair from this stitch make *linen stitches* with all pairs to the right.
3. With the next adjacent pair to the left again work *linen stitches* with all pairs to the right.
4. Repeat step 3 until all left pairs have crossed over all right pairs.
5. PIN under the crossing of the center pairs and make a *linen stitch.* The pin is the center of the spider.
6. Repeat steps 2, 3, and 4 until all pairs are again crossed.
7. Continue working all pairs with TWISTS, forming the remaining legs.

Working the first row of linen stitches to the right (steps 1 and 2).

With the next pair to the left, linen stitches are made with all pairs to the right (step 3).

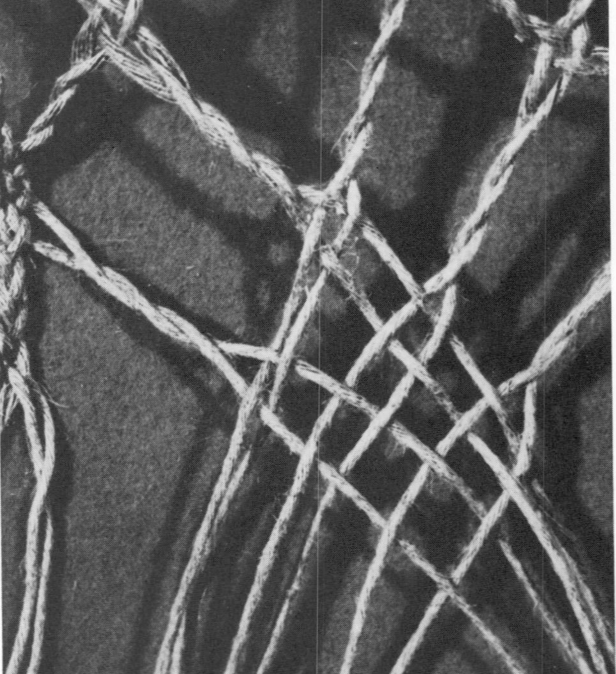

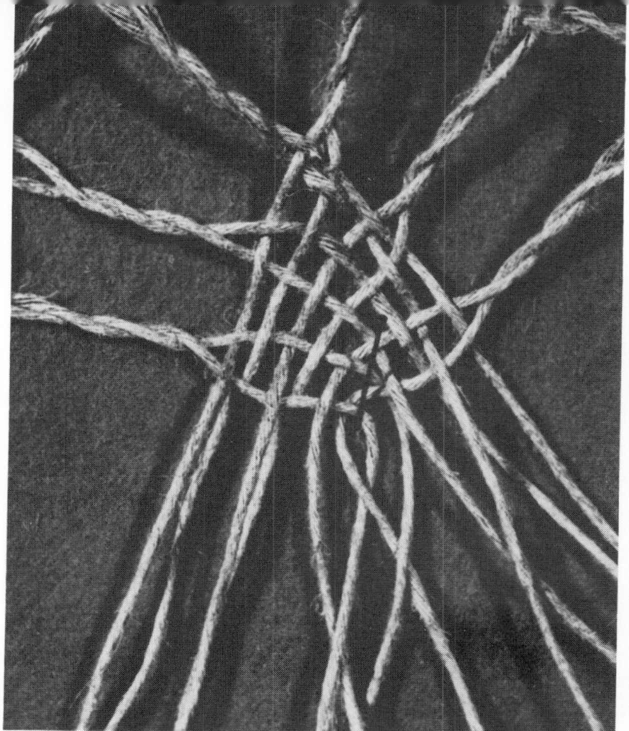

All left pairs have crossed to the right (step 4) and a linen stitch is made with the center pairs (step 5).

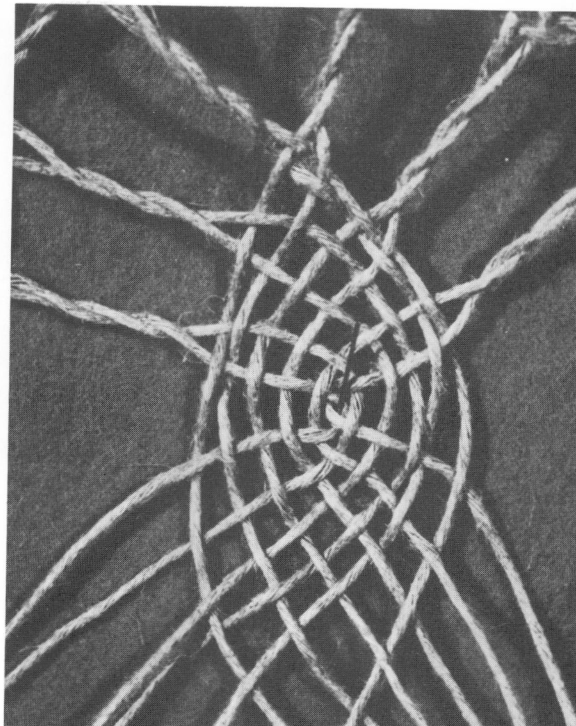

All pairs have again crossed so they emerge on the same side that they entered (step 6).

All pairs pulled tight and worked out with TWISTS *forming the remaining legs (step 7).*

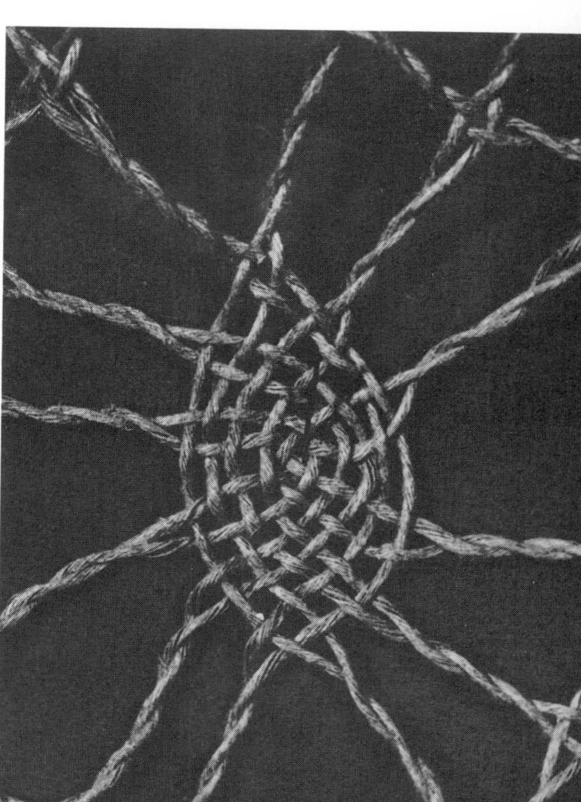

PICOTS

A "picot" is a small loop used as a decorative element as well as a means to change direction of a *braid*. A pair of threads is used, which is twisted, looped, and finally locked together securing the loop.

The picot is formed with a bobbin pair that extends beyond the edge of a worked design.

1. Take the extended pair from your work and make four to six TWISTS depending on the weight of your cord and the size of loop wanted.
2. Place a pin under the outer thread and rotate the pin causing the thread to loop around the pin. If the picot is on the right side of your work, rotate the pin counterclockwise. If the picot is on the left side of your work, rotate the pin clockwise. Insert the pin adjacent to the edge of the worked design.
3. Gently pull the loop thread down into place so it forms a loose loop. If done correctly, it will lie under the twisted length.
4. Now loop the second thread around the pin. This thread will lie on top of the twisted length.
5. Make a final TWIST with your pair and work it back into your design.

The picot should hold its shape after the pin is removed and should not slide back into the work.

Picots with large loops can be used to form a fringe edge. The triple picot, which is simply three picots in a row, each separated by a *whole stitch*, is another common design element. Both these picot variations are explored as edge techniques in Chapter 7.

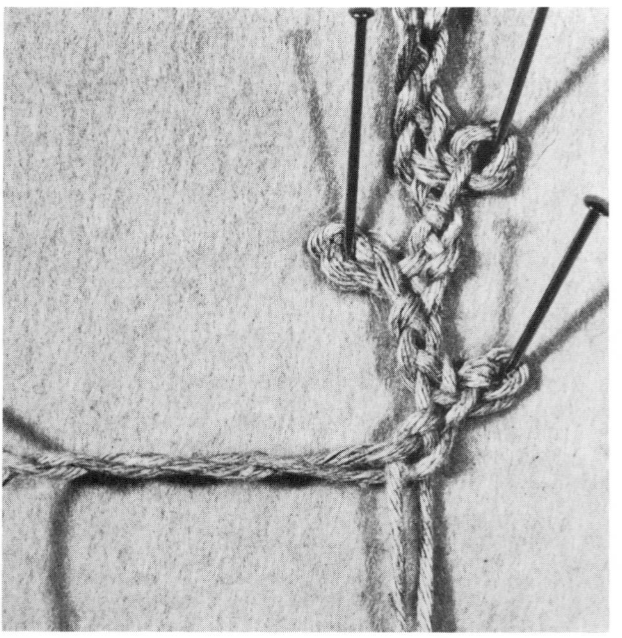

One pair is extended and given four TWISTS *(step 1).*

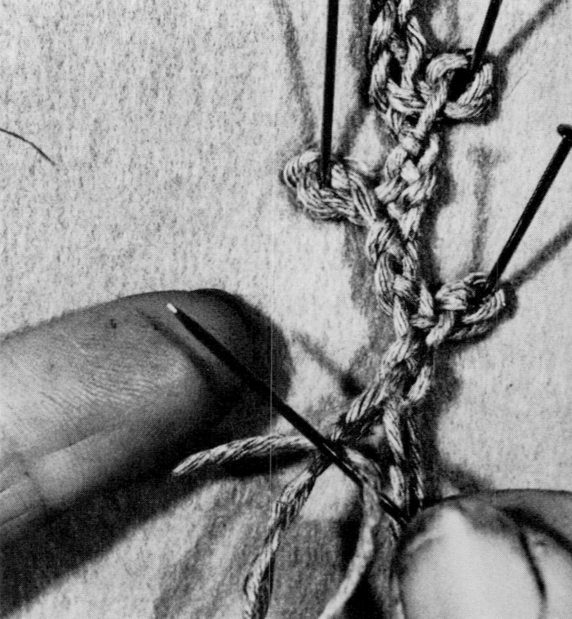

A pin is placed under the outer thread and rotated causing the thread to loop around the pin (step 2).

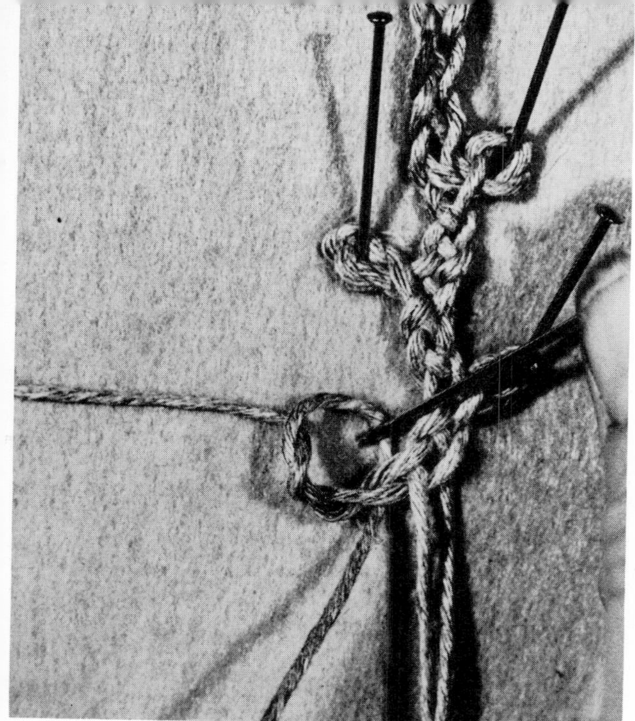

The pin is inserted adjacent to the edge of the worked piece (step 2). The loop thread is pulled down (step 3).

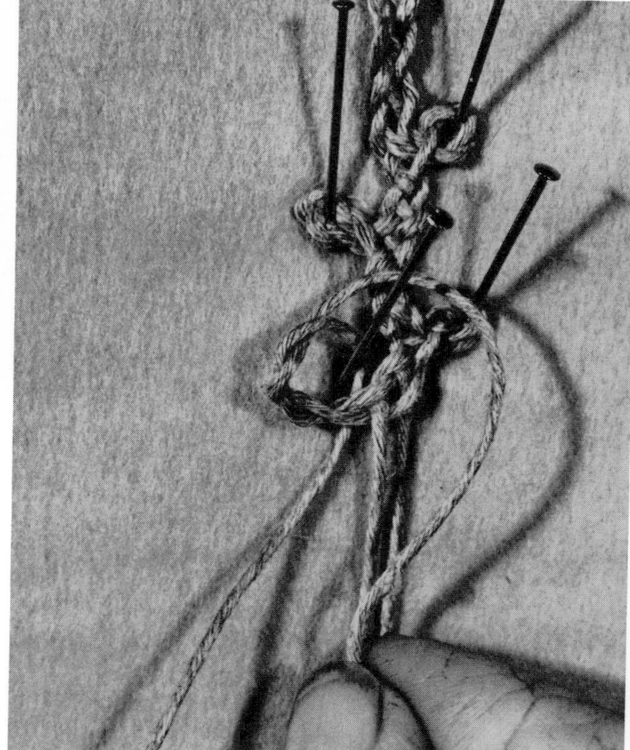

The companion thread is now looped around the pin. It lies over the twisted length (step 4).

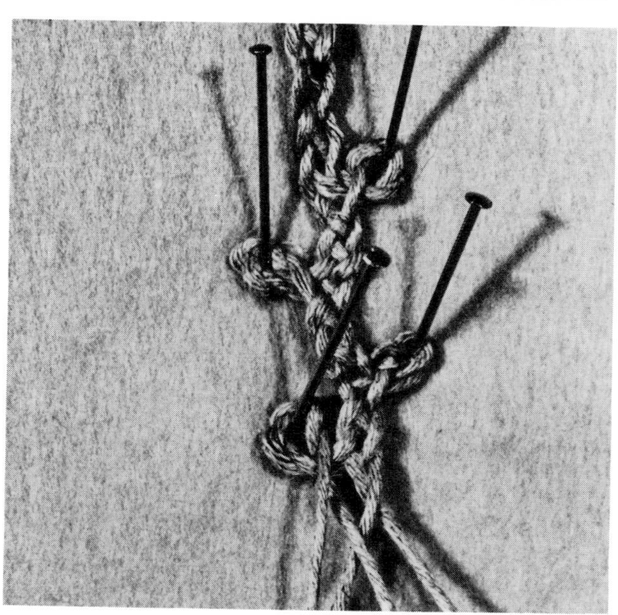

The picot pair is given a final TWIST *and worked back into the work (step 5).*

FILLINGS

A "filling" is a way of controlling a small dense area in a design. Many names have been given to fillings based primarily on their shape. Leaves, fans, and spots are common terms with further refinements in shapes bearing such precise names as the Cluny leaf (a long slender leaf), the Maltese leaf (a broad leaf), and the Torchon leaf (a triangular leaf). Four Maltese leaves radiating from a center point is a common lace motif and is referred to as a Maltese cross.

Most fillings are made with two bobbin pairs by forming a series of *leaf stitches*. If more bobbins are used, the additional threads are generally incorporated with the center thread of the three hanging or nonweaving threads.

In working a filling, shape is controlled by thread tension. The pulling of the weaver as well as the direction in which the outside hanging threads are pulled determines the shape. In working the *leaf stitches* (TWIST—CROSS—TWIST), hold the center hanging thread firmly in the direction in which you are working. Pull together or spread apart the two outside hanging threads after each row to control the shape. When beginning, keep the weaver in loose tension and pull up after every row, checking your shape.

At the completion of a filling you can continue working with your two bobbin pairs forming TWISTS or a *braid*. If the filling is to be at a termination, which is common with leaf shapes, the four threads can be terminated with an overhand knot with one thread wrapping around the others or all threads can simply be wrapped with another thread.

SQUARE: Keep your hanging threads parallel, i.e., evenly spaced as you work the weaver. Make a series of *leaf stitches* until the required length of the filling is made.

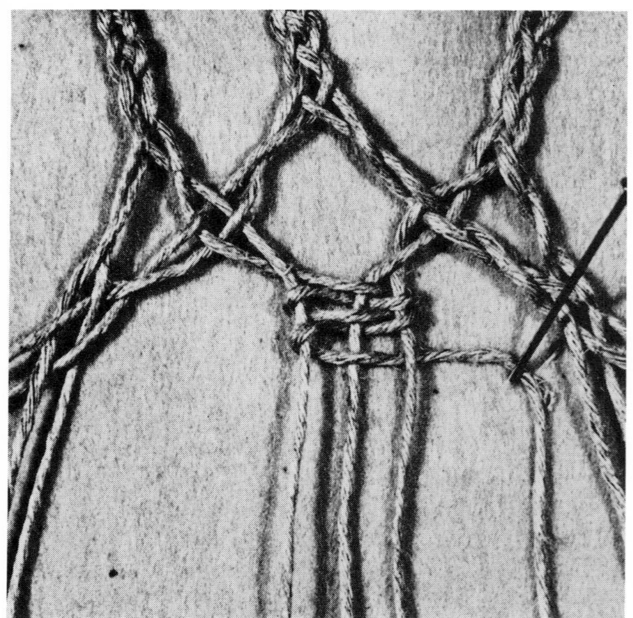

Making a series of leaf stitches with all hanging cords parallel forms a "square" filling.

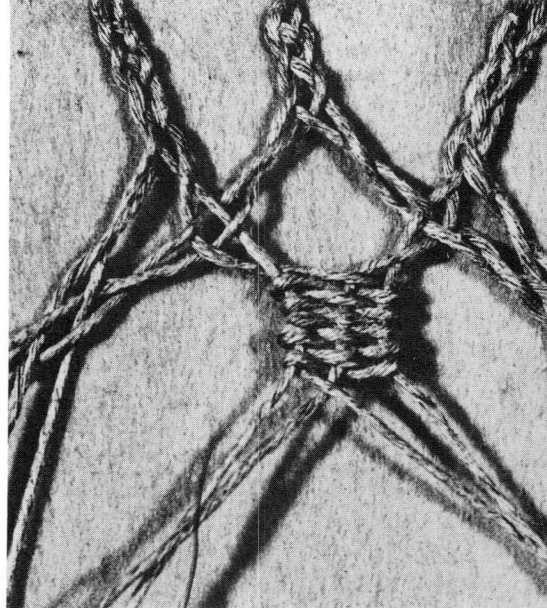

At completion of filling, combine the four threads into two pairs and make TWISTS.

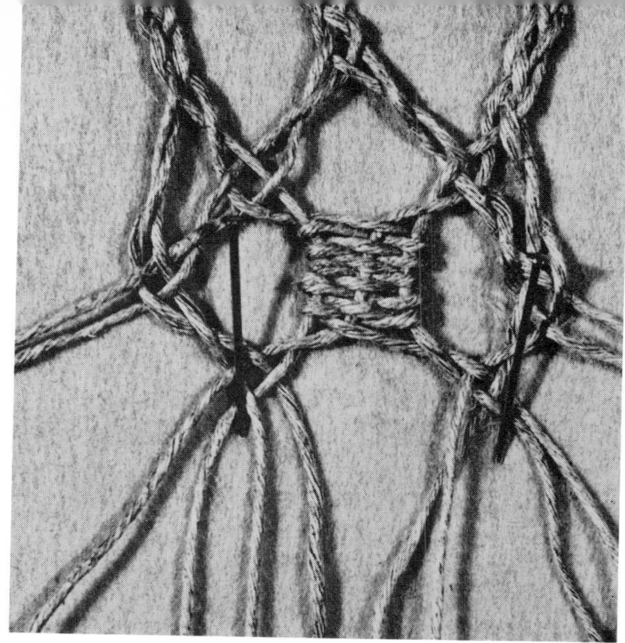

The completed square filling.

OVAL: Make a *linen stitch* with the two pairs and pull tight. Follow with a series of *leaf stitches*, narrowing and opening the outer hanging threads to form the desired shape. Narrow and complete with another *linen stitch.*

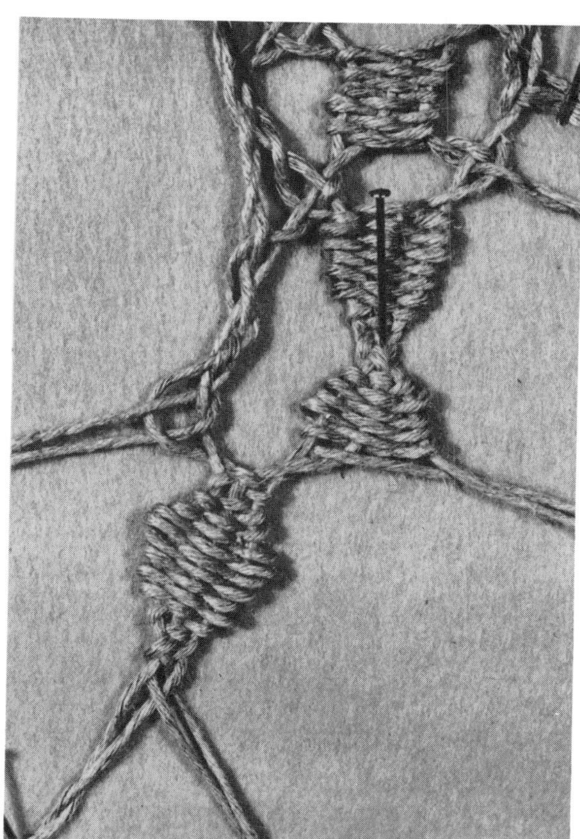

An oval or leaf shape begins and ends with a linen stitch.

TRIANGLE: Begin with a *linen stitch*. Follow with a series of *leaf stitches*, uniformly opening the outer hanging threads.

HOURGLASS: Begin with the hanging threads spaced apart. Make a series of *leaf stitches* while pulling the outer hanging threads uniformly together. When the outer threads come together make a *linen stitch* at the center of your shape. Continue with *leaf stitches*, uniformly spreading apart the outer hanging threads.

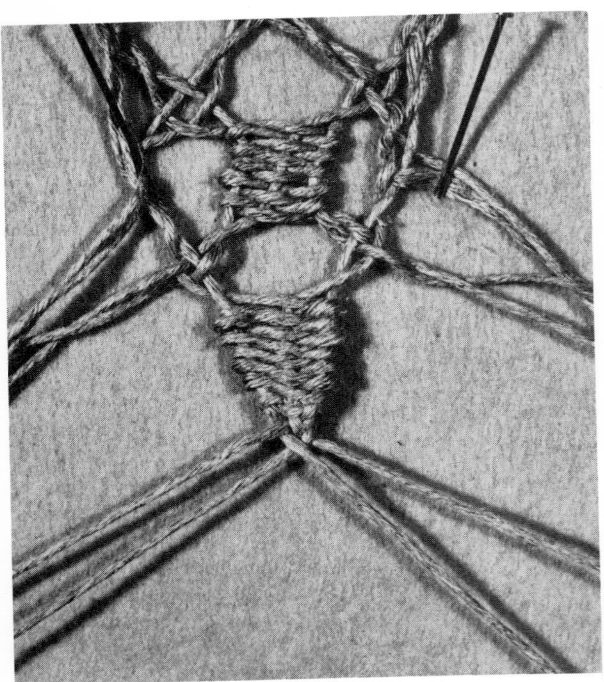

An hourglass shape is formed by bringing the hanging pairs together as you work your leaf stitches. At the center of the shape a linen stitch is made.

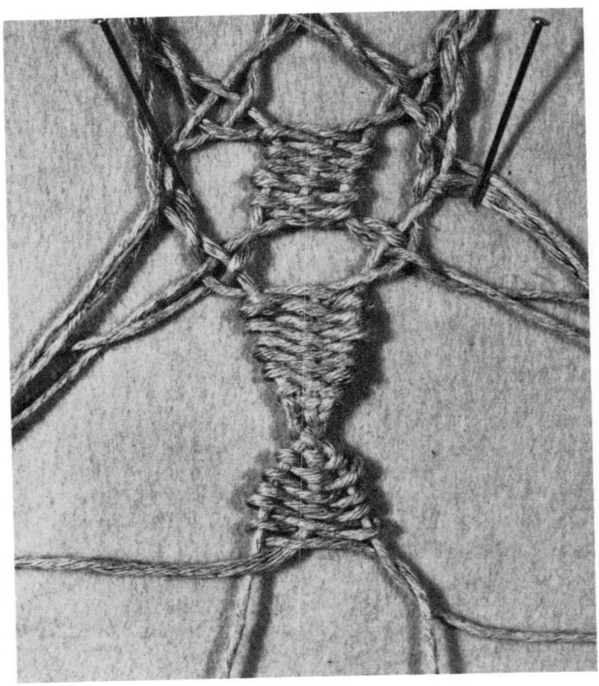

Complete the shape by working the hanging threads apart.

BASKET: The basket filling can be used where large shaped dense areas are desired. This filling also permits the adding of additional bobbin pairs to the work. As in other fillings, one weaver thread weaves back and forth.

Start with two bobbin pairs from your work. PIN one or more additional pairs on each side of these. An overhand knot at the pin location can be used as an accent. The stitch used is an extended form of the *leaf stitch* so all TWISTS are made with single bobbin pairs.

1. TWIST the center two pairs three to six times or until the TWIST reaches the level of the hanging pairs, which were added.

2. Take the center two pairs and CROSS. Working to the left, TWIST the left pair only, then CROSS this pair with the adjacent pair to the left. Again TWIST the left pair only. Continue in this manner until you reach the outside thread, ending in a TWIST position.

3. With the outside pair make another TWIST, then return weaver to the other side with the same weaving motions that you did in the first row. Pick up all hanging threads.

4. Continue weaving in this manner while shaping your filling. Pinning at the outside edge is helpful in forming the shape.

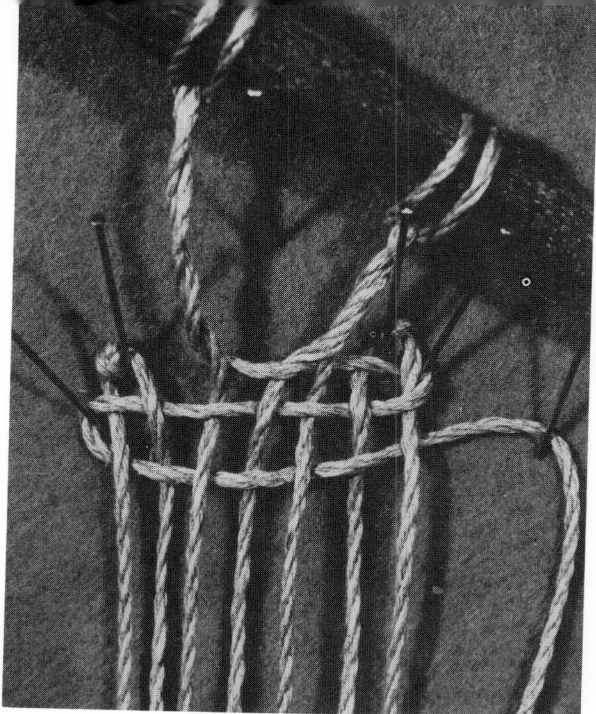

Beginning a basket filling with two added pairs.

A completed basket filling.

JOINING OF THREADS AND SPLICING

When a single thread or cord runs short it is often most expedient to join a new thread to the short end. Two methods to consider are splicing and knotting.

SPLICING: For the sake of practicality, only adhesive methods are considered. Splicing the softer and finer cords is simply done by overlapping the two ends and rolling them between your fingers with a small dab of fabric adhesive.

With larger and firmer cords, where overlapping produces too much bulk, cut half the plies of each end approximately ½ inch back. Coat the exposed ½ inch of each cord with a light coat of fabric adhesive and overlap the two pieces so they join forming an invisible splice. Put a dab of adhesive on your finger and roll the splice between your fingers. You can continue your work immediately.

Splicing a soft thread (wool) by overlapping the two ends and applying a small dab of fabric adhesive.

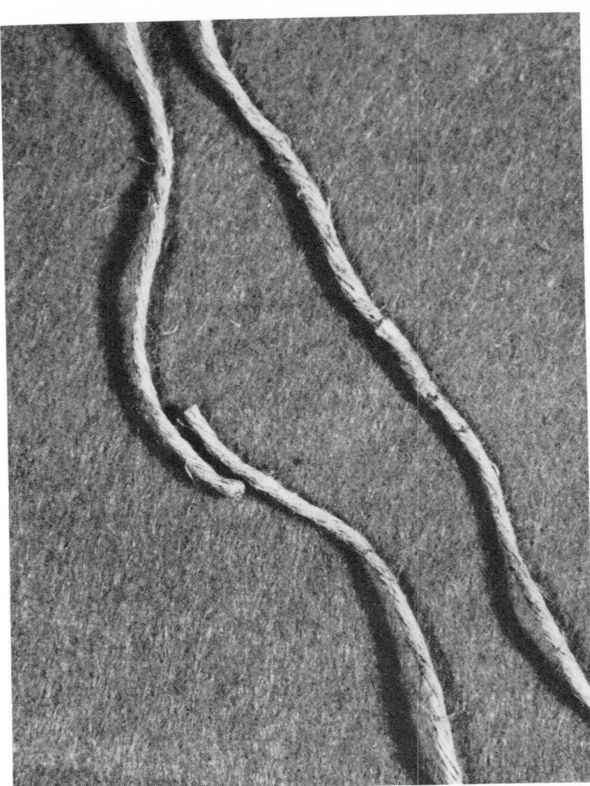

Splicing a thin thread by overlapping with a small dab of fabric adhesive.

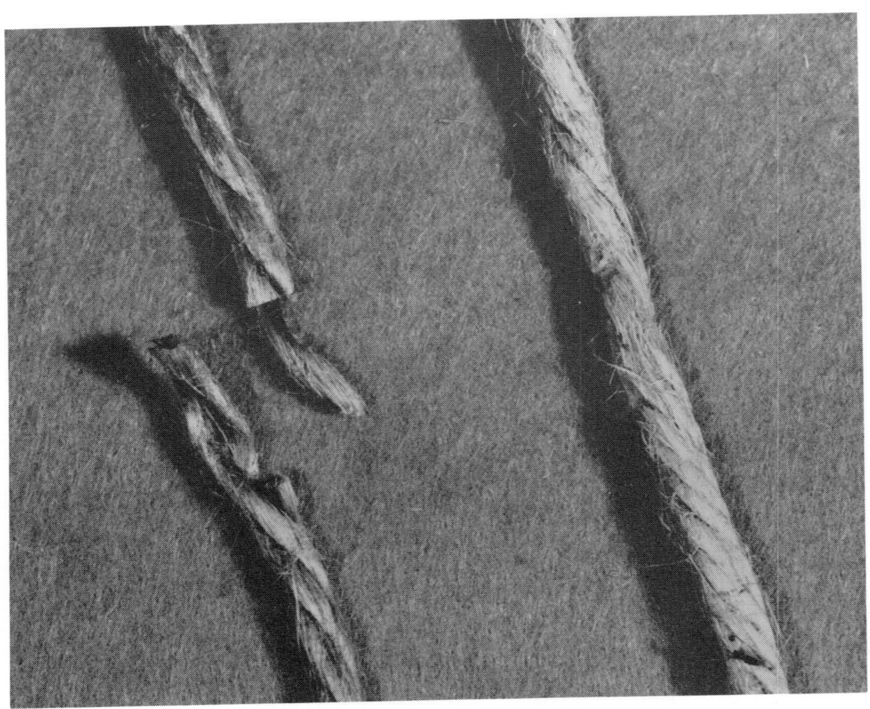

Splicing a heavy thread. Cut back half the plies of each end, coat with adhesive, and join.

WEAVER'S KNOT: Before the availability of the flexible fabric cements, threads were joined with a weaver's knot. With fine lace threads, this knot is virtually invisible. If you intend to dye your work, a knot is preferable to an adhesive splice as the adhesive will resist the dye.

The simplest method of making this knot is to make a slipknot in the end of one of your threads. Slip the end of the other cord through the loop formed and pull the slipknot tight, giving it a final tug. The two cords should intertwine forming a tight knot. Cut off the free ends close to the knot.

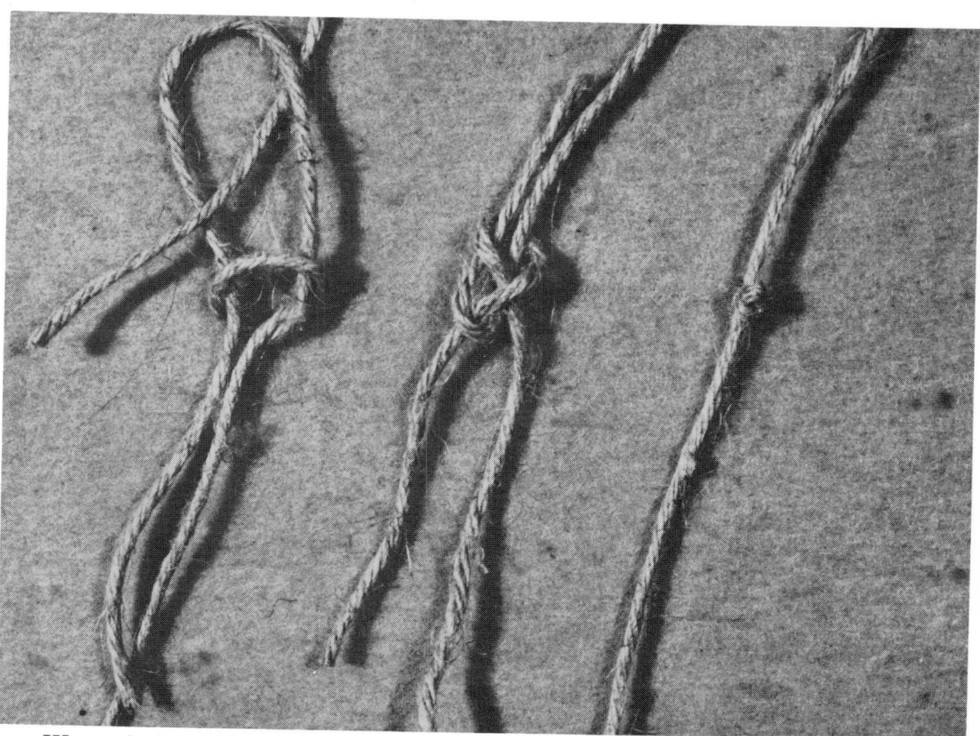

Weaver's knot. From the left: (1) Slip the end of one thread through the loop formed by a slipknot in the end of the other thread; (2) Pull the slipknot ends taut, interlocking the other thread; (3) Pulled tight you can cut the free ends close to the knot.

ADDING AND DELETING THREADS

Adding threads in bobbin lace is a relatively simple procedure because of the inherent integrity of the completed piece. Threads simply hung on a pin and worked as part of the piece soon become an integral part of the work. When the hanging pin is later removed, the new threads cannot be discerned from the old. In the same manner threads can be deleted. When not wanted any more, they are simply abandoned and after the work has progressed several rows, the loose ends can be cut close to the work. As all stitches are worked with pairs, threads are always added or deleted in pairs. In most cases, adding or deleting threads will change the density of a piece. With this in mind, select a location where the change in thread will work into the design.

Some general methods of adding threads are:

1. Hang a pair of bobbins on a pin and work them into your stitches. Added to the edge of a *weaving ground*, the new pair can be used as the weaver or as a hanging pair. After working a few rows, remove the pin and pull on the threads to eliminate the loop.

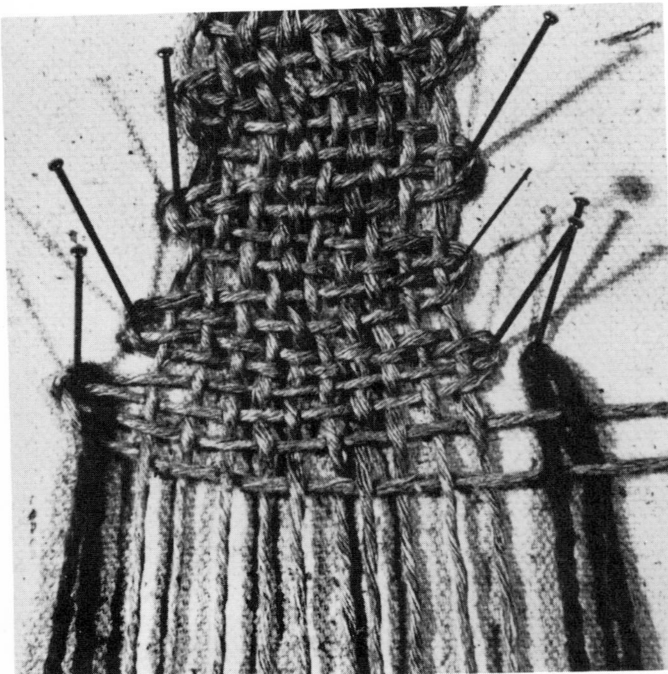

Pairs are pinned at the edge of a ground as a method for adding threads to the work.

2. Hang bobbins on another thread or threads. A new pair can simply be laid over the supporting thread, half hitched to it or, if two pairs are added, they can be secured with a *whole stitch*. When adding threads in this manner, it is a good practice to PIN in addition to hanging to keep the supporting thread from being pulled out of place.

Upper pin: a new pair added by making a linen stitch with an existing edge pair. Lower pin: a new pair added by laying it over an existing edge pair.

A new pair half-hitched to an existing pair.

3. Join a new pair to an existing pair with a *whole stitch*. An initial TWIST can be given the new pair prior to the stitch depending on the detail desired.

4. Two pairs can be added by making one or two *whole stitches* with these two pairs before entering them into the work. Placed in the center of a *whole-stitch ground* or similar mesh, the two pairs can be worked in opposite directions.

Two pairs added. These are joined by a whole stitch before becoming part of the work.

5. Fillings: A filling can be formed with two pairs. Pinned to your work, the hanging threads can then be used as two new pairs.

Two pairs added by making a filling before joining to the work.

Invisible adding of threads: These specific methods are more interesting as it is virtually impossible to detect these new threads.

Two pairs added to a braid.

The two new pairs combined with the original braid pairs to form two braids.

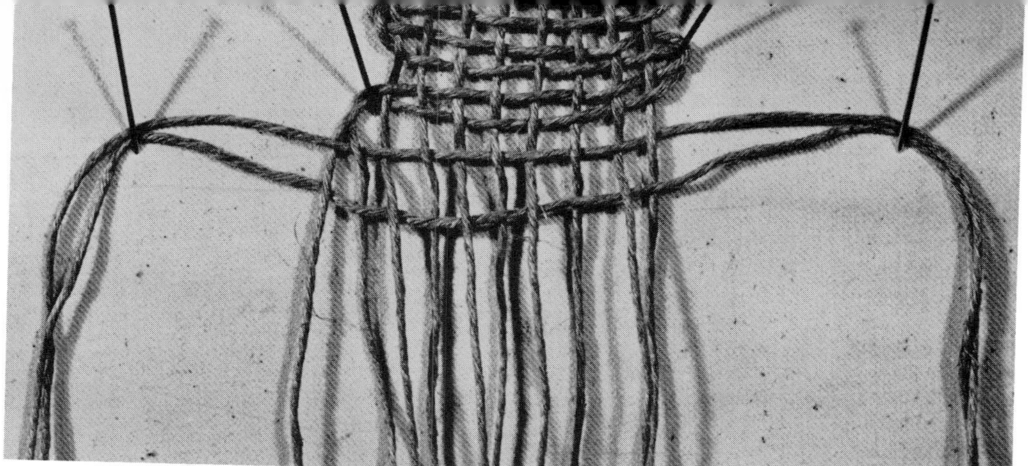

Adding two horizontal pairs.

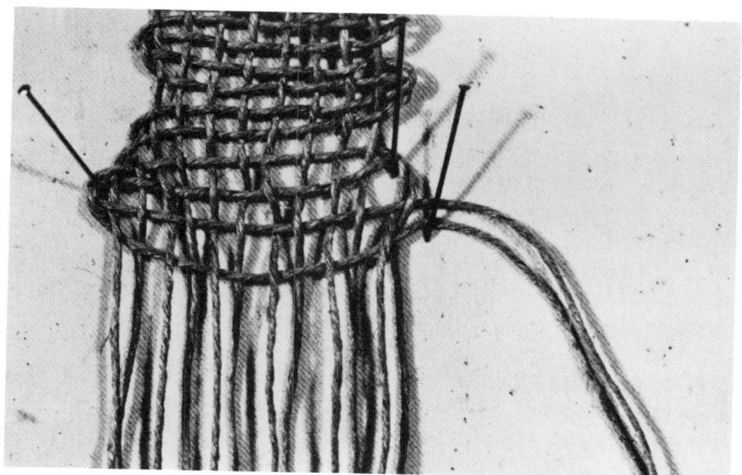

The two added pairs worked as part of the ground.

1. Adding a horizontal pair: Two new pairs are added by this method to a *weaving ground*. Hang two pairs to the left side of your work over a pin. Using a pair formed from the right bobbin of each of the two hanging pairs, work *linen stitches* with all hanging threads. Let this pair now hang on the right side as a hanging pair. Now use remaining two bobbins as a new weaver pair, continuing the work.

2. Adding edge pairs: This method ordinarily adds two pairs. If a piece is started by this method, four pairs will enter the work.

Invisible method of adding two pairs into the work. A linen stitch is made with one of the pairs (one thread from each of two added bobbin pairs) and an extending pair from the work.

The new pair worked into the piece.

Working two pairs into the work: Take one bobbin from each of your two new pairs and an extending pair from your work. Give each pair one or more TWISTS and then make a *linen stitch* and PIN. Work the new pair into the work. In the following row work the other pair from the *linen stitch* (original extending pair) into the work. Now take your other two new bobbins and using these as a pair, give them one or two TWISTS and combine with another extending pair from your ground.

Starting a piece: This method makes a very neat beginning for a shaped piece. Working with four bobbin pairs, take one bobbin from each of two pairs and give them one or more TWISTS. Do the same with two bobbins from the other two pairs. With these two twisted pairs make a *linen stitch* and PIN in place. These twisted pairs enter the piece as hanging threads. Combine each of the other two pairs with new pairs as described in the paragraph above.

It should be noted that the working face of your work is the back of your piece. Thus, all knots and other irregularities as well as cut ends, which are worked on this face, will not be obvious when the work is reversed.

SEWINGS

A "sewing" is a technique for joining two parts or pieces of lace and making them into one. The sewing is made as a piece is being worked and differs from a simple attachment with a needle and thread or for that matter with a separate pair of bobbins as used to join completed pieces.

To make the standard sewing, a bobbin pair from the piece being made is worked to the outside edge at a point where the joining is to be made. In the *weaving ground* this would be the weaver pair.

1. Give the extending pair one or two TWISTS.
2. Take one thread of this pair, form a loop, and draw it through the nearest opening in the edge of the part to be joined, forming a large loop. A crochet hook is a useful tool for this operation.
3. The bobbin of the companion thread of your sewing pair is now passed through this loop.
4. Pull both bobbins taut to secure the stitch.
5. TWIST the sewing pair and return to your working ground.

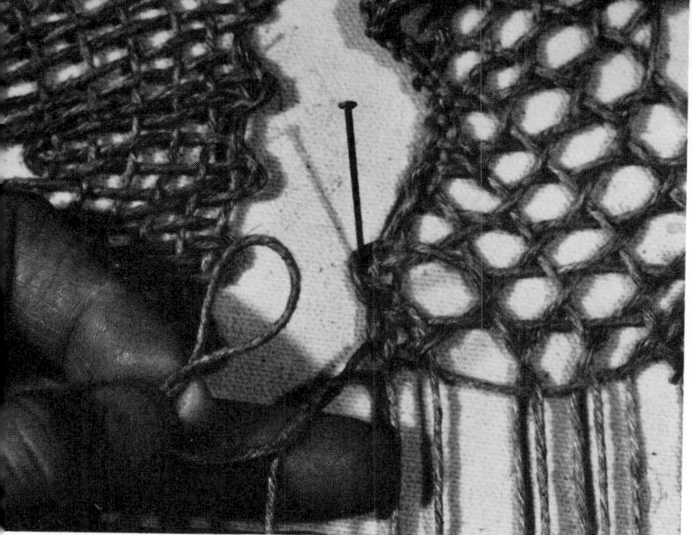

A loop formed with one thread of the sewing pair.

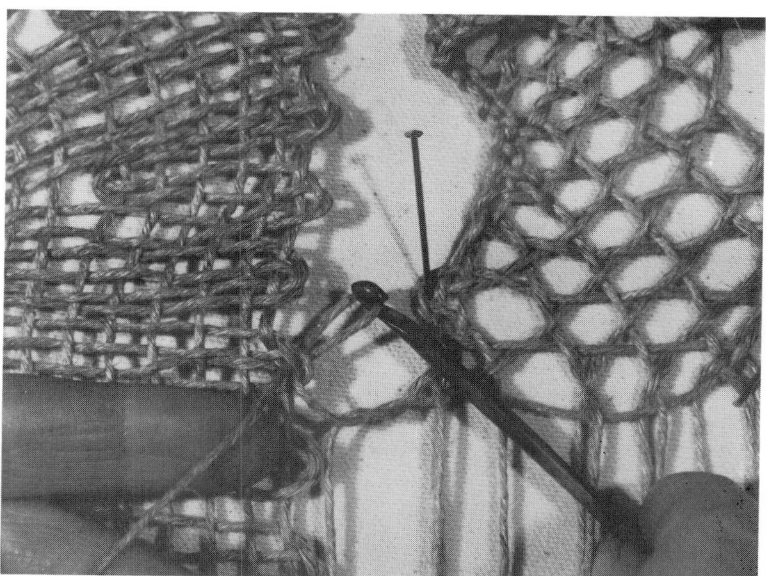

The loop is pulled through an opening at the edge of the part to be sewn.

The bobbin of the companion thread is passed through the loop.

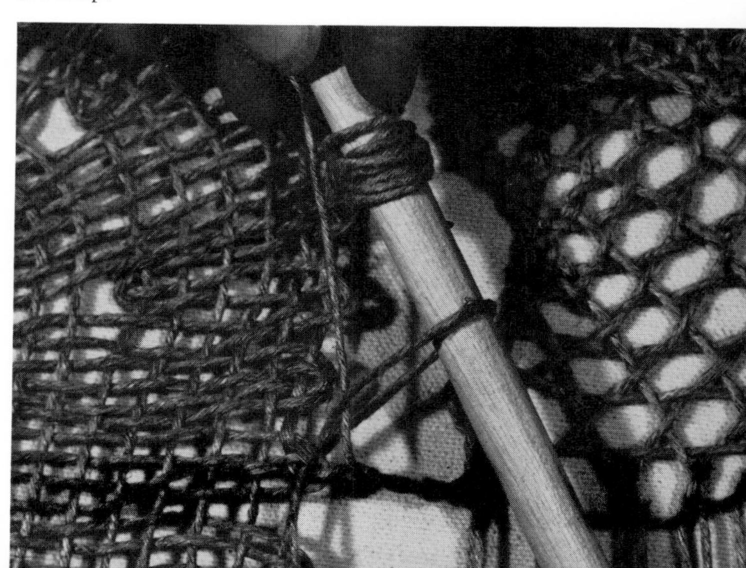

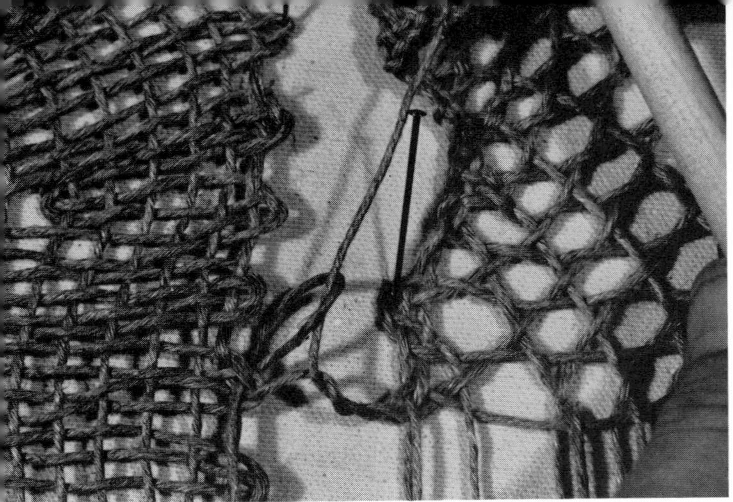

The pulling of both threads of the sewing pair will secure the stitch.

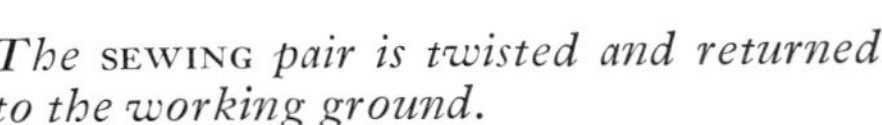

The SEWING *pair is twisted and returned to the working ground.*

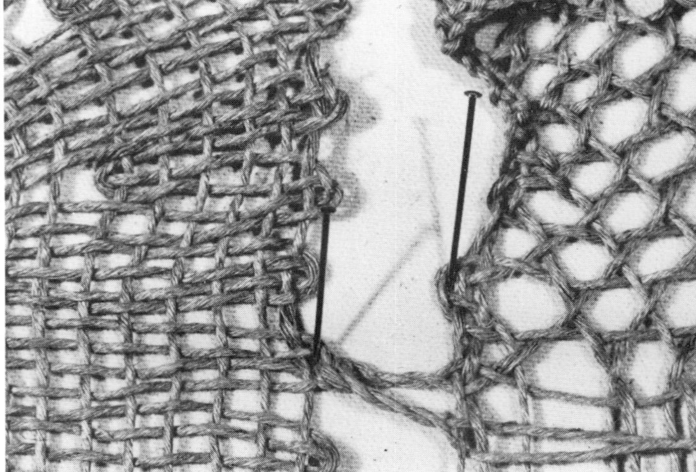

A traditional lace pattern (Idria bobbin lace style) where a continuous weaving ground tape is worked and, by sewings, is joined to itself.

To form open webs or other openwork an alternate sewing method is desirable as it will secure the sewing pair at any location.

1. Give the sewing pair enough TWISTS to bring it to the sewing point.
2. Loop one of the sewing threads under the threads to be sewn and the companion sewing thread.
3. Pass the bobbin of the thread that formed the loop through the loop.
4. Pull the loop-forming bobbin only, to secure the stitch.

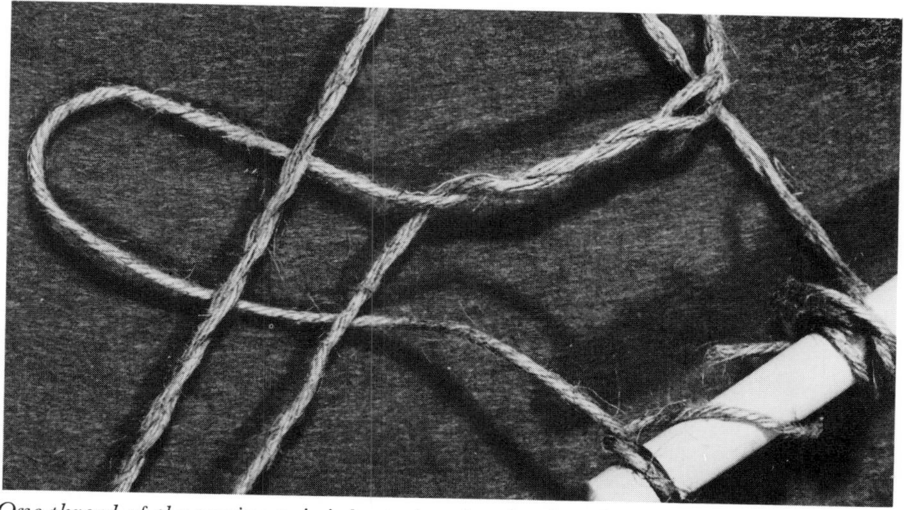

One thread of the sewing pair is looped under the threads to be sewn and the companion thread.

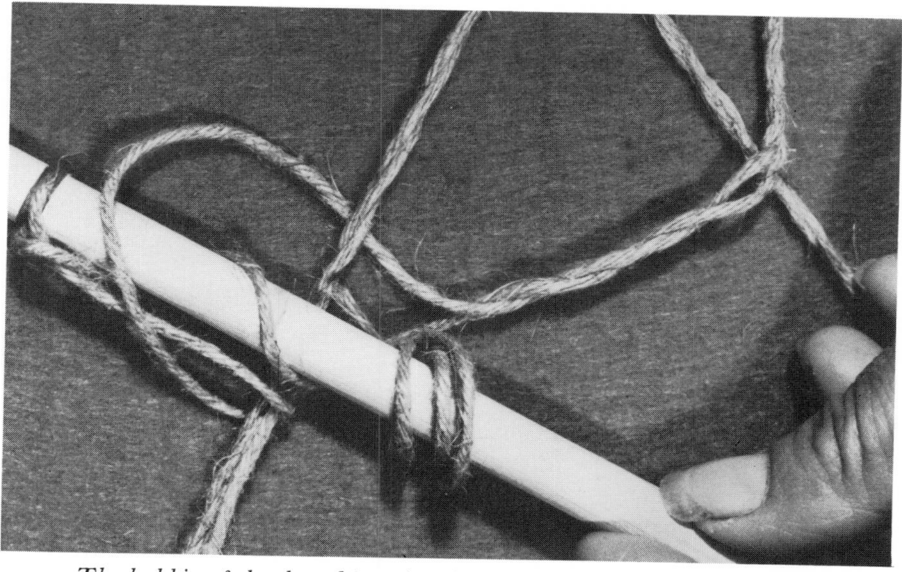

The bobbin of the thread forming the loop is passed through the loop.

Pulling the active bobbin secures the sewing stitch.

RAISED WORK

Raised work traditionally refers to a technique for making raised edges or designs in a style of bobbin lace known as Honiton lace. These raised edges would commonly be worked along the edges of leaves, flowers, and so on.

In addition to being merely a raised edge, the techniques permitted the carrying of relatively large numbers of threads across a piece of lace.

In contemporary lace, raised work, in addition to giving the work an additional dimension or strong line, can be used to form a strong edge on a belt or coat, or a sturdy handle on a bag.

TIED BUNDLE: This is the quickest technique for grouping a large number of threads. Care should be taken, however, for a uniform appearance.

One pair from your group of threads will be used for the binding. Tie this pair around all other threads, then pass them over and under the bundle in opposite directions so they cross on opposite sides. All crossings should be aligned and evenly spaced. The threads of the bundle can be straight or the entire group can be twisted before it is bound.

Tied bundle; all threads are bound by a single pair.

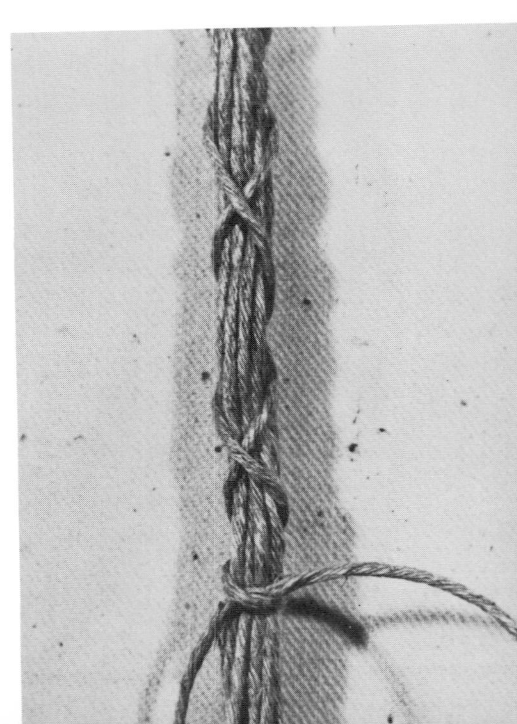

BRAID: In reference to raised work, a "braid" is a dense bundle of many threads. Three-strand and four-strand braids are the most common.

Three-strand braid: Divide all threads into three equal groups. Take the right group and lay it over the center group. Follow by taking the left group and laying it over the new center group. Repeating this sequence will extend the braid.

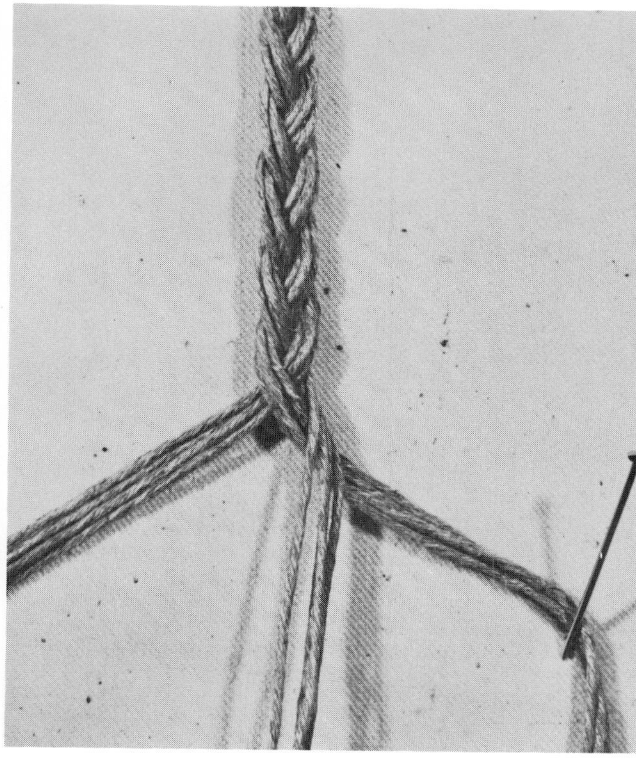

All threads are separated into three groups to form a three-strand braid.

Four-strand braid: Divide all the threads into four equal groups. Treating these four groups as two bobbin pairs makes a series of *whole stitches* forming a heavy braid.

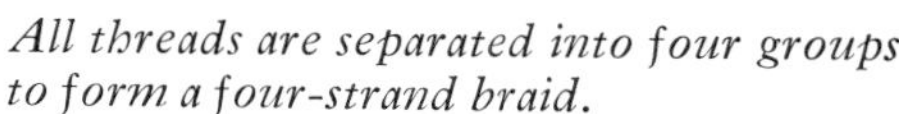

All threads are separated into four groups to form a four-strand braid.

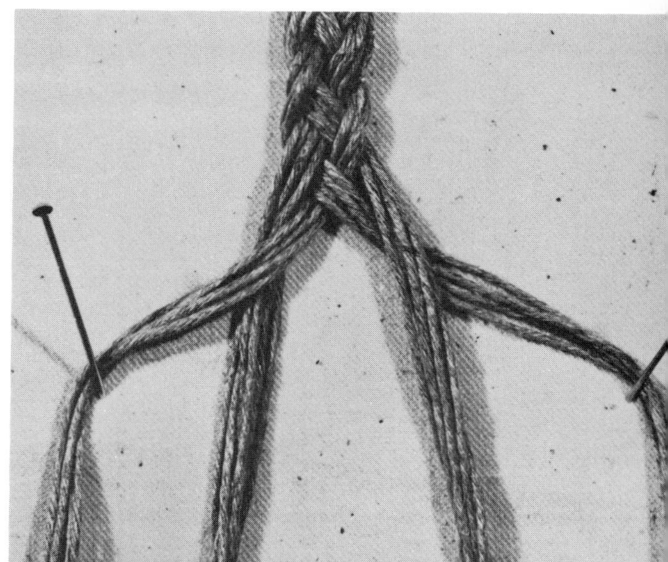

CABLE: A heavy twisted cord is easily formed with a large bundle of threads.

Divide all the threads into two equal groups. TWIST each group separately counterclockwise giving them a hard twist. Follow by twisting the two groups together in a clockwise direction forming the cable. This second twist motion should form naturally as a result of the first twist motions.

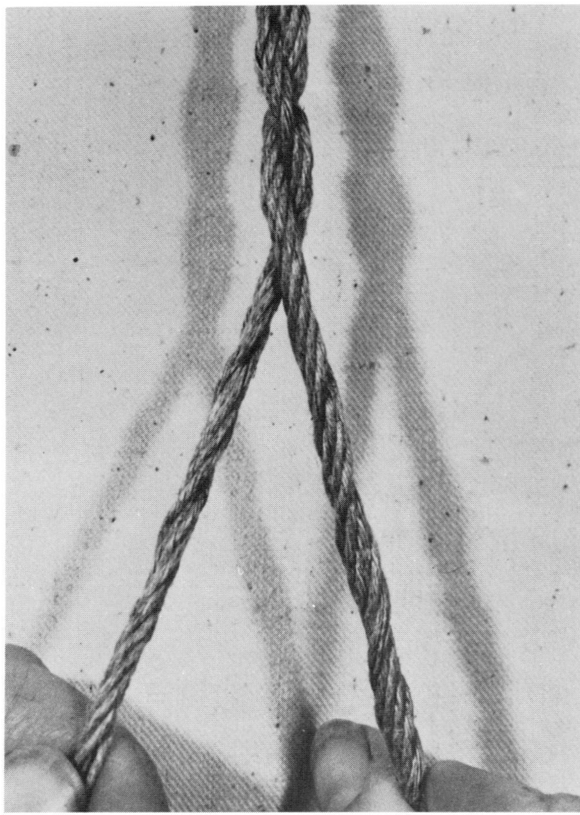

All threads are divided into two bundles to form a twisted cord cable.

STITCHED CABLE: This cable is somewhat more difficult to make but it is very handsome and quite strong. Hang all pairs from a pin. Use the left pair as the weaver pair.

Lay all pairs other than the weaver pair out evenly, keeping each pair separated by a pin. Work the weaver pair across all the hanging pairs with *linen stitches.* Give the weaver pair a TWIST and PIN to the left of your work, laying it over all hanging pairs. Again weave over all hanging pairs from left to right. Remove from left edge pin and pull each thread of the weaver separately, pulling the work into a tight tube.

This cable is worked best with five or six pairs. If more threads are to be incorporated into your cord, they can be treated as a core around which the other threads are woven.

Lay your core or bundle of threads in the center of the hanging threads that will be woven. Proceed as you did for the plain stitched cable with the weaver going under and over the core.

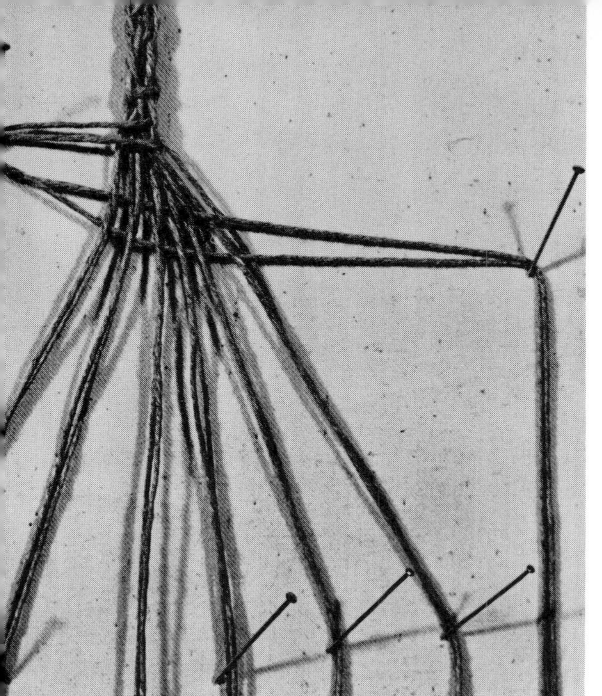

The weaver pair is laid over all hanging pairs going from right to left and then woven through all pairs when going from left to right. Note how all hanging pairs are separated by pins to keep them in order.

Pulling the weaver pair to form the stitched cable.

Working a pair into a stitched cable. The weaver goes over the new pair and works it as one of the cable pairs.

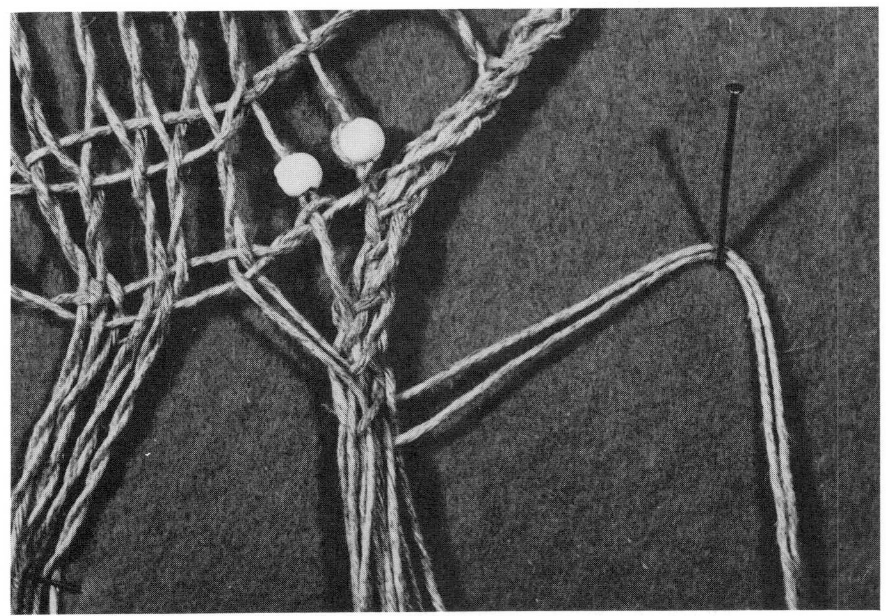

The weaver is pulled tight to complete the stitch.

Pairs are eliminated from the cable to balance for the added pairs. Eliminated pairs are left extended and finally cut off after several more stitches have been made. Note that piece is worked from the reverse side.

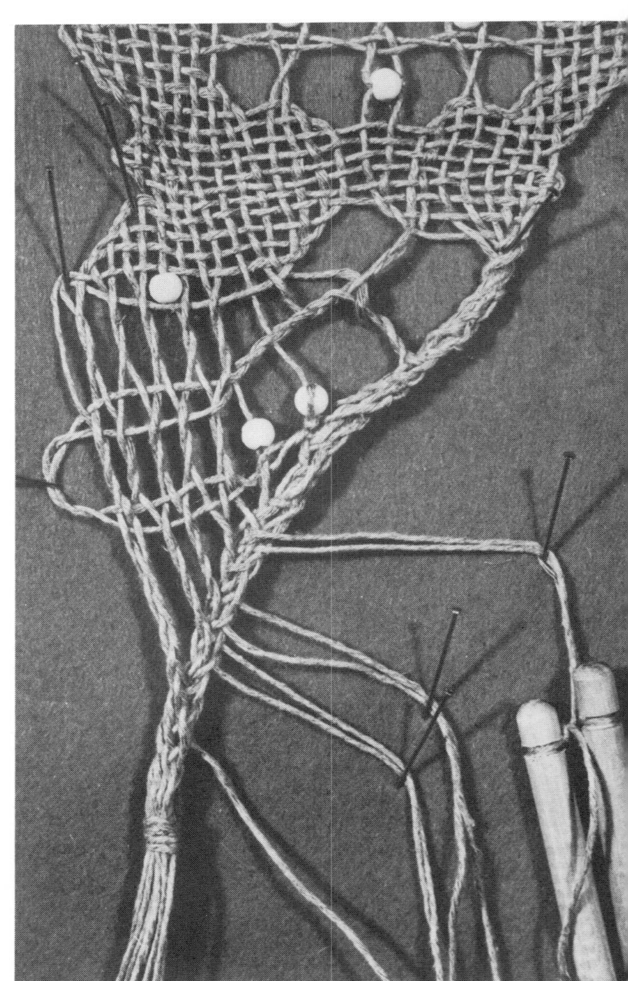

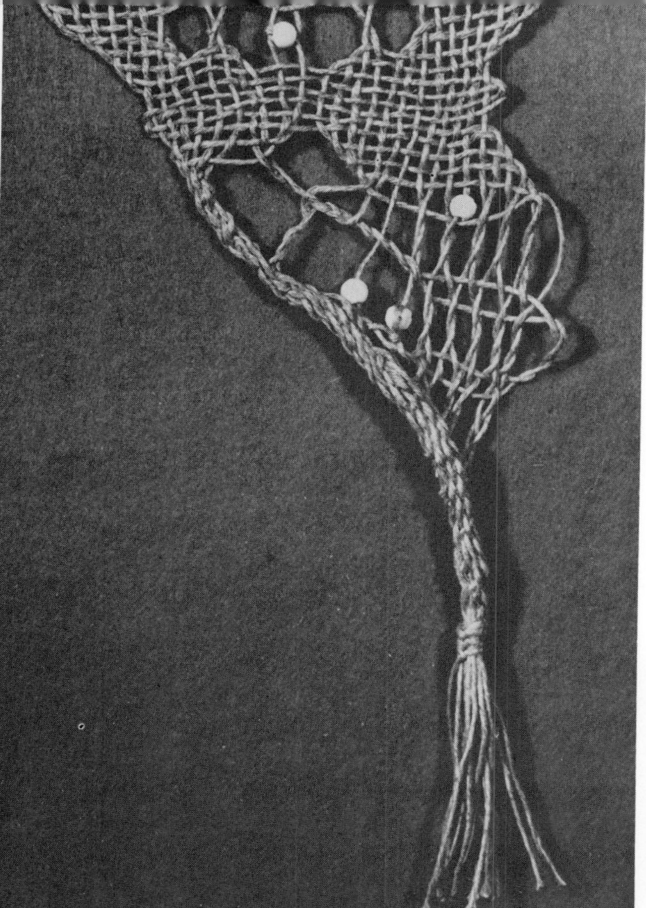

The completed piece from the right side.

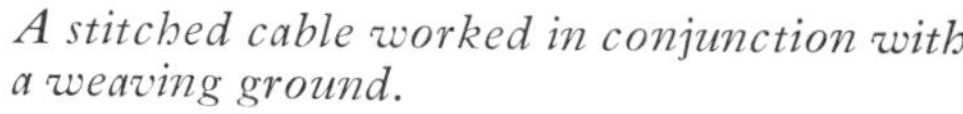

A stitched cable worked in conjunction with a weaving ground.

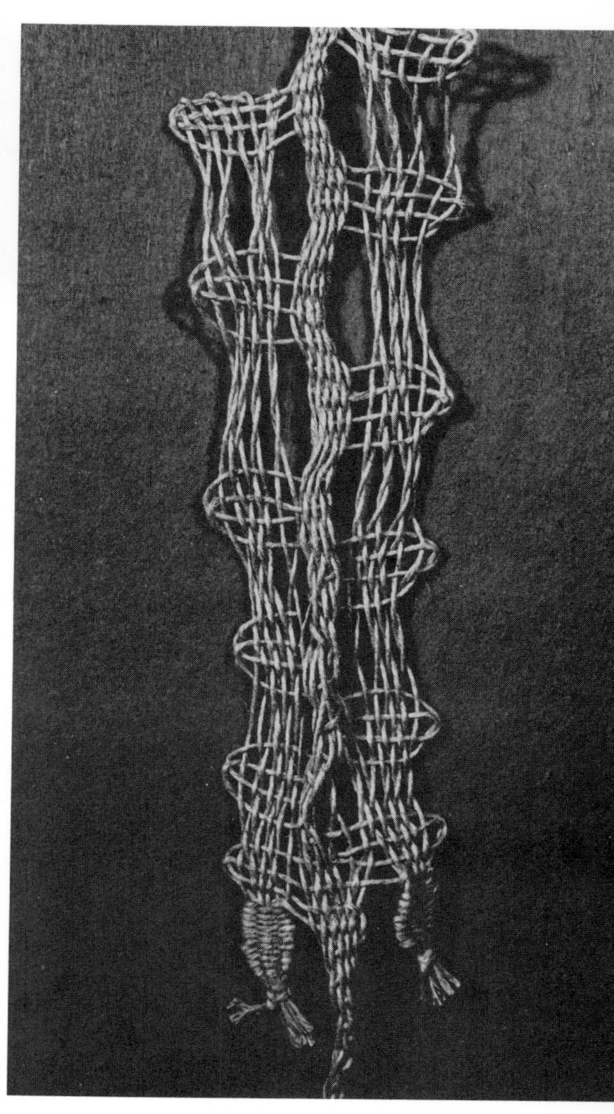

STEM STITCH, OR "TEN STICK": This is a dense narrow braid generally formed with five bobbin pairs, thus the name "Ten Stick." The ground was generally sewn to the outer edge of this band, which resulted in the band being raised and laying over the work. One side or edge of the braid usually has a plain or scalloped edge and the other side a tightly stitched edge. If worked to form a belt or strong band, both edges should be stitched.

Begin by hanging all five pairs on a pin. Take the left outside pair as the weaver and work *linen stitches* across all pairs. At the right edge a detail can be worked (see Chapter 7). Work the weaver pair back across all hanging pairs through the left edge. Now form your stitched edge:

Give the weaver pair and the edge pair a TWIST followed by a CROSS. Pin the outside pair out of the way and use the other pair from this stitch as the weaver. Note that one of the threads of the weaver pair has exchanged with a hanging thread.

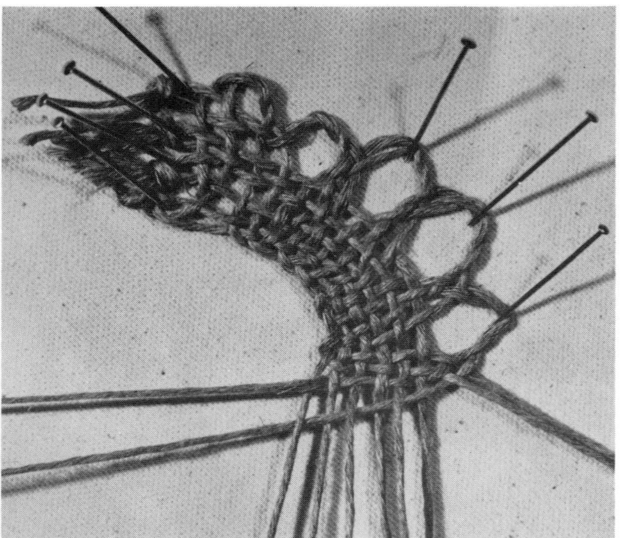

Stem stitch; the weaver pair is brought through the left edge.

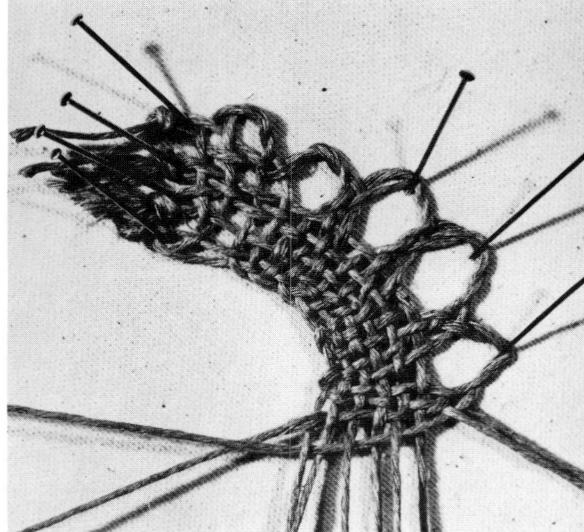

The weaver pair and the edge pair are TWISTED,

then CROSSED.

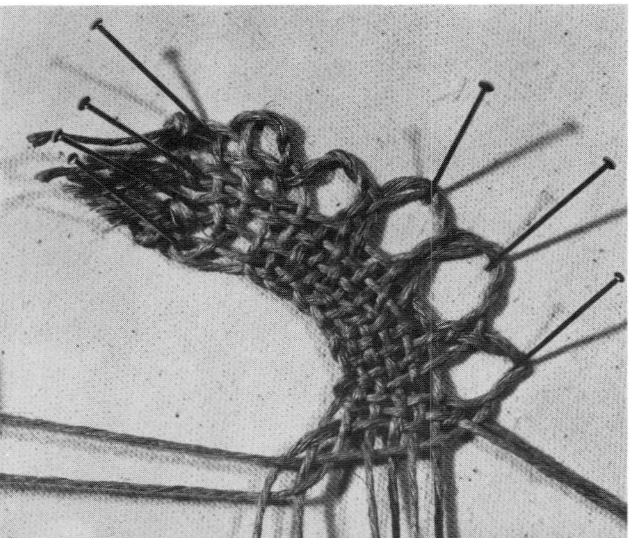

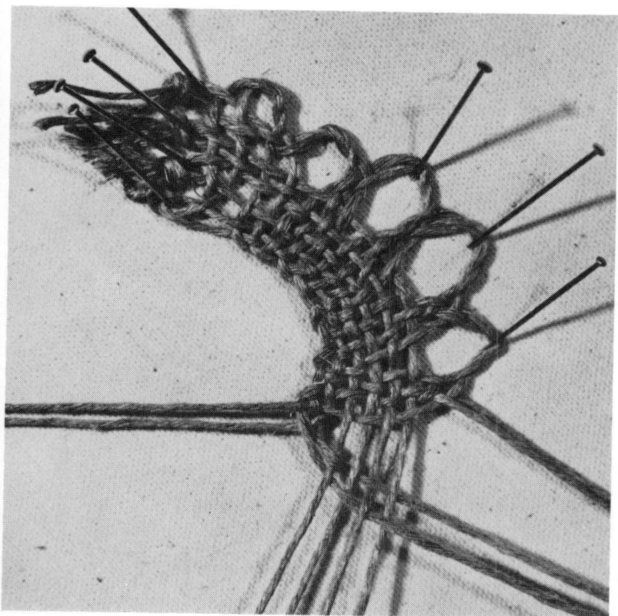

The right pair from this stitch is the new weaver, returning to the left edge.

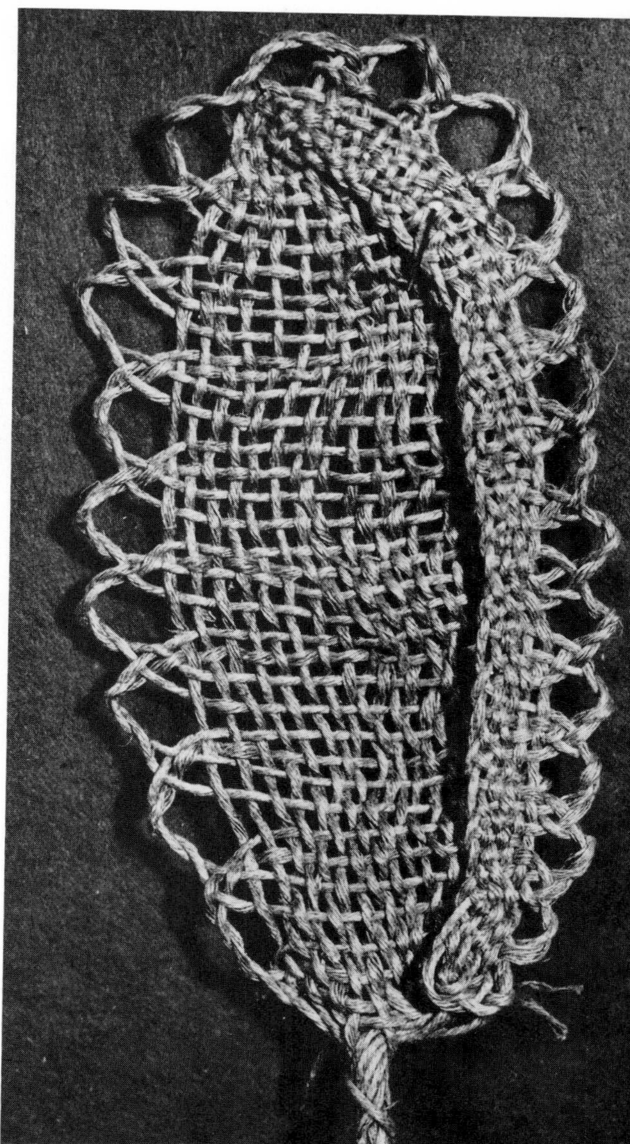

Stem stitch worked as a raised edge on a leaf design. The piece is worked from the reverse side with the weaving ground sewn to the outer edge of the stem stitch.

GIMP: Although not considered raised work in the traditional lace forms, a "gimp" is used to create a strong or distinct line in the work. A gimp is generally a heavier cord, although it can be a cord of a contrasting color or texture, which is laid into the work as you make your stitches. Typically, it is held in place by a TWIST on one or both sides of it by the crossing cords. In traditional lace, the gimp thread had a special bobbin that could easily be distinguished from the others.

A gimp can also be used as a bead-carrying cord to create special effects with beads. When used in this manner it is usually of the same material as the other cords.

Although a gimp thread can be worked as one thread of a pair, its companion thread being of the same material as the other threads, it is more commonly worked as a single thread, being woven in and out of its connecting threads.

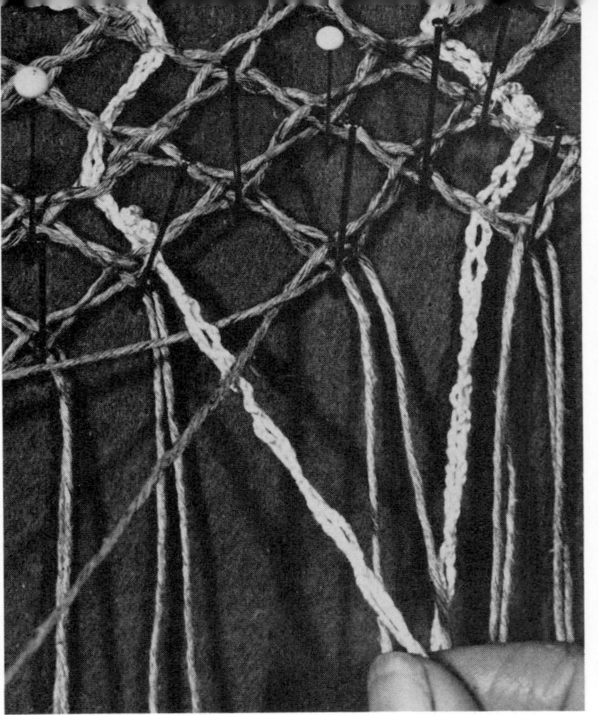

A gimp thread worked into a design by being laid between a working pair.

A stitch with the working pairs secures the gimp.

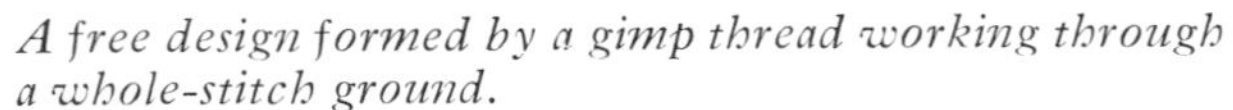

A free design formed by a gimp thread working through a whole-stitch ground.

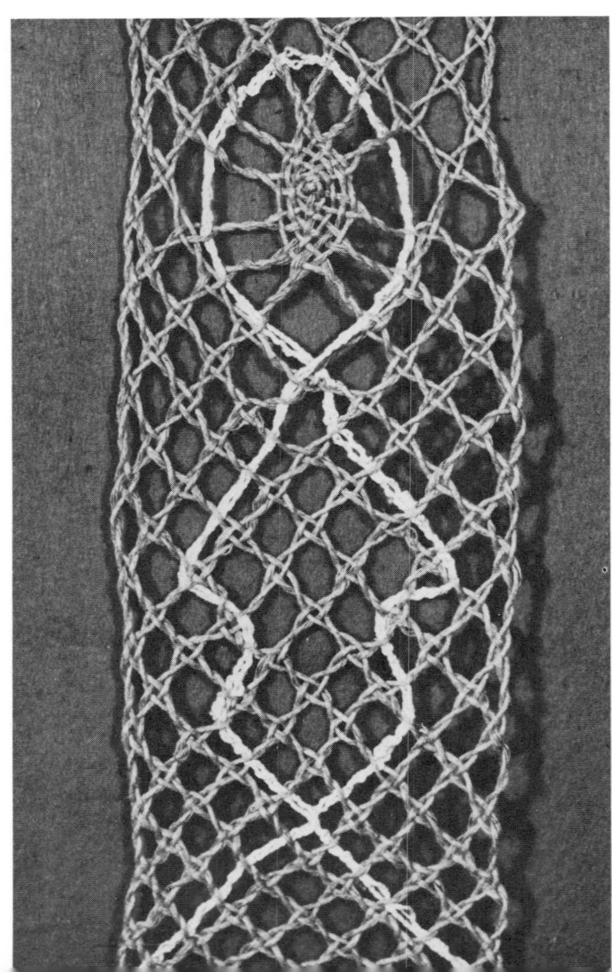

PLAITING

Plaiting can be considered as a *weaving ground* with all threads running diagonally. Worked without edge pins, plaiting will produce a dense strong band suitable for bag handles and belts as well as a design element. Worked with edge pins, the diagonal pattern can be left as an open mesh and treated purely as a design element.

If *linen stitches* are made across a row with each two adjacent bobbin pairs, with alternate rows being worked with the two adjacent pairs from the two stitches above, a plaiting will result.

The simplest method, however, for producing a plaiting is as follows:

Starting at the right edge:

1. With the right two pairs make a *linen stitch* followed by a TWIST with the right outer pair.
2. With the two adjacent pairs (third and fourth pairs from the right) make a *linen stitch.*
3. With the right pair from this stitch make *linen stitches* with all pairs to the right followed by a TWIST with this pair at the right edge.
4. Repeat steps 2 and 3 as many times as required until you have reached the left edge.
5. With the left edge pair make a TWIST and work across all pairs to the right followed by a TWIST with this pair at the right edge.
6. Repeat step 5 extending the plaiting.

As you work your plaiting pull the stitches into place, maintaining straight and symmetrical diagonal lines.

A linen stitch worked with the two right pairs followed by a TWIST *with the outer pair.*

A linen stitch made with the next two adjacent pairs. The right pair from this stitch makes linen stitches with all pairs to the right and ends in a TWIST.

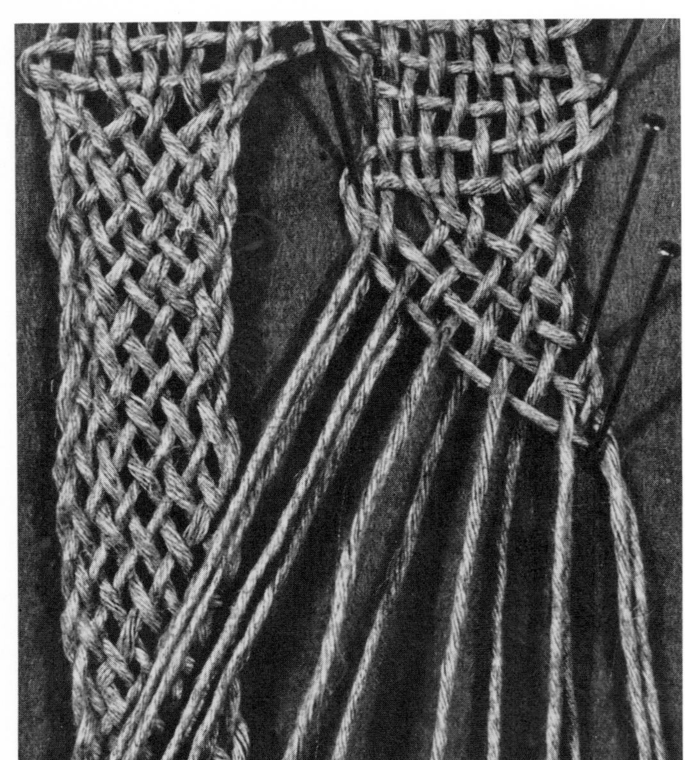

In a repeated sequence the left edge pair is given a TWIST, *then worked across all pairs to the right and finally given another* TWIST *at the right edge.*

Plaiting used as a design element.

An extended plaiting.

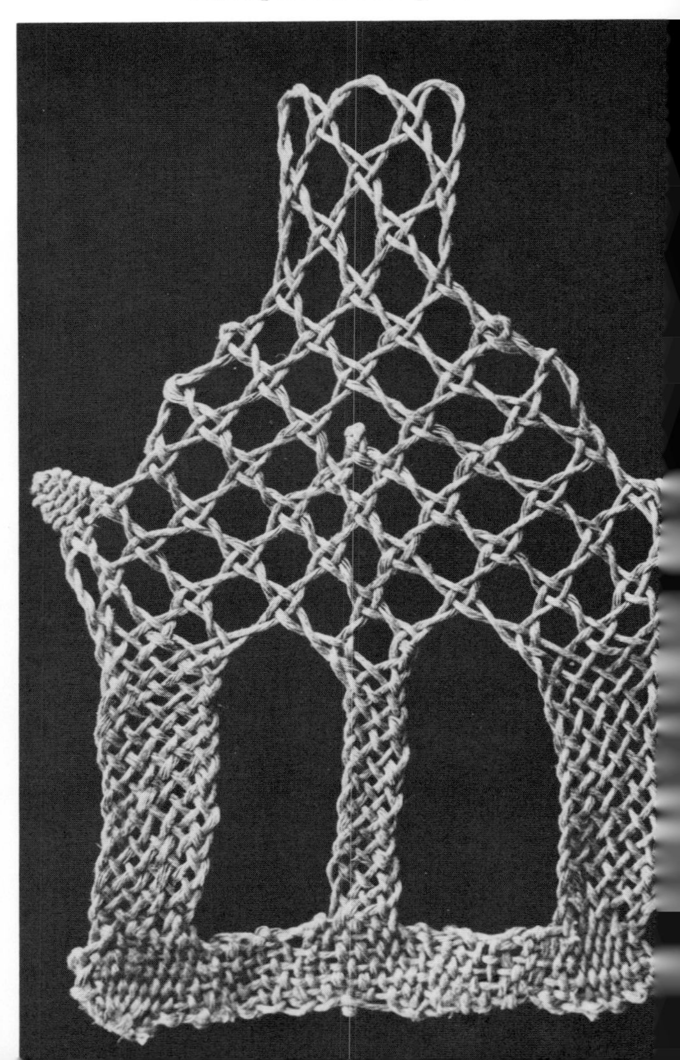

ENDINGS

Many endings are possible when working bobbin lace. Hanging cords can be looped, fringed, or simply knotted off. The latter method was the only way traditional lace threads were terminated. For looped or fringe endings, the cords have to be secured to keep them from untwisting. The two basic methods are by an overhand knot or knots with one of the hanging threads, or by wrapping with the same or a contrasting thread.

OVERHAND KNOT: With one of the hanging cords make a simple overhand knot over the other cords. Pull firmly downward so the tieing cord lays flat and together with the other cords. This knot is best repeated two or three times to adequately secure the ending as well as give the ending a more decorative detail.

Forming the first overhand knot with one of the hanging threads. Adjacent groups are bundled with a series of three overhand knots.

WRAPPING: A wrapping is a neat binding of the hanging cords. The same or a contrasting cord in terms of color and/or weight can be used, depending on the effect desired. The wrapping can be of any length or several wrappings, each separated by a short distance, and can be made to give a beaded effect.

1. With your wrapping cord, lay a loop at least twice the length of your wrapping distance over all cords to be wrapped. Let the short end of this loop extend about 1 inch below the start of the wrapping.
2. Holding the base of the loop and all cords to be wrapped firmly between thumb and forefinger, begin wrapping with the long free end of the wrapping cord. Wrapping should be firm and evenly spaced forming a neat tight coil.
3. At completion of wrapping, pull on the side of the loop that tightens the start of the coil. Pull to even up the start of the coil.
4. Take the wrapping end of the cord and feed it through the loop. Hold firmly while pulling opposite end of wrapping cord. Pull until loop is drawn inside of coil.
5. Clip off both ends of wrapping cord close to coil.

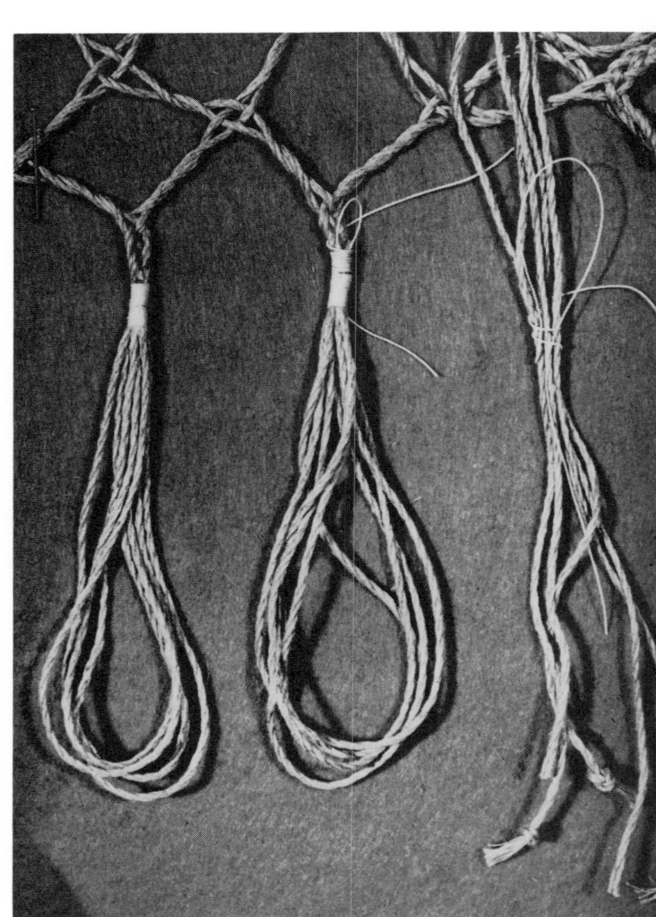

Binding groups of threads by wrapping. From the right: (1) A loop is formed and the first few turns have been made; (2) the loop has been pulled, tightening the start of the coil. The end of the wrapping cord is passed through the loop; (3) the lower end of the wrapping cord has been pulled tight, drawing the loop inside the wrapping. Free ends are cut, completing the binding.

Once your hanging cords are secured, they can be treated in various ways. Some cords, like nylon, can be combed out to form beautiful tassels. Wetting the cord will take out any kinks or waves. Various types of knots can be made in the hanging cords to create ending effects and give the individual cords additional weight. If a firmer edge is desired, the hanging cords can be looped back with the ends secured under your binding knot.

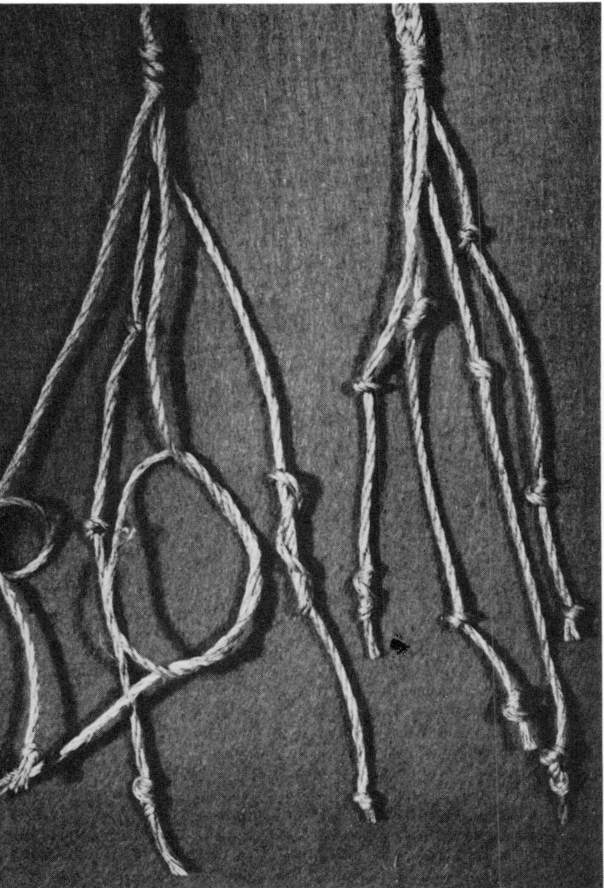

Hanging cords are knotted for a decorative fringe effect.

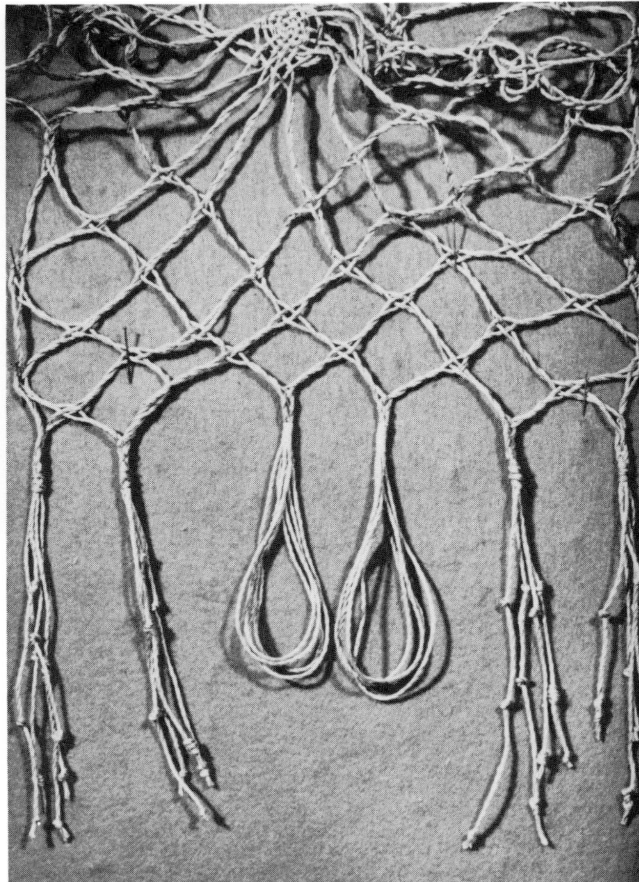

A variety of looped and knotted hanging threads.

TWISTED PAIRS: For a fringe ending, hanging pairs can be twisted together and left with a simple knot or bead on the end. To twist a terminating pair, take one thread in each hand and twist each of the threads individually in the same direction as their natural twist. When they have been given a hard twist, bring the two threads together and, while still holding the ends, twist them around each other in a direction opposite to the initial twist. A knot at the end will keep the pairs in the twisted position.

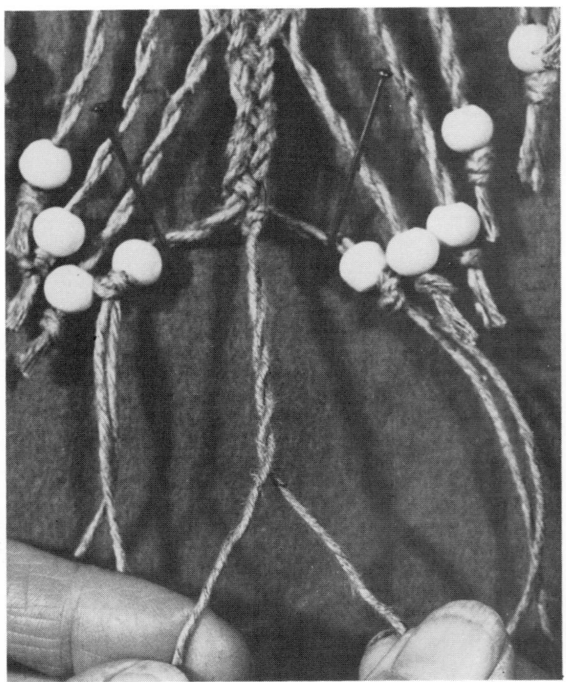

A pair of terminating threads is given a hard twist and then twisted around each other.

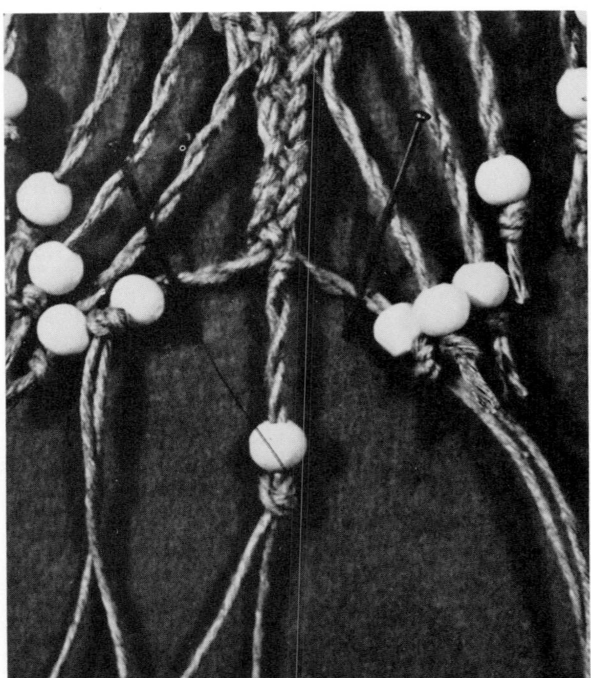

A bead is placed over the twisted pair and a knot secures the bead and the twist.

TERMINATING A CORD ON A FRAME: Half hitch the free cord ends to the frame, pulling securely. Twist the free end around the secured cord for a short distance and glue the two cords together with fabric adhesive. Cut off the free end. If desired, a wrapping can be added to cover the glued joint.

A pair of threads terminated on a frame by a half hitch and binding.

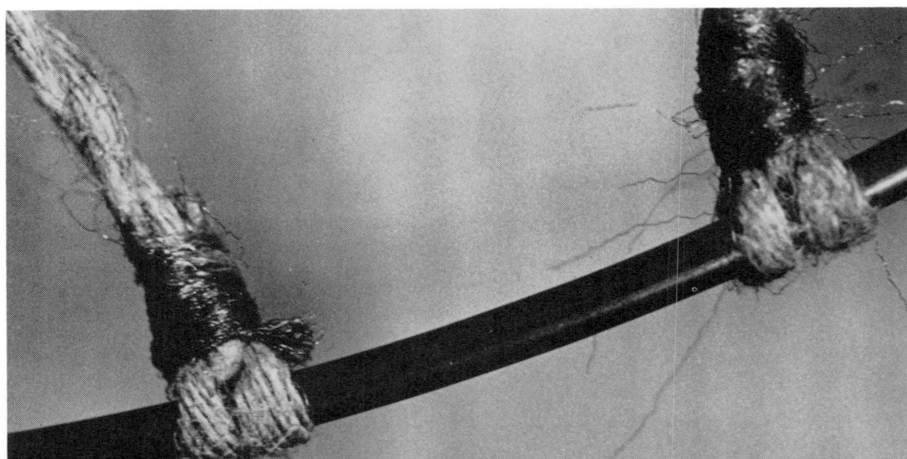

FIRM ENDING: A firm ending is often desirable as a termination when a fringe is not desired. Although ends can be knotted close to the edge, a neat selvage without knots is generally preferred. A firm ending is generally required for a belt, especially when a buckle is to be used. A firm ending is best worked from a *weaving ground*, as this ground provides the dense edge to conceal the loose ends. The general method is to take each hanging thread and weave it back through the ground four or more rows.

For a horizontal edge:

1. Cut all threads free of bobbins allowing a 4-to 5-inch free end.
2. Working one pair at a time, make a TWIST. Using a yarn-end weaver or crochet hook, return the free ends into the ground four or more rows. It is a good practice to terminate adjacent threads in different rows.
3. Cut off free ends close to the work.

If your edge gets too bulky, you can periodically cut hanging cords just before they reach the edge, without any return.

Making a horizontal termination. Cut ends are crossed over adjacent threads and fed back into the ground. Extended ends are cut off close to the work. A nail clipper is an excellent tool for this operation. It should be noted that the working face is the reverse side of the piece.

For a pointed termination: This makes a neat termination for the end of a belt. Simply weave out the weaver pair, and use one of the edge pairs as the new weaver for the following row. Repeat this process until all hanging pairs have been used and all weavers have been woven out. Work out pairs on alternate sides to produce a symmetrical point. Weave each terminated weaver pair back into the ground. These should be returned alternately both vertically and horizontally. As in the horizontal edge, all threads should be given a TWIST before they are returned into the ground. All threads should extend at least four rows back. When weavers are returned horizontally, they should be cut before reaching the opposite edge. It should be pointed out that all thread ends are worked out and cut off on the working side of your piece. This is ordinarily the back of the work. All knots and other irregularities should similarly be worked on this side of the work.

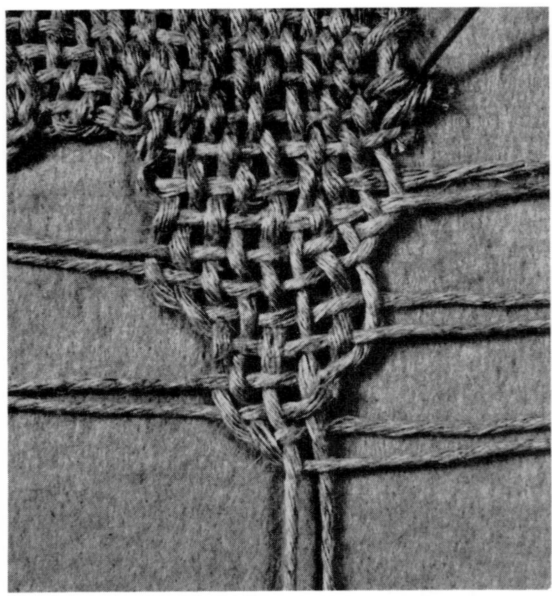

Making a pointed termination. The ground is shaped with dropped pairs extending from the work.

Extended pairs are worked back into the work with ends left extending.

All ends are cut close to the work.

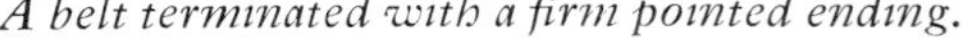

A belt terminated with a firm pointed ending.

WORKING WITH BEADS

Beads can be an integral part of bobbin lace adding detail and ornament to your designs. They can be placed on your working threads prior to winding your bobbins or they can be laid into the work afterward.

Beading working strands: Beads can simply be threaded onto your working strands prior to winding your bobbins. When a bead is required to be incorporated into the work, it is slid up and worked into a stitch.

If a particular line of beads is desired, thread all the beads on one strand and use it as a gimp, weaving it into your work.

If your beads are stranded to start with, a simple way of transferring them to your working strands is as follows:

> Glue with fabric adhesive one end of your bead strand to the end of one of your working cords. Transfer the number of beads to be worked onto a working strand by sliding them across the glued joint. Cut the bead strand free and wind your bobbin in the usual manner keeping the beads at the top of the wound bobbin.

Stitching beads into the work: A bead can be stitched into the work by either of two basic methods.

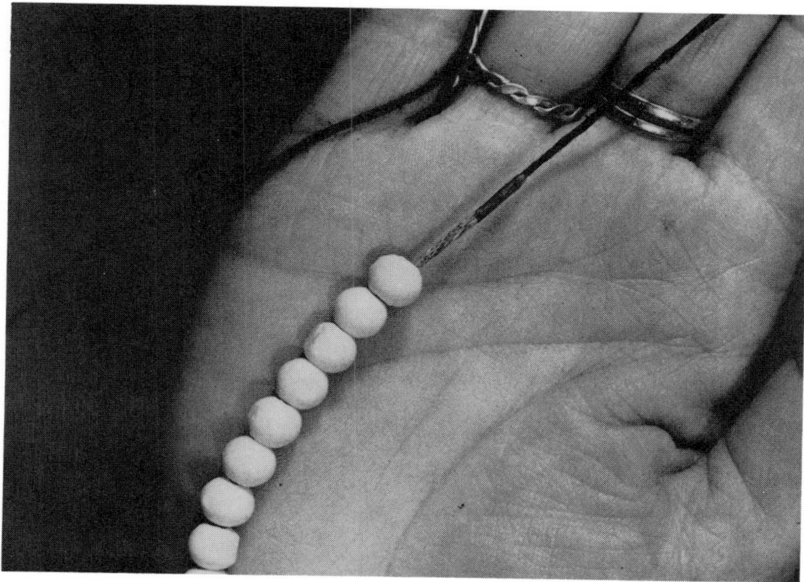

Beads are transferred from a beaded strand to a working strand. The threads are glued together and the beads are easily transferred.

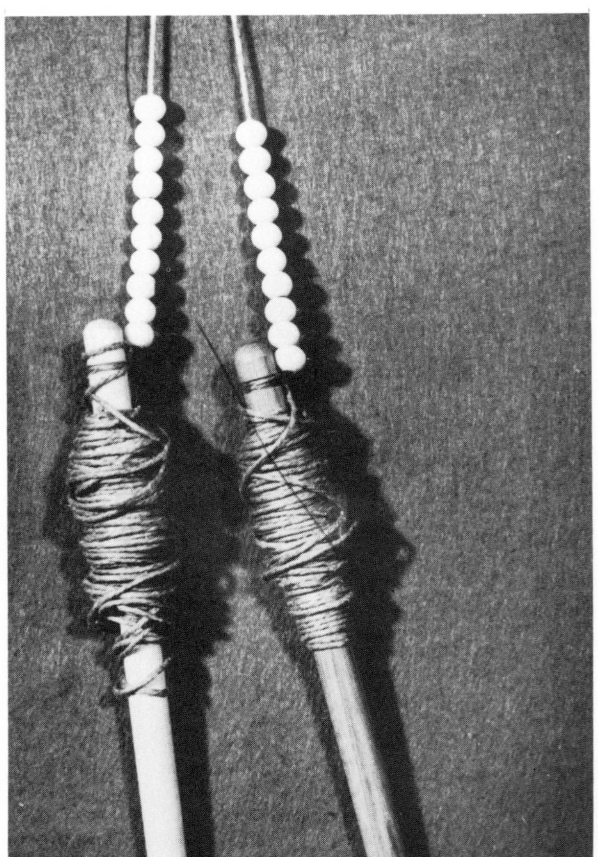

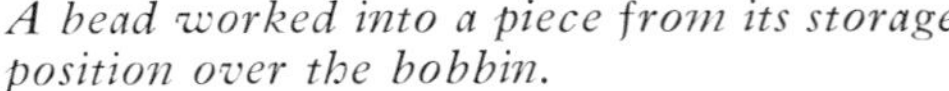

Beads threaded onto working strands resting above the bobbin.

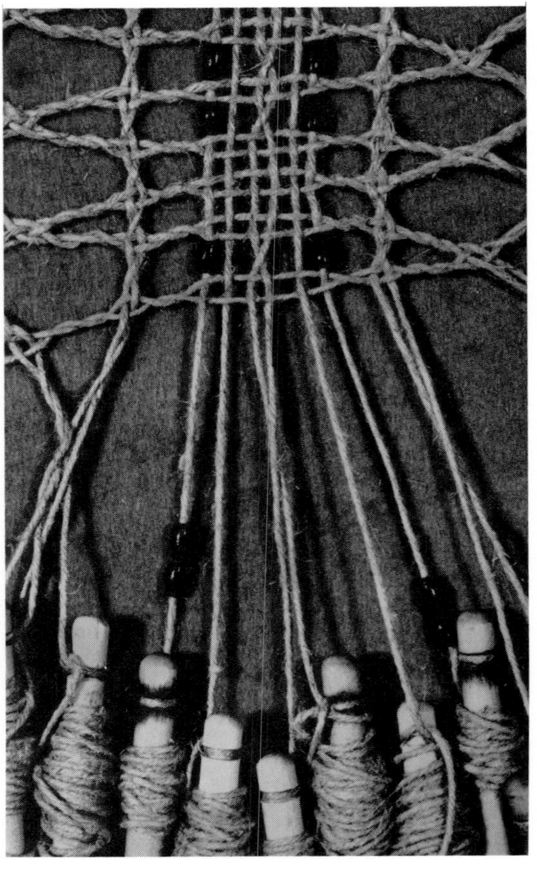

A bead worked into a piece from its storage position over the bobbin.

Working a bead between two threads: Pull a section of one thread through the bead with a crochet hook or other device so that a loop is formed. Pass the companion thread through the loop. Pull the initial thread tight, closing the loop and securing the bead.

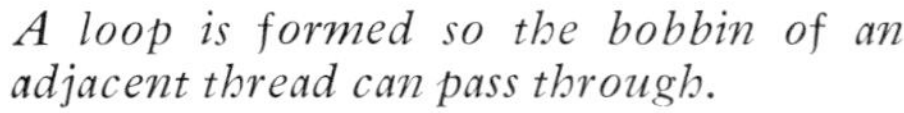

A loop is formed so the bobbin of an adjacent thread can pass through.

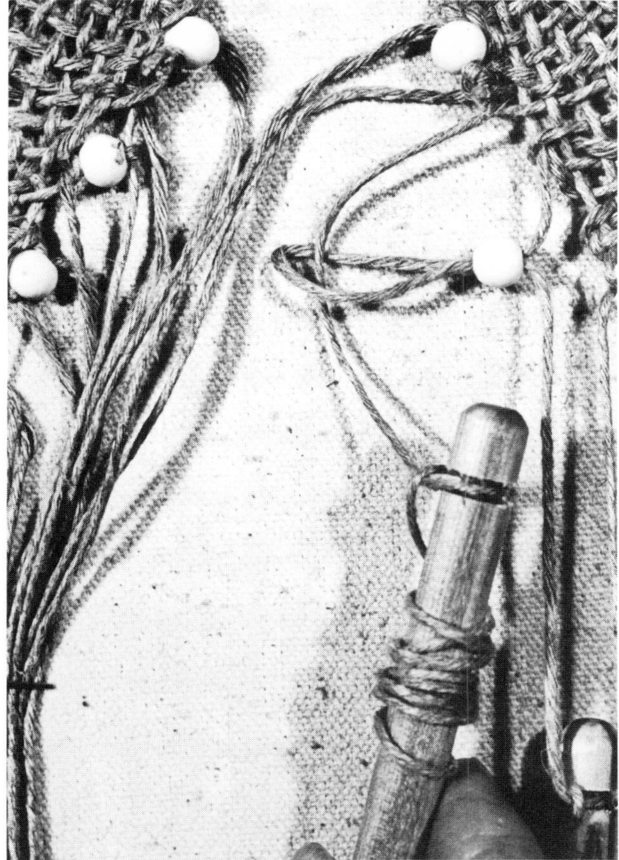

The adjacent thread is passed through the loop.

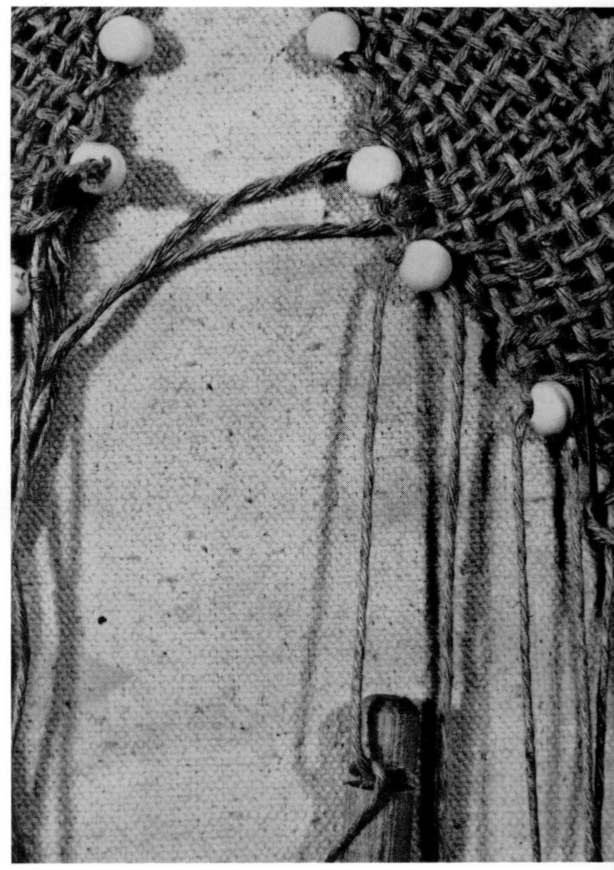

The thread that formed the loop is pulled tight, securing the bead.

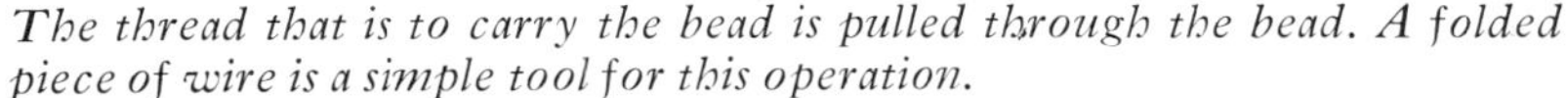

The thread that is to carry the bead is pulled through the bead. A folded piece of wire is a simple tool for this operation.

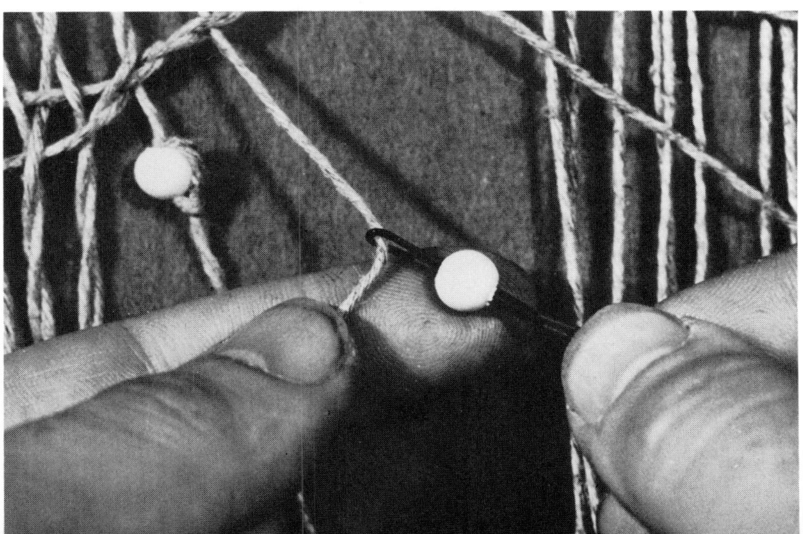

Working a bead with one thread: Pull a section of the thread through the bead forming a loop. Pass the bobbin through the loop formed, then pull tight securing the bead. Note that the thread will lay over the bead on one side, giving this technique a front and back.

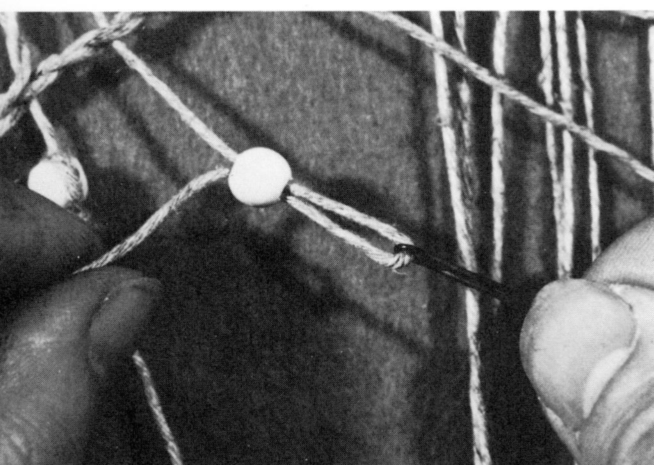

A loop is formed.

The bobbin of this thread is passed through the loop.

Pulling the thread tight secures the bead. The exposed thread extending around the bead will lie on the back side of the work.

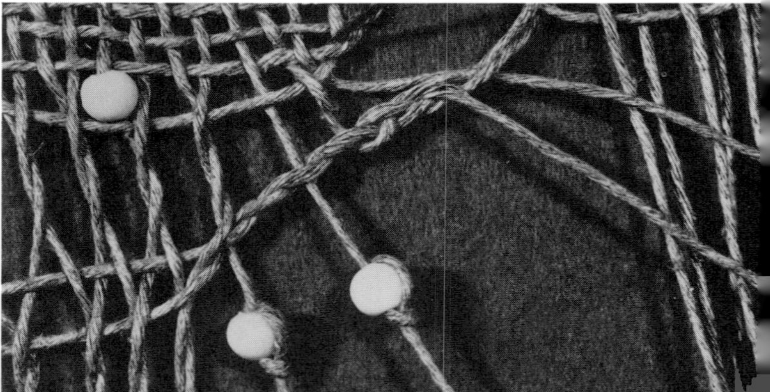

Additional Grounds

Chapter 6

The grounds of bobbin lace are virtually unlimited in number. Although the ground or mesh generally formed the background of a lace piece or an infilling between the designed elements, many details were themselves formed of these grounds. Shading and depth in a design was achieved by varying the type of ground.

Characteristics of grounds are:

Direction: The angular lines formed by the strongest ground lines.

Density: With any given thread, the ratio of open to solid areas will determine the density.

Scale: With any given thread, the relative size of the openings to the size of thread will determine the scale. For a specific density some grounds will have many small openings while others will have few large openings.

Color Pattern: If threads of various colors or textures are used, the individual threads will create a pattern in themselves as they weave through the mesh.

Thread Pairs: Each motif of the ground mesh is formed by a specific number of bobbin pairs. These can vary from two for the simpler grounds to eight or more for the more complex grounds.

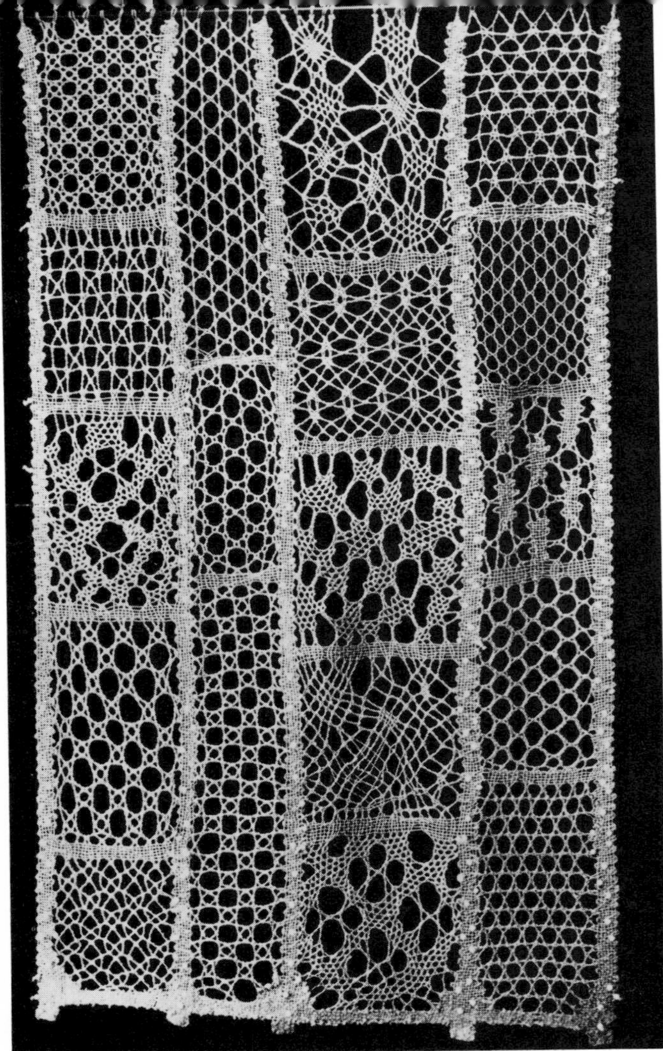

A curtain worked as a sampler of grounds. By the author.

Although the various named bobbin laces held to a few very specific grounds, contemporary lace can take advantage of the many sources available in terms of both time and place. And, of course, there should be no restrictions on experimentation as you explore the grounds of this chapter.

Although the grounds described can be worked over graph paper or a pattern for perfect uniformity, it is strongly advised that these aids be dispensed with. With the direction of the ground lines understood and the sequence of operations followed, it is not too difficult to pin by eye and still maintain uniformity. As you work these grounds, don't be afraid to experiment with your spacing. Most shapes and voids can be changed dramatically by simply changing pin locations. Adding or deleting TWISTS can be experimented with as a means to manipulate the design. Threads of different colors and/or materials can be used for design purposes as well as an aid in understanding the working of the ground. Contrasting threads will enable you to easily follow the course of any particular bobbin pair.

A useful technique in working your ground is to lay out the main direction lines on your board. Masking tape applied directly to your board is an excellent method of doing this. If your board has a cloth cover, the tape can be removed easily when no longer needed. Tape, outlining the extremities of your piece, will aso aid considerably in working to a specific shape or size.

THE PRINCIPLE of most of the regular grounds is that stitches or a specific sequence of stitches are made separately by a group of bobbin pairs. These groups are placed at uniform intervals in a row. In working the following row, the groups from the first row are divided to form new groups with one-half of the bobbins coming from the original right-hand group and the other half coming from the original left-hand group. This procedure is repeated for each succeeding row. For neatness and strength as well as spacing control, the threads connecting the stitches are either twisted or braided. Grounds formed by this method can be worked diagonally from right to left, or horizontally from left to right. The latter method is easier to follow and is the way the grounds of this chapter are described.

Designations referred to in this chapter are:

Rows: a row is a horizontal series of repetitive stitch groupings.

Columns: a column is a vertical row of repetitive stitch groupings.

Stitch: a particular sequence of motions (CROSSES and TWISTS) as described in Chapter 3.

The *whole stitch* is designated when the final TWIST of the stitch is critical to the ground design.

The *linen stitch* is specified when the number of TWISTS between stitches can be varied to change the scale or density of the ground without affecting its basic characteristics.

In describing these grounds, operations are given describing a particular sequence of basic motions or stitches as worked with one grouping of bobbin pairs. This sequence is then repeated across the row with all other groupings.

When you have worked several of these grounds and understand their rhythm, try designing a ground of your own. You can use some of the stitch sequences described in the previous chapter, or you can be completely innovative.

VIRGIN GROUND I

This popular decorative mesh was originally Flemish and belonged to the lace style known as Binche lace. As its use spread, it took on other names such as Cinq Trous, Fond de la Vierge, Point Carre, and Pin Check.

The *Virgin Ground* is essentially the linking of square blocks or motifs, joined at their corners, checkerboard fashion. The motifs are made up of five small holes, while the voids between the blocks form large octagons. Each motif requires four bobbin pairs, two of which enter on each upper corner.

Mount bobbin pairs in groups of two, equidistant across your top border, allowing two groups for each motif of the first row.

Working the first block of the first row:

1. Give all four pairs to be used for this motif an initial TWIST.
2. With the two center pairs make a *whole stitch* and then give each pair an additional TWIST.
3. With the two left pairs make a *whole stitch* and PIN. Do the same with the two right pairs. Give each inner pair an additional TWIST.
4. With the two inner pairs make a *whole stitch* and then PIN under the stitch.
5. With the two left pairs make a *whole stitch* and PIN. Do the same with the two right pairs.

This completes the stitches that form the first block in this row. Work across row, repeating steps 1–5 with each group of four pairs. Make the alternate blocks of the next row using the outer pairs from the adjacent corners of the two blocks above. In working this ground, be sure to maintain straight horizontal and vertical lines. PIN and pull all stitches as required to accomplish this. Note that all pairs used for the diagonals receive an additional TWIST.

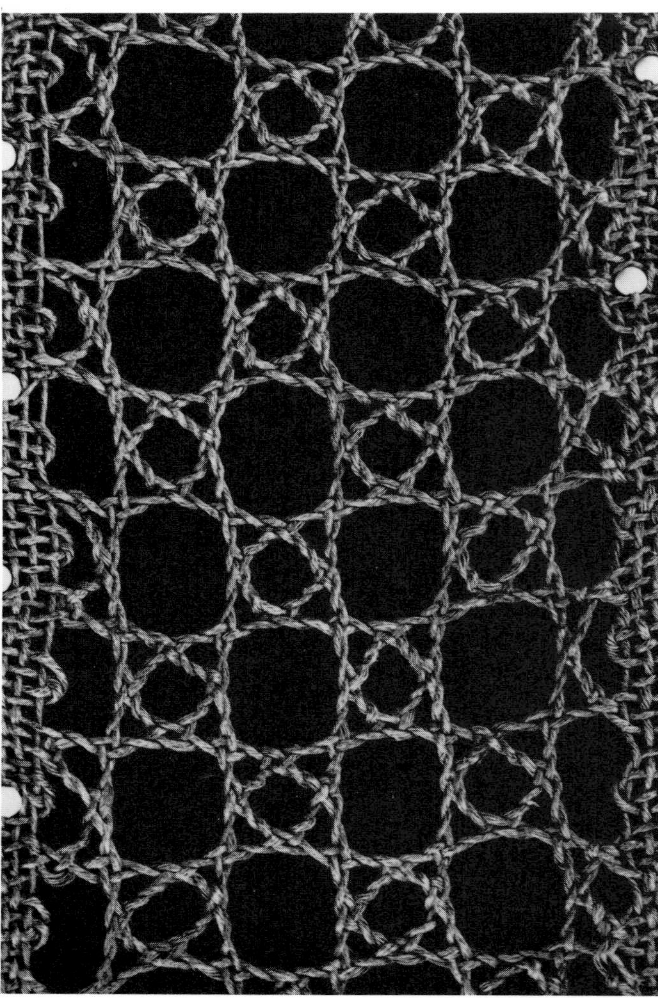

Virgin Ground I, each motif connected at the corners with a whole stitch.

A whole stitch formed with the two center pairs (step 2).

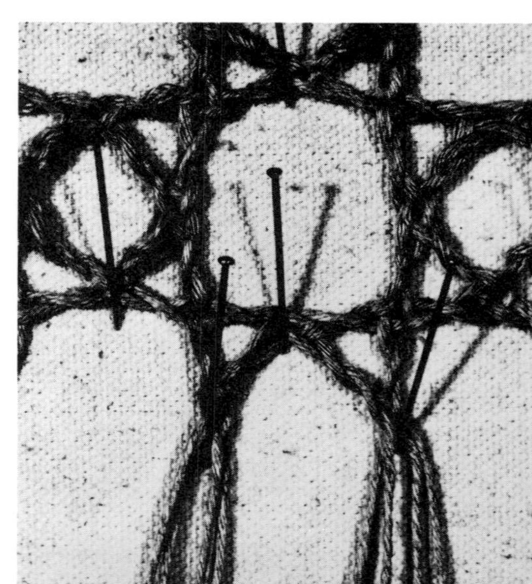

Whole stitches formed with the two left pairs and the two right pairs (step 3).

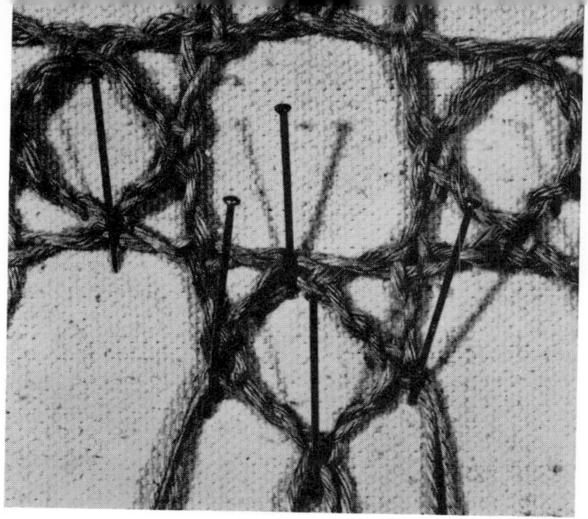

A whole stitch again formed with the two center pairs (step 4).

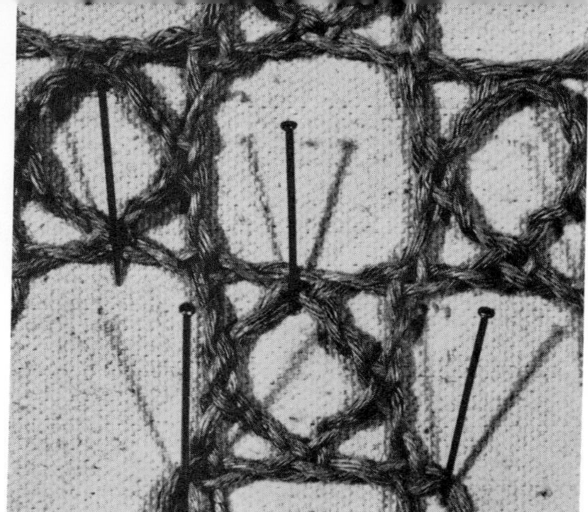

Whole stitches formed with the two left pairs and the two right pairs completing the block (step 5).

VIRGIN GROUND II

As the name implies, this is a variation of *Virgin Ground I.* While *Virgin Ground I* has a *whole stitch* connecting the worked blocks, this ground has a *half stitch.*

Each filled block requires four bobbin pairs, two of which enter at each upper corner. Mount bobbin pairs in groups of two, equidistant across your top border, allowing two groups for each worked block of the first row. These same pairs will form alternate blocks in the following row. This ground will be started at the top of the first block.

Working the first motif of the first row:

1. Give all four pairs to be used for this motif an initial TWIST.
2. With the two center pairs make a *whole stitch.* For all rows other than the first row, these will be the outer pairs from the adjacent corners of the two blocks above.
3. With the two left pairs make a *whole stitch.* Do the same with the two right pairs.
4. With the two center pairs make a *whole stitch.*
5. With the two right pairs make a *half stitch.* Do the same with the two left pairs.

This completes the stitches that form the block in this row. Work across row, doing steps 1–5 with each group of four pairs. In the following row form the alternate motifs using the two outer pairs from each of the adjacent motifs above.

Virgin Ground II, each motif connected at the corners with a half stitch.

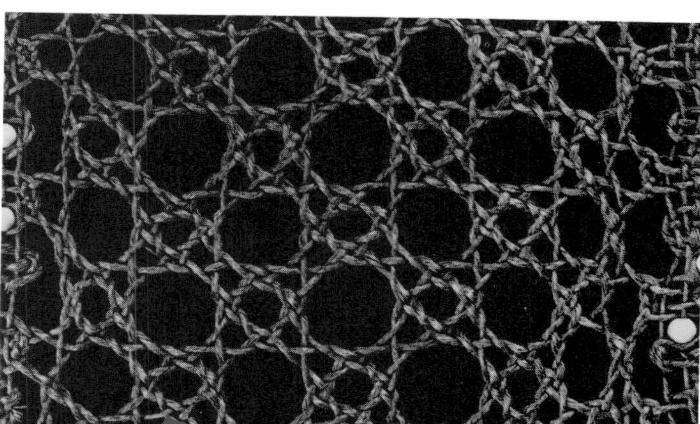

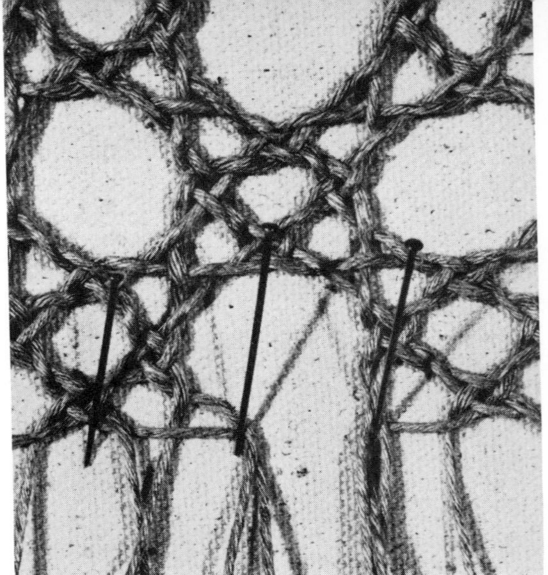

Half stitches completing two adjacent motifs.

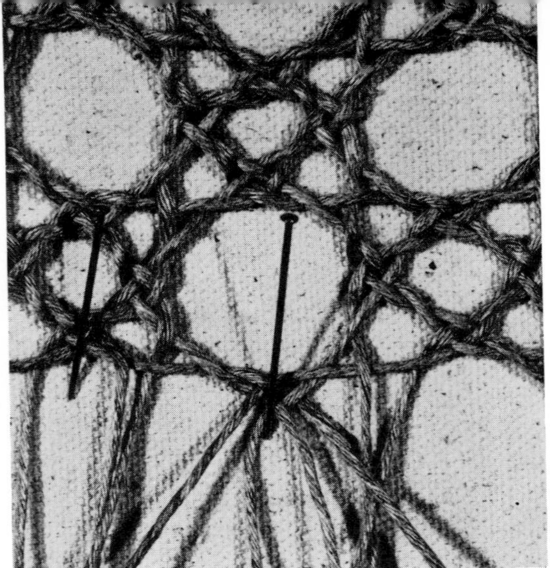

A whole stitch with the two center pairs starting a new block (step 2).

LATTICE

This *lattice* has strong vertical and horizontal lines and can be described as a series of rectangular blocks with crossing diagonals. The blocks are arranged checkerboard fashion with rectangular openings between the blocks.

Each block requires four bobbin pairs. These form the vertical and diagonal lines. An additional weaver pair is required for the horizontal closures. This pair weaves back and forth through the ground.

Mount bobbin pairs in groups of two, equidistant across your top border, allowing two groups for each block of the first row. Hang an additional pair, the weaver pair, with the first group of two bobbin pairs (upper left corner).

Working the first block with the first two groups of bobbin pairs (five pairs):

1. With the left pair (weaver pair) and the other two pairs (block pairs) at this same location make *linen stitches.*
2. With the two hanging pairs (block pairs) make a *linen stitch* below the weaver pair.
3. Give the weaver pair two TWISTS. With the next two pairs (right block pairs) and the weaver pair make *linen stitches.*
4. With the right block pairs make a *linen stitch* below the weaver pair.
5. With the two center pairs (inner block pairs) make two TWISTS —*linen stitch*—two TWISTS and PIN.
6. Give the outer pairs three TWISTS, bringing them down to the lower edge of the blocks.

Proceed across row with steps 1–6 with each set of four bobbin pairs. At the end of the row join the weaver pair to your border or bring it down with TWISTS to the lower edge of the blocks.

7. Repeat from step 1, working the weaver pair to the left, closing off all blocks above and forming alternating blocks below.

By varying the number of TWISTS between each stitch, manipulation of this ground is easily accomplished. The vertical and horizontal lines can be at regular or irregular intervals or they can become angular.

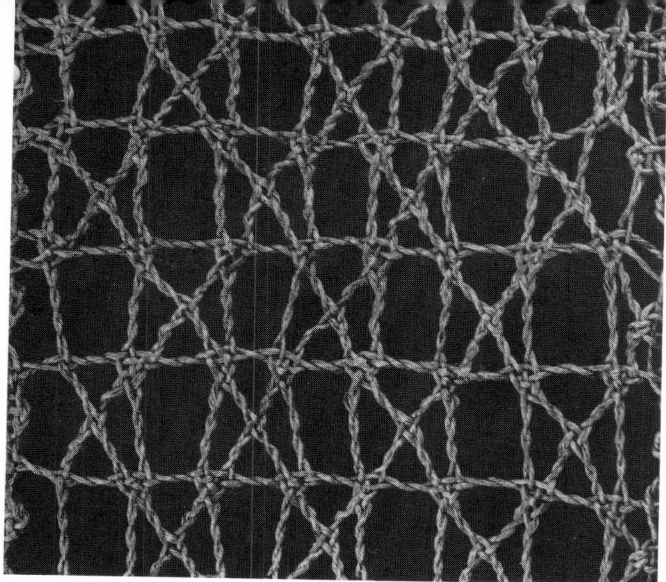

Lattice ground.

FEATHER GROUND

This ground can be described as vertical columns of staggered oval shapes that are crossed by diagonal lines. The entire pattern is formed by the crossing of twisted pairs, two pairs forming each crossing.

For each two adjacent columns, six starting bobbin pairs are required. Mount two bobbin pairs at the center of the first vertical column. Mount the other four pairs equidistant across the width of the oval of the adjacent column.

Working the two pairs over the first column:

1. With these two pairs (oval forming pairs of the first column) make a *linen stitch* followed by three TWISTS to each pair.

Working the four pairs over the second column:

2. With the two center pairs (diagonal forming pairs) make a TWIST—*linen stitch*—two TWISTS.
3. Give each of the outer pairs (oval forming pairs of the second column) three TWISTS. With the two left pairs make a *linen stitch* and TWIST. Do the same with the two right pairs.
4. With the two center pairs (oval forming pairs) make a *linen stitch* closing the oval. Give each pair three TWISTS.

Working the first column:

5. With the right pair of the first column (oval forming pair) and the left pair from the second column (diagonal pair) make a *linen stitch*. Give the left pair (diagonal pair) two TWISTS and the right pair (oval pair) three TWISTS.
6. Mount a new diagonal pair at the left border. With this pair and the adjacent pair (oval pair) make a *linen stitch*. This stitch should be aligned with the stitch on the opposite side of this oval (step 5). Give the oval pair three TWISTS and the diagonal pair two TWISTS.

There are now four pairs working in the first column. Working these four pairs repeat steps 2, 3, and 4.

This ground is easily worked if you follow your design in making the correct number of TWISTS between each *linen stitch*. Note that all oval forming pairs have three TWISTS between stitches except at the lower closing where they have only one TWIST. All diagonal pairs have two TWISTS between stitches within an oval and one TWIST when between ovals. As you work, keep your shapes formed by pinning after each stitch.

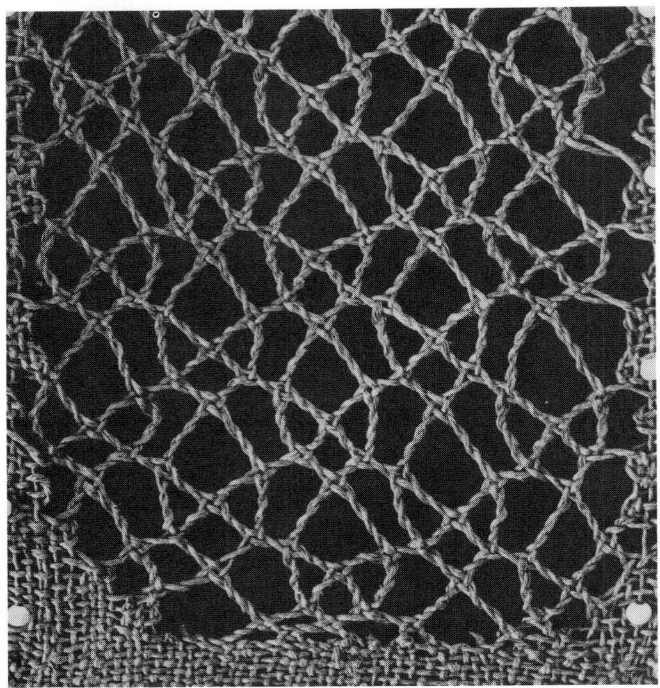

Feather ground.

ROSE GROUND (POINT DE MARIAGE)

This popular traditional ground is commonly found in the Chantilly laces. The pattern formed is a series of interlocking hexagonal openings that give it a honeycomb appearance. The hexagonal openings in adjacent columns are staggered.

Alternate columns of hexagonal shapes are worked. The adjacent or in-between columns are automatically formed by the joining of the worked columns.

For each worked column, four bobbin pairs are required. PIN these pairs equidistant across each worked column. All stitches in this ground are *half stitches* followed by a TWIST in each pair.

Working the first column:

1. Give all four hanging pairs two TWISTS.
2. With the two left pairs make a *half stitch*—PIN—TWIST—*half stitch*—TWIST. Do the same with the two right pairs.
3. With the two center pairs make a *half stitch*—PIN—TWIST—*half stitch*—TWIST.
4. Repeat step 2.

This completes the initial steps on the first column. Work across row, doing steps 1–4 for each worked column. Now join the working columns:

5. With the outer pairs of adjoining columns make a *half stitch*—PIN—TWIST—*half stitch*—TWIST. Work across row in this manner joining all worked columns.

Again working the first column:

6. Repeat from step 2.

In working this ground, shape the voids as you work, keeping your pin locations at the outer corners of the hexagonal shapes.

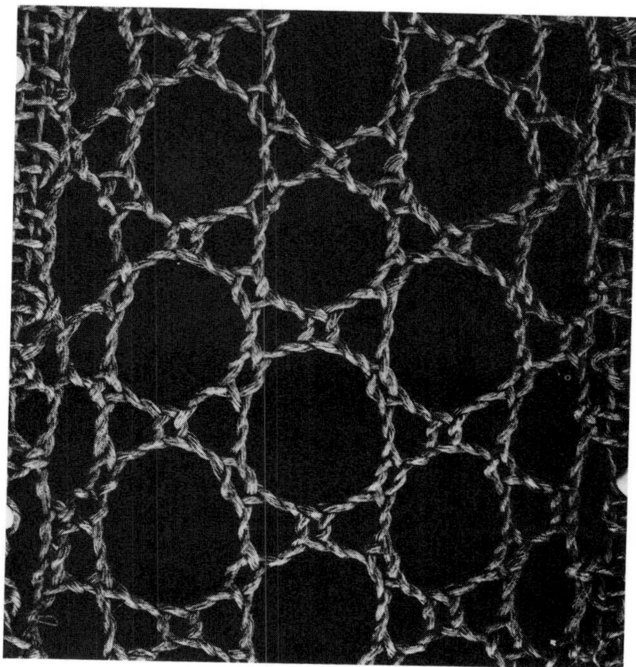

Rose ground.

ITALIAN SPIDER

This ground has as a motif a repeated spiderlike design. The design is formed by the crossing of pairs. Where four pairs intersect, the dense spiderlike motifs are formed.

Four bobbin pairs are required for each spiderlike motif of the first row. Allowing four pairs for each motif, mount all pairs equidistant across your top border.

Begin by working the outer pairs of all groups:

1. With the adjacent outer pairs of all groups make a TWIST—*linen stitch*—three TWISTS.

2. In the first and last groups give the outside pair adjacent to the border three TWISTS.

Now work the first group of four pairs:

3. With the two center pairs make three TWISTS—*linen stitch*—and PIN.

4. With the two left pairs make a *linen stitch*. Do the same with the two right pairs.
5. With the two center pairs make a *linen stitch*.
6. Repeat step 4.

This completes the upper half of the spiderlike motif. Work across row, repeating steps 3–6 with each group of four pairs.

Again work the outer pairs of all groups:

7. With adjacent outer pairs of all groups make three TWISTS—*linen stitch*—three TWISTS.

Now work the first group of four pairs again:

8. Repeat steps 4–6.
9. With the two center pairs make a *linen stitch* followed by three TWISTS.

This completes the final steps on the first spiderlike motif. Work across row doing steps 8–9 with each group of four pairs. Working the outer pairs again:

10. With the adjacent outer pairs of all groups make three TWISTS *linen stitch*—two TWISTS.
11. With the left pair from the above stitch and the adjacent pair to the left make a *linen stitch*—two TWISTS. Do the same with the right pair and the adjacent pair to the right.

You are now ready to form the spiderlike area of the next row. The motifs of this row will lie between the dense areas of the first row. The new working groups are now between the working groups of the row above:

12. With the adjacent outer pairs of all new groups make a *linen stitch*—three TWISTS.

Repeat all steps from step 3 on, forming the alternate motifs in the next row.

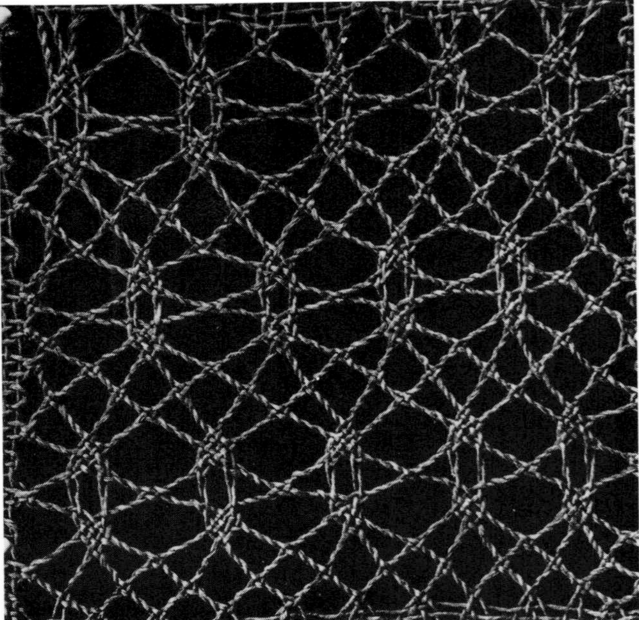

Italian spider ground.

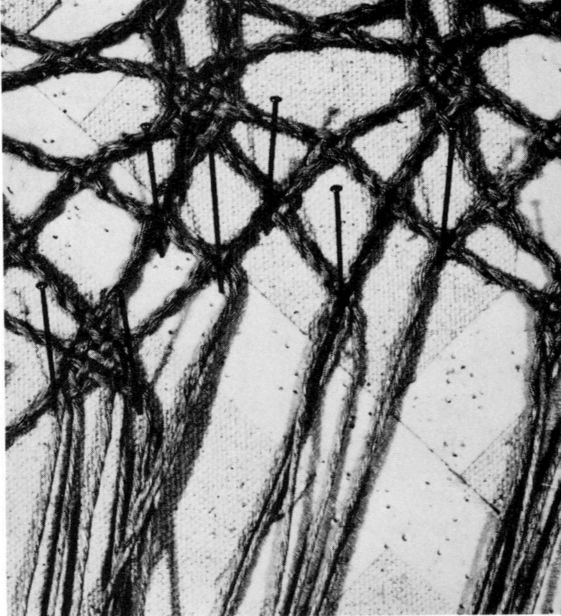

A linen stitch formed with the two center pairs (step 3).

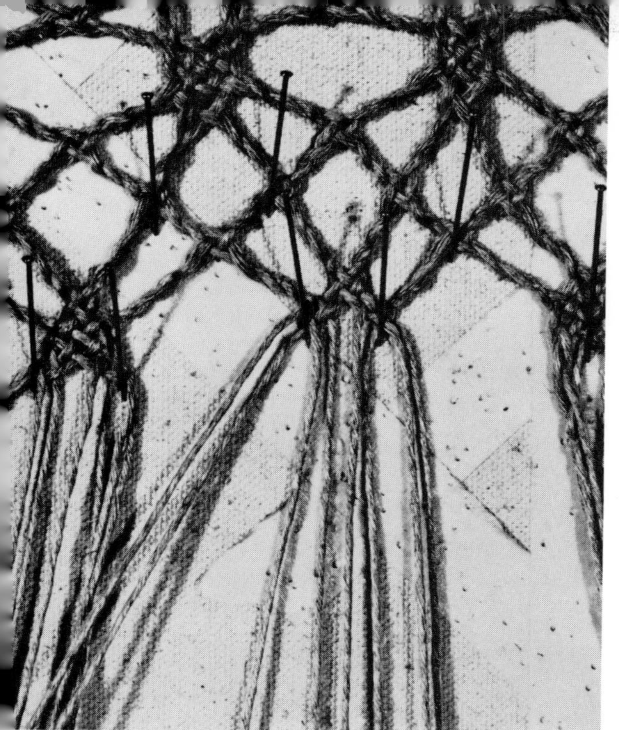

Linen stitches made with the two left pairs and the two right pairs (step 4).

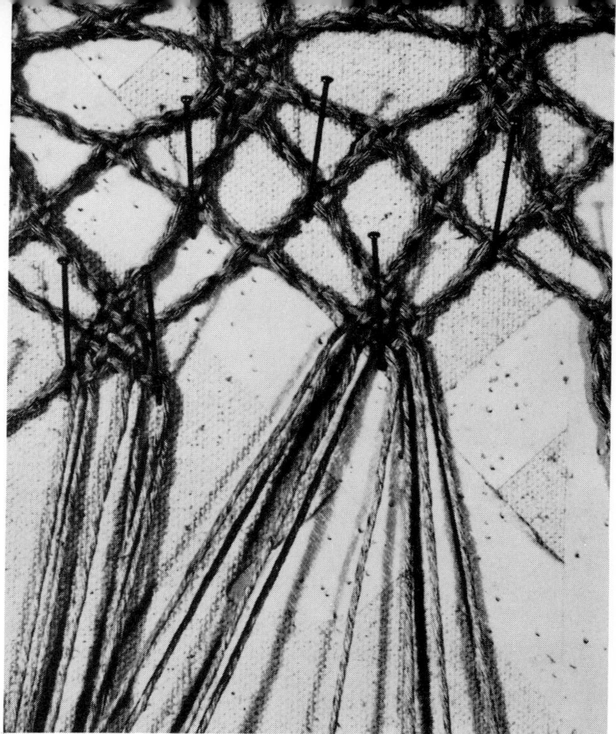

A linen stitch is again made with the center pairs (step 5).

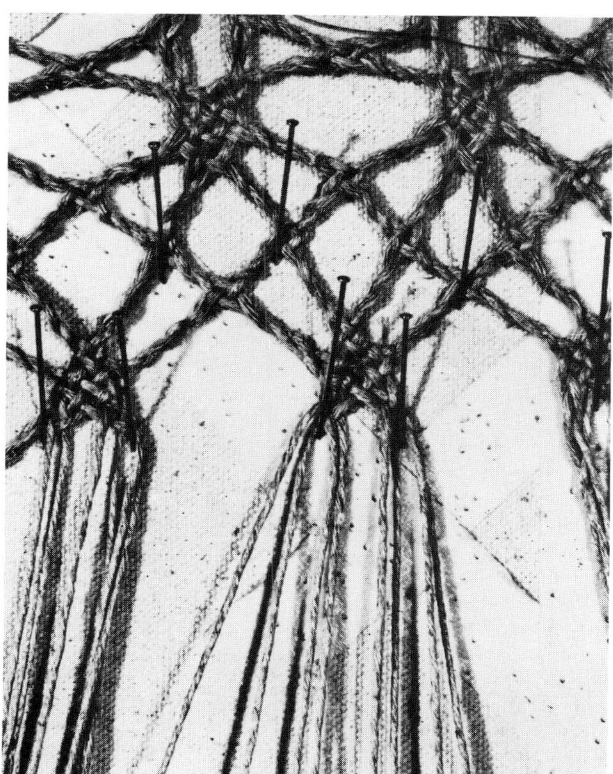

Linen stitches made with the two outer pairs (step 6), completing the upper half of the spider.

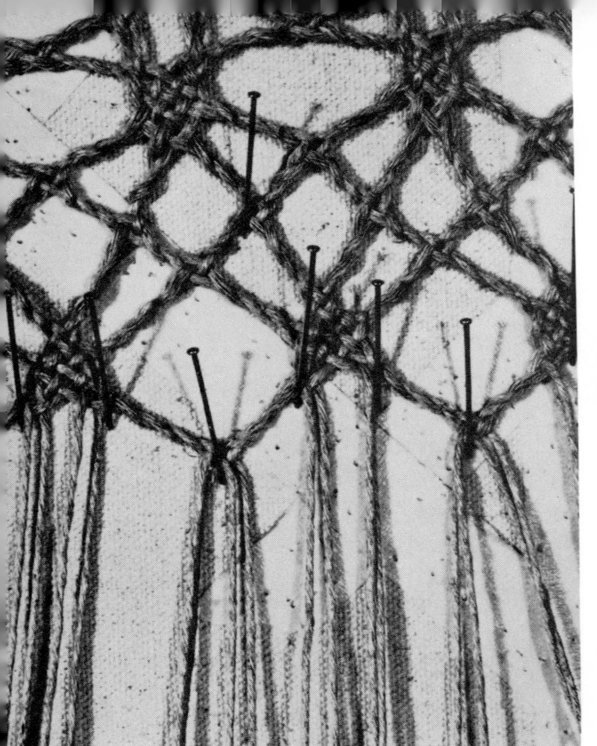

The outer pairs of adjacent groups are joined with a linen stitch (step 7).

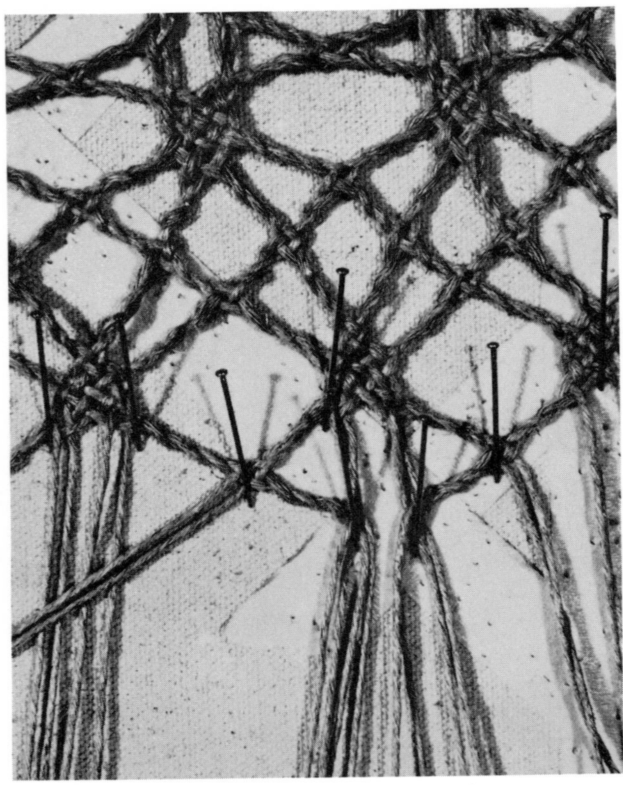

Linen stitches formed with the two left pairs and the two right pairs (start of step 8).

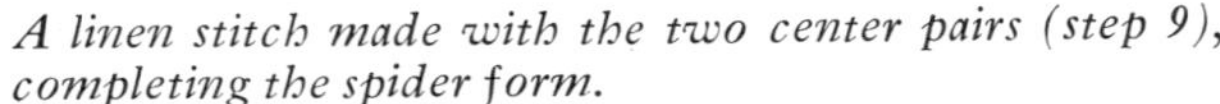

A linen stitch made with the two center pairs (step 9), completing the spider form.

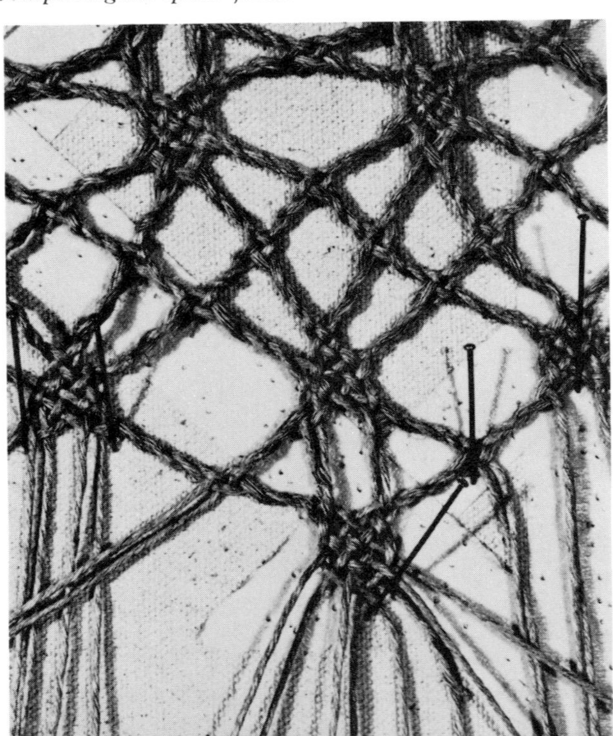

A linen stitch is made with the adjacent outer pairs (step 10).

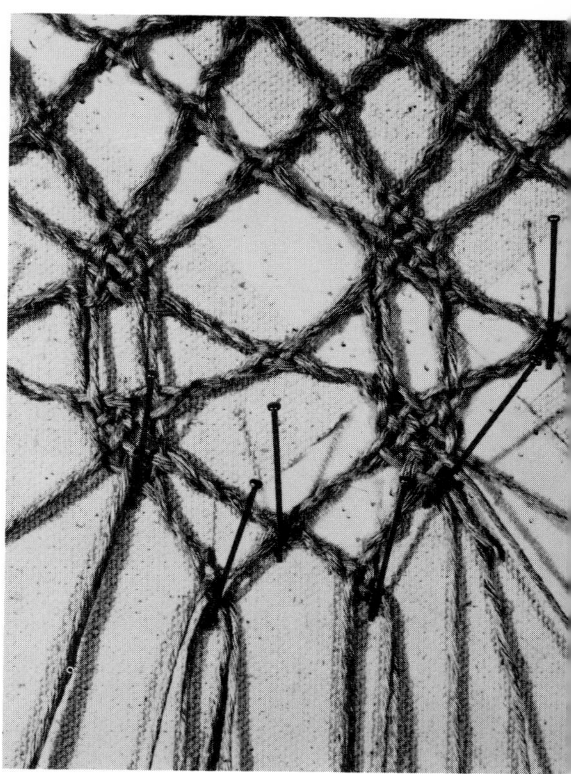

Linen stitches made with the two left pairs and the two right pairs of the alternate group (step 11).

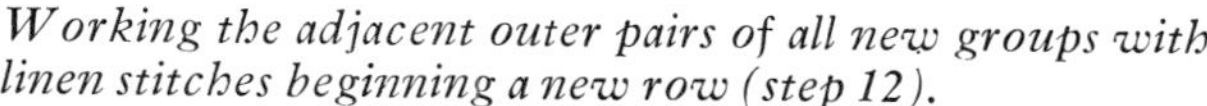

Working the adjacent outer pairs of all new groups with linen stitches beginning a new row (step 12).

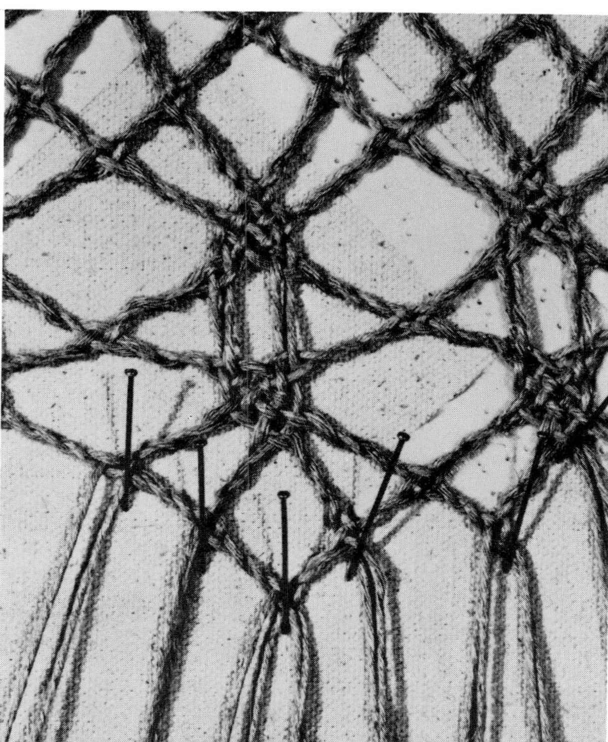

TRENTINO

A pattern of dense circular areas joined by *braids* forms the design. These dense areas can be run vertically in columns or they can be staggered in a checkerboard fashion.

Ten bobbin pairs are required for each dense area of the first row. The dense areas are made alternately with *linen stitches* and *half stitches.*

Over each dense area of the first row mount ten bobbin pairs in groups of two, equidistant apart.

Working the first group of ten pairs:

1. With the center two pairs make *linen stitch*—TWIST.
2. With the left center pair work across the two adjacent pairs to the left with TWISTS and *linen stitch.* The number of TWISTS will be determined by the outline of your dense area. Do the same with right center pair and the two adjacent pairs to the right.
3. With the two outer pairs on each side make a *braid* and join with the pairs from the center with *linen stitches.*
4. Give all hanging pairs two TWISTS and *linen stitch* with inner eight pairs until they all cross each other. End with two TWISTS.
5. With the outer pairs make TWISTS and *linen stitches* with all hanging pairs to enclose the circular area. Complete circle with a *linen stitch* with the two perimeter pairs.

This completes one dense area. The next dense area is worked in the same way except *half stitches* are used for the filling (step 4) instead of the *linen stitch.*

6. With the outer two pairs of each group make a *braid,* then cross the braided pairs of adjacent groups. *Braid* out again to form your new groups.

This ground works very well in contemporary designs as it can be as structured or unstructured as one wishes. Varying the length of the *braids* will permit specific location of the dense areas. The design is bold and strong, yet still retains the "lace" quality.

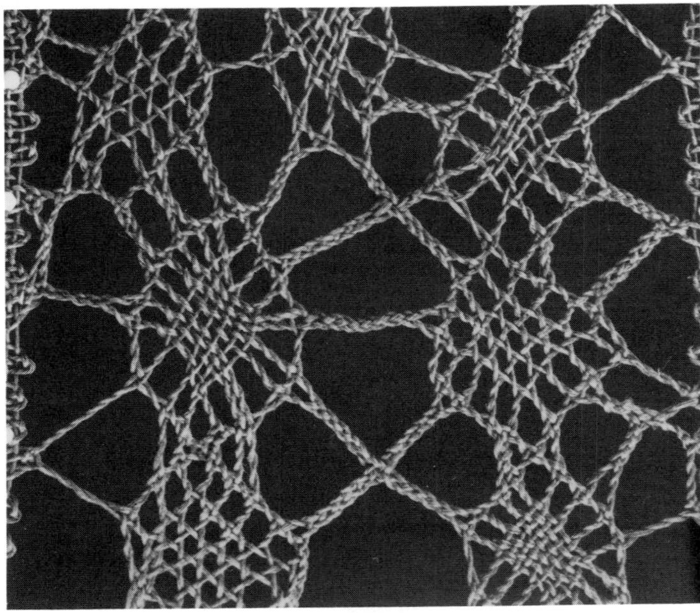

Trentino ground.

SPOTS

This ground consists of an irregular grouping of random sized and shaped spots joined by *braids* and/or twisted pairs. Each spot is formed with eight to sixteen pairs depending on the size of spot desired as well as the material used. Layout of the spots can be as random or regular as one wishes. This ease of manipulation lends this ground well to the freedom of contemporary lace expressions.

Hang all pairs for each spot of the first row in groups of two across the width of the spot.

Working the first spot:

1. With all groups of two pairs make *braids*, extending each *braid* to the perimeter of the planned spot.
2. Starting with the shortest *braid*, make *half stitches* picking up additional pairs from the other *braids*. For an oval shape, pick up a new pair in each row.
3. In a similar manner drop out pairs as you work to your desired shape.
4. Combine dropped pairs into *braids* or simply TWIST each pair, working toward the next spot.

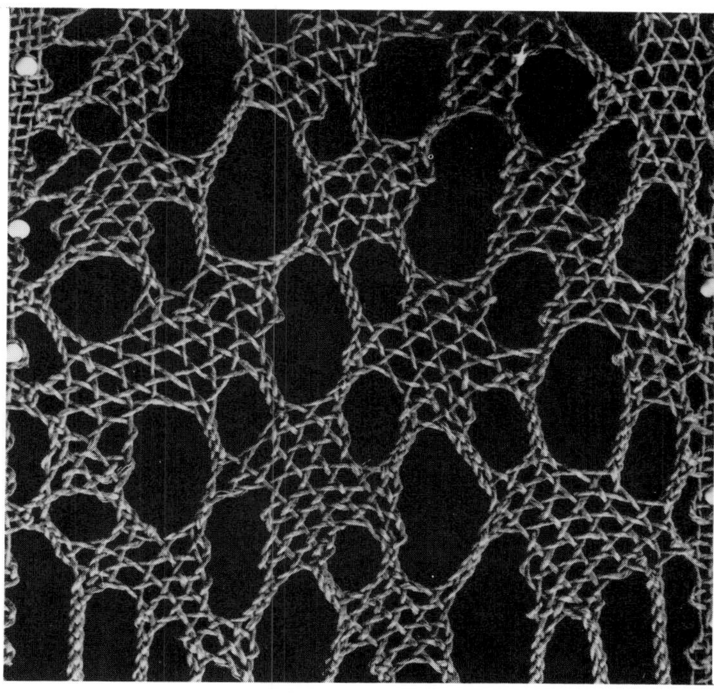

Spots ground.

COBWEB

This ground is formed by the crossing of twisted pairs, each crossing being made with three pairs. Horizontal and diagonal lines form triangular shapes, which in turn form larger hexagonal shapes.

One pair is required for each diagonal line. These are mounted in pairs across your top border. Another pair is required for the horizontal lines.

This pair weaves back and forth as the weaver, crossing the diagonal pairs. The first hanging pair will join the edge and become the weaver.

Working across the first row:

1. Take one pair from each of two adjacent mounting points and make two TWISTS—*half stitch* and PIN.

Bringing in the weaver:

2. Take the first pair and give it two TWISTS, then join it to the left border. Give it three more TWISTS and return it to the right as the horizontal weaver.

Work the weaver across the row:

3. With the weaver pair and the first two pairs that formed the half stitch in step 1, make a *linen stitch*. Give the weaver three TWISTS and make a *linen stitch* with the next two pairs. Work across row in this manner, joining all diagonals and weaver.

Complete the intersection:

4. With the same diagonal pairs that formed the first *half stitches*, make another *half stitch* (below the weaver) and PIN. Pull pairs to align your horizontal lines.

Continue working your ground by repeating from step 1, this time working your weaver from the right. Each time the weaver reaches an edge, join it to the edge and let it run vertical with TWISTS until it reaches the next row.

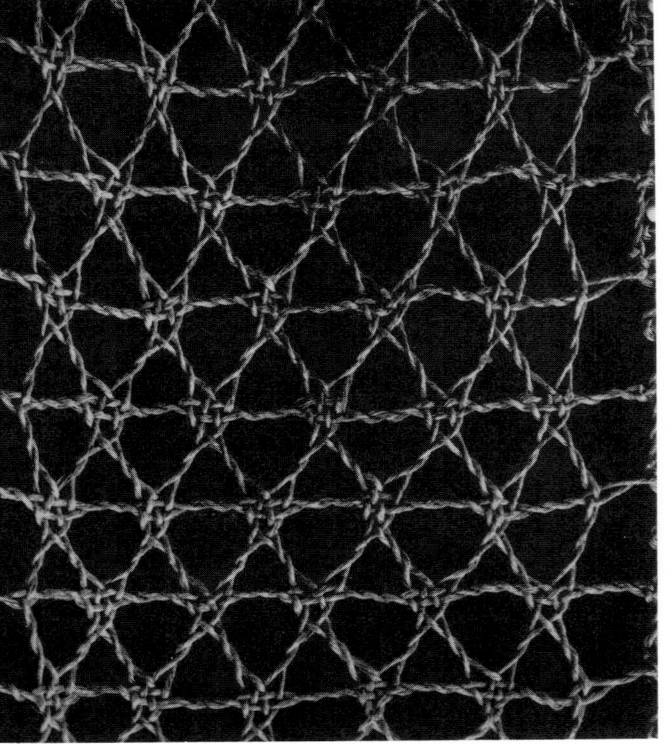

Cobweb ground.

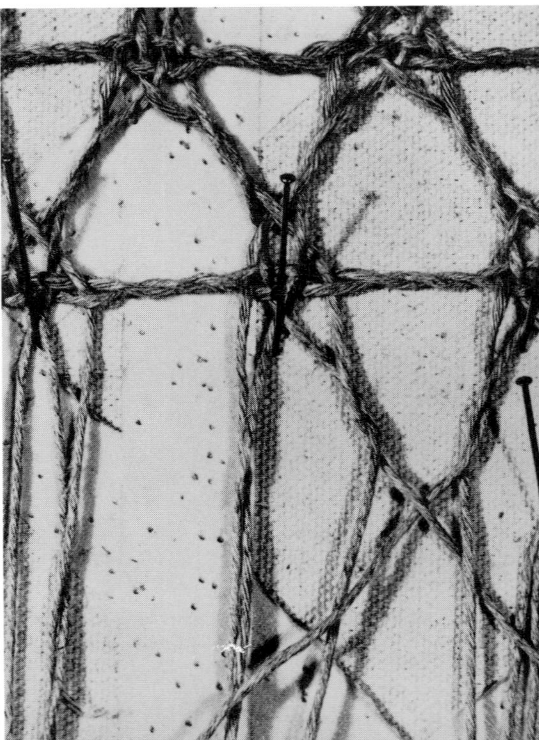

Two adjacent pairs joined with a half stitch (step 1).

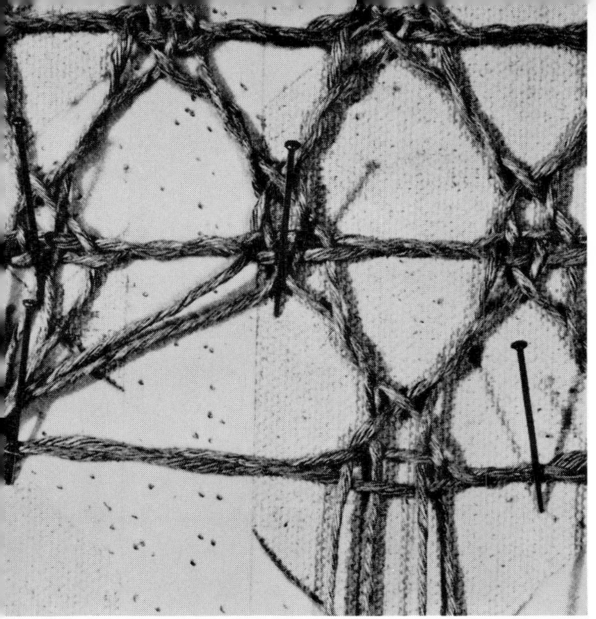

The horizontal pair (weaver) makes linen stitches with the two diagonal pairs (step 3).

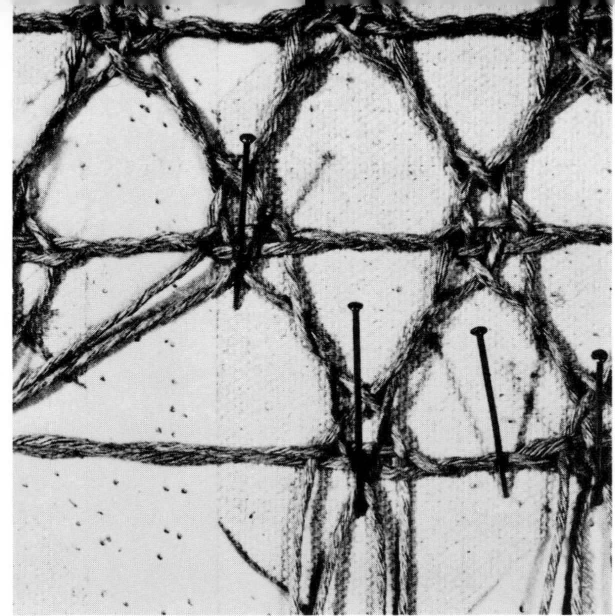

A half stitch is made below the weaver completing the crossing (step 4).

LILLE

This is a very basic lacy ground. It is formed in the typical fashion, with stitches in alternate rows staggered. As it has very little structure and distorts quite easily it should be used with caution. *Half stitches* form the basic stitch as they are formed with adjacent bobbin pairs.

Hang your pairs equidistant across the top border:

1. Give all hanging pairs two TWISTS.
2. With two adjacent pairs, make a *half stitch*—PIN—TWIST. Work across row joining each group of adjacent pairs.
3. Work the following row in the same manner using the adjacent pairs from each of the two above adjacent stitches to make your new stitch.

It should be noted that each *half stitch* ends in one TWIST. The additional TWIST called for results in two TWISTS between each crossing. This one added TWIST should be considered a minimum. Two or more TWISTS can be added after each *half stitch* to modify as well as strengthen this ground.

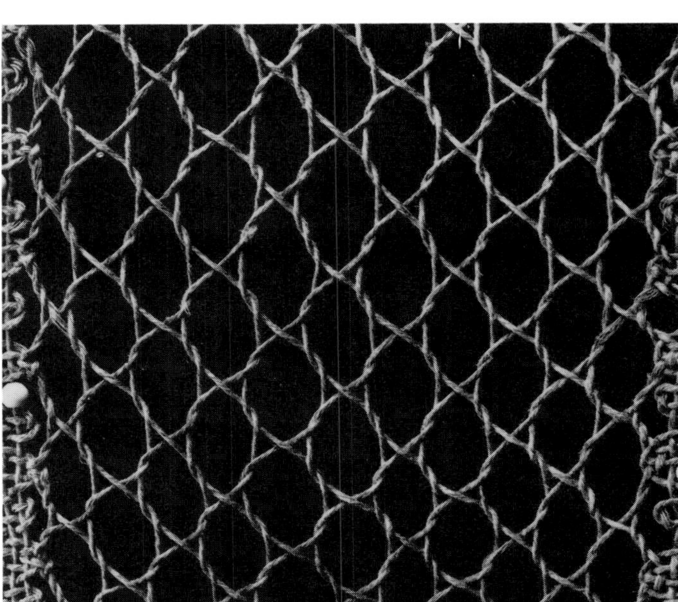

Lille ground.

VALENCIENNES (VAL) GROUND

The Valenciennes ground has a bold, strong appearance with interconnecting *braids* forming heavy lines and large openings. The size of the openings are determined by the length of the *braids*. In traditional lace the length of the braids in this mesh would identify the particular lace area where it was executed. The oval or diamond shapes formed create an overall honeycomb pattern.

Each oval of the first row requires four bobbin pairs for the two *braids*. Mount all pairs, in groups of two, across your top border. An edge pair is required at each edge to join the ground to the edge.

Working across the first row:

1. Work each group of two pairs with two *whole stitches* forming a short *braid*. PIN after the last stitch to hold in place.
2. With the two inner pairs of two adjacent *braids* make a *whole stitch* and PIN.
3. With the two left pairs make another *braid* (two *whole stitches*). Do the same with the two right pairs.
4. In alternating rows at the outer edges, join the edge pair and the outer pair of the adjacent *braid* with a *whole stitch*.

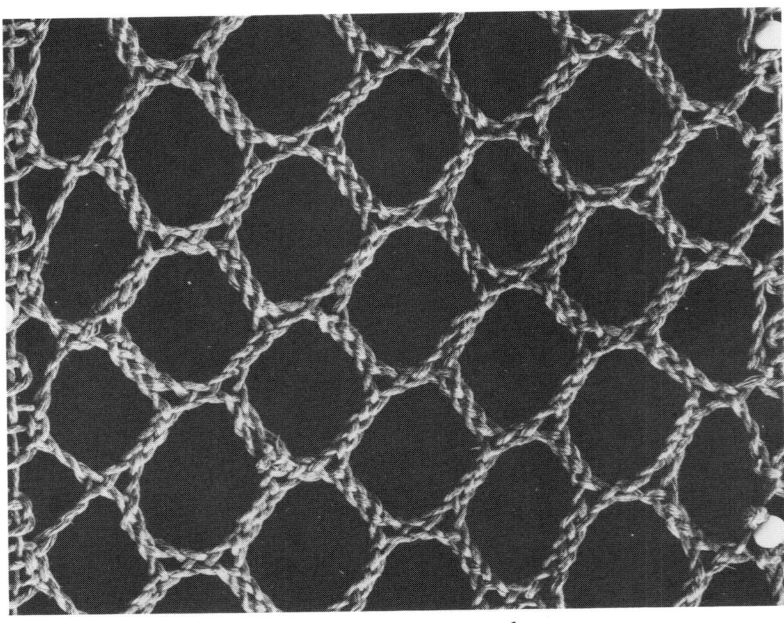

Valenciennes ground.

FRENCH GROUND (POINT DE PARIS)

This simple ground is formed by pairs crossing with *whole stitches*. The pattern can be thought of as a series of crosses between straight lines. These lines can either run vertically or horizontally. The crosses, which are staggered in each row or column, form an overall pattern of interlocking six-pointed stars.

To make a ground with horizontal lines, two pairs are required for each crossing in the first row. In addition, one weaver pair is required, which runs horizontally crossing the angular pairs. Hang pairs equidistant across your top border.

Working across the first row:

1. Give all hanging pairs a TWIST.
2. With each group of adjacent pairs make a *whole stitch.*
3. Mount the weaver pair at the left border and give it a TWIST. With the weaver pair and all other pairs make *whole stitches,* working the weaver pair to the right border.
4. Using the adjacent pairs from each of the two adjacent crossings from the row above, make *whole stitches* forming the crosses of the next row.

To work this ground with vertical lines, hang four pairs for each alternate column. Two are for the vertical lines and two for the crossing lines. Hang bobbin pairs in groups of two, equidistant across your top border. As above, work *whole stitches* for each crossing.

In working this ground, PIN at all intersections maintaining straight lines. Add additional diagonal pairs at your left border to complete the pattern.

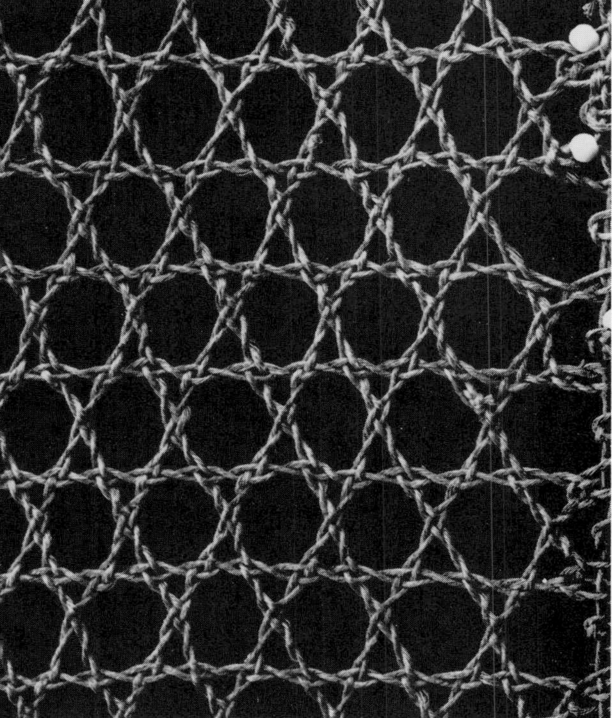

French ground: horizontal lines.

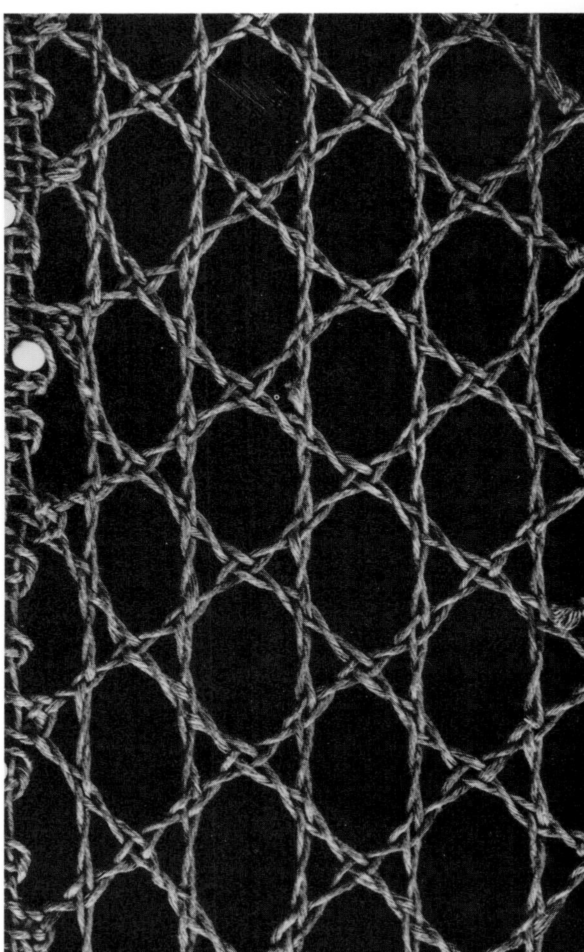

French ground: vertical lines.

A LILLE JOUR

This is a bold yet delicate ground. A checkerboard arrangement of alternating motifs forms the pattern. A dense *linen stitch* motif alternates with an open lacy motif worked as in the *Rose Ground.*

Four pairs are required for each motif of the first row. In addition, an edge pair is required at each edge, which joins the outer columns to the edge.

Working the *linen stitch* motif, mount all four pairs adjacent to each other:

1. Using the second pair as the weaver, work a *weaving ground* with these four pairs giving two TWISTS to the weaver pair at each edge. Work four rows ending with the weaver pair at the left. The twists at the end of each row can be varied to control the shape of this motif. Work alternate columns in this fashion.

Working the *Rose Ground* motif in the alternate columns, mount two pairs at the center and one pair at each outer edge of each column:

2. With the two center pairs make a *half stitch*—TWIST—*half stitch* —PIN.
3. With the two left pairs make a *half stitch*—TWIST—*half stitch*— —PIN. Do the same with the two right pairs.

Now join adjacent columns:

4. With the right outer pair from your *Rose Ground* motif and the weaver pair from the adjacent column make a *half stitch*—TWIST—*half stitch*—PIN.

Work alternate columns across row in this fashion. In all columns other than the first column, the outer pair from the *Rose Ground* motif combines with the weaver pair of the adjacent *linen stitch* motif.

Returning to the *linen stitch* motif of the first column:

5. Hang in your edge pair in line with the weaver pair. Give the edge pair one TWIST and the weaver pair two TWISTS. With these two pairs make a *half stitch*—TWIST—*half stitch.*
6. With the weaver pair work across with *linen stitches* to the right. Return the edge pair to the edge.

Joining the other side of adjacent columns:

7. With the left outer pair from the *Rose Ground* motif and the adjacent weaver make a *half stitch*—TWIST—*half stitch*—PIN.

Working the *Rose Ground* motifs again:

8. With the two left pairs make a *half stitch*—TWIST—*half stitch*—PIN. Do the same with the two right pairs.
9. With the center pairs make a *half stitch*—TWIST—*half stitch*—PIN.

This closes the first *Rose Ground* motif. The four hanging pairs will now form the alternate *weaving ground* motif in this column. The left center pair will be the weaver pair.

Returning to the *weaving ground* motif of the first column:

10. Take the weaver pair and work three rows of *linen stitches* with the weaver ending at the edge.

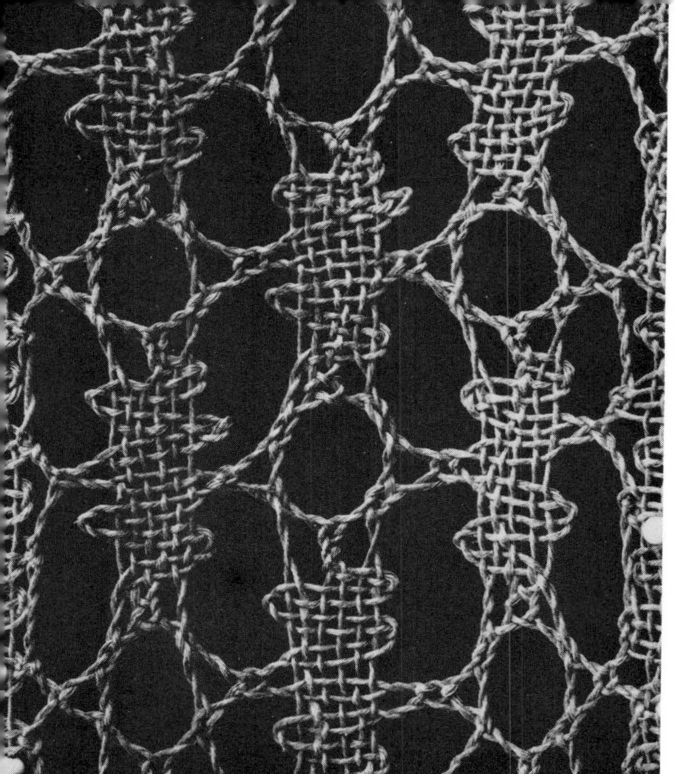

A Lille Jour ground.

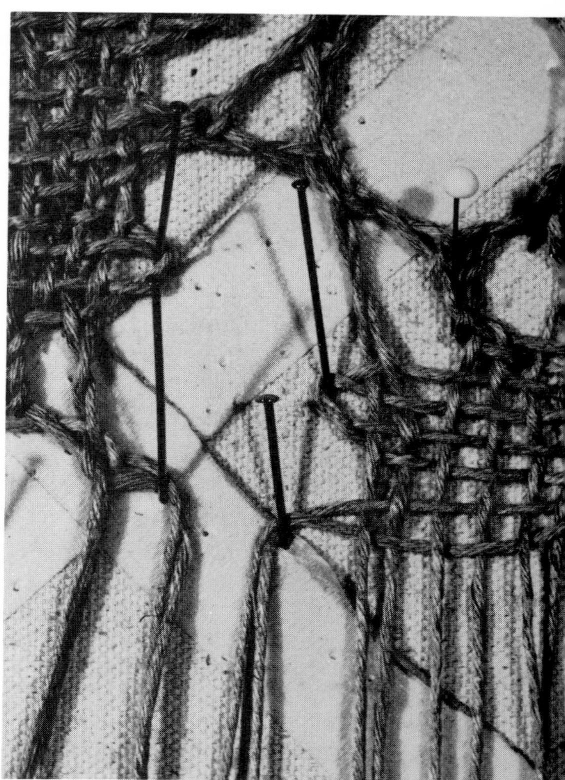

Working four rows of the linen stitch motif (step 1).

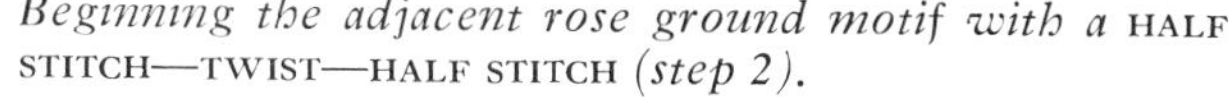

Beginning the adjacent rose ground motif with a HALF STITCH—TWIST—HALF STITCH *(step 2).*

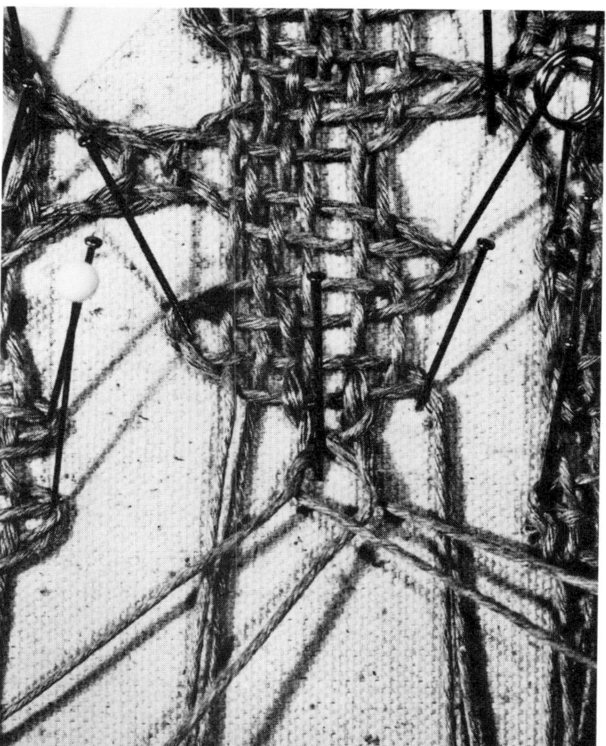

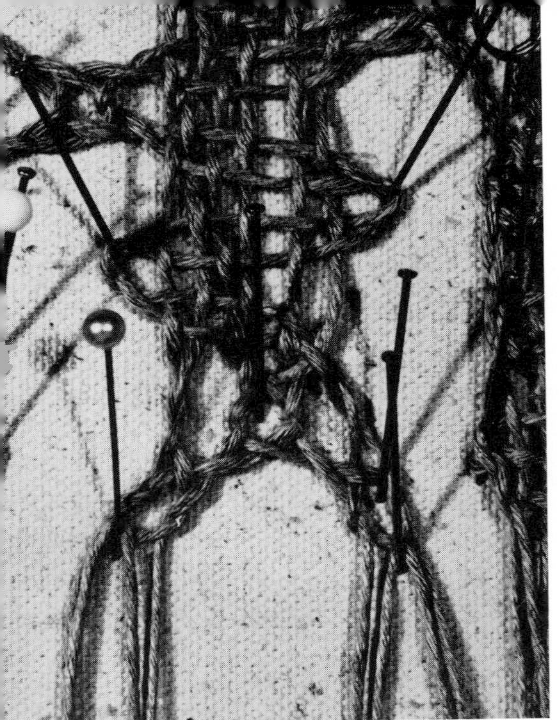

Making half stitches with the two left pairs and the two right pairs (step 3).

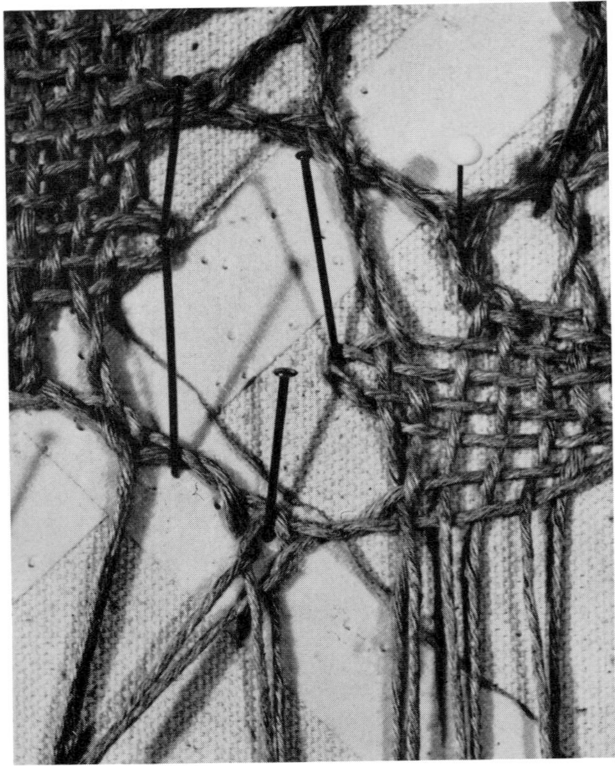

Joining the two adjacent motifs with half stitches (step 4).

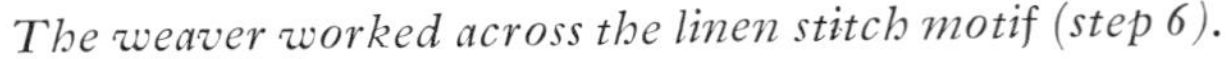

The weaver worked across the linen stitch motif (step 6).

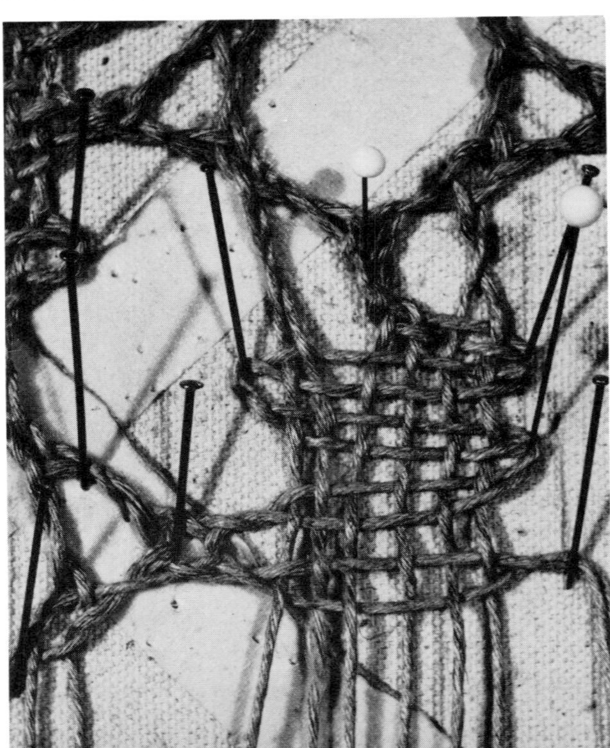

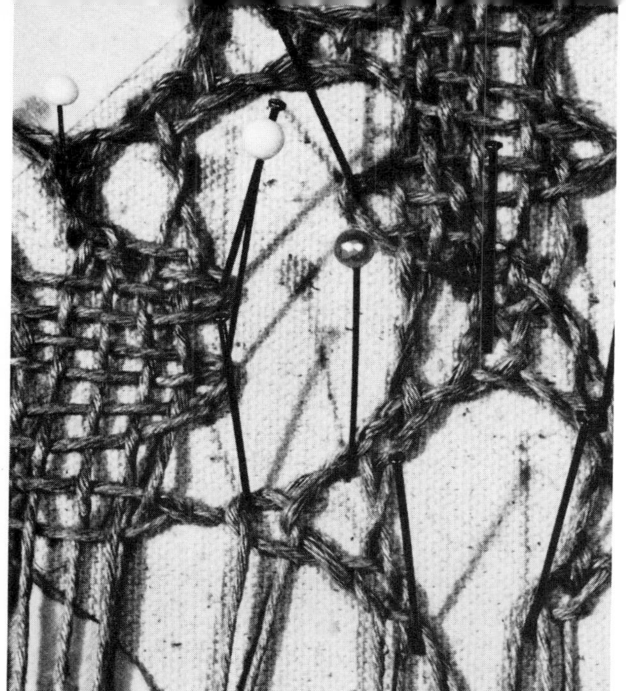

Working the two adjacent motifs or columns together with half stitches (step 7), followed by the working of the two left pairs and the two right pairs of the rose ground motif (step 8).

Half stitches worked with the two center pairs completing the rose ground motif (step 9).

Working three more rows of linen stitches completing the linen stitch motif (step 10). The first half stitch of the new rose ground motif has been made with the two center pairs.

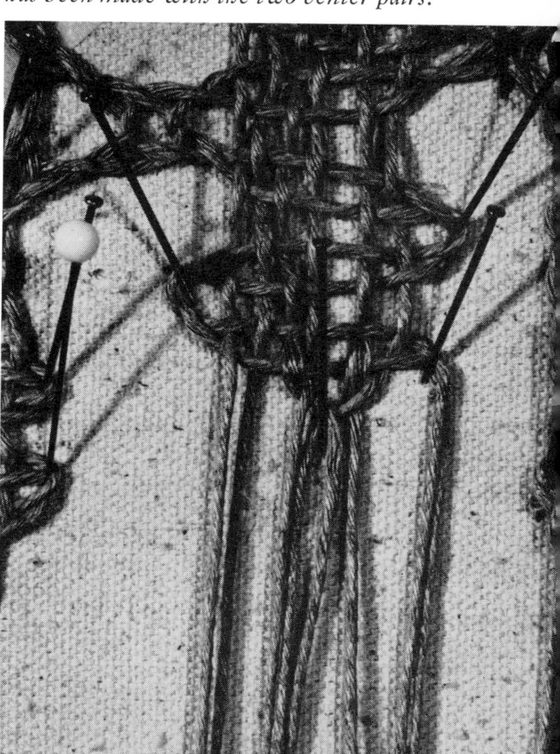

This completes the first *weaving ground* motif. The four hanging pairs will now form the alternate *Rose Ground* motif in this column. When working the *Rose Ground* motif in the first column, the edge pair joins with the left pair of this motif, joining the motif to the edge.

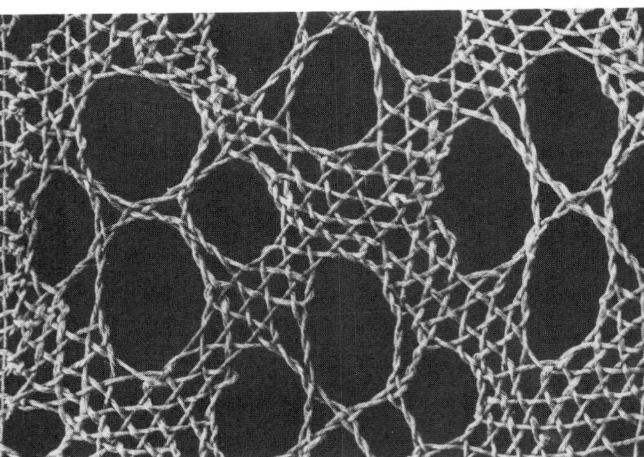

Half-stitch clover ground. Half stitches worked along the diagonal lines and interlocked forming clover-shaped openings.

Fond de Brides ground. A loosely structured ground made with random joining of twisted pairs and single threads.

A group of experimental grounds. Otto *Lange, Dresden, 1930.*

Explorations Within Grounds And Edges

Chapter 7

While any ground or edge can simply happen, following a systematic rhythm of stitches and stitch spacing, unlimited possibilities are open in terms of explorations within the rhythm of a ground or edge.

GROUNDS

The *weaving ground* that is traditionally used for dense areas and narrow tapes can be used as the basis for many stitch combinations, which cannot only provide design elements within the ground framework, but can change the basic density of the ground. While the following techniques demonstrate several methods illustrating this approach, any of them repeated in some sequence can become a new ground in itself.

A weaving ground study worked in two colors. By the author.

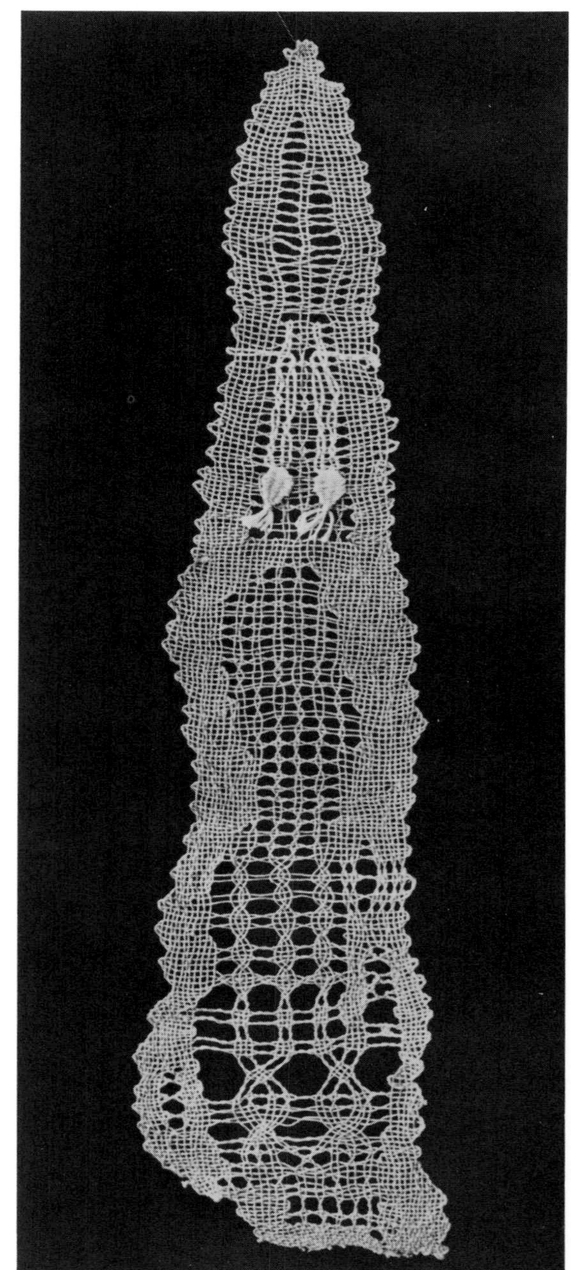

A hanging based on explorations of the weaving ground. By the author.

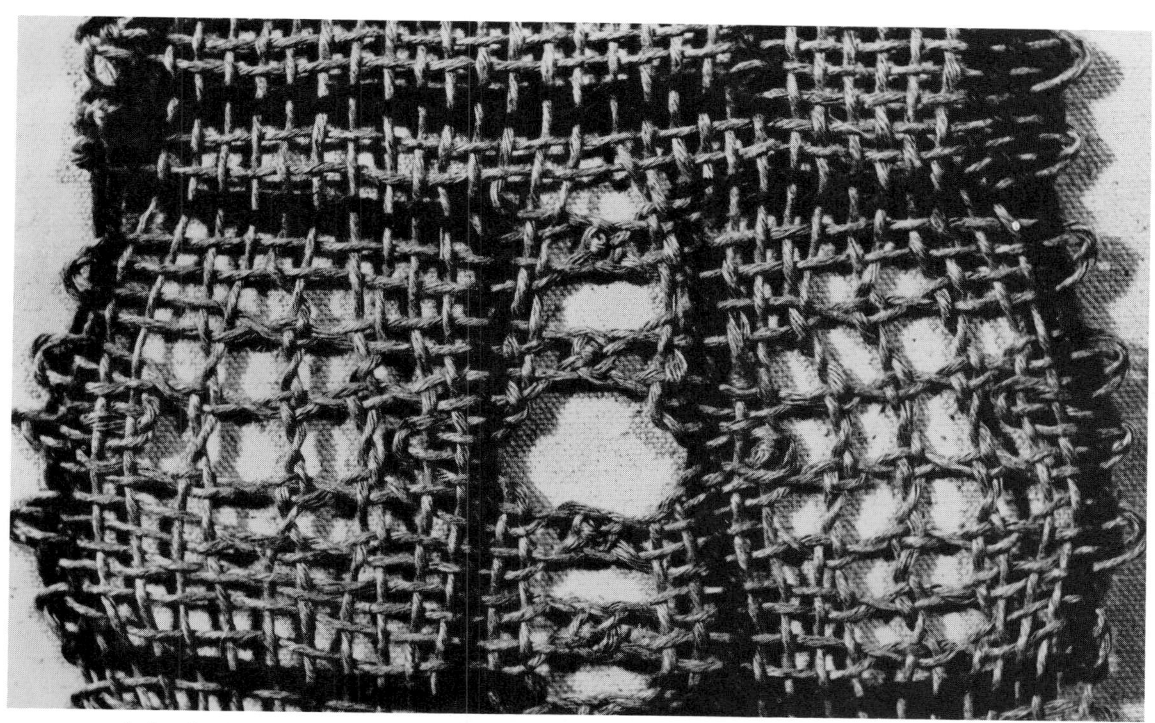

A detail of openings within a ground. Note the design formed by the exchanging of weaver and hanging threads.

Exchanging Weaver and Hanging Threads

By using contrasting threads, designs can be formed by simply manipulating the course of the contrasting threads within the ground. Threads can work vertically down or horizontally in either direction. These manipulations can be made with any pair of threads or any single thread.

1. To exchange a weaver pair and a hanging pair: Make your normal *linen stitch*, then lay down your weaver pair and pick up the hanging pair used in this stitch and use it as the new weaver. Two pins are generally required, one to the side of each hanging thread where it changes direction. After weaving two or three additional rows, the pins can be removed. It should be noted that the exchanged hanging pair will work in the same direction as the old weaver pair. This procedure is an excellent method for exchanging pairs when the threads on one of the pairs run short.

2. To exchange a weaver thread and a hanging thread: Make your normal *linen stitch*, then lay down the weaver thread that is to be exchanged and pick up one of the hanging threads to be used as the new weaver thread. If the hanging thread lies on top of the weaver, lay the weaver thread back over this thread. If the hanging thread lies under the weaver, simply drop the weaver.

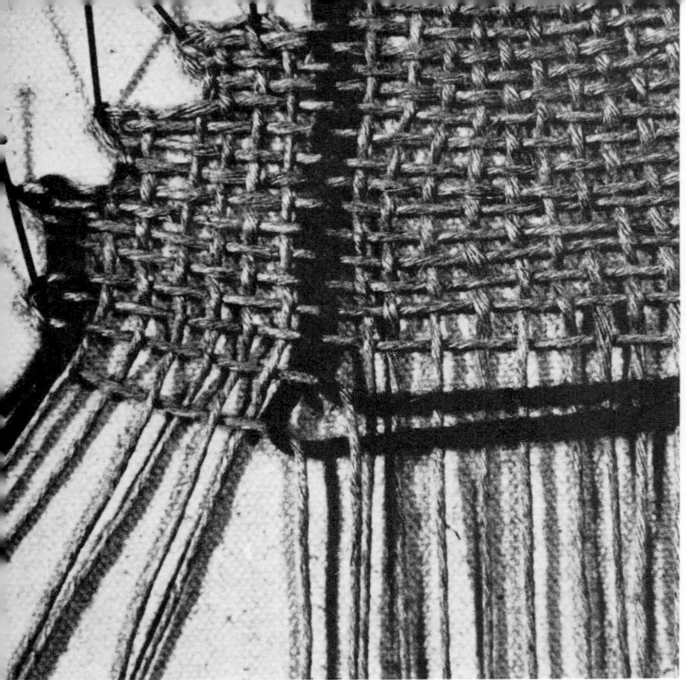

Exchanging a weaver pair and a hanging pair.

Changing the direction of contrasting color threads by exchanging hanging pair with weaver pair.

Opening the Ground

To change the density within a ground without obvious distortions, certain bobbin pairs must be removed or relocated.

1. A horizontal weaver can be eliminated by returning the weaver when it reaches the area to be opened up. Periodically, of course, the

Opening a ground by working the weaver to the outer edge and leaving it as a hanging pair. The next inner hanging pair is used as the new weaver.

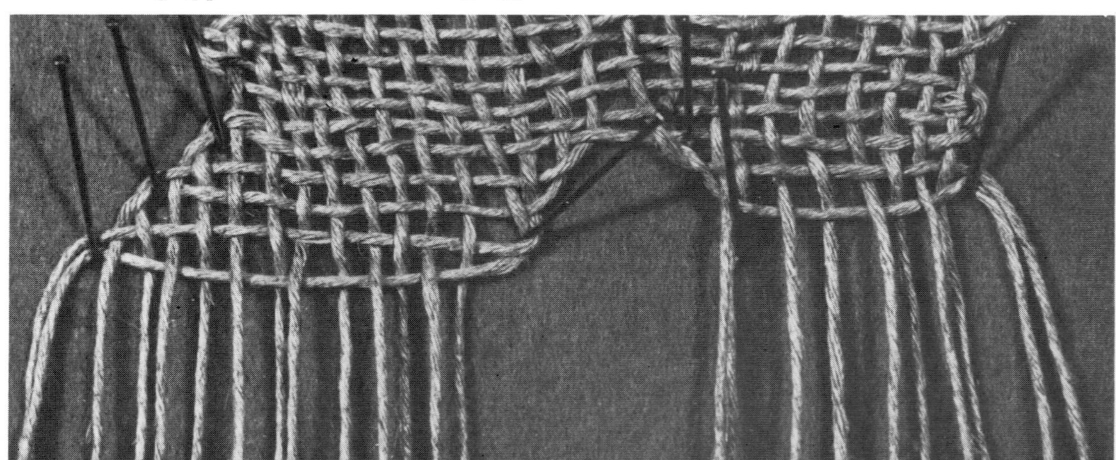

weaver should run through to the opposite edge to tie the work together.

2. A hanging pair can be eliminated by giving it a TWIST and then weaving it out to the edge as a weaver. This can then be left as a hanging pair or it can return again as the weaver. If inner hanging pairs are continuously woven to the outside, the ground will open up at a 45° angle.

Twisting Pairs

With the ground opened up, the remaining threads can be manipulated by TWISTS to create patterns and secure the threads in position. Some combinations are:

1. TWISTING the weaver pair while keeping hanging pairs plain: This can be done every row or can form a rhythm by alternating with plain weavers.

2. TWISTING hanging pairs while keeping weavers plain: As above, the TWISTED pairs can alternate with plain pairs.

3. TWISTING weaver pairs and hanging pairs: If TWISTS are made after every stitch, the result will be very much like the *whole-stitch ground* but with all lines running vertically and horizontally rather than diagonally. By alternating twisted pairs with plain pairs, unlimited patterns can be designed. Varying the number of TWISTS between stitches can be used as a technique for opening the ground.

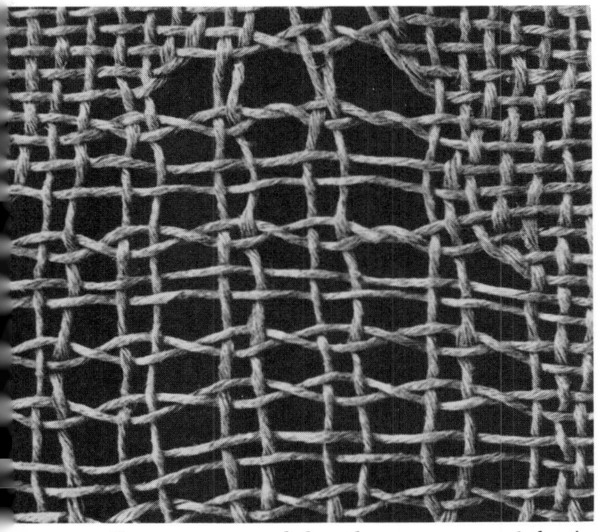

Patterns created by the TWISTING *of horizontal threads.*

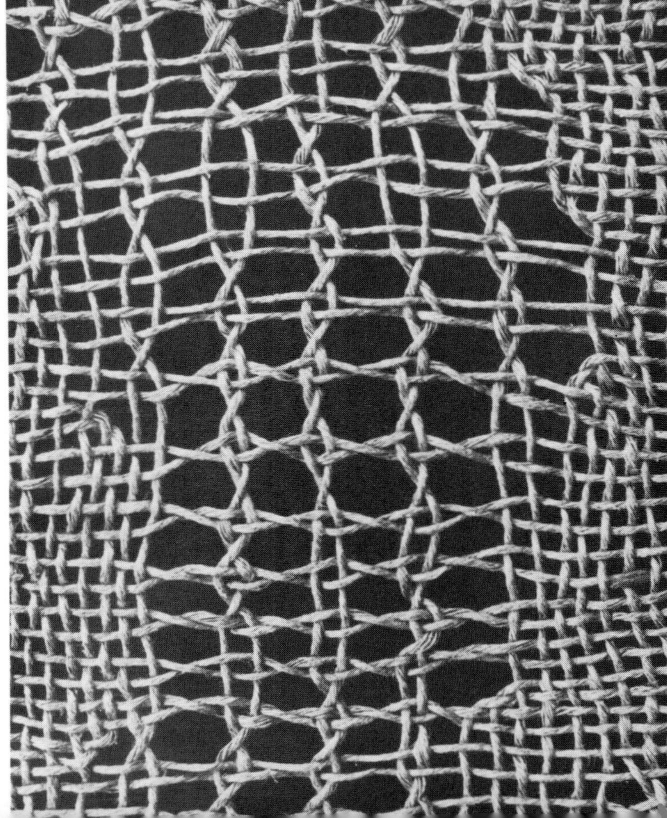

Patterns created by the TWISTING *of both vertical and horizontal threads.*

The TWISTING *of vertical threads to open up a ground.*

The TWISTING *of horizontal threads to open up a ground.*

Pair Groupings

Two pairs of hanging or weaver threads can be worked together as a unit to form "spot" motifs.

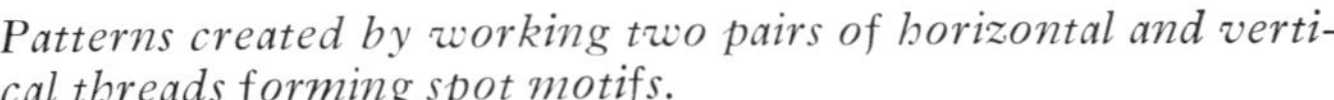

Patterns created by working two pairs of horizontal and vertical threads forming spot motifs.

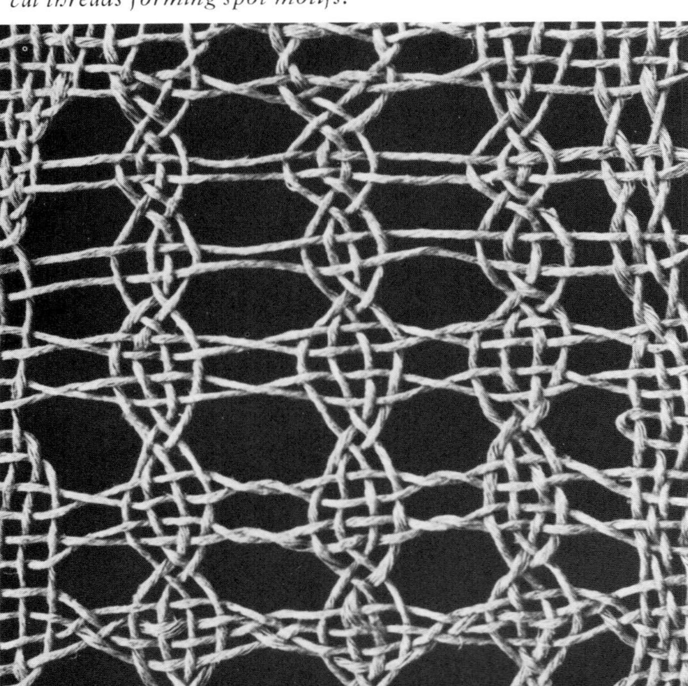

1. Working two hanging pairs: Work two adjacent hanging pairs with a *linen stitch*. This can be followed by one or more rows of horizontal weavers and then followed by another *linen stitch* with the original two hanging pairs. For a variation the weavers can be TWISTED between groups.

2. Working two weaver pairs: Take one of the hanging pairs and work it into your opening as a second weaver pair. With the two weaver pairs make a *linen stitch*, working horizontally. Follow with *linen stitches* with one or more groups of hanging pairs, and then follow with another *linen stitch* with the two weaver pairs.

Blocks

Patterns of dense blocks can be worked by separating groups of *linen stitches* with TWISTED pairs.

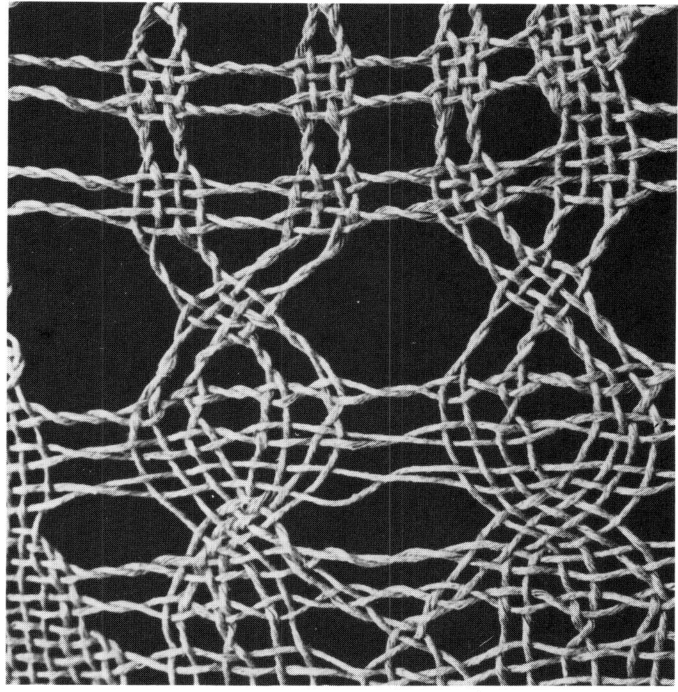

Block motifs formed by separating groups of linen stitches with TWISTED *pairs.*

1. Square blocks: For a uniform checkerboard pattern, use as many weaver pairs as hanging pairs in forming the block. Give all pairs a uniform number of TWISTS between the blocks. Blocks are worked with *linen stitches* with all crossing pairs.

2. Diamond blocks: Diamond-shaped blocks are worked without weaver pairs. Two groups of hanging pairs are crossed by *linen stitches* and the groups in turn are separated by TWISTS in all pairs. This stitch or pattern is worked in the same manner as the upper half of the "Spider" described in Chapter 5. This technique can be used as a tool to explore other shapes. It can be used with or without TWISTS.

Holes

Holes or small openings can be formed within a weaving ground without distorting the weave.

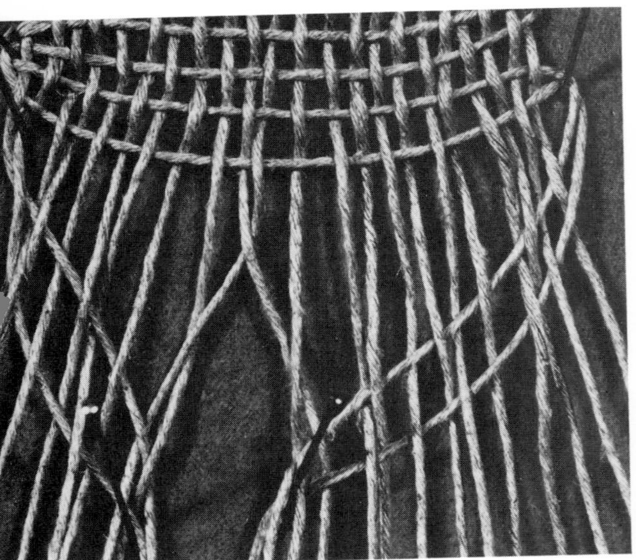

A hole formed by making CROSS—TWIST *motions with two adjacent hanging pairs. Two weavers are formed that work from opposite sides to the opening.*

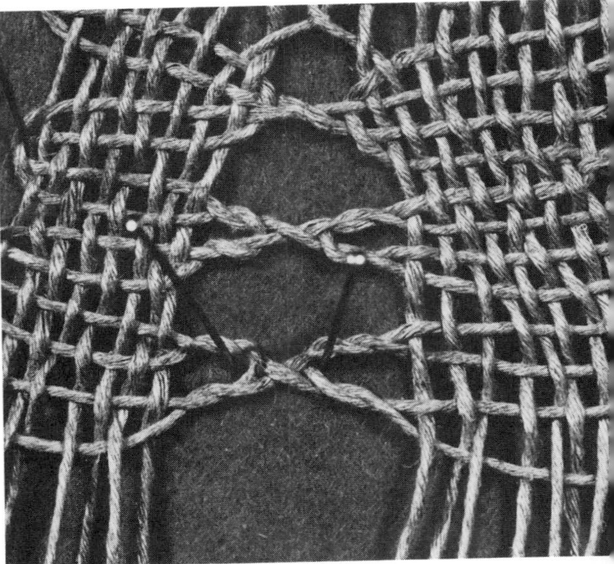

A half stitch is made with the two weavers and then they are returned in opposite directions to the ground.

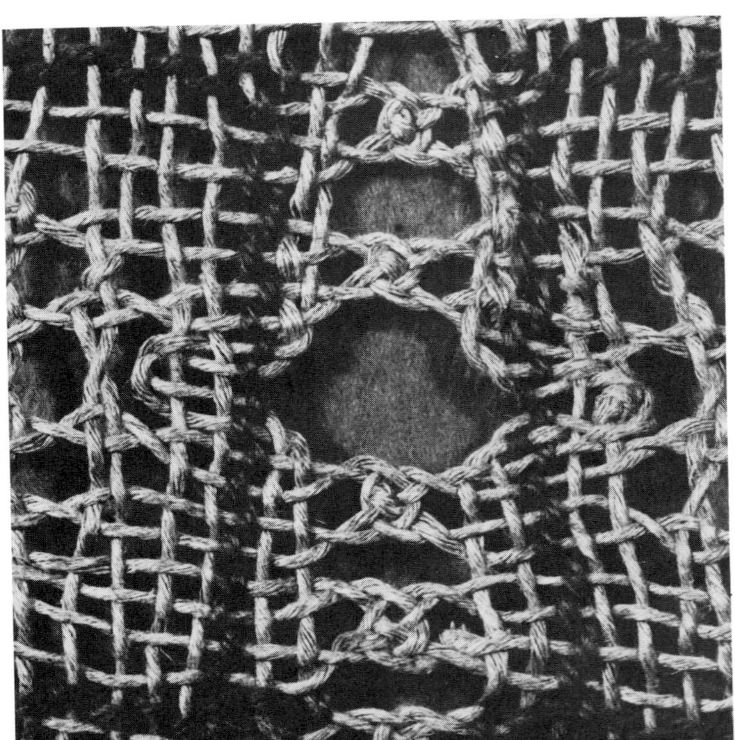

A pattern of holes made by linen stitch crossings of two weaver pairs.

1. *Half-stitch* crossing: Working with two adjacent hanging pairs, make a CROSS followed by a TWIST. Create an additional weaver pair that will enter from the side opposite that of the regular ground weaver. Weave both weaver pairs to the hole, making *linen stitches* with all hanging pairs including the TWISTED pairs. Where the two weavers come together, at the opening, make a *half stitch* (CROSS—TWIST) and work the new formed weaver pairs back out.

2. *Linen-stitch* crossing: Two weaver pairs are again used as above. Weave both weaver pairs to the hole and then give each pair a TWIST followed by a *linen stitch* and then PIN in place. Make another *linen stitch*, give each pair a TWIST, and return the weavers back out. For a neat stitch pull tightly around the pin.

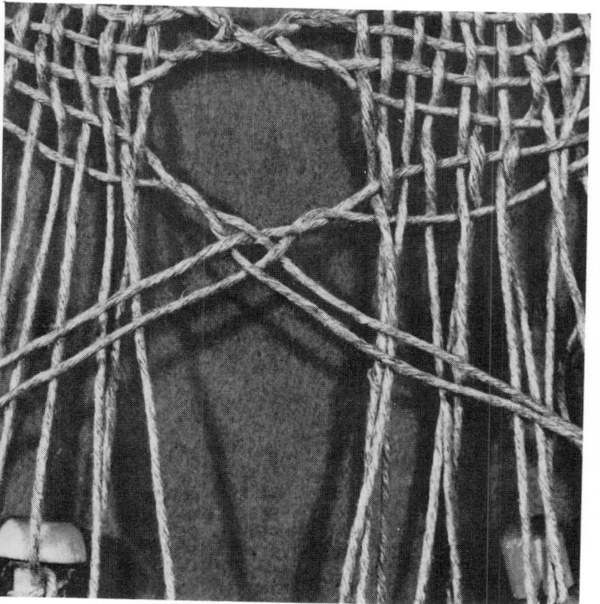

A linen stitch is made with the two weaver pairs at the opening.

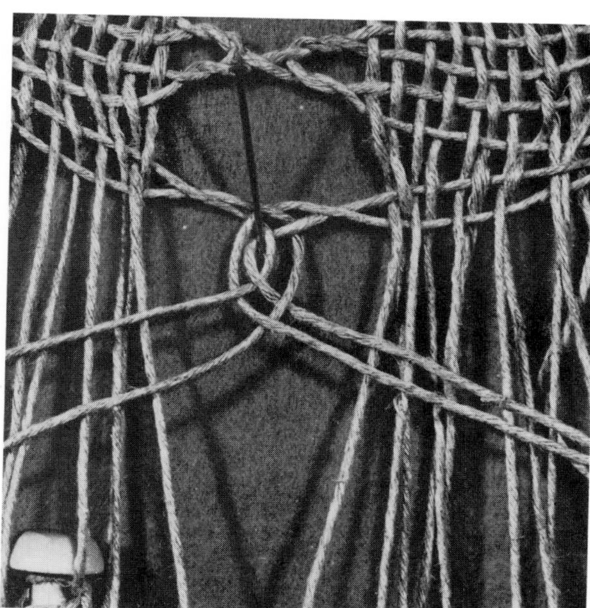

A pin is placed and another linen stitch is made.

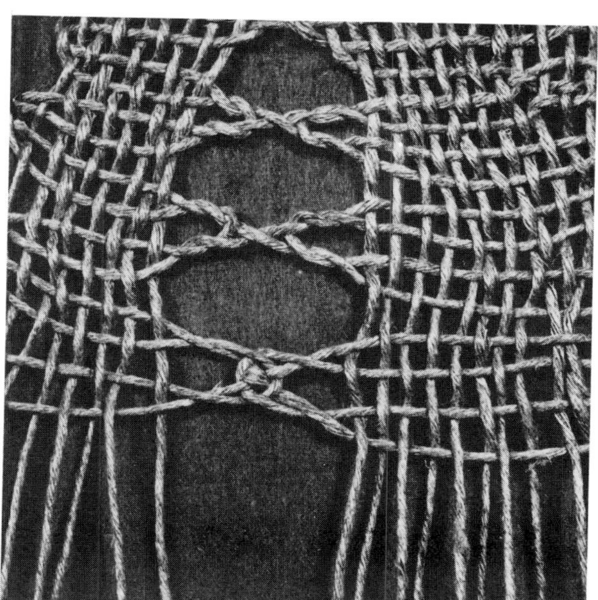

The stitch is pulled tight and the weavers are returned in opposite directions to the ground.

Detail of a traditionally executed lace collar showing the use of holes as a design element. Author's collection.

EDGES

The finished edge of a piece of bobbin lace has always been given special consideration. Whether straight, scalloped, or fringed, many stitch combinations can be used to explore the finishing of an edge.

All edges demonstrated in this section are formed outside of a *weaving ground*. The weaver pair will be referred to as the borrowed pair from this ground, which will be used in working an edge. An edge, of course, can be formed outside of any ground. When working other grounds, the borrowed pair will be from the last stitch of any row. Many edges are formed with this borrowed pair by itself. Other edges require additional edge pairs. These extra pairs are pinned out from your ground edge where they become joined to your weaver.

The edges demonstrated are in no way meant to be conclusive. Though some are shown primarily for detail, others are shown to illustrate some of the many combinations of motions of which bobbin pairs are capable.

Different cords, in terms of color and/or texture, where extra pairs are required, can be used for special design effects in working these edges. They will all also make clear the path the various pairs take as they weave in and out of your ground.

A decorative edge worked as part of a collar design. By the author.

Loop Edge

This edge is formed with the weaver pair and one extra pair. The extra pair is pinned approximately one twist length out from your ground edge.

1. Give the weaver pair a TWIST, then make a *whole stitch* with the extra pair.
2. Give the weaver pair three or more TWISTS, loop back, and make another *whole stitch* with the extra pair.
3. Give the weaver pair a final TWIST, and then rejoin it with the ground to form the next row.

Extra TWISTS can be added to the weaver or extra pair to control loop size and spacing.

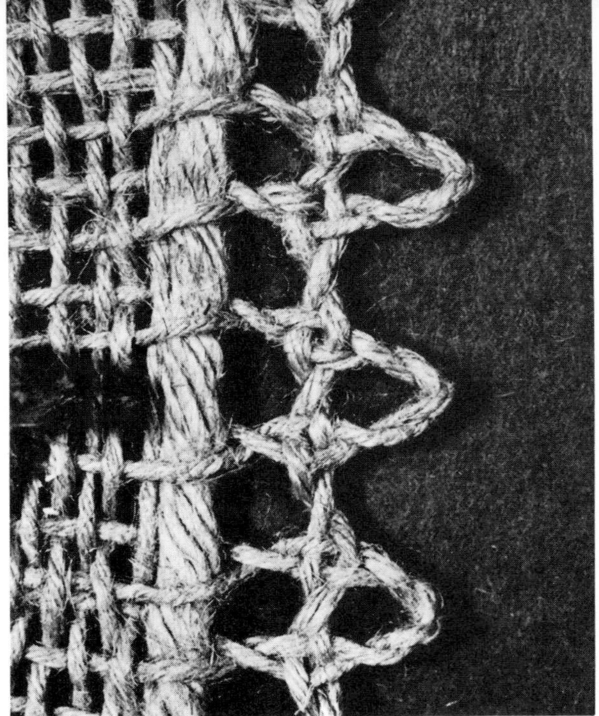

Loop edge; formed with one extra pair and the weaver pair.

Fringe Edge

This edge is the same as the loop edge except that additional TWISTS are given to the weaver pair after it crosses the extra pair. For uniformity, PIN the loops at their extremity. When the pin is removed, this loop will generally twist on itself forming a single fringe element.

Fringe edge.

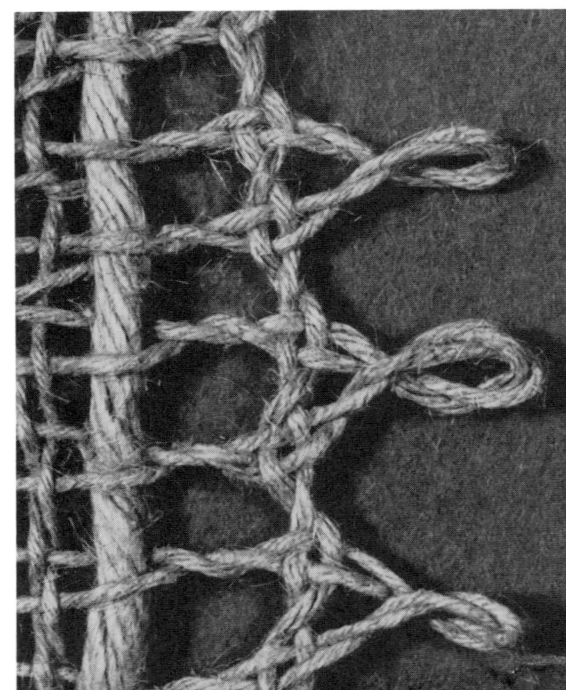

Spot Edge

PIN an extra pair adjacent to your ground as for the loop edge.

1. Give the weaver pair a TWIST, then make a *linen stitch* with the extra pair.
2. Give the weaver pair another TWIST and make another *linen stitch* with the extra pair.
3. Give the weaver pair one more TWIST and work back into the ground.

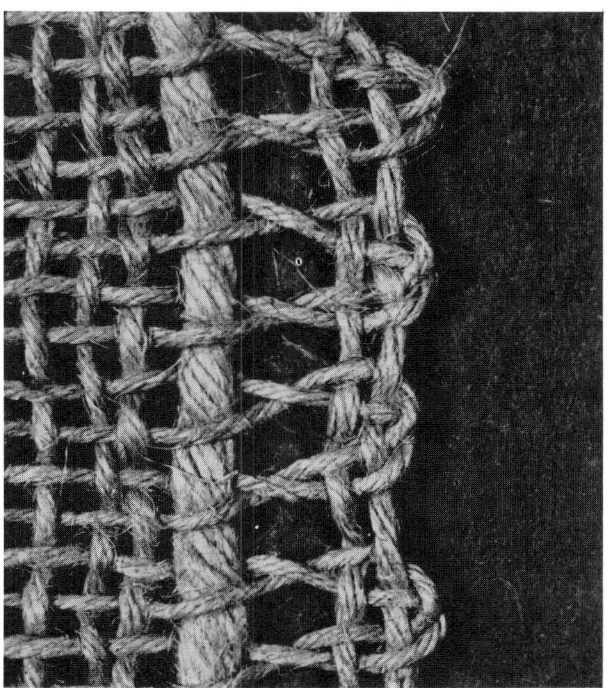

Spot edge; formed with one extra pair and the weaver pair.

Picot Edge

The picot can be formed as part of the ground edge or spaced out by using an extra edge pair as shown.

1. Give the weaver pair a TWIST, then make a *linen stitch* with the extra pair.
2. Make a picot with the weaver pair (see Chapter 5).
3. Make another *linen stitch* with the two pairs, being sure to pull the picot into place.
4. Give a TWIST to the weaver pair and work it back into the next row of the ground.

To make a picot directly against the edge of a ground, simply form a picot with the weaver pair after the last stitch of each row.

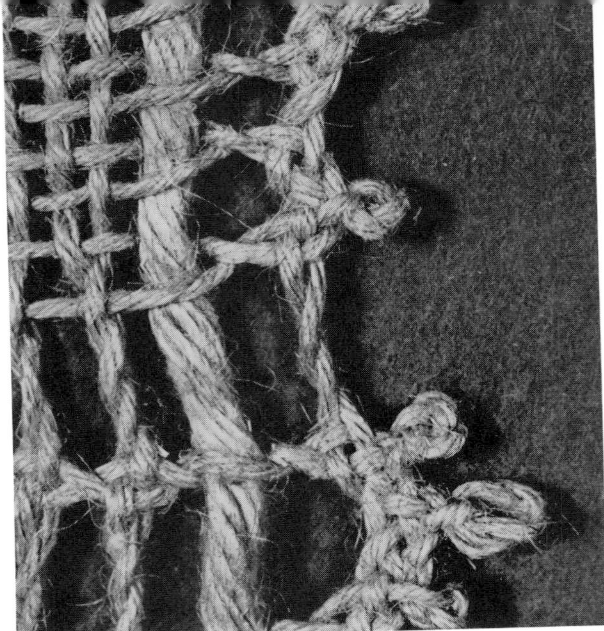

Single picot edge and triple picot edge.

Triple Picot Edge

Again working with an extra pair.

1. Make a single picot, as in the *picot edge*, with the weaver pair.
2. With the weaver pair and extra pair make a *linen stitch.*
3. With the extra pair make another picot, giving it one or two extra TWISTS for a larger loop.
4. With the two pairs make another *linen stitch.*
5. With the weaver pair make a final picot.
6. With the two pairs make another *linen stitch*, followed by a TWIST with the weaver pair before returning it to the ground.

This edge detail takes up a wider spacing than a normal ground row. To make up this distance in the ground, the hanging pairs can be given TWISTS or the weaver pair can weave an extra row between the edge picots.

Completion of the first picot of the triple picot edge. The picot is made with the weaver pair.

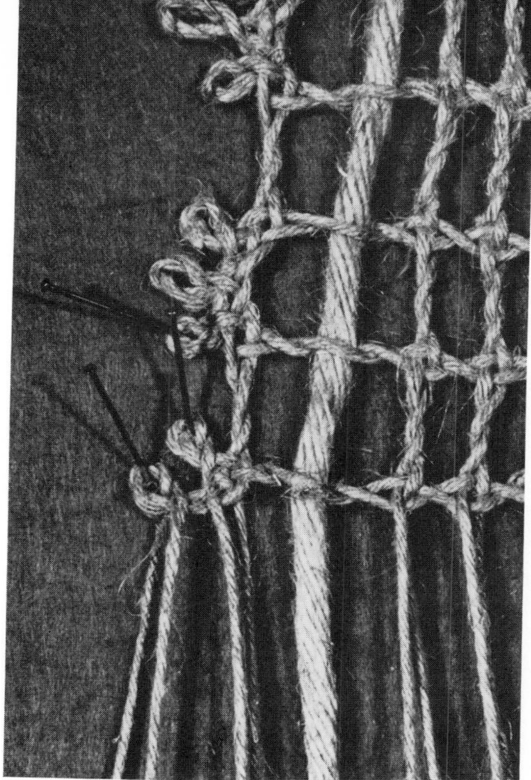

A linen stitch is made with the weaver pair and the edge pair. The second picot is then made with the edge pair.

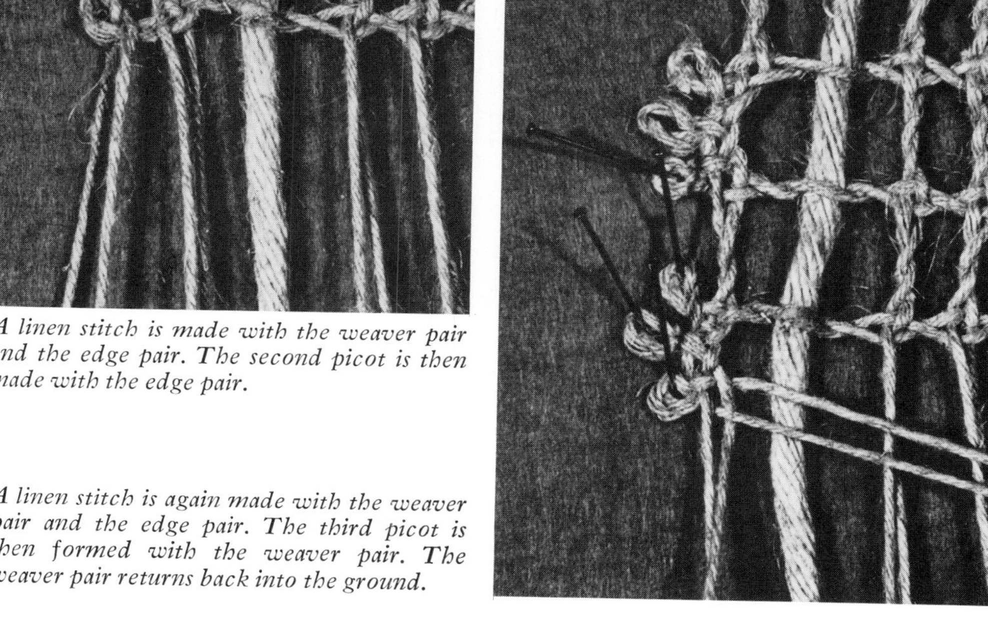

A linen stitch is again made with the weaver pair and the edge pair. The third picot is then formed with the weaver pair. The weaver pair returns back into the ground.

Alternate Weaver Loop

This is one of several edge details where the weaver pair alternates with an extra pair. Contrasting color cords are very effective when working these edges.

Two extra pairs are used to create a double loop with large open areas. PIN these pairs the distance of two TWISTS apart and the same distance from the ground edge. The outer extra pair interchanges with the normal weaver pair at each row.

1. Give the weaver pair two TWISTS and make a *whole stitch* with the inner extra pair.
2. Give the weaver pair two more TWISTS and make a *whole stitch* with the outer extra pair.
3. Give the outer extra pair (now the weaver pair) two TWISTS and make a *whole stitch* with the inner extra pair.
4. Give the weaver pair two TWISTS, returning it to the ground.
5. The outer hanging pair (the former weaver pair) is now given two TWISTS and is ready to form the next edge stitch. For a scalloped edge, give this pair extra TWISTS, letting it loop out, before making the next *whole stitch*.

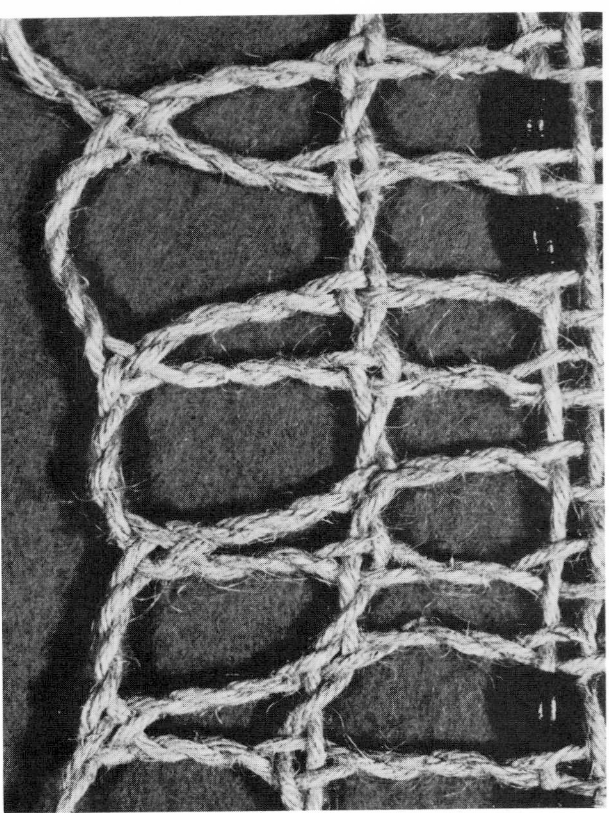

Alternate weaver loop: formed with two extra pairs and the weaver pair.

The weaver pair and inner pair are crossed (step 1).

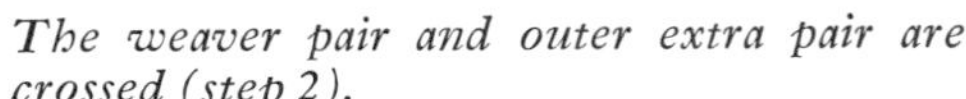

The weaver pair and outer extra pair are crossed (step 2).

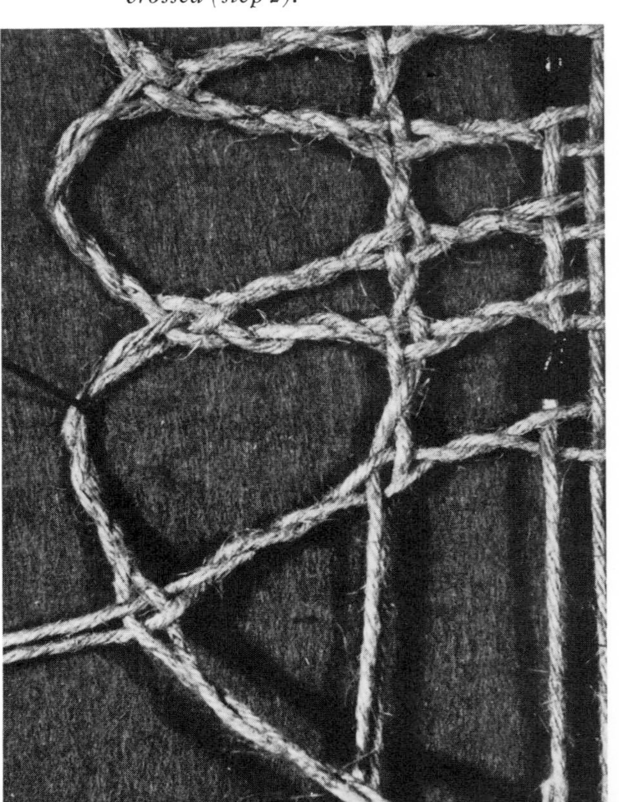

The outer extra pair (the new weaver) and inner extra pair are crossed (step 3). The new weaver returns to the ground.

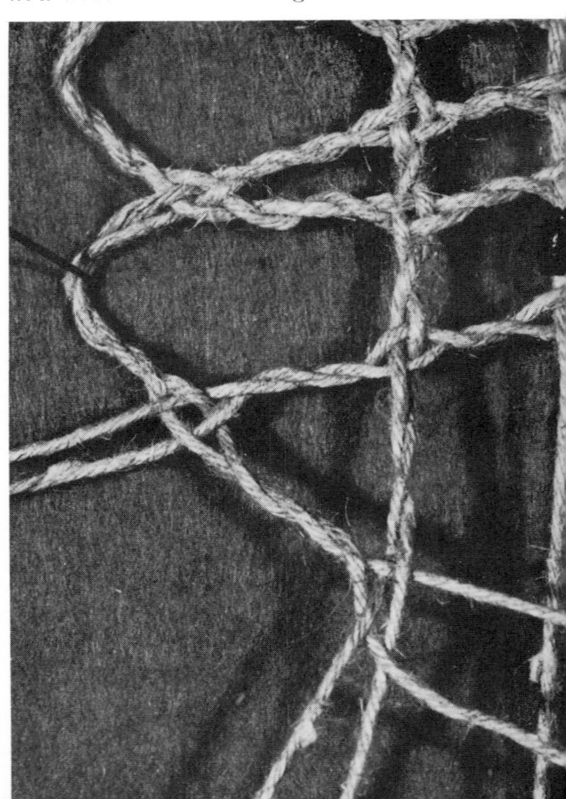

Alternate Weaver Gothic

Two extra pairs are again used and pinned as in the *alternate weaver loop*. The two extra pairs and the weaver pair interchange, forming Gothic archlike loops.

1. Give the inner extra pair two TWISTS and the outer extra pair three TWISTS. Make a *whole stitch* with these two pairs and PIN at the outer edge.
2. Give the outer extra pair three TWISTS and the inner extra pair two TWISTS. Give the weaver pair two TWISTS.
3. With the weaver pair and the inner pair make a *whole stitch* followed by two TWISTS with both pairs.
4. Work the inner pair back into the ground as the new weaver pair.
5. With the inner pair (the former weaver pair) and the outer pair make a *whole stitch*, repeating step 1.

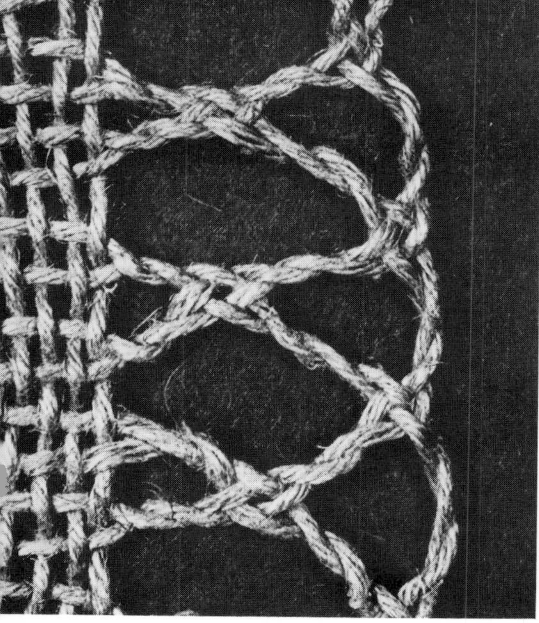

Alternate weaver Gothic: formed with two extra pairs and the weaver pair.

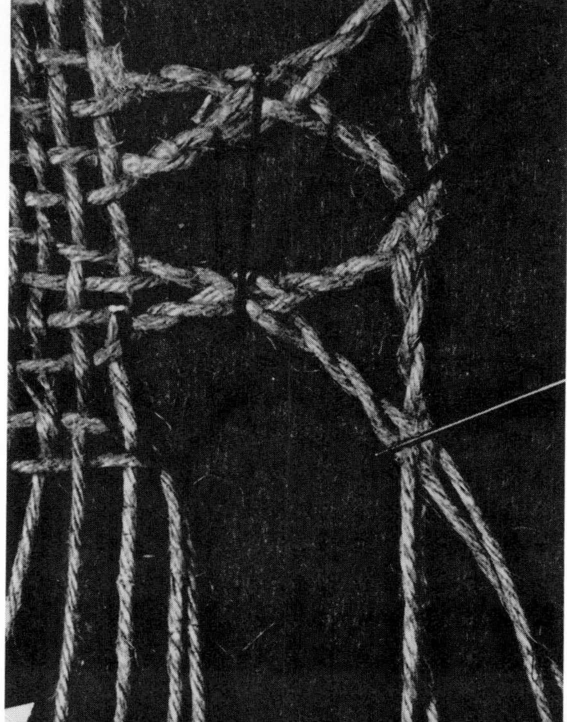

The inner extra pair and the outer extra pair are crossed (step 1).

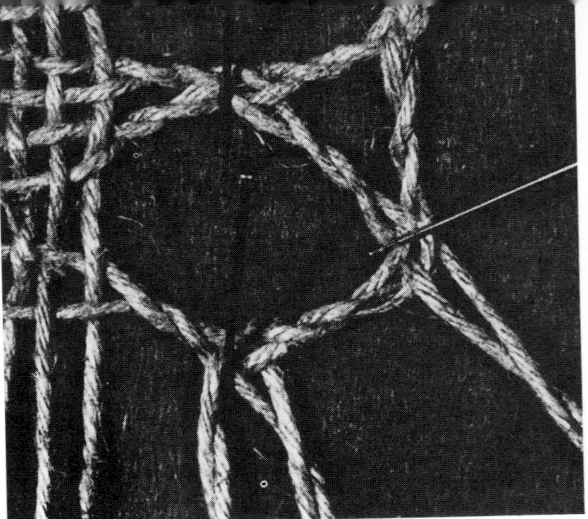

The weaver pair and the new inner pair are crossed (step 3).

The inner pair is worked back into the ground as the new weaver (step 4).

Gothic Heart

Work as in the *alternate weaver Gothic* with two extra pairs.

1. Give two TWISTS to the inner extra pair and three TWISTS to the outer extra pair. Make a *whole stitch* and PIN at the outer edge.
2. With the weaver pair from the ground, make an edge picot and return the weaver pair back into the ground.
3. In the following row, where the weaver pair returns, bring it out and work into the edge as in the *alternate weaver Gothic.*

Gothic heart: the alternate weaver Gothic combined with a picot.

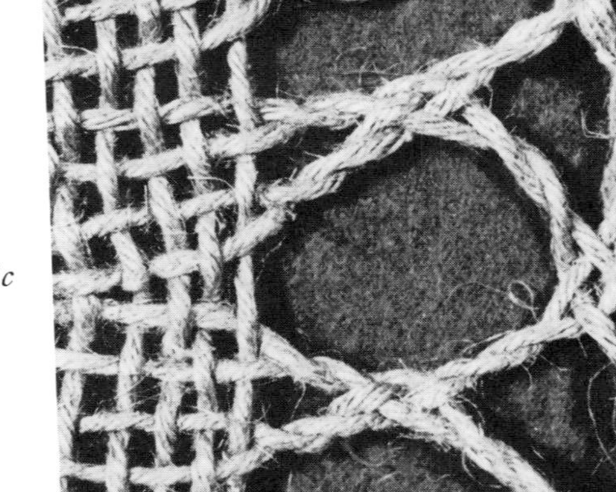

Crossed Loop

This edge requires three extra pairs. Two of these pairs together with the weaver will interchange. PIN the extra pairs next to the ground edge. PIN two of these pairs on one pin two twists out from the ground and PIN the third pair three twists out from these pairs.

1. Give the outer extra pair four TWISTS and one of the inner extra pairs two TWISTS. Make a *whole stitch* with these pairs followed by four TWISTS with the outer pair and two TWISTS with the inner pair.
2. Give the weaver pair two TWISTS, and the unused extra pair one TWIST. Make a *linen stitch* with these two pairs.
3. With the center two pairs make a *linen stitch.*
4. With the inner pairs make a *linen stitch.*
5. Give the inner pairs two TWISTS and work into the ground as the new weaver pair.

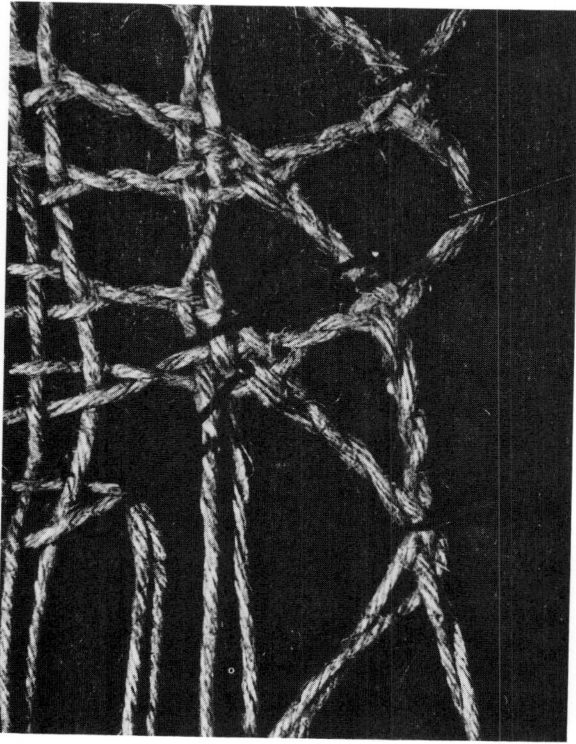

Crossed loop: formed with three extra pairs and the weaver pair. The outer extra pair and the adjacent inner extra pair are crossed (step 1).

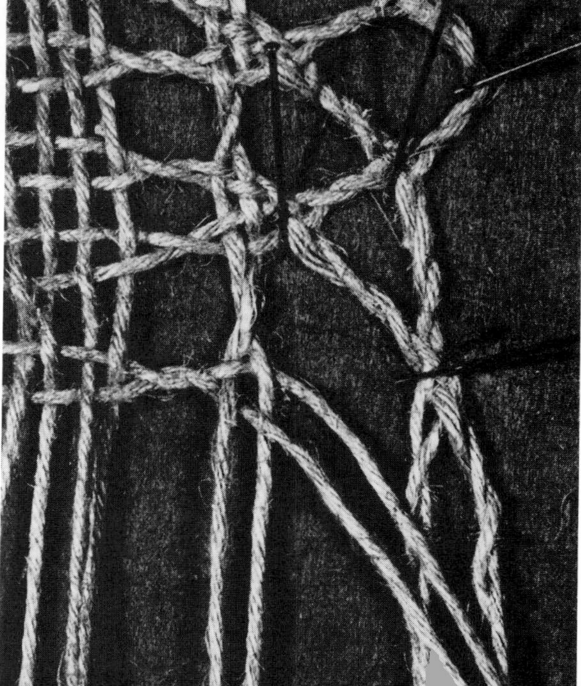

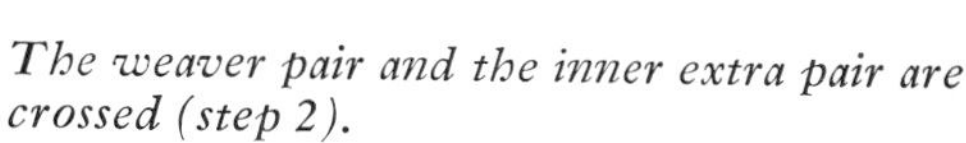

The weaver pair and the inner extra pair are crossed (step 2).

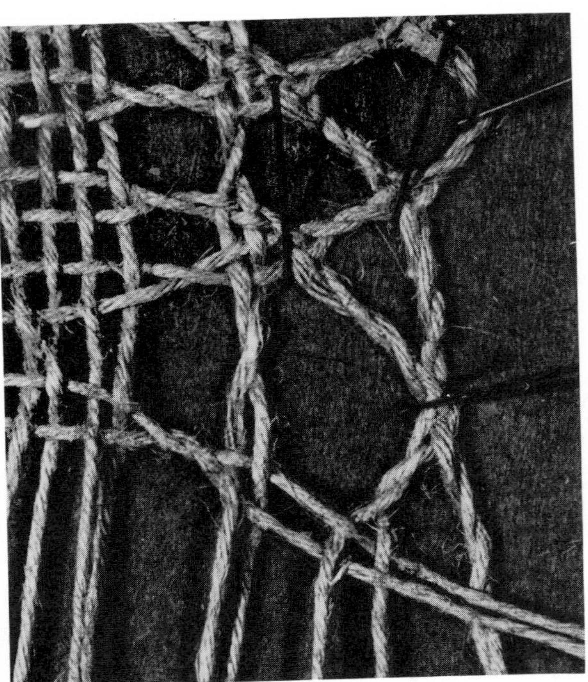

The center two pairs are crossed (step 3).

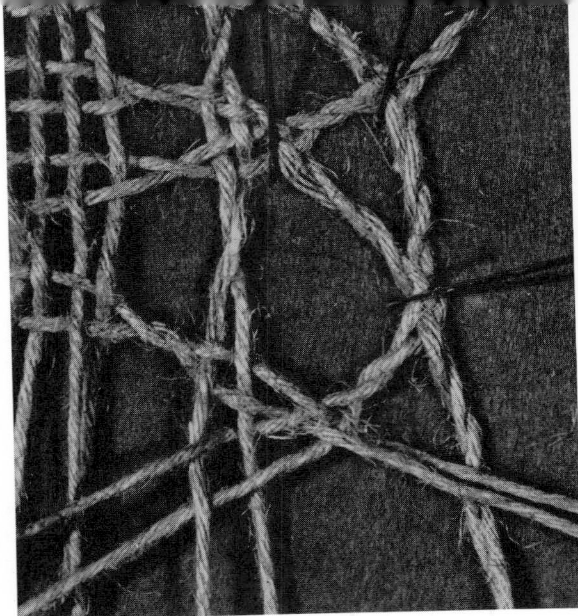

The two inner pairs are crossed (step 4).

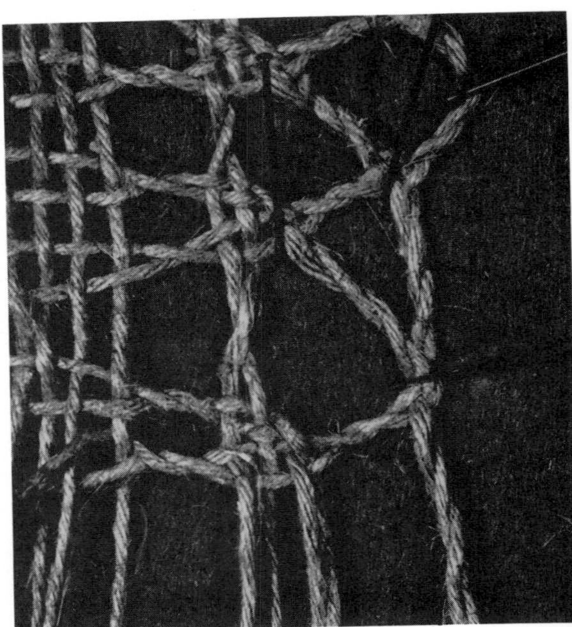

The inner pair is worked into the ground as the new weaver (step 5).

Double Loop

This edge requires two extra pairs. Both these pairs, together with the weaver, will interchange. PIN one extra pair adjacent to the ground edge and the other extra pair two twists away.

1. Give the outer extra pair six TWISTS and the inner extra pair two TWISTS. Make a *whole stitch* with these two pairs.
2. Give the inner pair two TWISTS. With this pair and the weaver pair make a *linen stitch*. The weaver pair now becomes the inner pair and the inner pair becomes the weaver.
3. Work the new weaver pair back into the ground.

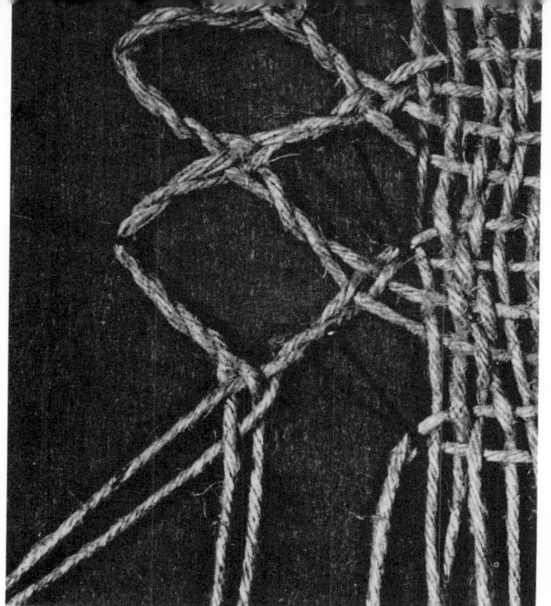

Double loop edge: formed with two extra pairs and the weaver pair. The outer extra pair and the inner extra pair are crossed (step 1).

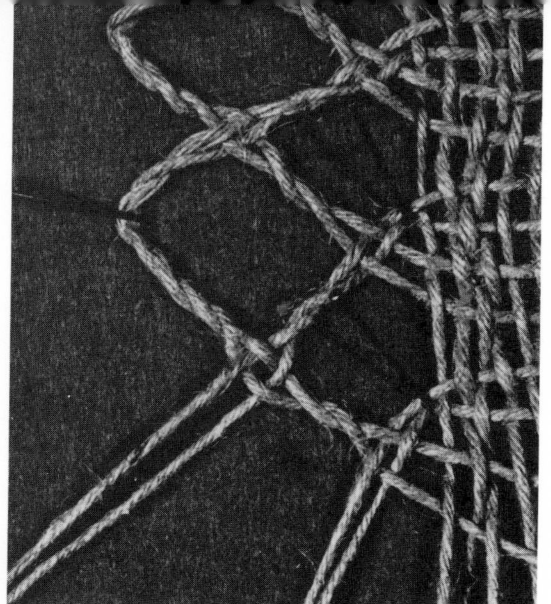

The inner pair and the weaver pair are crossed (step 2). The new weaver is worked back into the work.

Single Loop

One extra pair is required. PIN this pair adjacent to the ground edge. This pair and the weaver pair will interchange.

1. With the weaver pair and the extra pair make a *linen stitch.*
2. Return the weaver pair into the next row of the ground.
3. Give the extra pair six TWISTS.
4. Take the weaver pair from the following row of the ground, and with the extra pair make a *linen stitch.* The weaver pair now becomes the extra pair and the extra pair becomes the weaver returning into the ground.

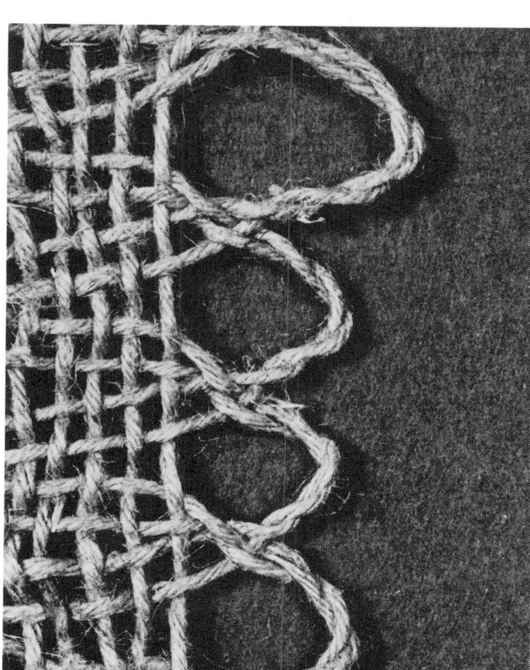

Single loop: formed with one extra pair.

Braided Loop

The *braided loop* gives a firm hard edge. The basic loop requires one extra bobbin pair that is pinned adjacent to the ground edge.

1. With the weaver pair and the extra pair, make a *braid* to any distance out from the ground edge.
2. Form one or more picots with the outer pair of your *braid.*
3. Continue the *braid* working back to the ground edge.
4. Let one pair return into the ground as the weaver pair. Join the other pair with the weaver pair from the following row for the next loop.

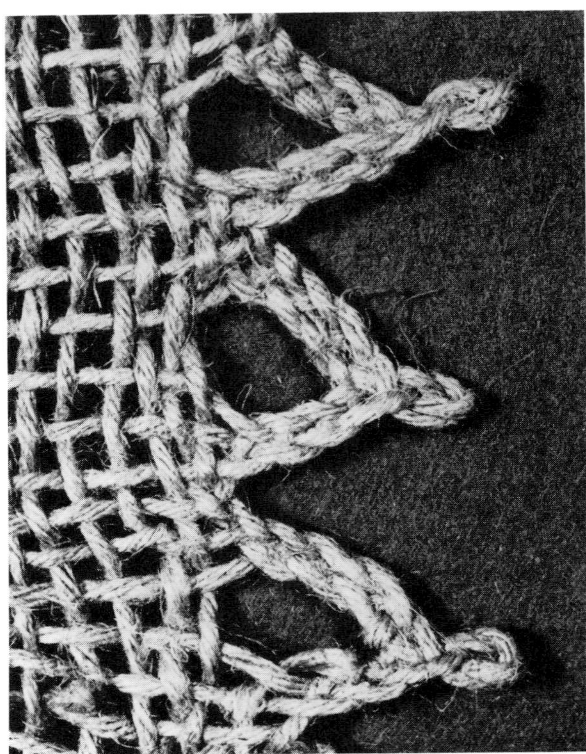

Braided loop: formed with one extra pair.

Cut Fringe

This fringe permits use of contrasting threads. One extra pair is required that forms the entire fringe. For a heavier fringe, multiple threads can be used for this extra pair. PIN the extra pair adjacent to the ground edge.

1. With the extra pair and the weaver pair make two *whole stitches.*
2. PIN the extra pair any distance out from the ground edge, the distance determining the length of the fringe.
3. Return the extra pair back to the ground edge. With this pair and the weaver pair make two *whole stitches.*

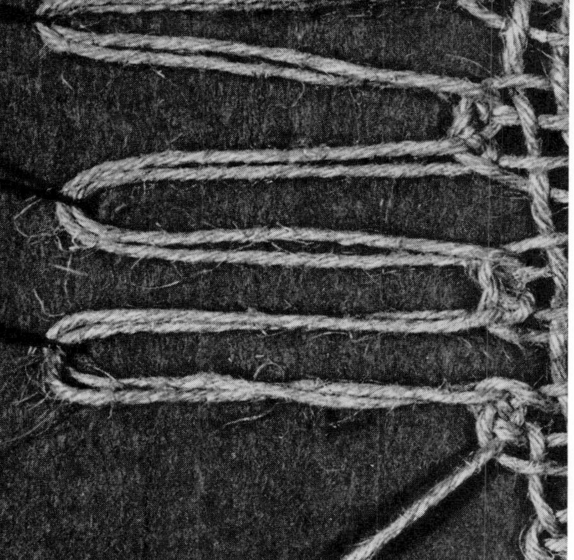

Cut fringe: formed with one extra pair. The extra pair and weaver are joined and then the extra pair is pinned out from the edge.

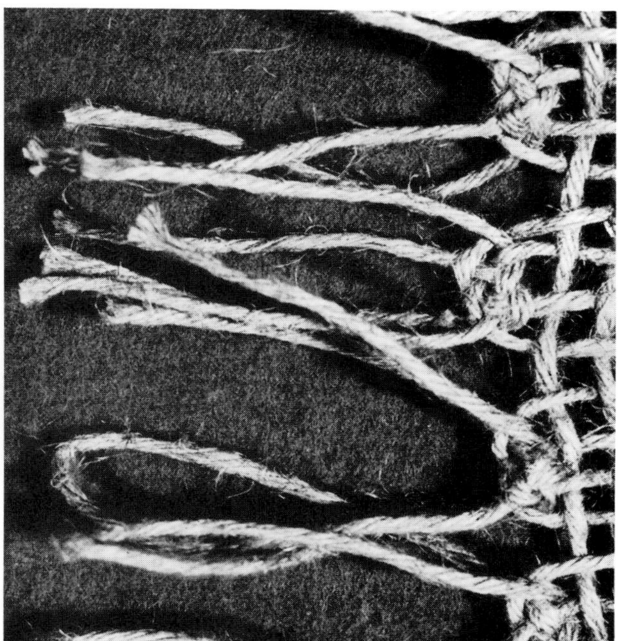

The finished fringe can be cut or left looped.

Picot Fringe

A twisted or cut fringe can be made by making a series of large looped picots and pinning out from the edge of the work, Making a fringe in this manner uses the weaver pair rather than an added fringe thread.

CONTOURING

Contouring refers to a planned curving of a relatively narrow ground or tape. The *weaving ground*, which is commonly used for tapes, is the one that is usually considered when contouring is desired. Most regular grounds, however, can be curved in a systematic way.

The prime objective when forming a contour is to keep the overall density the same throughout the curve while at the same time maintaining a logical arrangement of the ground lines as they work around the curve.

For wide or gentle curves, the outside pins can be spaced slightly further apart while the inside pins can be spaced slightly closer together. It will appear normal to see some crowding along the inside edge and some separation along the outside edge. When working around a curve, radial lines should always be considered. These are the lines running from the center of the curve to the outer edge. In a *weaving ground* the weaver pair should follow these lines. In other grounds each row of stitches should follow these lines.

The Weaving Ground

Various techniques can be considered when curving a *weaving ground.*

1. Tight curving of a narrow band. Bring the weaver pair past the inner edge pair. Drop the edge pair and return the weaver, making the

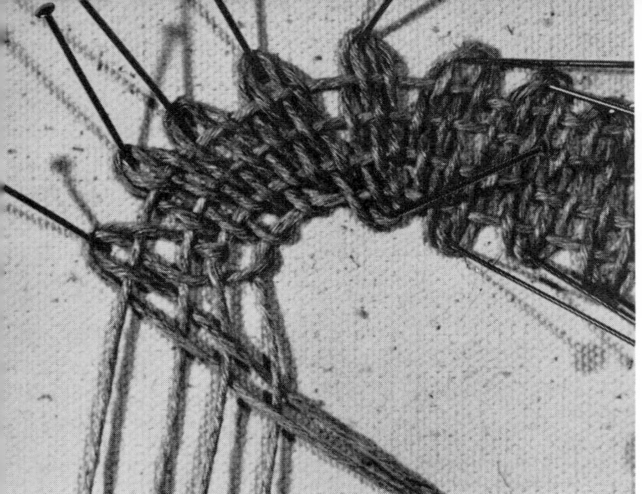

To curve a narrow band, the weaver is brought past the inner edge.

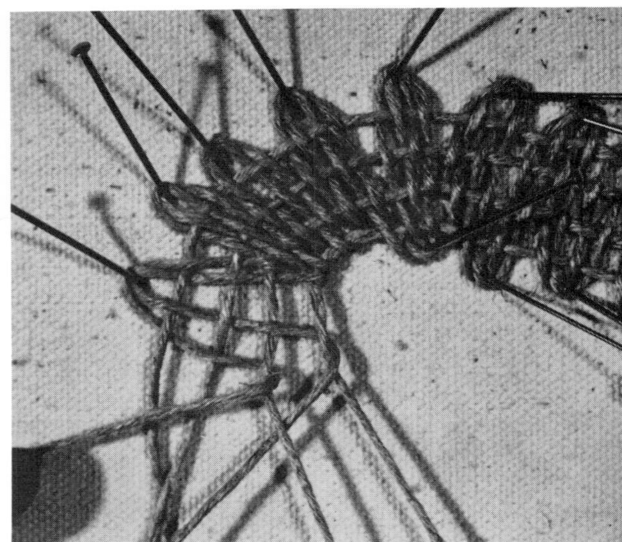

The edge pair is dropped and the weaver returns without weaving the edge pair again.

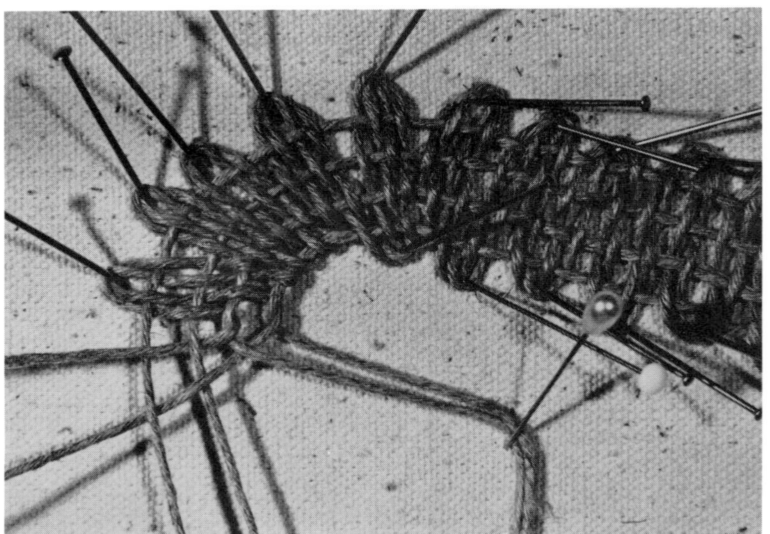

The edge pair is pinned to maintain tension and keep the curve smooth.

first return stitch with the second hanging pair from the inner edge. In other words, the inner hanging edge pair is combined with the weaver pair only once for each two rows of the weaver. PIN the inner edge pair to keep the stitches uniform.

2. Tight curving of a wide band: In a uniform pattern, weavers working from the outer edge to the inner edge should be returned before reaching the inner edge. The point of the return and how many weavers reach the inner edge will be determined by the width of the band and the tightness of the curve.

3. *Turning stitch*, for a tight curve in a dense narrow band: This particular stitch is a standard method of working a narrow band, called

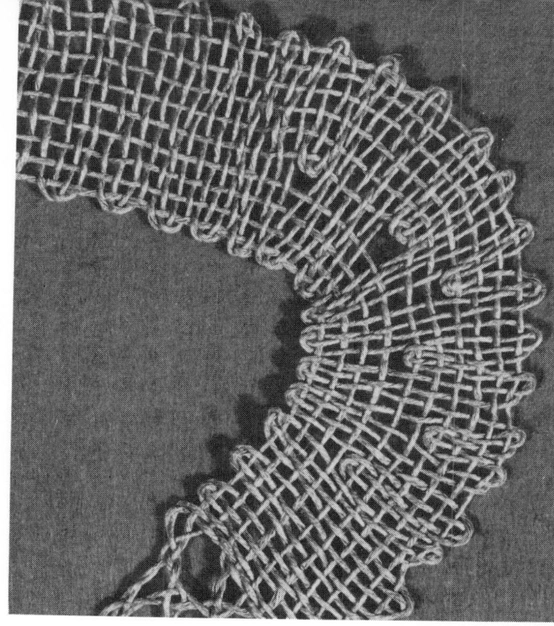

Curving a wide band of a weaving ground.

a *stem stitch*, in forming leaves and floral shapes in a bobbin-lace style known as Honiton lace. The *stem stitch* was typically worked with four to six bobbin pairs. The outer edge of the band has a plain or regular *weaving ground* edge while the inner edge is formed with a *turning stitch*. When the band changes direction to curve the opposite way, the *turning stitch* is made on the opposite side. PINNING is generally not required on the edge where the *turning stitch* is made, as the stitch is pulled firm forming a secure and tight edge.

TURNING STITCH: Work the weaver pair across all pairs to the inner edge. Without pinning, take the *weaver pair* and the *inner edge* pair and make a TWIST followed by a *half stitch*. For tight curves the TWIST motion before the *half stitch* can be eliminated. The pair outside the inner edge is pinned out of the way and the other pair from the *half stitch* is returned as the weaver. Refer to section on Raised Work, Chapter 5.

The Half-Stitch Ground

Closely akin to the *weaving ground*, similar manipulations can be worked in curving this ground. Due to the regular diagonal line pattern, handsome curved lines are formed by the diagonal threads as they work around the curve. When the weaver, and its complementary bobbin, is returned before it reaches the inner edge, holes, or openings, are formed in the ground at the point of return.

Curving a wide band of a half-stitch ground.

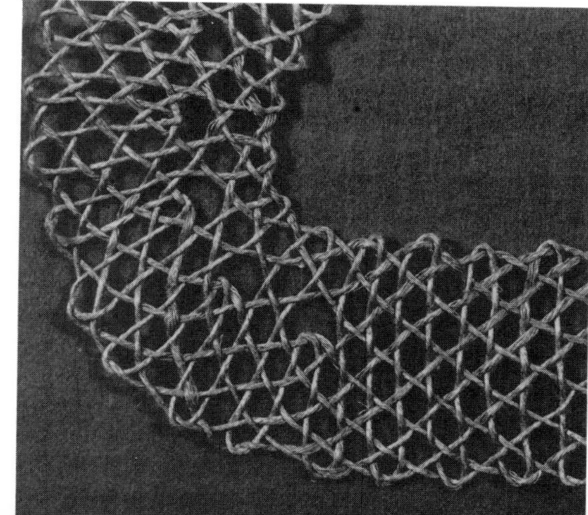

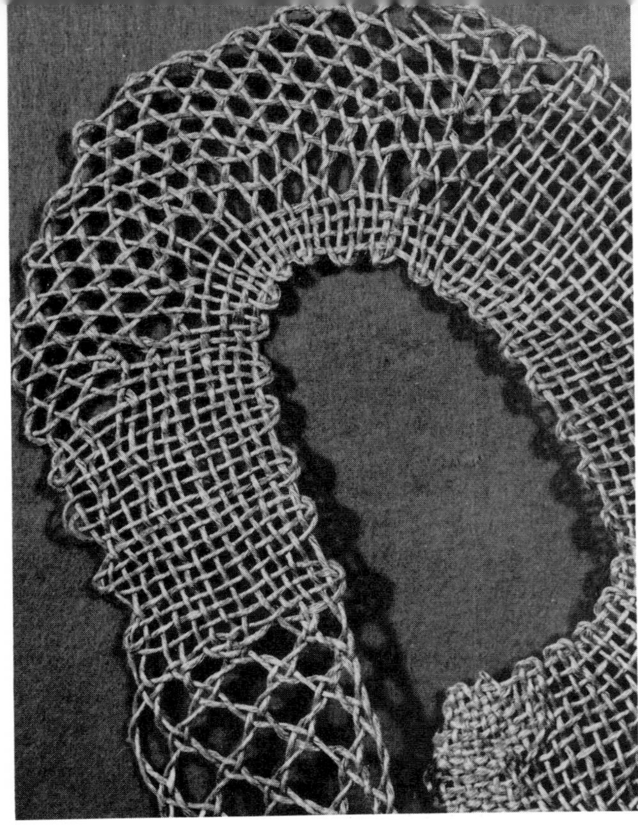

Combining the linen stitch and half stitch in a curve.

TURNING STITCH: The *turning stitch* can also be used to curve a narrow *half-stitch ground.* Working toward the inner edge, make *half stitches* across the ground with all pairs except the inner edge pair. With the unworked edge pair and the working pair (with the weaver) make a *linen stitch,* follow with a TWIST, and then a *half stitch.* The inner edge pair is pinned out of the way and the other pair from your stitch is worked back into the ground.

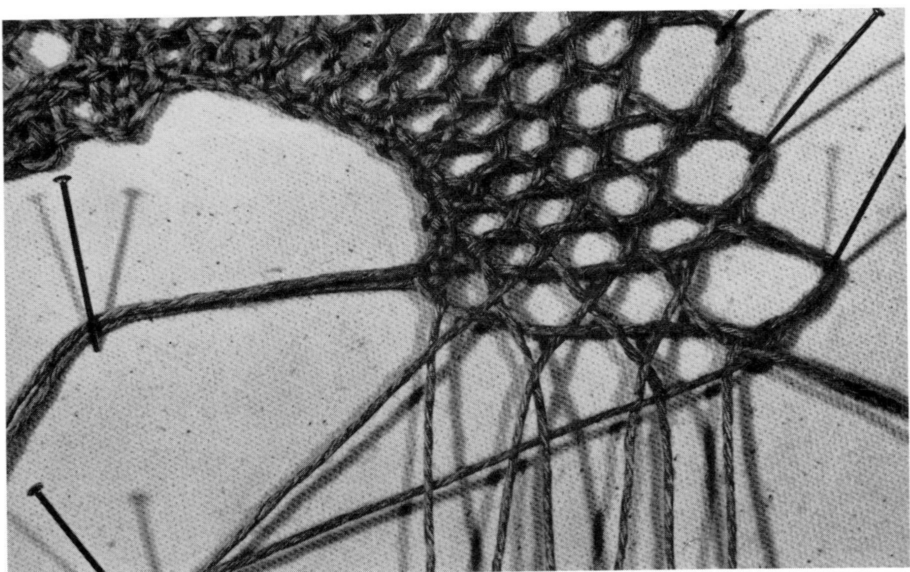

A half-stitch band curved with a turning stitch. A row of half stitches is worked across the ground with all pairs except the inner edge pair.

A linen stitch is made with the inner edge pair and the last working pair. This is followed by . . .

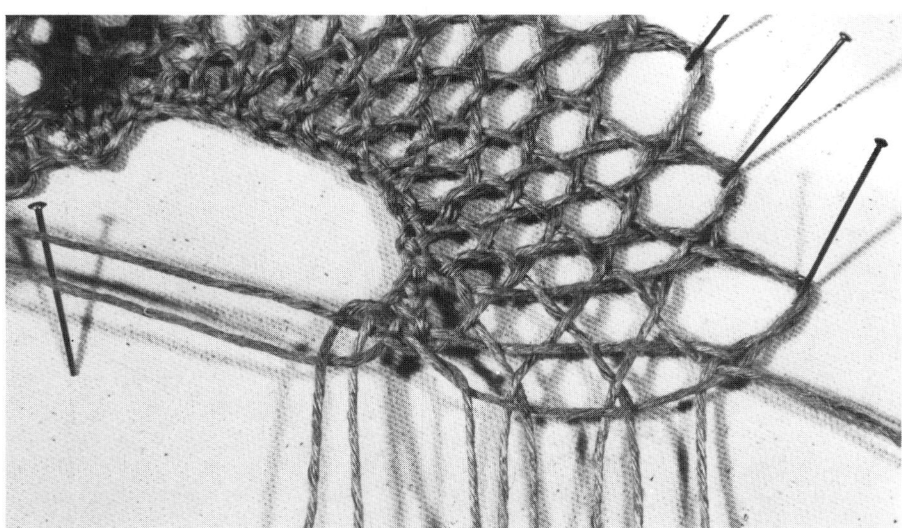

. . . a TWIST *and a half stitch.*

The inner edge pair is pinned out of the way and the other pair is worked back into the ground,

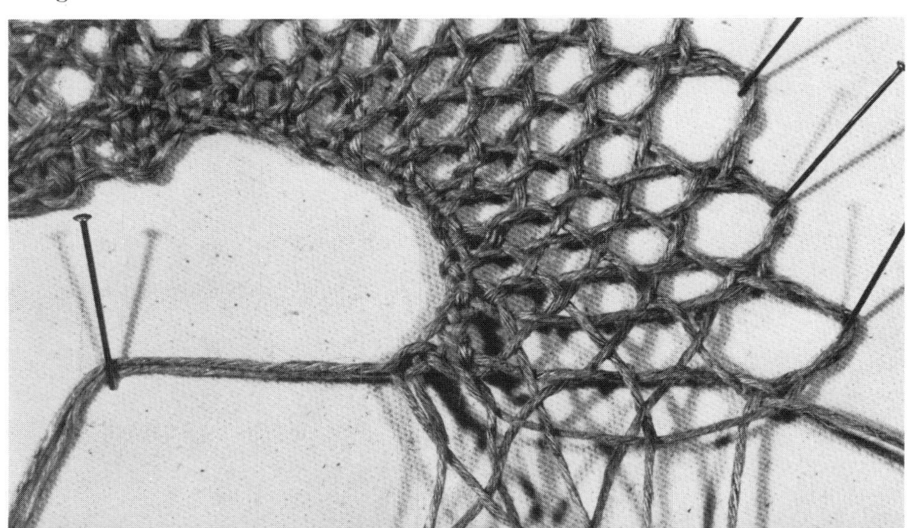

The Whole-Stitch Ground

The *whole-stitch ground* and related grounds, which are formed with adjacent groups of bobbin pairs from the two adjacent stitches above, are manipulated by varying the distances between the crossing points. Typically, this is done by varying the number of TWISTS after each crossing. At the inner edge a single TWIST is given, which is part of the normal working ground. For a tighter curve, this TWIST can be eliminated by working a *linen stitch* instead of a *whole stitch* at the crossing. As the stitches progressively reach the outer edge, additional TWISTS are systematically added after each stitch. In locating the individual stitches, keep in mind the radial lines. Each row of stitches should fall on one of these lines.

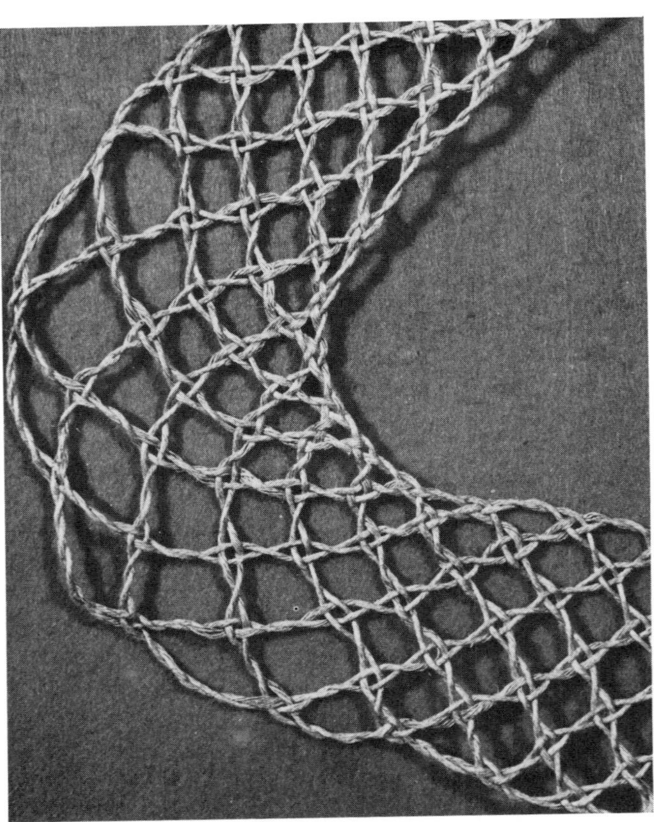

curving a band of whole stitches. Note how the number of twists varies between the crossings.

Working Techniques

Chapter 8

The complete freedom that contemporary bobbin lace affords the textile worker permits many approaches to the execution of any piece. Taking advantage of some of the many unique characteristics of bobbin lace, the worker will be able to use to his advantage this new tool for expression in the textile media.

A piece can be formed from the finest of threads or the heaviest of ropes or any combination of these. Pieces can be two-dimensional and self-supporting or supported in tension within a structural framework. In the same manner three-dimensional forms can be conceived.

Although each piece will require its own particular working technique, some of the more general techniques will be discussed in this chapter. As you work any particular piece, explore new methods, forget the rules, and find the easiest means to accomplish the final project.

DESIGN CONCEPTIONS

Some specific characteristics of bobbin lace might well be considered before approaching a particular project. These can be listed as:

1. Patterns or textures can be created by simple repetition of stitches or sequences of stitches.
2. Shapes can be developed easily by adding and/or deleting threads.
3. The direction of any thread can be changed as it is worked through a piece.
4. Designs can be executed as solid filled areas similar to those of weaving, as lacy or semiopen filled areas, or as completely open skeletal forms. These approaches can be used independently or combined within a piece.
5. Designs can be abstract, using any number of stitch combinations, or they can be representational, depicting images from real or imaginary sources.

Fine threads of various textures and materials worked in three dimensions. "Doublefaced Decadence." Caroline Beard.

In executing a design, the threads or cords can be thought of as the lines from an artist's pen. The greater the number of lines, the denser the area. While the graphic artist can terminate his lines by lifting the pen, the lacemaker must think of each line as coursing through the entire piece. Where the graphic artist works with a single line, the lacemaker is concerned with many lines running in unison. Where the lacer's lines or threads meet or cross, a special thing happens as an affair between these threads is considered. Such an affair can be a simple crossing with TWIST or CROSS motions or an encounter with an elaborate rhythm of stitches.

In thinking of the various materials available, texture and color should be a definite consideration. Cords of different colors or of contrasting textures or values can be a useful design tool. While the various threads can be left free to wander through a piece to form whatever design or rhythm that happens, it is entirely possible to control these threads and work them through a piece by plan. When two pairs of threads are worked, a *half stitch* will always interchange one thread of each pair while a *whole stitch* or *linen stitch* will keep the original pairs together.

A detail showing some of the rich involvement of threads. "Doublefaced Decadence." Caroline Beard.

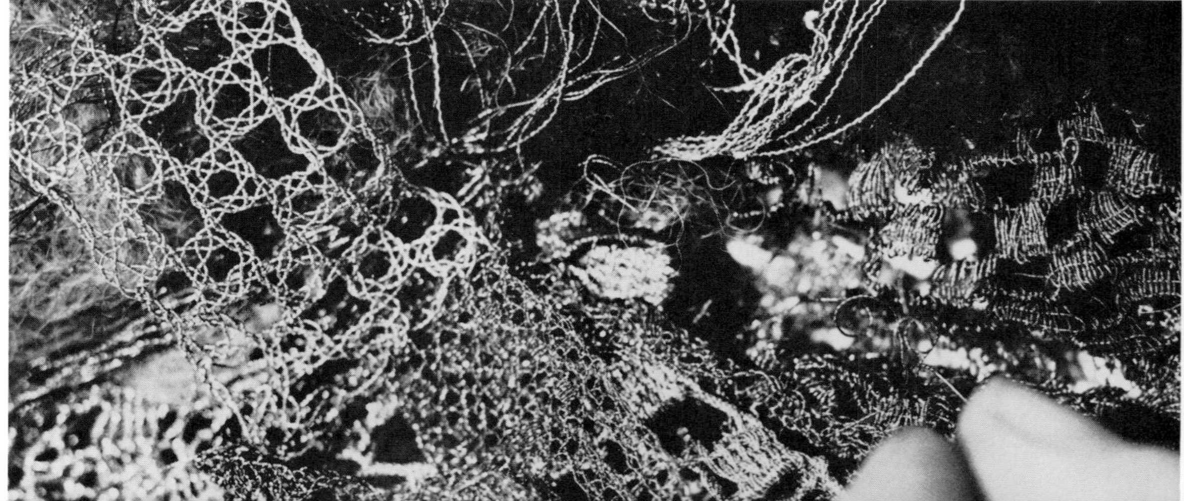

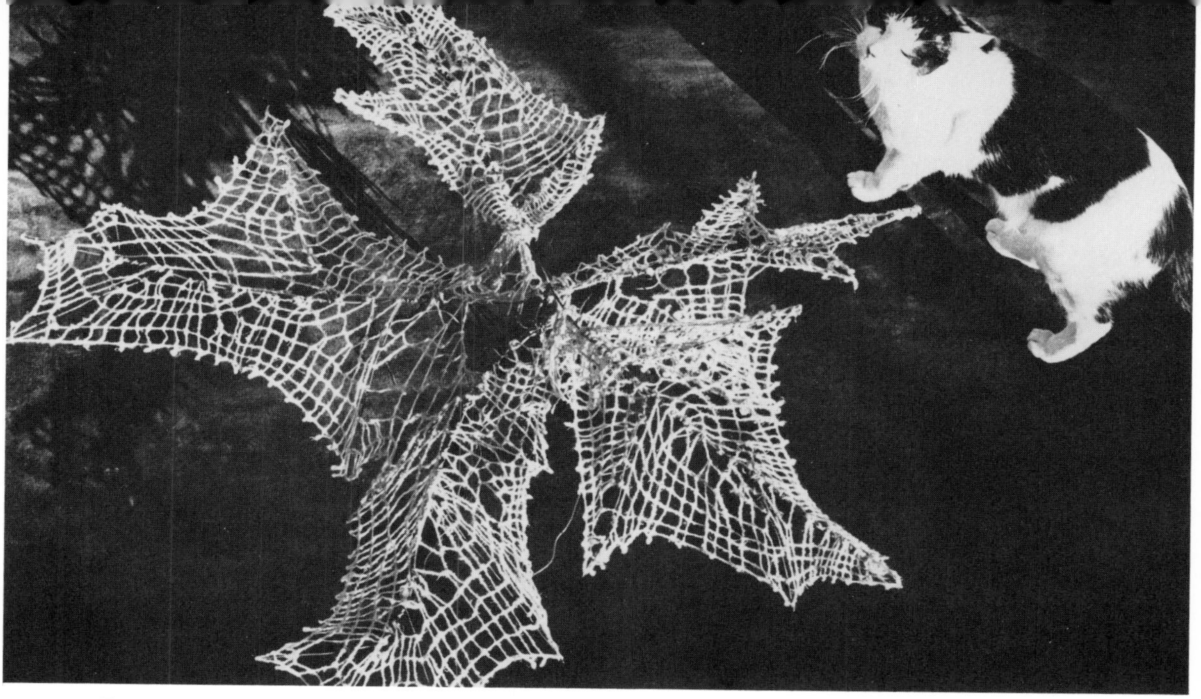

Lace webs of linen supported on a structural wire frame. "Lace Weed." Lydia Van Gelder.

Pictorial designs of great detail worked from the finest of threads. Shading and depth are created by varying the grounds within the forms. "Rabat" from the Regency Period (France about 1720). From the Alfred Lescure Collection, after Overloop.

Pictorial representation using the fine threads as pen lines. "Voile ou Tableau," Empire Period (France about 1810). From the Alfred Lescure Collection, after Overloop.

Rich texturing reminiscent of the lines from an artist's pen. Note how the forms are held in place by the simple indiscrete mesh ground. "Volant" from the Regency Period (France about 1720). From the Alfred Lescure Collection, after Overloop.

Great richness and detail by using many lace grounds. "Voile de Benediction," Louis XV Period (France 1765–1770). From the Alfred Lescure Collection, after Overloop.

Detail from "Voile de Benediction."

Twentieth-century pictorial representation in lace. Joannes Chaleye, 1910, Le Puy, France.

A floral composition worked with the weaving ground and half-stitch ground. Joannes Chaleye, 1910, Le Puy, France.

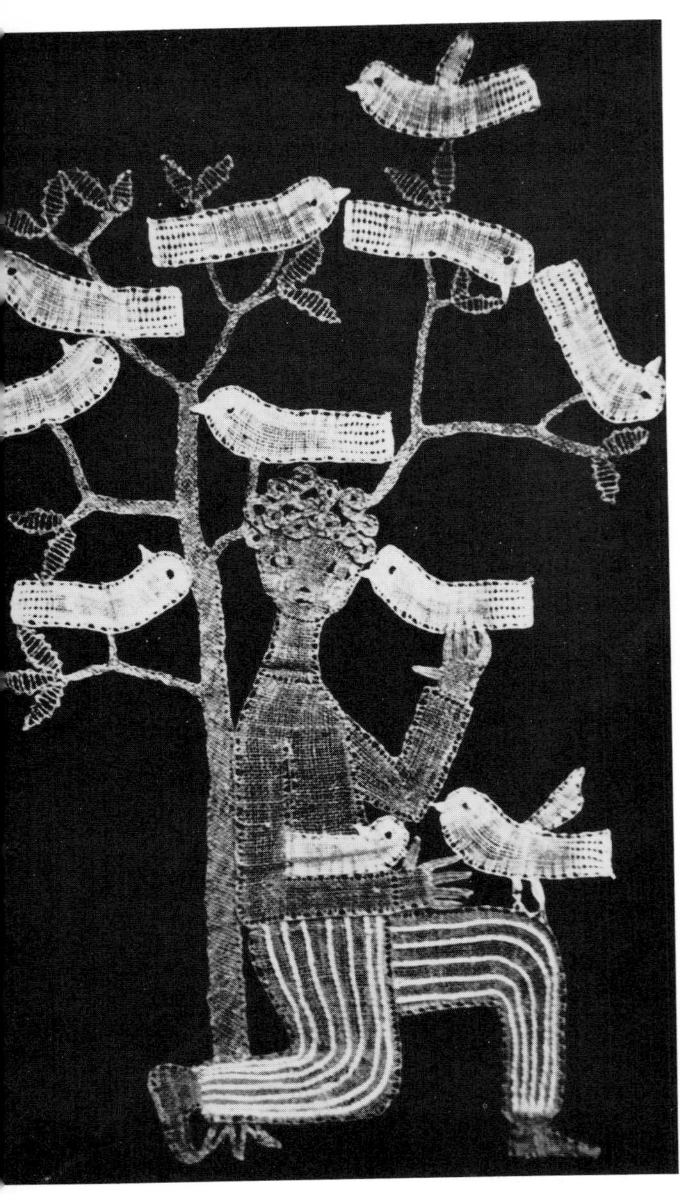

Figures worked in a contemporary style using fine threads of various textures and colors. Luba Krejci, Czechoslovakia. Traveling exhibit, 1965.

Spatial involvement using plastic can-separator rings, nylon monofilament, and waxed linen. Three views. Christina Santner, 1972.

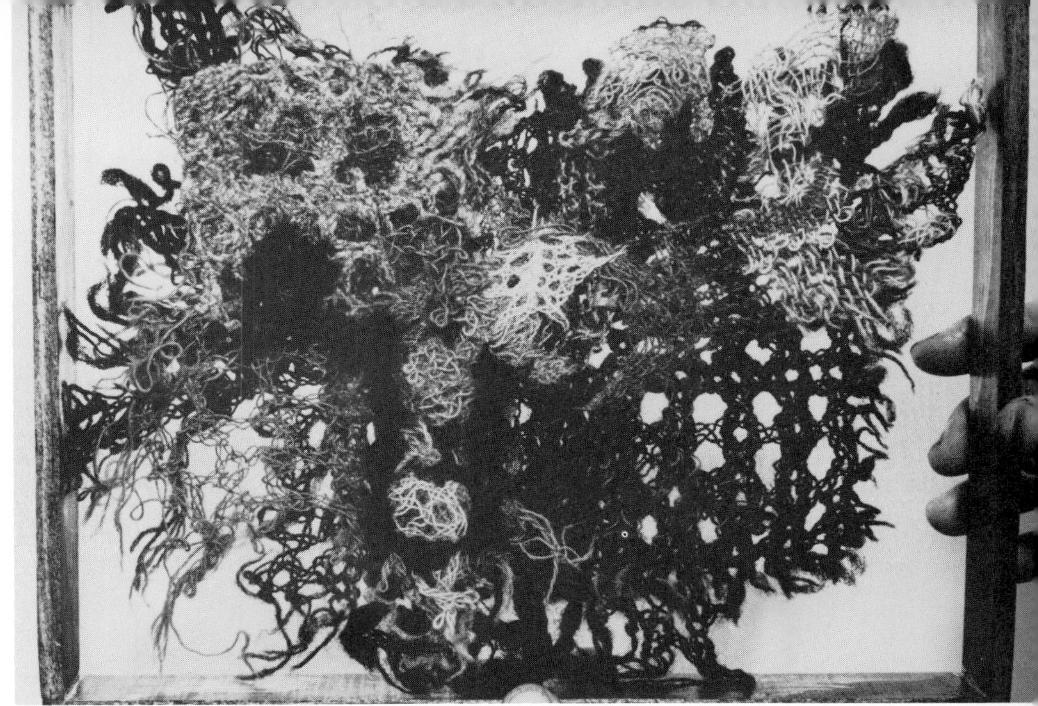

A multilayered composition. "Junius Fragment." Carolyn Beard.

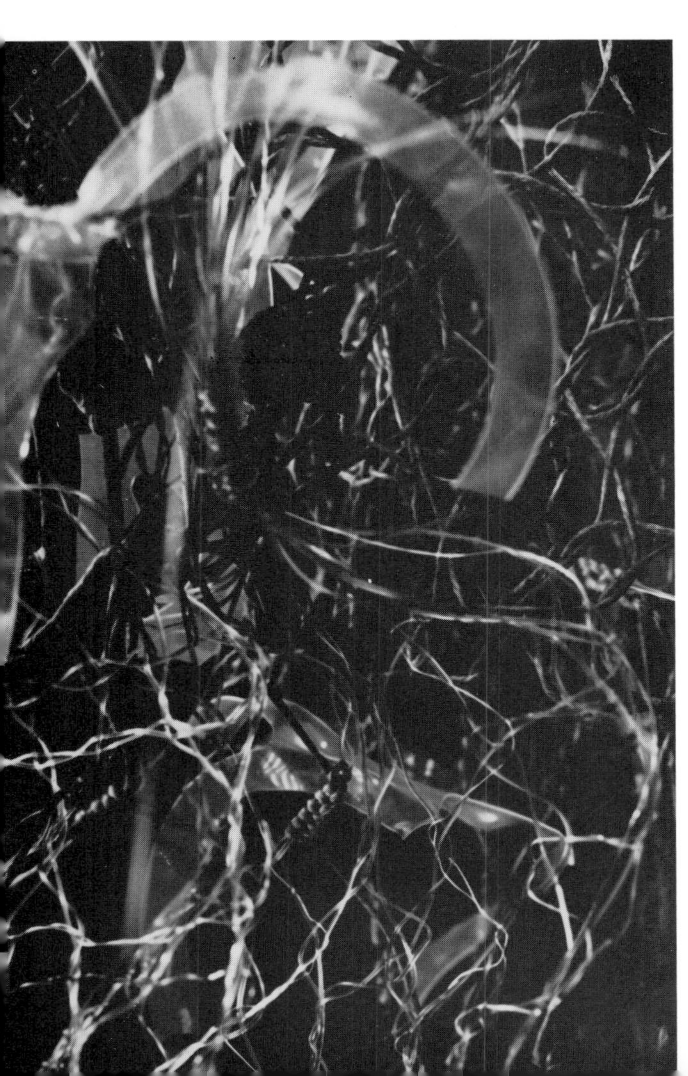

Self-supporting three-dimensional forms using wrapped cords of various materials. Three views. Sharon Bazis, 1972.

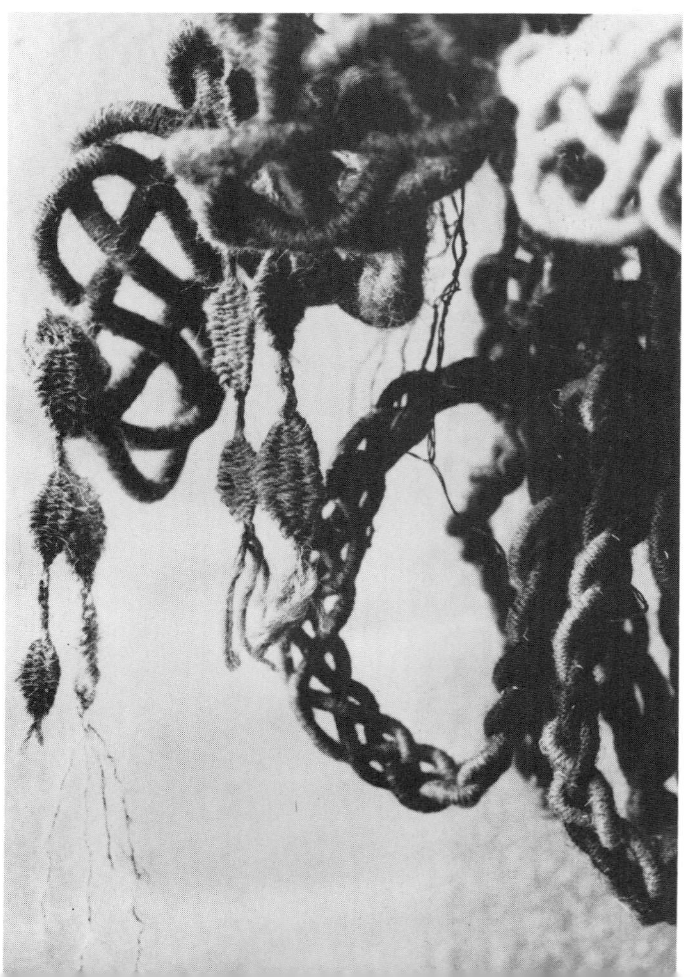

The free twining of bobbin lace expressed in cane, waxed linen, and fur. Three views. Christina Santner, 1972.

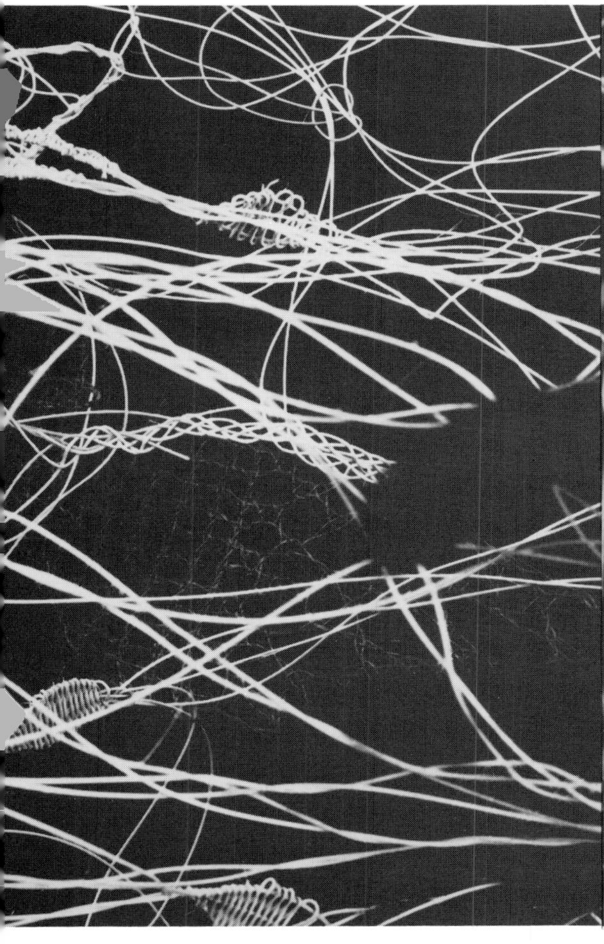

A child's purse in wool yarn. Irene Jarvis, 1972.

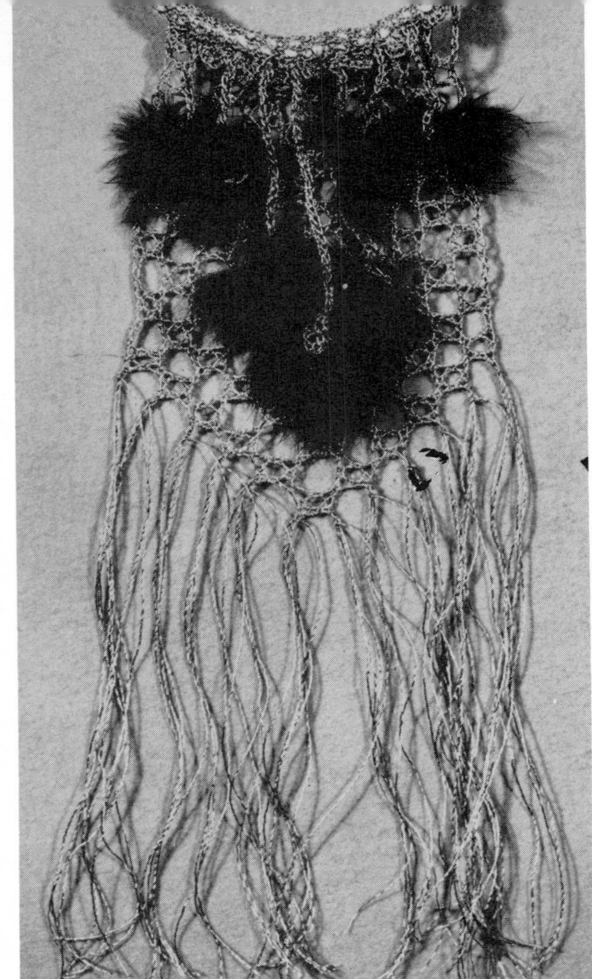

A neckpiece of gold thread and fur. Clarise Bois, 1972.

A feather basket. Lydia Van Gelder.

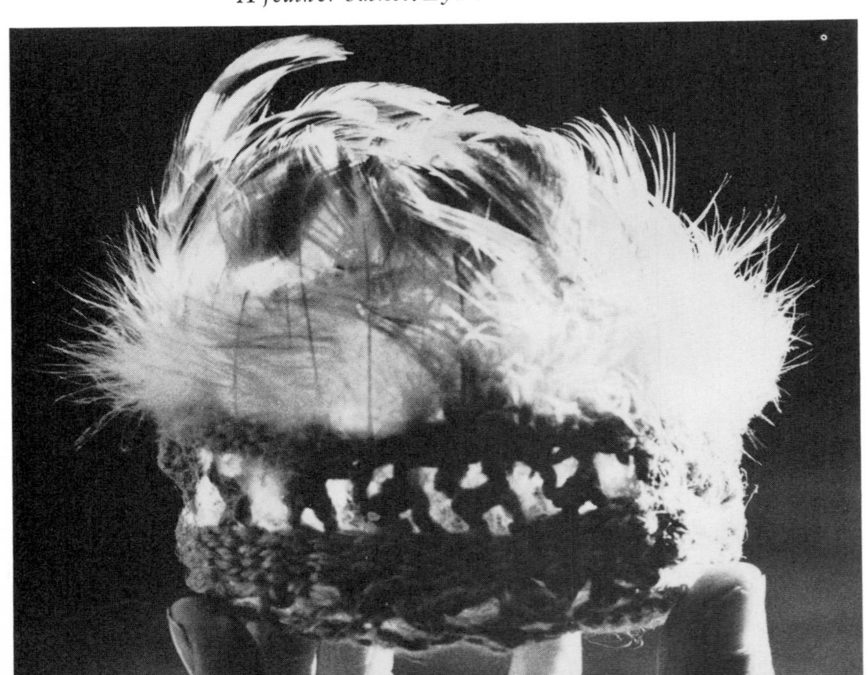

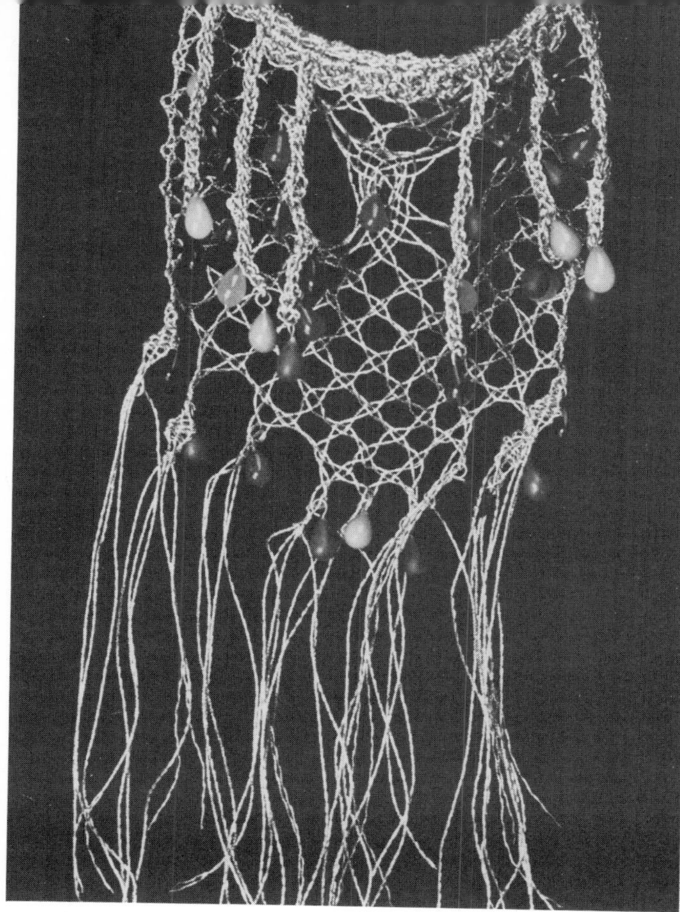

A neckpiece. Gold threads and beads. Clarise Bois, 1972.

A child's jacket of wool yarn. Irene Jarvis, 1972.

A traditional native hat worked from grass. Portugal.

Animal forms in a wire frame. Threads of various textures, materials, and colors. Lydia Van Gelder.

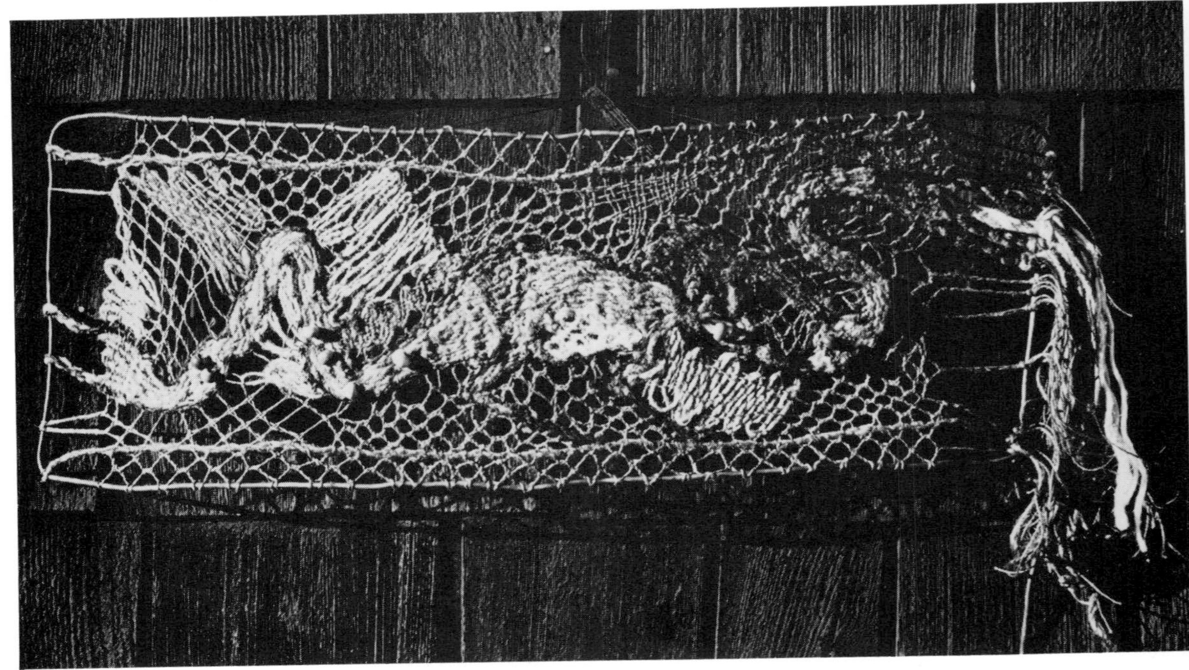

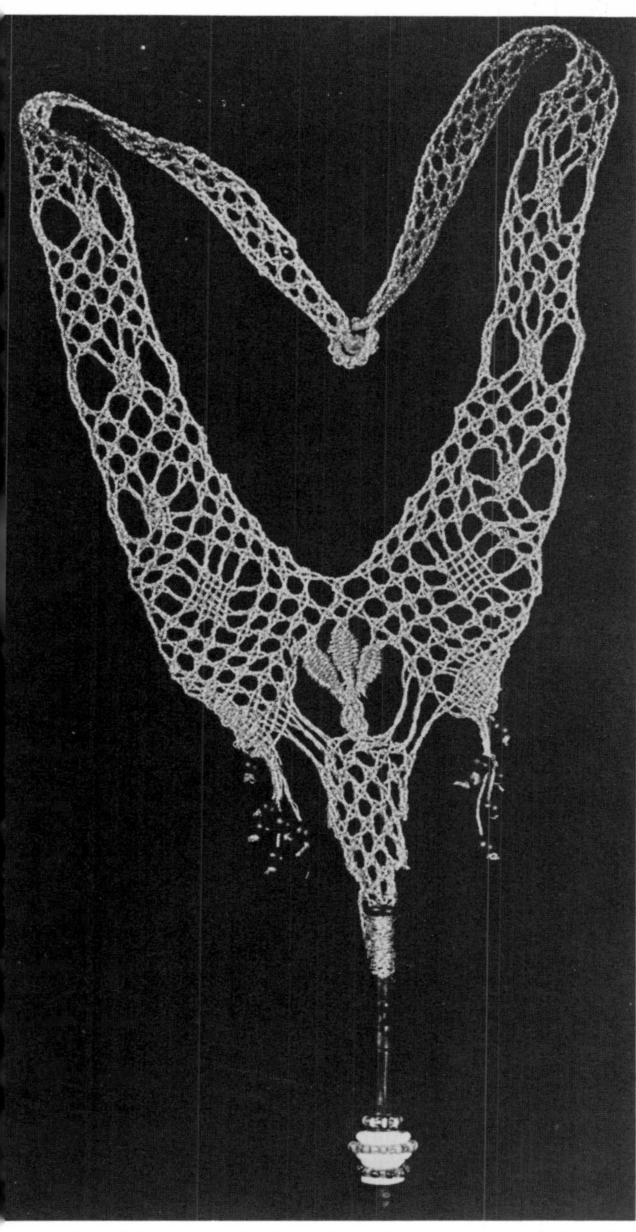

A necklace of gold threads and an ornamental bobbin. Kaethe Kliot, 1973.

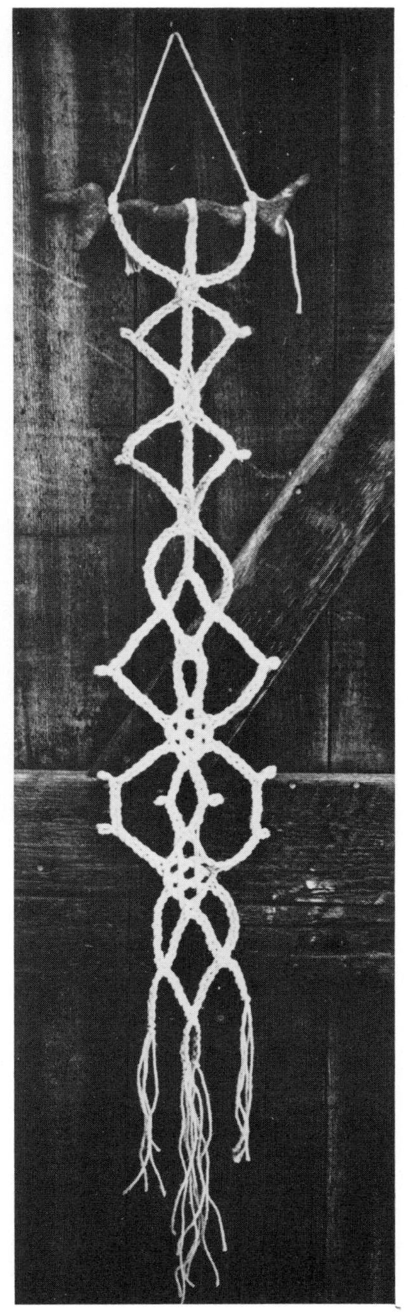

A wall hanging in bobbin lace illustrating an open skeletal approach. Linen threads are worked with braids and picots. Kaethe Kliot, 1972.

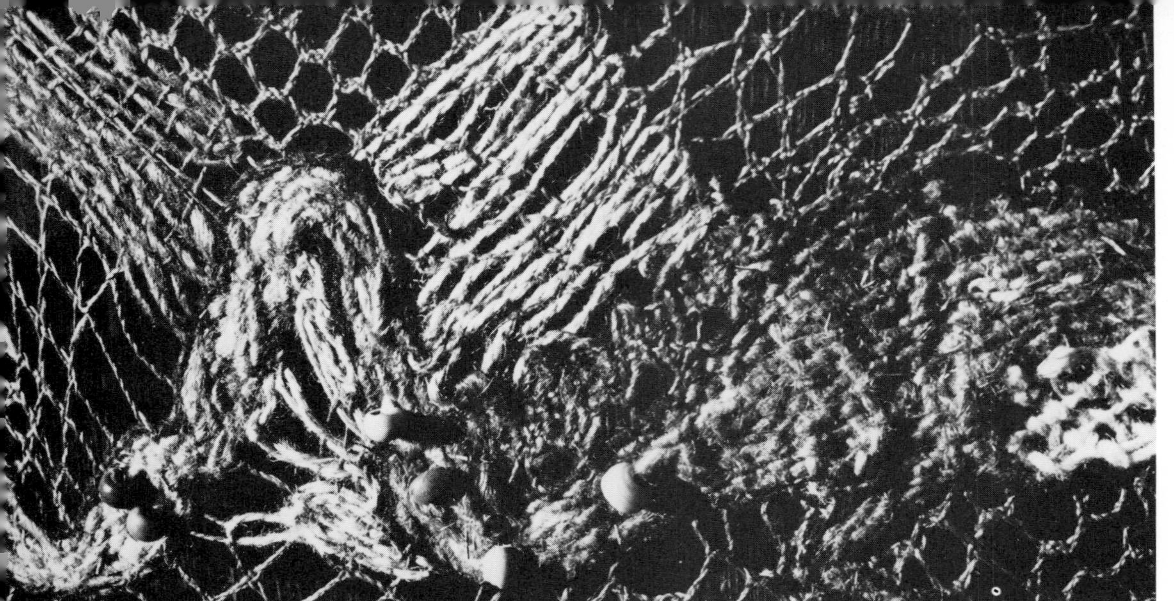

Detail showing how the various threads are manipulated to control line and color. Lydia Van Gelder.

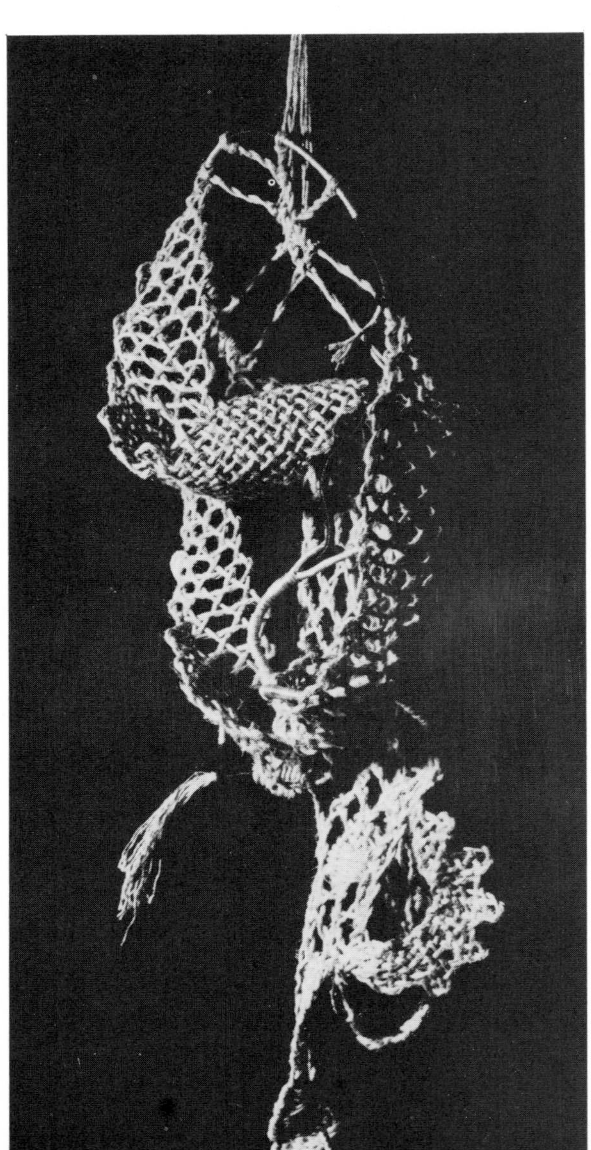

A three-dimensional hanging of natural linen and dyed silk. Shape is controlled by wrapping sections of the linen with silk threads. Kaethe Kliot, 1973.

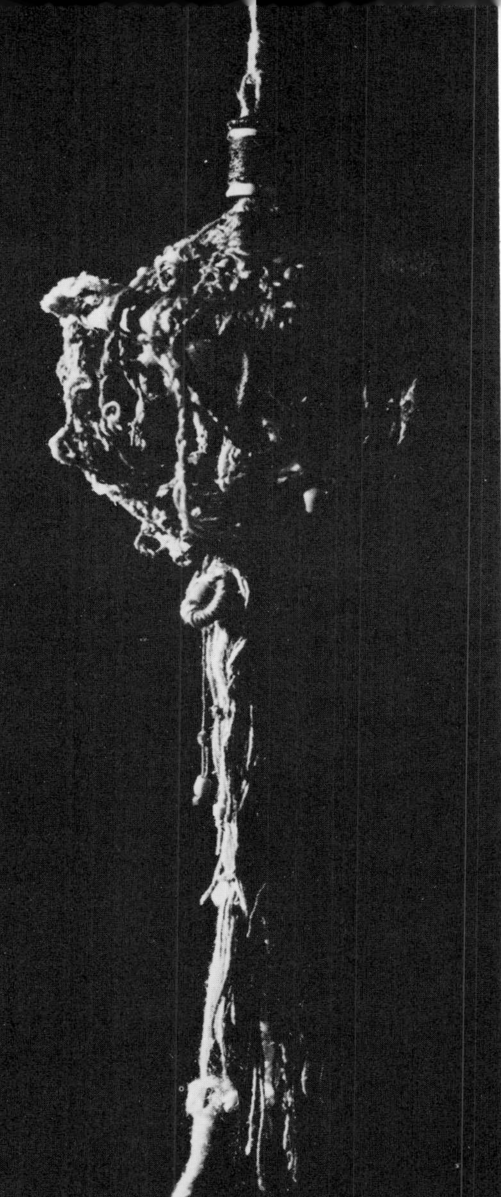

A playful lantern in textured threads and beads. Helen Dietge, 1973.

A joyous hanging of various yarns, bells, and beads worked within a teak and brass frame. Helen Dietge, 1973.

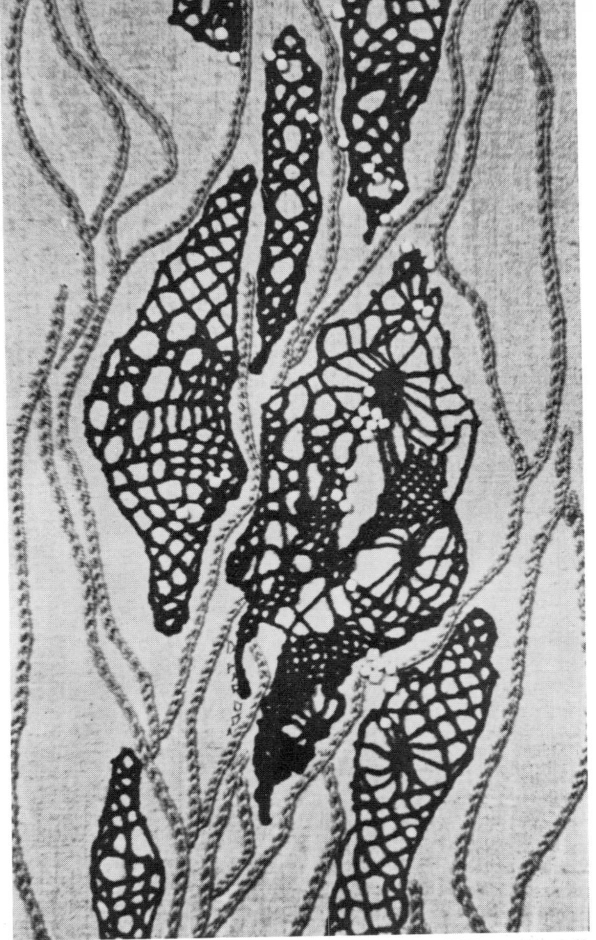

Bobbin lace used as a tool of stitchery. "Tree Bark." Dorothy P. Pardon. Photo: Gary Mitch.

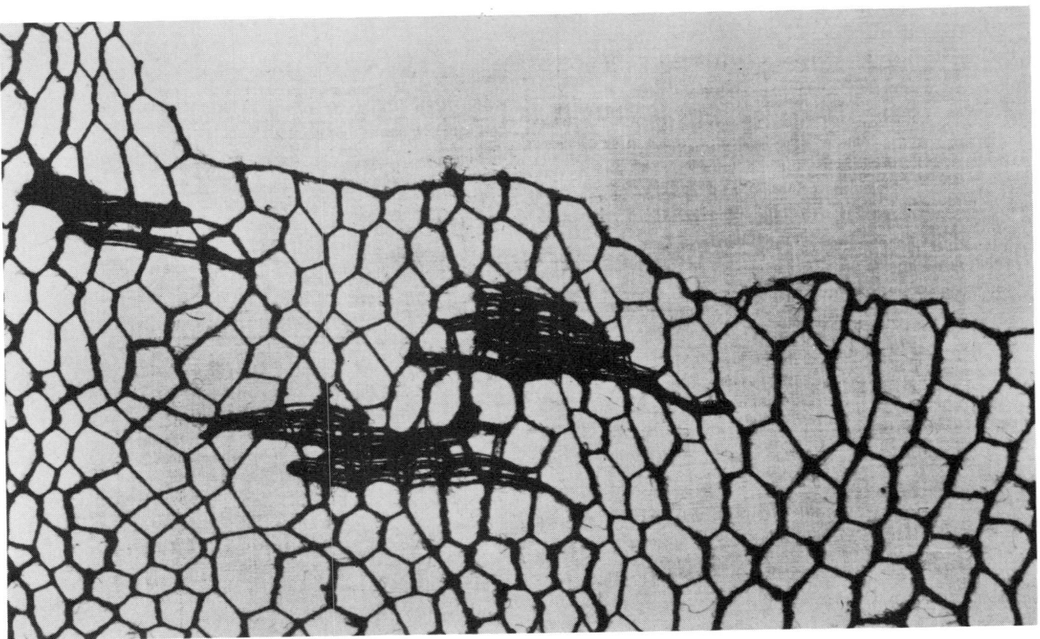

The delicate quality of an ink sketch expressed in lace. "Snow on the Mountain." Dorothy P. Pardon. Photo: Gary Mitch.

Exploring the freedom of line and dimension. "Basket of Flowers." Mary Ellen Cranston-Bennett. Approximately 14 inches across. Photo by artist.

Several grounds used to create a great richness and depth in a two-dimensional design. "Flower." Mary Ellen Cranston-Bennett. Photo by artist.

Textured homespun yarns and gold threads used to create a free lace expression. Approximately 30 by 40 inches mounted on plexiglass. "Typography." Mary Ellen Cranston-Bennett. Photo by artist.

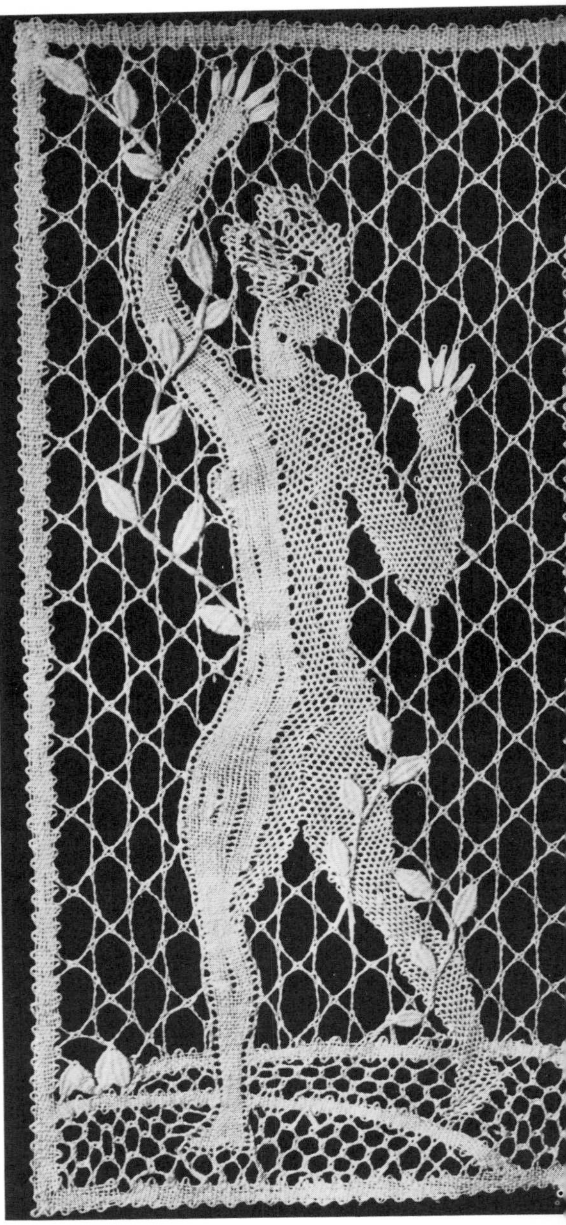

our tapestries in bobbin lace worked over a detailed pattern in fine linen. Each piece approximately 7 inches high. esign, pattern, and execution by Gertrude Biederman.

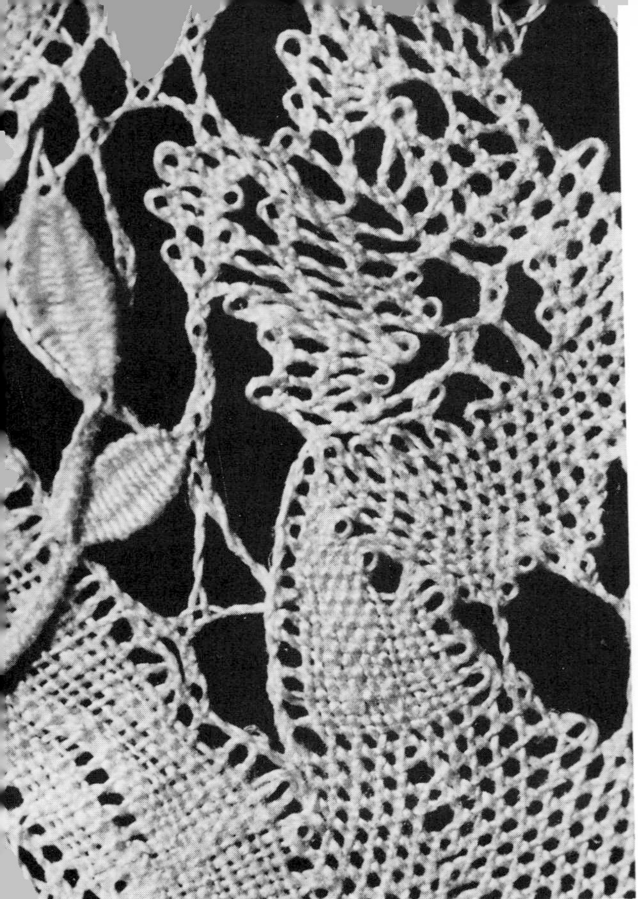

Detail of "Woman" showing the flow of threads. Gertrude Biederman.

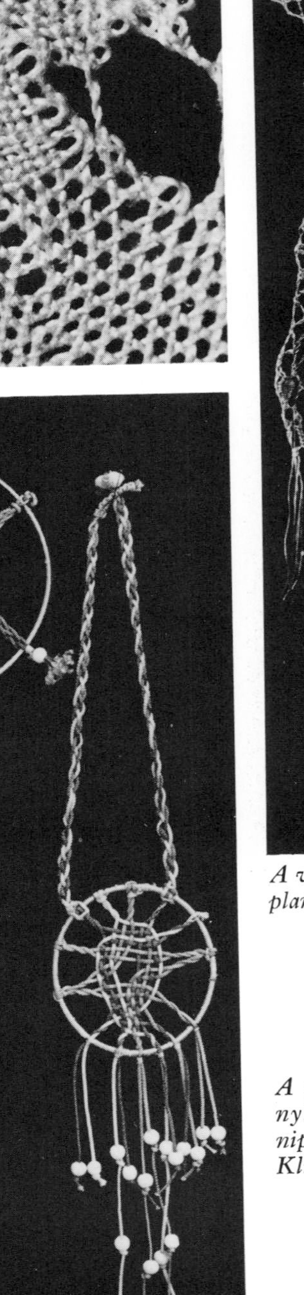

A window curtain in waxed linen and jute with three plants. Christina Santner.

A group of neck pendants worked in dyed braided nylon. The threads of various colors have been manipulated to form strong controlled patterns. Kaethe Kliot.

A playful form using monofilament nylon on a found piece of seaweed. Kaethe Kliot.

A self-supporting three-dimensional form of polypropylene and two feathers suspended from a single line of wire awakens to the gentlest air current. Lydia Van Gelder.

WORKING ON A BOARD

The lace board, which is basically a flat fibrous board that can easily be pinned and that will hold the pin firm, is probably the most useful tool for working bobbin lace. Although boards of this type can be purchased in sizes up to 4 by 8 feet, sizes up to 2 by 4 feet will be found most useful. The smaller sizes can be supported by a table or floor stand while the larger sizes can be mounted on or hung from a wall.

Grid lines, to act as a guide in working your stitches, can be either drawn directly on the board or on a paper overlay, on which the design can also be drawn. If you cover your board with cloth fabric, strips of masking tape can be used for your grid lines.

If working a large piece from many directions, it is often easier to set your board horizontal, supported by a table or stool. To maintain tension, let your weighted cords hang over the edge. A stretched spring secured along the edge of your board is a good tool for keeping the threads aligned.

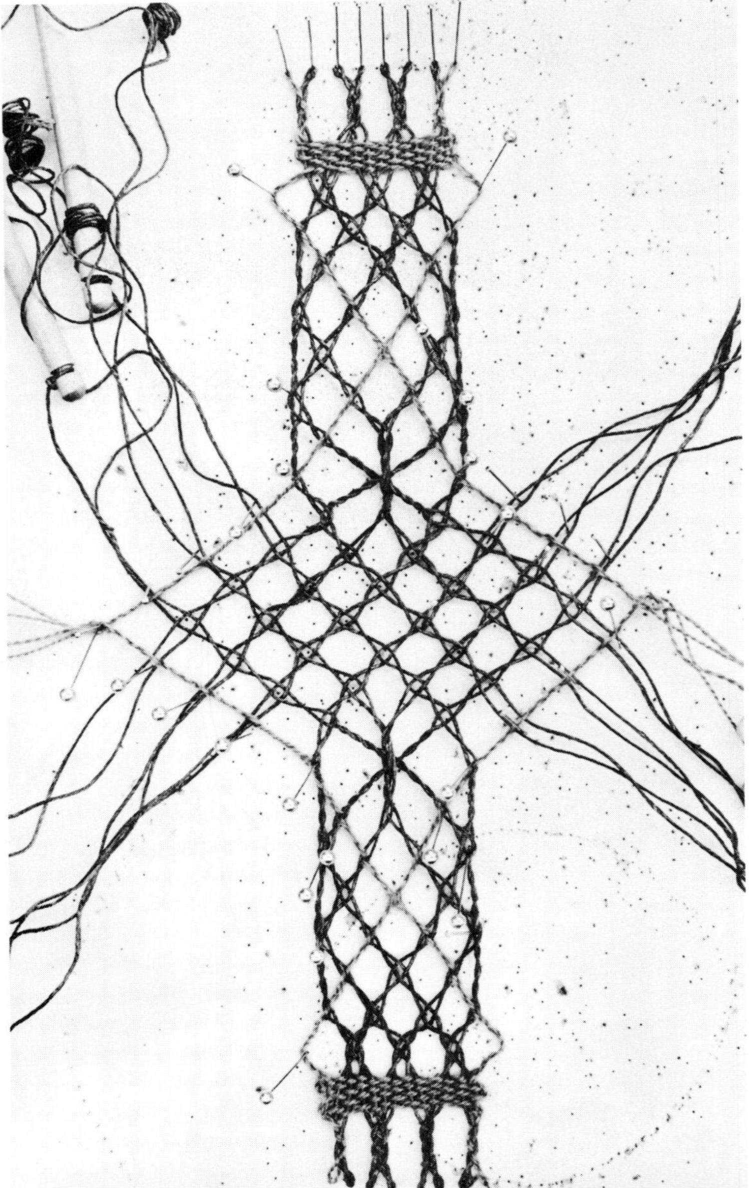

Working a piece from two ends toward the center. The piece was worked with the board in a horizontal position.

The finished hanging with threads terminated on a wire frame. Lynn Turner, 1972.

SUSPENSION TECHNIQUES

Working large-scale or environmental pieces will almost always require use of suspension techniques. The techniques will vary somewhat depending on the size and type of cords used but basically will require weighted cords suspended from some rigid frame. The cords can be wound onto bobbins or, for larger cords, weights can be attached to the cords by clothespins or other similar devices. In some cases, due to the weight of the cord itself, additional weights will not be required.

To keep threads organized, a warp spacer beam will be found useful. This is a length of wood with closely spaced notches to hold the threads. The beam can be left hanging or clamped to the side and out of the way.

As sections are worked, temporary ties will often be necessary to keep the worked sections in place. As infilling grounds are completed and sewn to the previously worked sections, the temporary ties can be removed.

In some cases, as detail or material demands, sections can be worked independently on a board and later sewn into the piece.

Other working methods will certainly be devised as new forms of lace are worked. Most large pieces will require combinations and use of most of the techniques described.

Screen of marlin, waxed linen, and monofilament worked entirely in suspension. "Life Cycle." Kaethe Kliot, 1972.

Detail of screen.

Forming the screen by working the heavy threads without bobbins. Note the winder used to hold the long ends of the working threads.

Temporary ties are used to hold the completed section in place until the ground is completed.

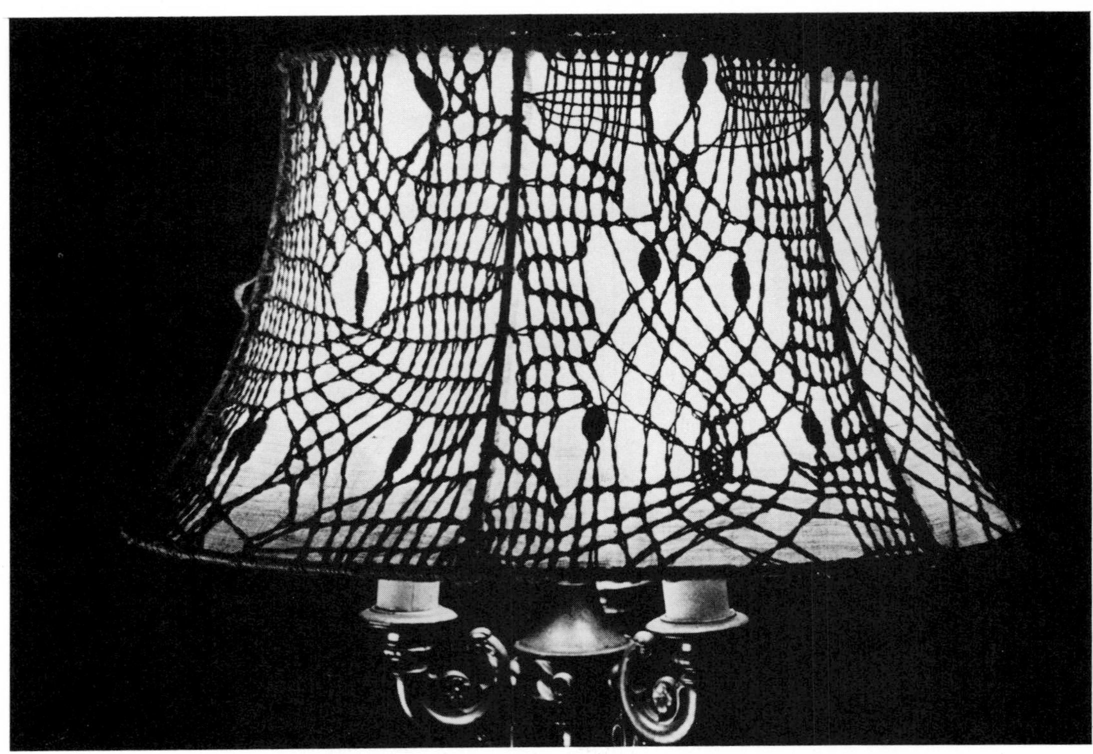

A lampshade made with linen cord worked in suspension directly on a wire frame. Jennifer Kaufman, 1972.

A hanger for a pot is worked in suspension directly over the pot with the pot in an upside-down position.

The finished pot and hanger.

WORKING WITH A SKETCH

A sketch indicating general form or shape should precede any lace project. Often a photograph, a painting, or even a three-dimensional object can serve as the nucleus of your design. As you conceive your forms, plan the structural supporting elements of your piece. Consider whether the fabric of lace is to be self-supporting or merely the skin, which is supported by a structural skeletal framework. As bobbin lace permits a similar freedom of design as does the paint and canvas of the painter, the initial concept or sketch should similarly be considered as important and an integral part of the work. You can work directly from your sketch, improvising as necessary, or you can go a step further and prepare a full-size cartoon.

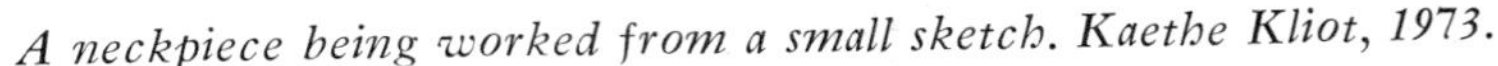

A neckpiece being worked from a small sketch. Kaethe Kliot, 1973.

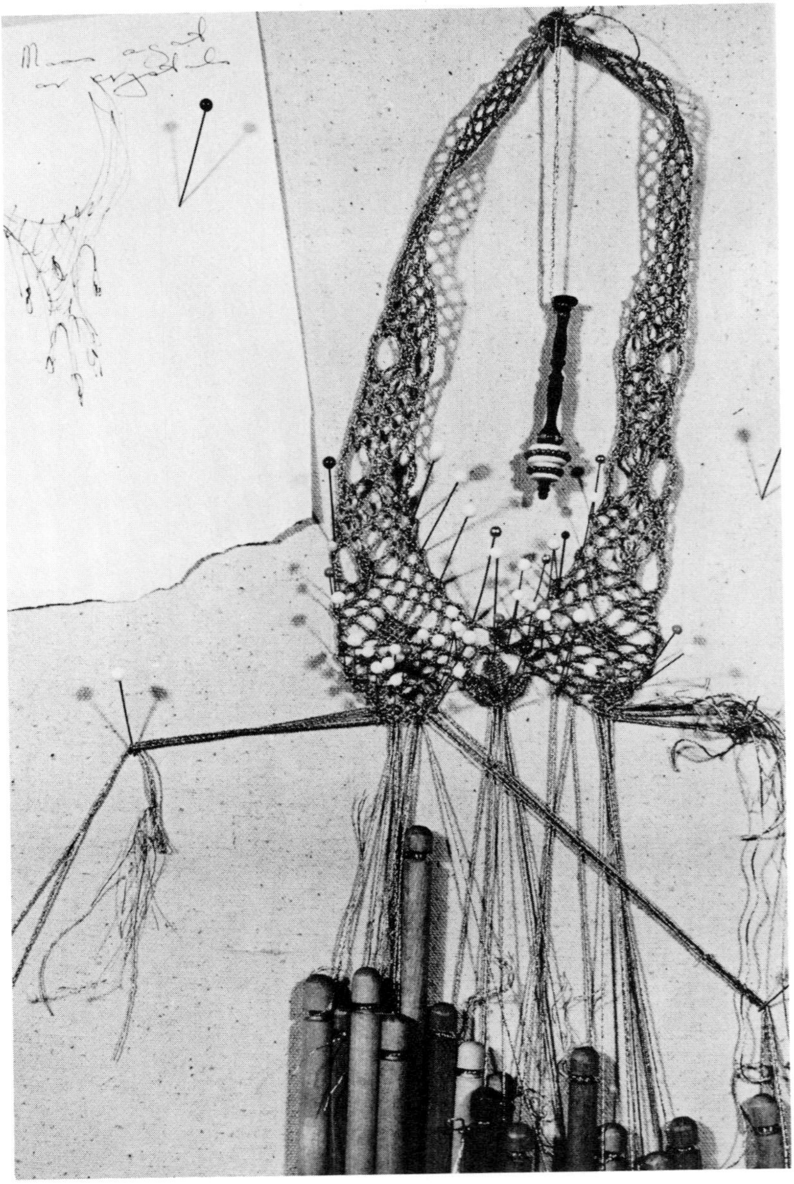

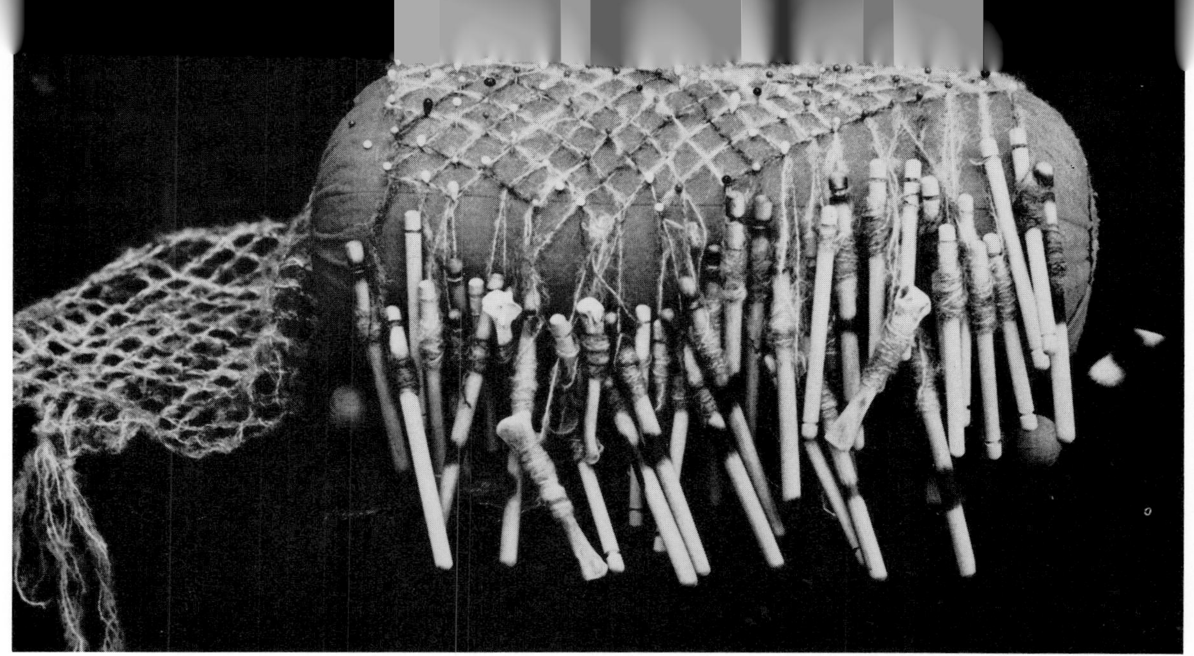

Worked simply as a repetitive ground, a scarf is formed from mohair as a continuous ribbon on a tubular pillow.

WORKING FROM A CARTOON

A cartoon is simply a sketch or drawing, in full size, of the intended piece. It can be as casual or detailed as one wishes. Drawn full size on a heavy paper, the lace is worked directly over it. Notes or graphic designations can be made to indicate types of stitches or densities desired in specific areas. This technique permits much more freedom in executing a piece as compared to a detailed pattern.

A lace tapestry being worked directly over a full-size cartoon. Drawn on tracing paper, the cartoon was then glued to a stiffer board.

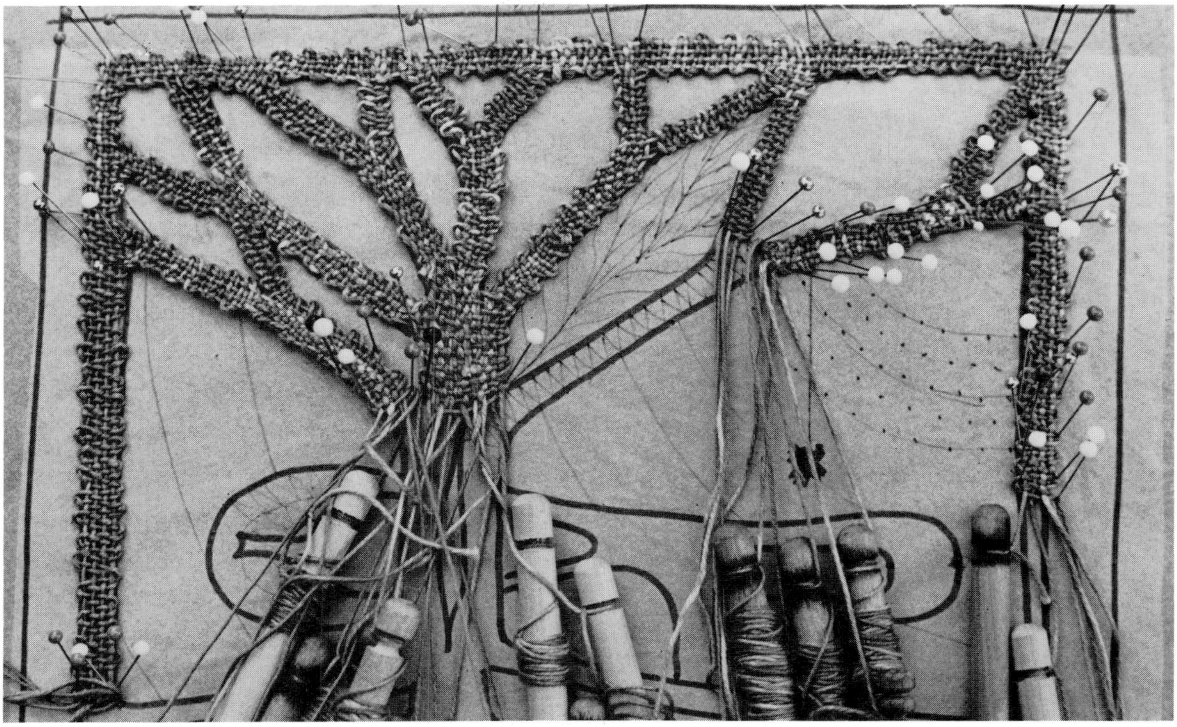

A cartoon drawn on index weavng card stock. Only the outline shape is indicated.

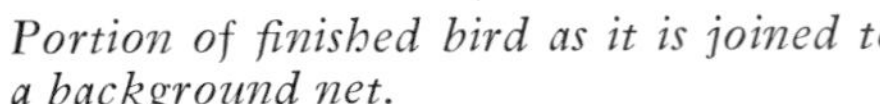

Portion of finished bird as it is joined to a background net.

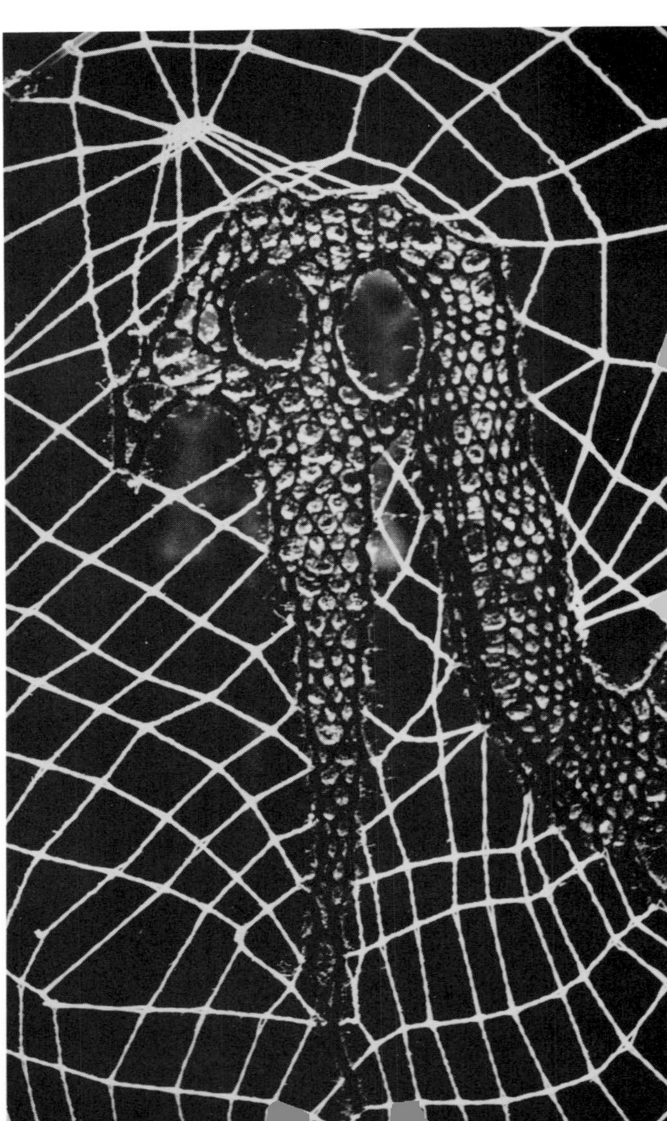

WORKING WITH A PATTERN

The pattern, which was the indispensable tool of traditional lacemaking, should at least be understood, if not used, by the contemporary lacer.

If any piece or design is to be repeated or shared, the pattern is still the indispensable tool. As the lace is worked directly over the pattern, the layout is always full size. Every PIN location is designated by a dot, which in turn locates the center of a stitch, or, for a *weaving* or *half-stitch ground*, the change in direction of the weaver thread(s). Lines connecting these dots show the course of the weaver pair. Outlines of shapes on a pattern are used to show the extent of "spider" or "filling" stitches. Letter designations are generally used at the top or beginning of a pattern to locate starting bobbin pairs. Number designations are generally used within the pattern to indicate the specific sequence of stitches. A heavy solid line is used to show the placement of "gimp" threads.

Although an experienced bobbin lacer can work from a pattern without any further explanation, a photograph or sample of a finished piece is most helpful. Many published patterns are presented with specific written directions in addition to a picture. Some of the common designations used in written patterns are:

h t or h th	:	*half stitch (half throw)*
w t or wh th	:	*whole stitch (whole throw)*
c	:	CROSS
t or tw	:	TWIST
sel	:	Selvage. A finished edge of a piece usually referred to when sewn to another piece.
close	:	Completing a stitch after a PIN. This is generally a repeat of the same stitch that was made before the PIN.

Bobbin pairs are generally referred to by number as counted in sequence starting at the left edge.

As the appearance of a finished piece is dependent on the thread used, a notation as to the gauge and type of thread should be given.

To duplicate an existing piece of lace, it is a simple operation to copy the piece on an office copying machine, and then to use the print as your working pattern. Cementing the print to a stiff board will extend the life of the print and minimize tearing.

A lace collar being worked on a detailed pattern. The design was drawn on one-half of the pattern and then transferred in a symmetrical fashion to the other half by folding and pricking through each pinpoint. Pattern and design by Gertrude Biederman for author.

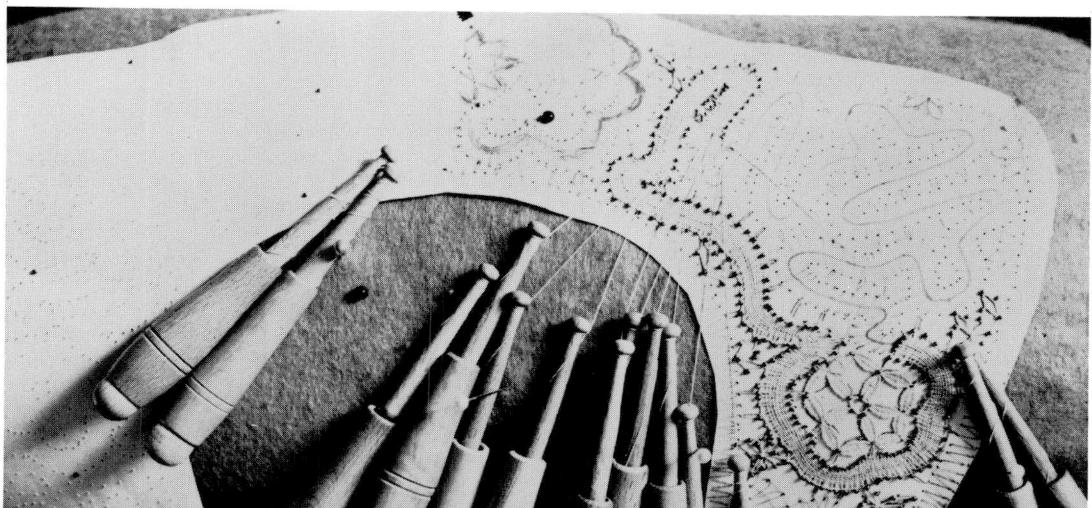

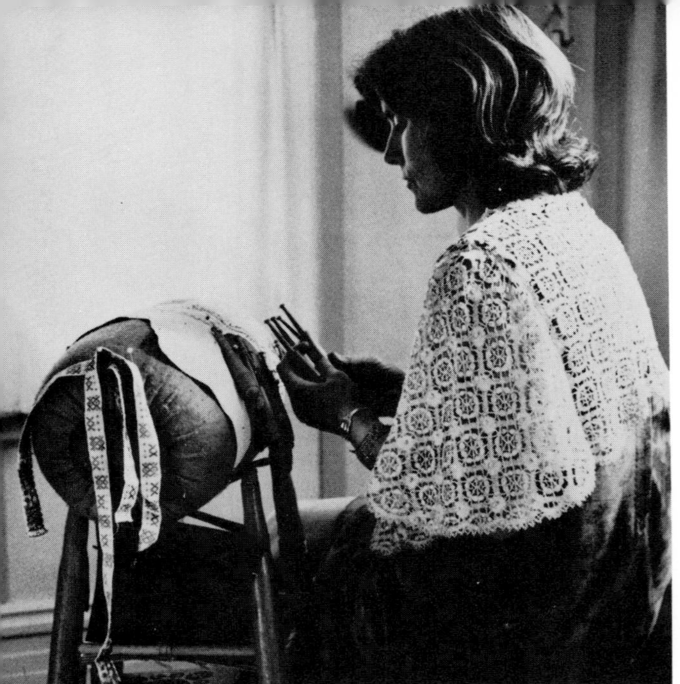

Collar being worked in traditional manner by author.

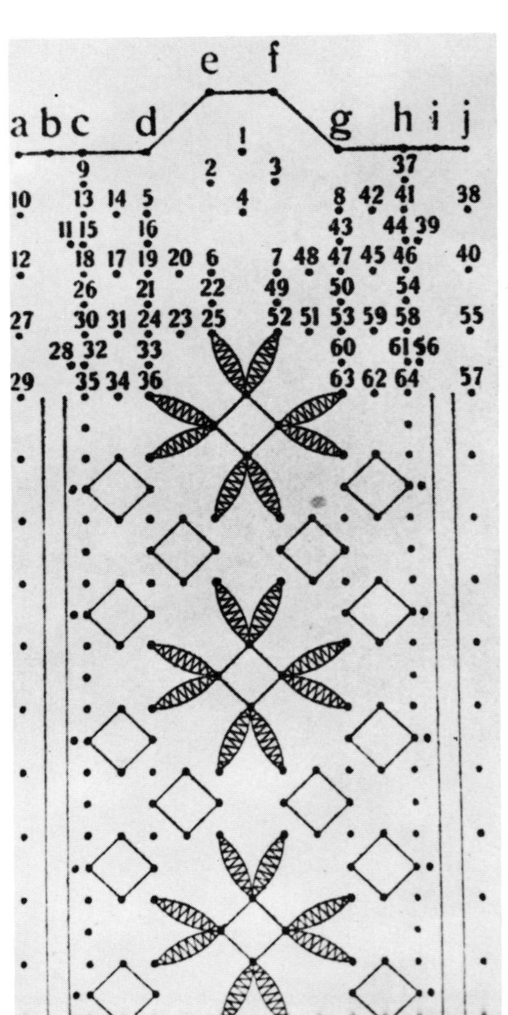

A detailed published pattern and photo of finished piece. From Die Kloppelspitzen, *1st series, DMC library.*

A more complex pattern for a border of various grounds and stitches and the accompanying photo. The lacer could work from the pattern alone but would need the photo to differentiate the various grounds. From Die Kloppelspitzen, 1st series, DMC library.

A variety of contemporary patterns that can be purchased.

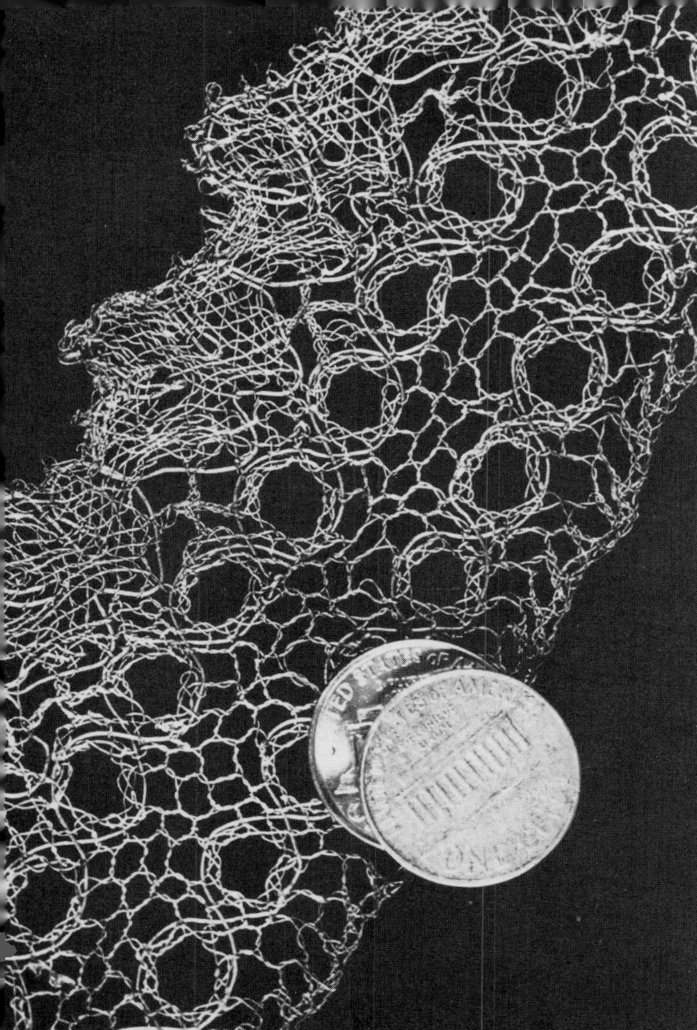

Detail of a fine lace edging that could only be worked from a pattern. Author's collection.

Lace doily. Worked from a pattern by the author.

STARTING A PIECE

The starting of a piece can be crucial as the start often determines the ease of the working and terminating of the piece.

Traditional lace was always simply started by hanging threads on pins that were later removed. This is still a satisfactory method for many two-dimensional designs, although it does not allow for any specific hanging or use of the piece. If a piece is to be hung, some method of hanging should be considered and made integral with the piece.

For a hanging piece starting threads can be mounted on a rod or hanger. If the piece is to be supported within a structural frame, the threads can either be mounted on the frame and worked across or to the center, or they can be joined at some central point and worked out to the frame.

When starting from some central point as might be the case for a hanging planter support, all threads can be mounted on a small ring or simply interlocked to form a structural center. Where hardware is necessary for a piece such as a belt, the buckle can serve as the mounting for your threads. This not only solves the starting of the piece but solves the problem of attaching the buckle.

A neck pendant worked on a wrapped brass ring. Dyed braided nylon in three colors. Kaethe Kliot.

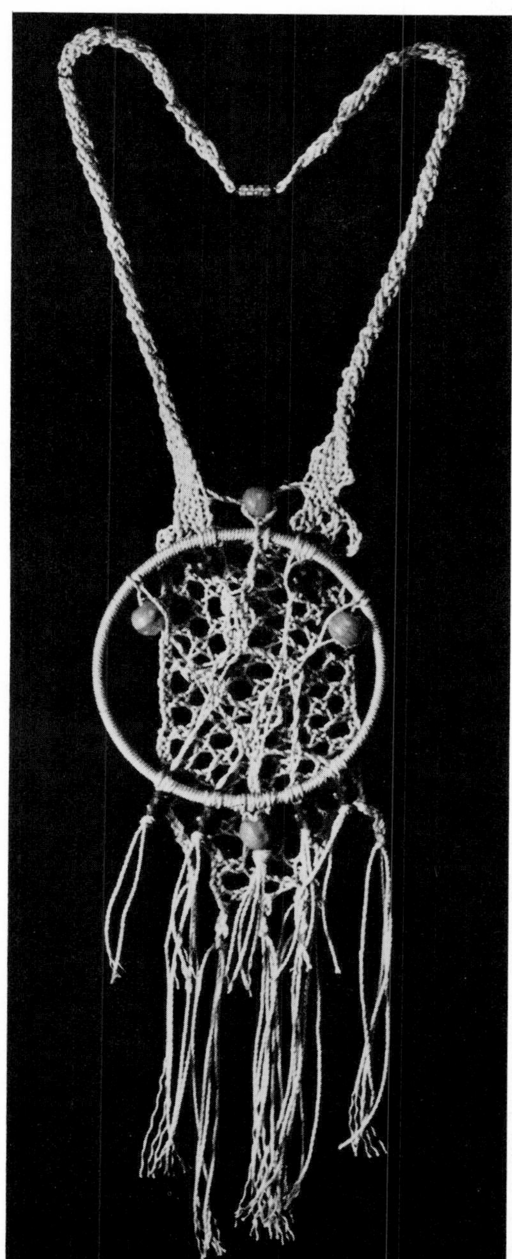

A neckpiece combining a self-supporting lace ground backdrop and a structurally supported motif within a ring. Neck strap is formed as a lace rope. Clarise Bois.

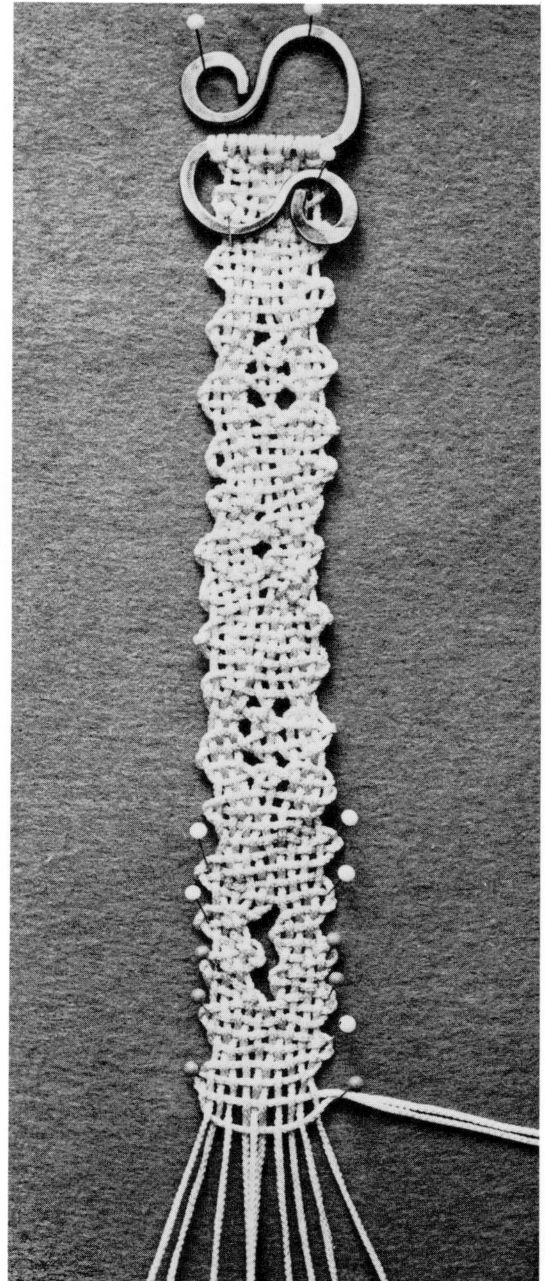

Starting a belt from a free-form friction buckle.

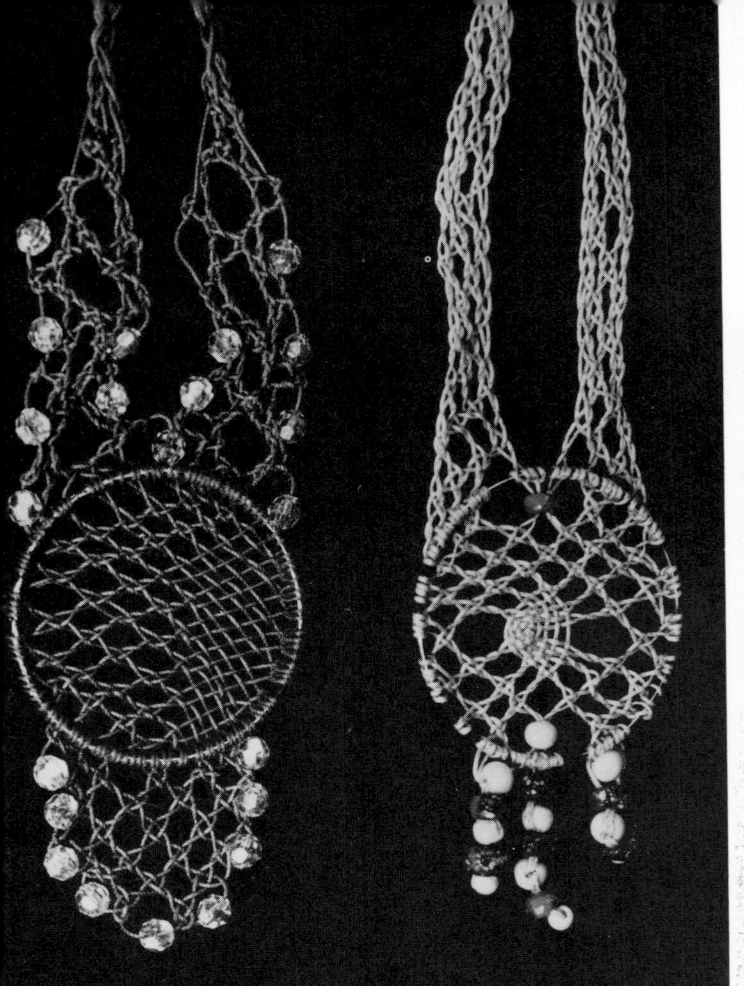

Two necklaces worked within a rigid ring. Irene Jarvis.

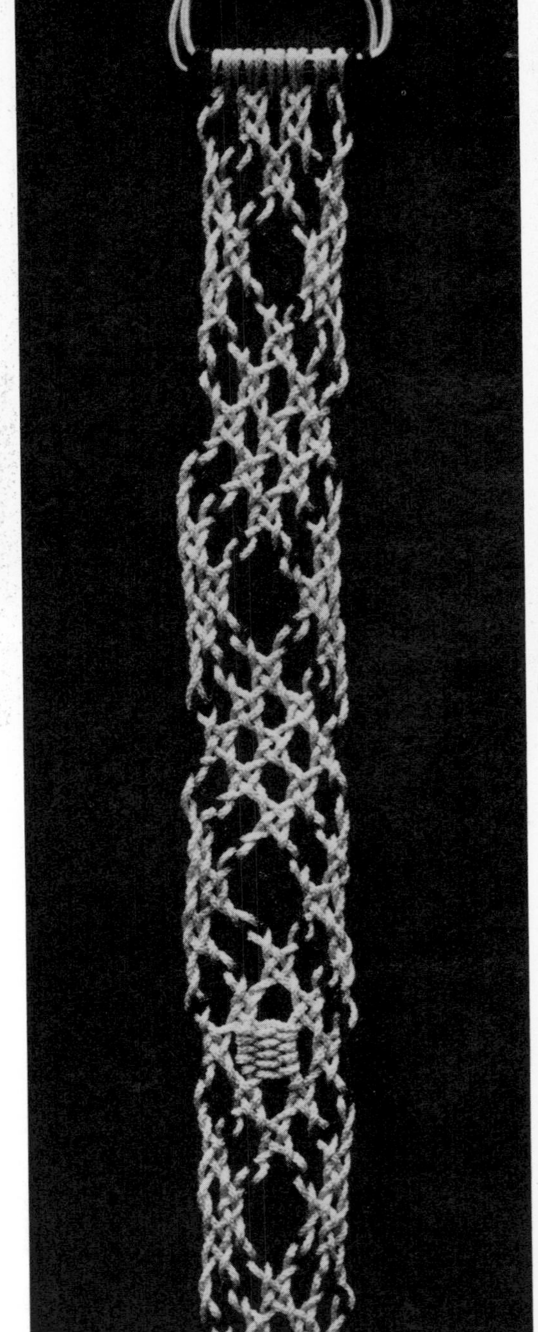

Starting a belt from two "D" rings.

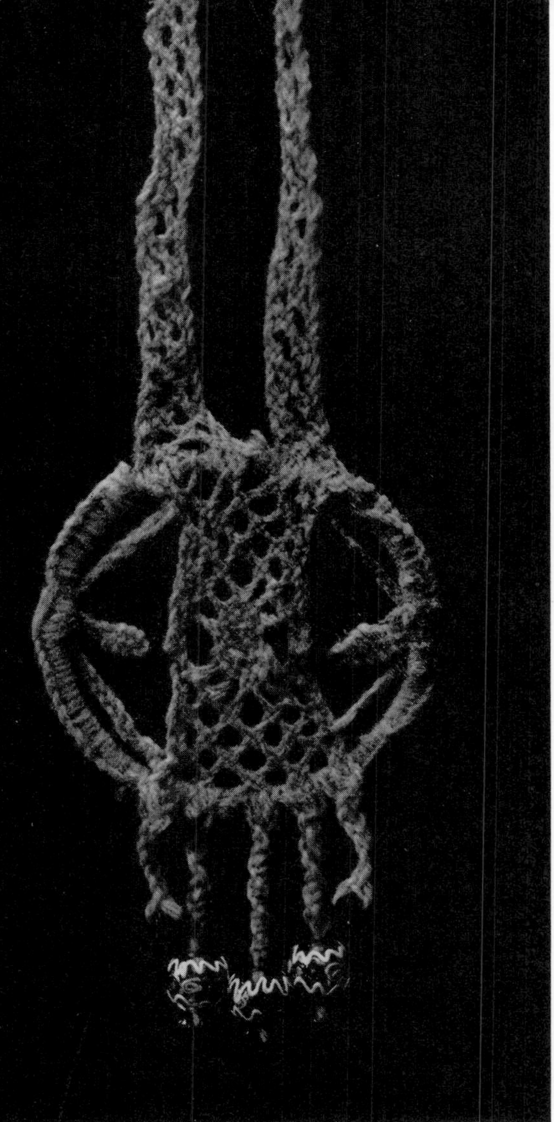

A pendant in wool. Irene Jarvis.

Starting a belt from a ceramic buckle. Material is seine twine, which was dyed while still wound in a ball.

An iron frame serving as a base for a lace seat. Kaethe Kliot.

A method of interlacing bobbin pairs where work is to be begun from a central point and worked outward. Virtually any number of threads can be joined in this manner. After threads are interlocked they are pulled to form a close structural center.

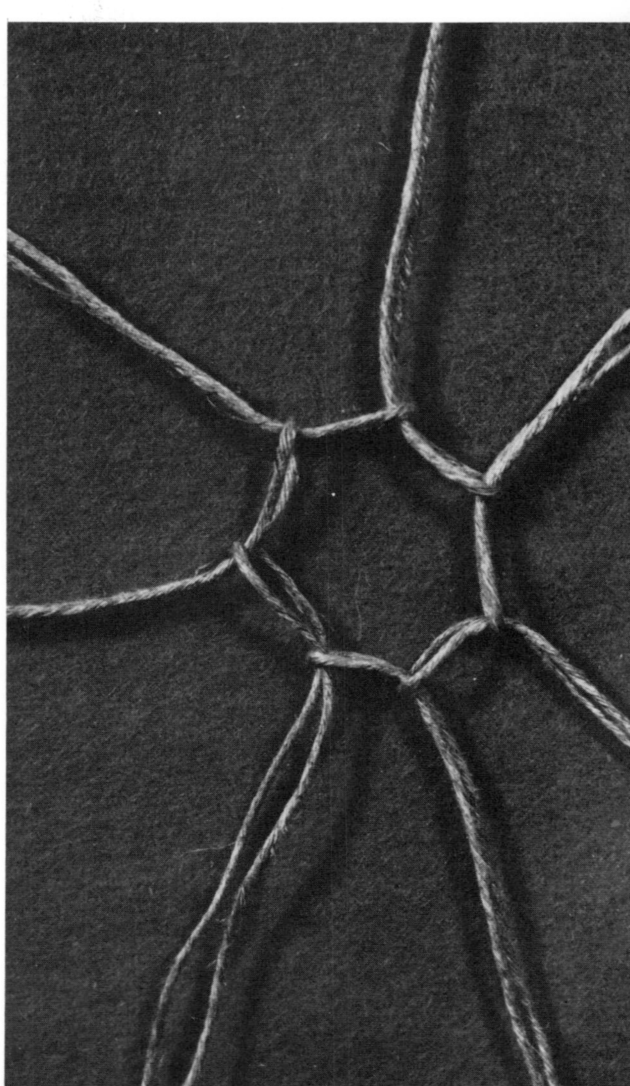

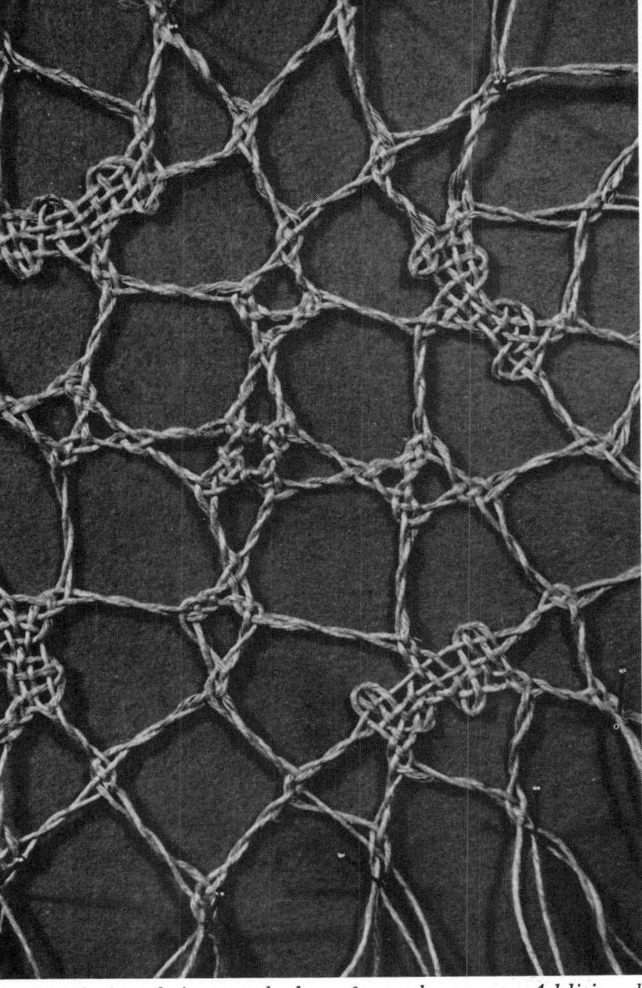

A piece being worked out from the center. Additional threads have been added by "invisible" techniques as the work proceeds outward.

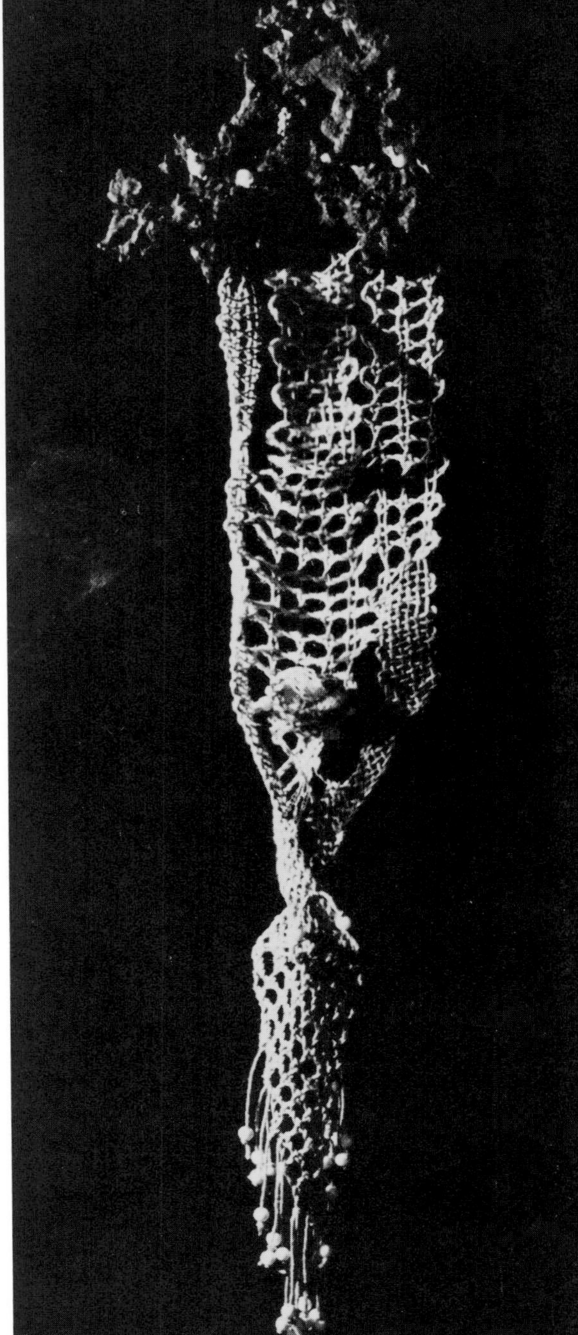

A hanging started from a fragment of iron slag. "Basket of Old Lace." Kaethe Kliot.

Lace worked on and integrated with driftwood. Three pieces by Kaethe Kliot.

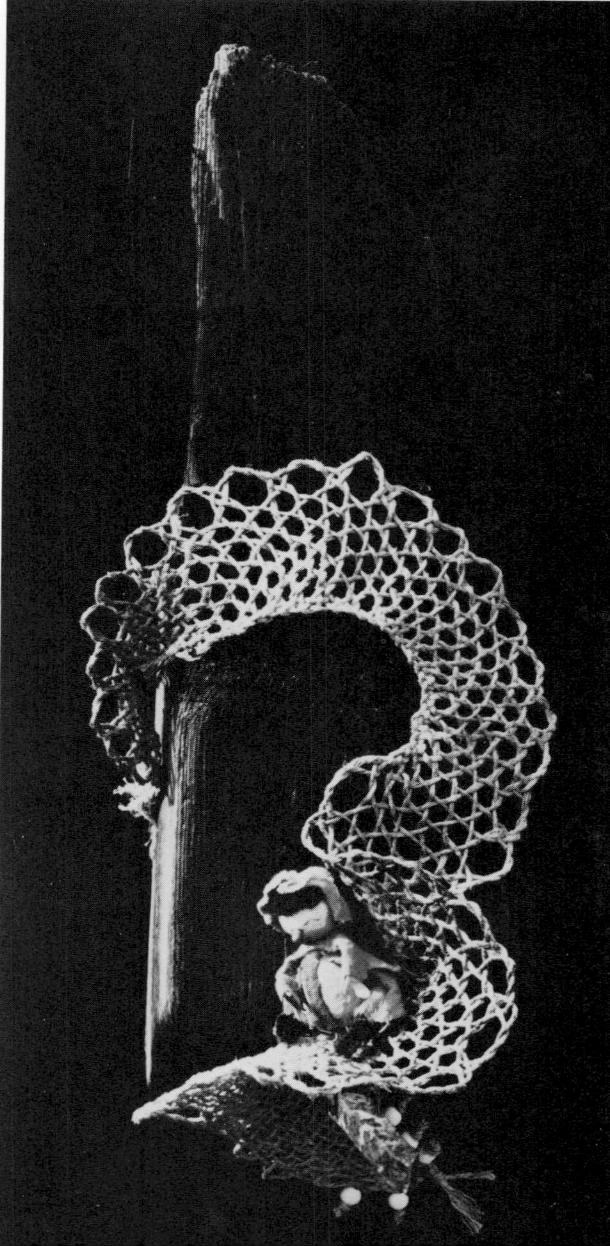

WEAVING TERMINATIONS

One theory as to the origin of bobbin lace is that it most likely evolved from its use as a finishing of a woven-cloth edge. Terminating a woven piece has always been a challenge. While the cut warp threads could simply be tied and left hanging, these hanging threads invited fringing by either knotting or twisting and braiding techniques. As the flexibility of the twisting and braiding techniques was explored, the edge was soon to take on the major effort and become independent of the woven fabric.

A fringe can be formed by any pattern of stitches using the extending warp threads. To further manipulate the termination, additional bobbin pairs can be worked between the normal warp threads. These can simply be pinned in place, worked into the fringe, and the pins finally removed. These added threads can match the warp or weft threads or be of some complementary texture or color.

Extending warp threads are often too short to wind onto bobbins. The bobbins can be secured to the hanging threads by a half hitch, taping, or by securing the threads to a small notch or saw cut in the bobbin.

Some examples of terminations to a woven piece. Note how in the unworked section threads of contrasting color have been added.

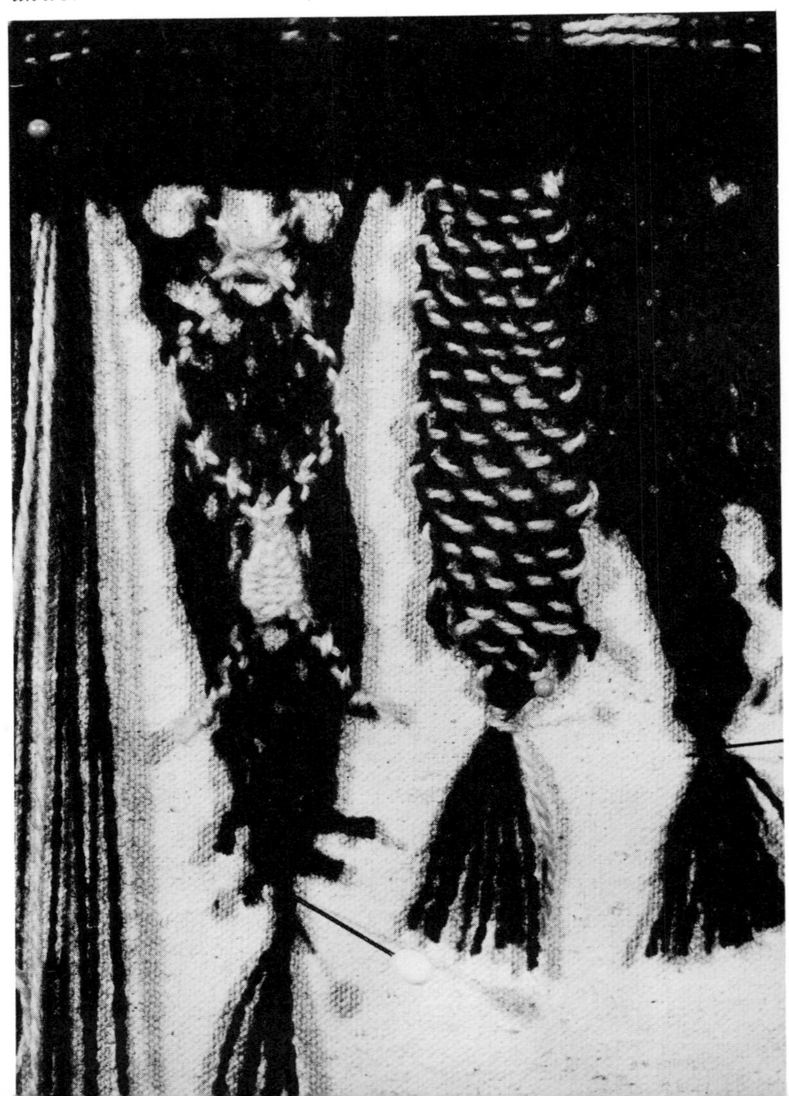

Bibliography

Anchor Manual of Needlework. Charles T. Branford Company, 1968.

Brooke, Margaret L. *Lace in the Making.* Albert & Charles Boni, 1925. Techniques.

Caplin, Jessie F. *The Lace Book.* The Macmillan Company, 1932. History.

Caulfeild, S. F. A. *Encyclopedia of Victorian Needlework.* Reprinted Dover, 1972.

Channer, C. C. *Lacemaking, Point Ground.* Dryad Press, 1970. Techniques and patterns of traditional English lace.

———, and Roberts, M. E. *Lacemaking in the Midlands.* 1900. Luton Museum and Art Gallery. History.

Ciba Review. Many articles covering history, fashion, traditions.

Close, Eunice. *Lacemaking.* Foyles, 1951. Traditional lace techniques.

De Dillmont, Therese. *Encyclopedia of Needlework* (DMC). France. Techniques.

Druk, Derde. *Lace (Kant).* Rijksmuseum, Amsterdam, 1966. History.

Freeman, Charles. *Pillow Lace in the East Midlands.* Luton Museum, 1958. History.

Gubser, Elsie H. *Bobbin Lace.* Robin and Russ Handweavers. Techniques, traditional lace.

International Old Lacers. Bulletins published six times a year. Traditional lace.

Johanson, Sally. *Knyppling.* LTs Forlag, 1969. Techniques.

Jourdain, M. *Old Lace.* B. T. Batsford, Ltd., 1909. History.

Kellogg, Charlotte. *Bobbins of Belgium.* Funk & Wagnalls Company, 1920. History.

Kielberg, Sina. *Laer at Kniple.* Berlingske Forlag, 1972. Techniques.

Lowes, E. L. *Chats on Old Lace and Needlework.* Frederick A. Stokes Company, 1908. History.

Maidment, Margaret. *A Manual of Handmade Bobbin Lace Work.* Reprinted Paul P. B. Minet, 1971. Techniques.

May, Florence Lewis. *Hispanic Lace and Lace Making.* Hispanic Society of America, 1939. History.

Mincoff, E., and Marriage, M. S. *Pillow Lace: A Practical Handbook.* J. Murray, 1907. Techniques.

Palliser, Mrs. Bury. *A History of Lace.* Sampson, Low, Son and Marston, 1864.

Tod, Osma G. *The Belgian Way of Making Bobbin Lace.* O. G. Tod Studio. Traditional techniques.

———. *Bobbin Lace Step-By-Step.* O. G. Tod Studio, 1969. Traditional techniques.

Van der Meulen-Nulle, L. W. *Lace.* Merlin Press Ltd., 1963. History.

Von Henneberg, Freiherr Alfred. *The Art and Craft of Old Lace.* B. T. Batsford, Ltd., 1931. History and analysis.

Whiting, Gertrude. *A Lace Guide for Makers and Collectors.* E. P. Dutton & Company, 1920. Analysis.

Wright, Doreen. *Bobbin Lace Making.* Charles T. Branford Company, 1971. Traditional techniques.

Wright, Thomas. *The Romance of the Lace Pillow.* Reprinted Paul P. B. Minet, 1971. Colorful history.

Sources For Supplies

Materials for contemporary bobbin lace can be the same ropes, cords, yarns, and twines as used in weaving and macramé. In addition to the yarn and weaving shops, you should try cordage companies, hardware stores, fabric shops, garden supply centers, variety stores, and so on.

Some of the tools and equipment specifically relating to bobbin lace will be more difficult to locate. The following sources are listed as having materials and/or equipment relating specifically to bobbin lace.

E. BRAGGINS & SONS
Silver Street
Bedford, England

Fine threads and equipment relating specifically to traditional bobbin lace.

FREDERICK J. FAWCETT, INC.
129 South Street
Boston, Massachusetts 02111

Fine lace threads and linen cords.

OSMA G. TOD STUDIO
319 Mendoza Avenue
Coral Gables, Florida 33134
Materials and equipment for traditional lace.

ROBIN AND RUSS HANDWEAVERS
533 North Adams Street
McMinnville, Oregon 97128
Materials and equipment for traditional and contemporary bobbin lace.

SOME PLACE
2990 Adeline Street
Berkeley, California 94703
Materials and equipment specifically designed for contemporary bobbin lace. Retail and wholesale.

Index

CS means Color Section